BECKHAMPTON

BECKHAMPTON

THE MEN AND HORSES OF A GREAT RACING STABLE

PAUL MATHIEU

RACING POST

First published in 2015 by Racing Post Books

27 Kingfisher Court, Hambridge Road, Newbury, RG14 5SJ

10 9 8 7 6 5 4 3 2 1

A catalogue record for this book is available from the British Library.

ISBN 978-1-910498-29-3

Cover designed by Nathan Bines

Typeset by J Schwartz & Co

Printed and bound in the UK by CPI Group (UK) Ltd, Croydon, CR0 4YY

www.racingpost.com/shop

Contents

Author's notes

Monetary worth

At the time when Billy Treen began to train at Beckhampton, the pound sterling was worth, depending on which benchmark is used, anything between £88 and £3,635, compared to £1 today. The option used in this book is based on the measuringworth.com 'purchasing power calculator'. It corresponds to the Retail Price Index. That option produces the £88 to £1 comparison between 1835 and 2014. The firm make the caveat that few of the contents of the RPI's shopping basket today even existed in 1835, or for that matter 1935. How would Treen have received the news that the 2015 RPI basket included for the first time e-cigarettes, streaming music subscriptions and protein powder? Almost the only things he'd recognise are bacon, milk and bread. Here and there, for emphasis, today's values are noted alongside contemporary pounds and guineas.

Illustrations

Thanks to all those who have helped by providing photographs, drawings and maps. They're credited alongside the individual illustrations. While every effort has been made to trace the copyright holder of each image, it hasn't been possible in all cases. The publishers will be happy to rectify any omissions, including in future editions of the book.

CHAPTER ONE

Billy Treen and the Beckhampton Inn

By Fashion out of Isolation, by Crossroads. That's the pedigree of Beckhampton, home to so many of the British turf's greatest racehorses and trainers. Fashion was represented by Bath Spa, which in the late eighteenth century became a magnet for London society, to take the waters and to preen in the current vogue. Isolation, because Beckhampton is wrapped in exposed downland. Crossroads, since it sits at the point from which two roads lead westwards towards Bath.

The Regency fashionistas' journey from London to Bath and back was long, uncomfortable and sometimes dangerous. Wealthy travellers had their own coaches. For the rest, the only option was to take a public coach. The roads were unsurfaced and turned to deep mud after rain.

To maintain timetables, the coaches needed back-up teams of horses along their routes, while the passengers demanded regular stops to relieve and feed themselves. Both parties' needs were answered by coaching inns. For the owner of a pub on a popular route, the coaches provided a guaranteed income, so the inn on the crossroads in Beckhampton prospered. It was half-way between Marlborough and Devizes and it offered a choice of roads to Bath: west to Calne along what became the A4, or south-west through Devizes. Along these routes ran coaches with come-ride-me names like 'The Favourite', 'The Star' and 'The New Day'. Their Beckhampton stop was described by a London paper:

> "[Readers from] the olden time of stage coaching may remember the Beckhampton Inn, where the two roads to Bath divide, and just where the traveller enters one of the most open and bleak reaches of the Wiltshire Downs. [The inn] stands between the two roads, a large square brick-built house, roomy, but plain, and bearing somewhat the aspect of a hostel that had seen better days. [On] either side facing the diverging roads was an entrance by which [the] considerable traffic arising from coach passengers made its entrance and exit. An immense range of stabling – far more extensive and of a more substantial character than was required or used for the coach horses which 'stood' there – was to be seen at the back of the house. The whole appearance of the place reminded one of the habitation of generations of rich old-fashioned squires, whose means, talents and energies had been perseveringly devoted to horses and hounds.
>
> "The Beckhampton Inn was at that time famous for potent ale. Winter travellers who were about to encounter the sharp breezes over Cherhill Downs or Roundway Hill, as well as those coming 'up the road,' who had passed over those exposed districts, [would] fortify or solace themselves with a glass of the strong Wiltshire beer, known by the genuine name of Kennett Ale."

Sometimes the passengers needed more than a sip of Kennett to help them over the downs. In the 1830s, when the Beckhampton Inn was beginning its transition from a coaching house to a training yard, George Neate was riding back from Devizes market when he was the victim of 'A highway robbery about a mile from the Beckhampton Inn.' Three men waylaid him, stole £50 in cash and double that in cheques, and made off. Their daring served notice that the threat of highwaymen persisted into Victorian times. Bad weather was a routine inconvenience for coach passengers, especially over the downs. Snowfalls could make the roads impassable. A county paper told a gleeful tale of privation and profit in the 1770s:

"The late heavy fall of snow has been the cause of many diverting scenes between [Bath] and London. The people of fashion, anxious of becoming in town to appear in the circle at St James's on Her Majesty's birthday, set off full of courage and fierceness of mind to face the bleak winds."

Many got no further than the Beckhampton, "[An] inn which was filled with a variety of good characters. The men did everything in their power to relieve female distress, for the women really appeared in a prodigious fuss to get to London in order to show their feathers and [finery] on the birthday. This was not the only difficulty they had to struggle with. As night drew on, it was discovered that the house had but few beds, and many were the petitioners for those few. The women, who of course were first to be accommodated, soon engaged every bed in the house, and left the gentlemen to appoint a committee to know [where] their tired carcases were to be deposited. Upon enquiry, orders had been given to litter down two rooms for masters and men, and happy were some to throw themselves down and forget the fatigues of the day. The people of the house thought it a good opportunity of providing against a bad day, and charged their customers accordingly. Eggs [were] a shilling apiece; half a dozen boiled potatoes were set down in the bill at three shillings, and other articles in proportion."

Mine host knew a captive audience when he saw one. In our money, that would be £6.20 per egg and £18.60 for the plate of potatoes.

Most good things come to an end, and for the coaching services the bell was tolled by the arrival of the railways. Their impact in Beckhampton, as elsewhere, was seen in the prices paid for turnpike leases. The income from turnpikes was sold off annually in advance. In and around Beckhampton and the adjacent village of Avebury there were four toll gates and two weighbridges. The leaseholder charged coaches and other traffic to pass through. In 1808, the auction of the toll rights around Beckhampton raised £1,720 (£120,000 today). When Bath Spa station opened in 1840 and the Great Western Railway came into being, the value of Beckhampton's road tolls collapsed. A dozen years later they were abolished: there was nothing left to collect.

At the tipping point between a busy staging post and an isolated country pub, a young horseman called William Treen took an interest in the 'immense range of stabling' behind the inn. It was 1835. Treen was 26. He hailed from Devon, 'had a natural taste for horses and riding,' and as little more than a boy, he was apprenticed to the largest stable in the south of England, that of John Day at Danebury near Stockbridge. It could have been to his disadvantage. The Day clan – father John and his sons John and William – were crooks. It's been said that, "There were few racing scandals in the middle of the nineteenth century in which a member of the Day family was not implicated." As for John Day junior, who held Treen's indentures, 'Whenever it was to his financial advantage, he broke faith with the owners for whom he rode and trained.' He was hardly an ideal role model, but as he rode 16 classic winners and trained seven more, there was plenty to learn if a lad kept his eyes open and his mouth shut. Treen developed into an excellent lightweight jockey. He rode his first winner at Stockbridge aged 14, and for the next few years plied his trade round long-past courses like Dorchester, Tavistock, Wells and Weymouth. Lord Palmerston was among Day's owners at the time. Treen rode several winners for him, including a three year old called Grey-Leg, who won four races in 1825. Years later, when Palmerston was foreign secretary, he commanded Treen to ride a relay of horses, as fast as he could, to a Channel port to collect a newly-arrived peace treaty.

After Treen had served his time with Day, he went back to Devon to train a few horses for the country meetings, riding them himself. He was notably successful, riding four winners in an afternoon at the Bridgwater and Plymouth meetings in the early 1830s. He had a particular knack for keeping his horses sound. For one of his owners he sent out an old horse called Coronet to win 17 races in five seasons. Treen had achieved enough to show he was ready for a bigger challenge. He found it at Beckhampton. The inn's landlord John Watts had suffered a 'reverse of circumstances.' The Salisbury paper announced an auction of, '*The stock of good and sweet casks, brewing utensils, a capital 100-gallon copper furnace, hops, malts, part of the household furniture and other effects of Mr Watts, quitting the Beckhampton Inn*'.

Beckhampton was thought to be the remotest training yard in England. The *Mirror* wrote:

> "Passing along the Wiltshire downs [we] finally arrive at the *ultima Thule* of training in England, the stables at Beckhampton where Treen [presides]. Beyond, westwards, except at Cheltenham and one or two unheard-of oases in Devon, all is desolation, and the foot of the racehorse finds no resting-place."

The Victorians were fond of the notion of 'ultima Thule'. The phrase meant 'beyond the known boundaries'. The implied remoteness might not have been helpful to Treen, but he did everything he could to make a success of his new venture. He'd taken on the licence of a large inn; he was trainer and jockey to his small string; and for extra income he took on the post of clerk of the course for the Devizes and North Wilts races. He was even a sponsor, putting up £20 for the winner of the Beckhampton Inn Stakes. His hands-on role as mine host is noted in a report of the 1836 end-of-season dinner of the White Horse Cricket Club, held at the Beckhampton: 'Many loyal and appropriate toasts were drunk in the course of the evening, and the party separated in the best feelings, and highly pleased with the liberal entertainment of Mr Wm Treen.'

If it's true that every trainer needs one good horse, it helps to get started with a rich patron. Treen was lucky enough to acquire both. The owner was one of the stand-out eccentrics of the first half of the nineteenth century, the irrepressible Fulwar Craven. The horse was his filly Deception. Craven was known for his unruliness, his dress sense and his racehorses, in that order. Men's fashion in those days was conformist, with small accessories adding personal touches. A handful of dashers ignored convention:

> "Among the throng [on the racecourse] might be discerned a figure that divided attention even with [Count] D'Orsay the Dandy, and everywhere he went there were nudgings and whisperings. He was a man past his prime, but with a handsome, devil-may-care face and defiant eye, reddish whiskers and reddish flowing hair, surmounted by a white hat of abnormal height carelessly cocked on one side; he wore a brown coat with brass buttons, from the breast pocket of which hung a gaudy bandanna; light drab breeches and gaiters, the latter pulled down at the calf to show 2in or 3in of pink silk stocking, and a frilled shirt with a huge jewelled brooch set in it. As he sauntered by towards the paddock, sometimes with a purple jacket – his racing colours – hanging over his arm, you would hear a running fire of whispers: *'That is Fulwar Craven.'*"

Craven had three tilts at the turf. His first winner was as far back as 1808 at Newmarket. Two years later he had a strongly fancied filly called Janette in the Oaks. She was clearly the best horse in the field – and won the Gold Cup the following year – but went lame in the classic, and even so was only narrowly beaten. Craven, who had a short attention span, turned his back on racing and devoted himself to town and country pursuits. When in town, he was, 'A rake and a libertine.' At his Wiltshire estate he hunted his own pack, went rabbiting with his tenants, and staged prize-fights. His return to racing was notable for another Oaks contender, Miss Jigg, who was thought a certainty for the 1824 renewal. Her supporters included the bluest of blue bloods, and after she'd disappointed, the Duke of Gloucester muttered, "Well, Craven, we're all ruined by this fine Miss Jigg of yours." To compensate, Craven had a money-spinner, a 600 guineas buy called Longwaist, who was a multiple winner as a three year old. The following year he progressed further, mopping up five Gold Cup races at a series of country courses; winning two stakes races at Newmarket; not least, finishing a close second in the Ascot and Doncaster Cups. However, Craven never hid his opinion that Longwaist wasn't within 7lb of top class, and he was happy enough to sell the colt to his friend 'Mad Jack' Mytton for 3,000 guineas.

Mytton began his adult life by arriving at university with 2,000 bottles of port; continued it crawling naked with a fowling piece across the ice on his lakes in mid-winter, to surprise ducks at daybreak; and hastened his demise by setting fire to his nightshirt to see if that would stop a persistent hiccup. It did. On one escapade, Mytton and Craven together tossed a drunken stranger through a shop window.

Craven fell out with his trainer soon after selling Longwaist, and had a second sabbatical from racing. A few years on, he met Treen and sent some horses to Beckhampton. The partnership flourished, winning 14 races in 1838, their first year together. Treen rode half of them. The highlight was a four-timer at Cheltenham's summer meeting. A few weeks later a friend, riding past Beckhampton, saw Craven and called out, "Have you anything worth having here, Craven?" "Yes, I have." "And what is it?" "A filly I'm going to win the Oaks with," was the unexpected reply. The filly, a bay daughter of Defence, out of Lady Stumps by Tramp, was named Deception. She'd run four times as a two year old for another owner, the last of them at Goodwood, where she was second. At that point Craven bought her. Trained for the first time by Treen, she made one more appearance that season, beating a small field at Salisbury.

At the end of the winter and into the following spring, Deception's improving home work convinced Craven and Treen that she was the best horse in training. She was entered in the Derby as well as the Oaks, and Craven decided to win both. The Derby was her first race as a three year old, and her final preparation could hardly have gone worse: on the eve of the race, she was coughing. It was only one ingredient in a devil's broth of rumour and gossip. The winter favourites for the race had either not trained on, or been beaten all ends up in the 2000 Guineas. A number of the runners were making their racecourse debuts. One of them, Bloomsbury, had been the subject of controversy since he was foaled. Bloomsbury was bred by Robert Ridsdale, who acquired wealth by corrupting everyone he could – jockeys, trainers and officials. Eventually, retribution called on Ridsdale. His horses all went under the hammer. Just one foal was unsold – 'an ugly little scrap' by a moderate sire, Mulatto – and that was Bloomsbury. The colt was taken and trained by Ridsdale's brother, William. Nothing had been heard of Bloomsbury since, and he didn't seem likely to run at Epsom, not least because Lord Chesterfield had threatened to scratch him. William Ridsdale had been training for Chesterfield, but the two fell out, and a dispute arose over the ownership of Bloomsbury. The spat was resolved, with the proviso that Chesterfield was refunded all his entry costs.

The race and its aftermath surpassed the build-up for drama and dispute. The weather at Epsom was, 'Composed of frost, snow, hail, rain and a north-east wind as sharp as a Damascus blade.' So far as could be seen through the snow, the field dawdled along, Deception always in the leading group, until gathering momentum on the incline to Tattenham Corner. Once into the straight, Treen set Deception alight. She leaped into a lead of several lengths. Coming into the last two furlongs, only two rivals had made up any ground on her. Deception held off one of them readily enough, but the other was Bloomsbury, and close home he wore her down to win by a length. Immediately after the race, Deception was made odds-on for the Oaks, to be run two days later.

The Derby was followed by a storm of disapproval for Treen's aggressive ride on Deception. The next day, he was jocked off Deception in the Oaks. His replacement was his former master, John Day. Fulwar Craven told the press he had no reason to feel dissatisfied with Treen's ride on Deception; his filly was beaten by a better horse. He said that he engaged John Day, "Purely out of deference to the public, who have backed my mare to a large amount, and who are anxious to have a more experienced jockey on Deception. In all other races in which the weight will permit, Treen will continue to ride my horses."

It was a generous sop to Treen's self-esteem, but it told little of the turmoil developing behind the scenes. On the morning of the Oaks, an objection was lodged against Bloomsbury in Fulwar Craven's name. It claimed that the colt's pedigree had been misrepresented in his Derby entry. The *Racing Calendar* described Bloomsbury as, 'by Mulatto, out of St Giles's dam (Arcott Lass),' while the *Stud Book* listed him as, 'by Tramp or Mulatto.' Tramp was a much more highly-rated stallion than Mulatto. On this pinhead, saints and sinners danced together for months.

The objection was little to do with Deception and much about betting. A coterie of heavy-staking aristocrats had fastened onto Bloomsbury as a risk-free 'lay'. The first card in their hand was the likelihood that Lord Chesterfield would scratch the colt. When Chesterfield relented, there was a technicality to fall back on – Bloomsbury's breeding was not as described. Lord George Bentinck and Lord Lichfield were prominent among those with an interest in Bloomsbury's demotion. Their insurance policy was to cover their liabilities by backing Deception to win the Oaks. To ensure nothing was left to chance, Bentinck paid Fulwar Craven £400 to put John Day on the filly, in place of Treen. Deception won the Oaks in a canter.

Meanwhile, the Epsom stewards were struggling with the objection against Bloomsbury. The rule was clear. If a horse was objected to before 10 am on race day, it was up to its owner to prove his horse's identity. If the objection came later, as this had done, the onus was on the objector to prove the grounds for disqualification. On the Monday, William Ridsdale advised the stewards that his witnesses to prove Bloomsbury's pedigree were ready. He said some of them had travelled a long way and their lodgings were costly: could the stewards please hold their enquiry without delay? The officials sent a letter to Craven advising him that the enquiry would be held at the Spread Eagle in Epsom the following day. Ridsdale and his team were ready, and gave their evidence. There was no sign of Craven. The stewards had no option but to find in favour of Ridsdale. They addressed a letter to Edward Weatherby, the holder of the stakes. It read, *"Bloomsbury was qualified to start for the Derby, and [his] owner is entitled to the stakes."*

Ridsdale set off to see Weatherby. In the reverse direction rode Bentinck, carrying a missive from Craven to the stewards: he hadn't had time to gather witnesses, and wanted proceedings halted. At about this time the stewards' letter to Weatherby was pinned up in Tattersalls. Settling of bets on the Derby began. It was interrupted by the arrival of Craven, who read out his own letter to the stewards, with the result that no one who'd backed Deception would settle – and nothing was paid out to supporters of Bloomsbury. The *Morning Herald* sighed: "The Bloomsbury affair still keeps the market in a feverish state, and will in all probability prevent a complete settlement for several months." The paper added, "There are always shabby people [who will] seize, or invent, any pretence for keeping their money in their pockets." *Sporting Review* sneered that it was, "A pleasant thing for [losers over the race] to defer, if they can, the payment of their bets to the day of judgement."

Weatherby presided over an arbitration meeting. The stewards begged both sides not to involve lawyers. Lord Lichfield protested that he was having trouble getting people who knew the facts to come forward and testify. He added that he didn't recognise the stewards' authority in the matter. At which point the officials saw that, 'No decision of ours would be binding on the parties, and therefore it is useless to proceed further.' Ridsdale promptly sued Lichfield. He had his day in a Liverpool court at the end of August. A colourful collection of witnesses for both sides – stud workers, farmers, cattle dealers, a chemist, even a 'clerk in the Secretary of Lunatics office' – gave confusing and contradictory evidence as to the exclusive (or not) nature of Mulatto's jump on Arcott Lass. Pages had been torn out of stud books. Robert Ridsdale's records had been burned after his bankruptcy. There was an allegation of witness tampering. Still, the jury gave a northerners' verdict, favouring the plain Yorkshireman Ridsdale over the lordly southerner Lichfield.

Bloomsbury ran twice at Ascot, after another unsuccessful objection to his breeding. First he beat three opponents in the Ascot Derby, then a single rival in a sweepstakes. Having won his first three races, he only won one other. At Doncaster he was down the field in the St Leger and then last of three in another race at the meeting: cracked heels were blamed. The following year he was a close third in the Gold Cup, having pulled hard all through the race; beat three rivals at Liverpool at 2–7; and finished an honourable second under a big weight in the Cesarewitch. In his final season he ran only twice, including fifth of six in the Gold Cup. The balance of his form fell short of what could be expected from a Derby winner. A growing murmur around the racecourse offered an explanation. It was that the previously unraced Bloomsbury wasn't eligible to run in the Derby: he wasn't a three year old. The breeding of Robert Ridsdale's 'ugly scrap' had no relevance at all. 'Bloomsbury' was said to have been an older horse, identity unknown, imported from Ireland. *Baily's Magazine* reflected:

> "There was something very queer about Bloomsbury, no doubt. His pedigree was open to grave suspicions. His owner's name did not smell sweet in the nostrils of men. Every racing man at that time was as persuaded that Bloomsbury was not the correct age, as he knew that two and two made four. There was only one difference of opinion, and that was as to whether he was a four or five year old, the popular belief holding to the latter."

If this sounds far-fetched, it wasn't. Stud records were haphazard in those early days. Other Derby 'winners' besides Bloomsbury were the subject of conjecture – among them Little Wonder, the next year. In 1844, in the greatest of Derby scandals, the first past the post, Running Rein, was shown to be a four year old called Maccabaeus. A generation earlier, Lord Egremont's trainer confessed on his deathbed that he'd won the Derby twice with four year olds, by the simple ruse of slipping a promising two year old into the Petworth yearling paddocks. As there were up to 300 horses at the stud, and management was lax, discovery was unlikely. Unfortunately, the man didn't say which two of Egremont's five Derby winners were the 'old 'uns.'

Deception had a busy time after Epsom, making nine further appearances over distances up to three miles. She won four times, including a feature race at Goodwood, and walked over twice. In all nine races, she was ridden by Treen. Fulwar Craven spent some of her proceeds on large gold brooches with enamel portraits of Deception and Longwaist. To complete the spectacle of Georgian bling, he took to carrying a large gold snuff box. A few weeks after the excitements of Epsom, Craven made an appearance at the Cheltenham Police Court. The report read:

> Fulwar Craven, magistrate of Cheltenham, and a gentleman named Throgmorton, were charged with being drunk and disorderly. Mr Craven, although one of the accused, took his seat on the bench with the magistrates who had to decide on the case.
>
> Policeman Smith stated: "This morning about one o'clock I saw the large doors at the Plough Hotel open. There [were] a lot of gentlemen in the street making a great noise with a lot of girls. I went up to them and cautioned them. Several of the gentlemen went away, and all the girls with the exception of one. Fulwar Craven was making use of very obscene language towards her. I cautioned the girl, and I saw her as far as the lamp. I advised her not to go back. Fulwar Craven and the other gentleman came to me and damned my eyes for interfering with the girl."
>
> The Magistrate: "The charge on the book is for being drunk and disorderly. Now if that is your charge, it is a simple case of drunkenness, and Mr Fulwar Craven will answer the charge the same as other people."
>
> Mr Craven: "Was I drunk?"
>
> Policeman Smith: "Yes you were, Sir. This other gentleman [raised his fists] and said the first person who touched Mr Fulwar Craven, he would knock down."
>
> The Magistrate: "Ah! A common case of disorderly conduct."
>
> Policeman Smith: "I took Mr Fulwar Craven to the door of the Plough, and he was so disorderly that I was obliged to obtain the assistance of four policemen to take him to the station-house. [The accused] were both very drunk."

Policeman Millard being sworn, said: "Mr Craven came to me and said, 'Do you know who I am?' I said, 'Yes, Mr Fulwar Craven, the magistrate.' He said, 'Yes, I am a magistrate, and will teach you so. I do not usually sit on the Bench, but I will in future. I am too respectable to sit with the rest.' With the assistance of four policemen I took [him] to the station house."

The Magistrate: "This case, which is a drunken case, is decided. You must each pay five shillings and costs, and I have no doubt you will do it willingly, for you are well able to. There is a great deal more made of the case than there ought to be."

The money was paid and Mr Throgmorton left the [court], but Mr Craven remained on the bench.

The magistrate, a Mr St Clair, lived a sheltered life if he thought the case would draw little attention. Craven was a prominent man of fashion, a racehorse owner, a noted eccentric – and a magistrate, his entitlement as a land-owner. For him to thumb his nose at proceedings by insisting, hung over, on his right to sit on the bench was the icing on the cake. From as far afield as Dublin, it was reported, 'The affair at Cheltenham [where] Mr Fulwar Craven was fined by his brother magistrates for being drunk and disorderly in the streets, occupies a considerable share of public conversation throughout England.'

Craven retreated a little from the public's gaze, but his appetite for low life was unquenchable. It was said of him that, 'After attending races he would gather together a party of rough 'uns and entertain them to their hearts' content.' He founded a corn exchange in Hungerford, to boost farmers' income, but he'd sit at the trestles outside the town's pubs, regaling the rustics with tall stories and egging them on to drink and fight. His companion in similar scrapes was a police inspector. The pair became notorious for mischief in the Berkshire market towns, until it seems to have dawned on them that one day they might face a higher judgement than that of a magistrates' court. The policeman became a Methodist preacher, howling hymns from soapboxes and proclaiming sobriety. Craven retired to his estate. That was the end of his colourful ventures into racehorse ownership.

Treen seemed likely to be forever haunted by Deception's defeat in the Derby. Had the true status of her conqueror Bloomsbury been known, Deception would've won the race and been recognised as the exceptional filly she was. Weight for age allowances are intended to even out the differences in maturity and strength between horses of different ages. In June, when the Derby is run, a horse aged four years or over should give 20lb to a three year old. Because of William Ridsdale's presumed chicanery, Deception was beaten a length while at a 20lb disadvantage.

At the time, though, Treen's main irritant was the continued belief that he'd ridden a stinker. A stranger asked him if he'd been to the Derby? Yes, said Treen. "Then I suppose you saw the jockey nearly fall off Deception, and lose the race?" "I rode her myself," Treen replied, gritting his teeth. It must have seemed to him that he'd be burdened forever with the tag of, 'The jockey who threw away the Derby.' Luckily for him and for Beckhampton, he was wrong: there was one man at Epsom that day who formed a most favourable impression of Deception and her rider.

CHAPTER TWO

William Gregory and Fred Swindell

An Oxford degree course isn't necessarily a path to ruin, but William Gregory nearly made it so. He was the heir to a 5,000 acre estate in County Galway. He was head of school at Harrow, and narrowly missed the top entrance scholarship to Christ Church College. In later life, he became a long-serving MP and was knighted for distinguished public service. But at Oxford, "A circumstance occurred [which] exercised a most fatal influence over my whole future life." He visited friends at Cambridge. They took him to see Newmarket and its stables, "Showed me all the favourite horses for the great events, introduced me to one or two jockeys and sent me back full of racing information. From that day I deserted my old studious friends, and thought of nothing but Epsom and Newmarket."

Gregory sat his degree the following year: "I had every reason to expect getting my first class, the great object of Oxford ambition – the credentials, in fact, for the start of an ambitious young man in life. I had left Christ Church and had gone to New Inn Hall [where] unfortunately, no discipline was observed. I could do as I liked. The consequence was that I went to the Newmarket spring meetings, and afterwards [rode] from Oxford to Epsom on relays of hacks, cantering all the way. There I saw Bloomsbury win the Derby during a snowstorm, and there I won £300 on him, which confirmed my fatal love of racing."

Gregory introduced himself to Treen at Epsom, and asked the trainer to buy him some yearlings. Gregory would've had a longer career on the turf if his gambling urge had been kept to his own horses, trained by Billy Treen. But he listened to anyone with a tip, and he bet without regard to the horse, the race or the opposition. Sometimes it came off spectacularly. Two years after Bloomsbury, he won over £5,000 on the Derby favourite Coronation. Gregory was in Rome before the race, but felt it necessary to come back to England, 'To make financial arrangements in case he was beaten.' A month before, Coronation had been 10–1. On the day of the race, when Coronation opened at 4–1 and was returned at 5–2, Gregory "Still continued to back him, even till he was saddled, [so] my losses would have been very heavy had he been beaten." Coronation won by an easy three lengths. Years afterwards, Gregory sat at a dinner next to an elderly lord who recalled a young man in the Jockey Club stand after Coronation's victory. The young man was totting up his book. When he finished his calculations, he said to himself, but audibly: 'Well, I'm sure I don't know how I shall spend all this money.' It was Gregory. His parents were at a dinner party not long after the Derby. Talk turned to the big race, and a fellow guest said he'd heard, 'One of the heaviest winners was a young Irishman, hardly down from Oxford – name of Gregory.' Not the best aid to his parents' digestion. Two years later, Gregory had another coup in the Derby, when a friend with an unconsidered outsider, Cotherstone, asked him to work a £1,000 commission. Gregory got his friend £22,000 to his £1,000. He backed Cotherstone for another £5,000 himself. It won.

The best horse that Treen saddled for Gregory was the result of outrageous luck. One wet Newmarket morning, Gregory was hurrying to the warmth of the Jockey Club rooms. Richard Tattersall was selling off some yearlings in the High Street – 'draggle-tailed, miserable-looking.' Gregory paused for long enough to note a tall chestnut colt, and left a 'Buy' instruction. When he came out, the chestnut was his for 15 guineas. As a two year old he ran three times, unnamed, in Treen's colours. His performances were lamentable: last of five in a Goodwood claimer, third of four at Bath and Marlborough. The colt, now named Clermont, not surprisingly started his three year old season on a low handicap mark. His work on the Beckhampton gallops was far better than his public form. Gregory and Treen mapped out an ambitious plan: to win five valuable handicaps in five weeks in March and April. First Clermont ran in the Great Northamptonshire Stakes, carrying just 4st 7lb. He was clearly 'expected,' starting at 5–2 favourite to beat 16 others. He failed by half a length. Undeterred, William Gregory had another thump on Clermont in the Newmarket Handicap, where he started at 3–1 favourite in a field of 19. He carried 4st 10lb and Treen's son William Jnr, and won cleverly by a length. Clermont was bogged down in soft ground at Bath in the Somersetshire Stakes, odds-on but only third, and three days later lined up for Epsom's Great Metropolitan Handicap. He won by a neck. Finally in the Chester Cup, Clermont again floundered, finishing out of the money for the first time. Two wins and two places from his five runs were meritorious enough; it might have been more but for a rain-soaked spring. There'd been a good reason for Clermont's derisory sale price: he had shocking forelegs. He simply couldn't go through heavy going.

Gregory had two other horses which made lively contributions to racing gossip of the time; one was a nondescript brown colt called Papageno. Treen's other patrons included a commission agent called Fred Swindell. He placed the bets of wealthy men who wanted the best prices and the least publicity. Among them was Sir Joseph Hawley. He was opinionated and belligerent, and although Swindell made him a great deal of money, Hawley was born to find fault. The men settled one dispute by agreeing to a £200 match at Newmarket. Mr Weatherby held the stakes. Shortly before the race, Sir Joseph's horse went wrong. Swindell heard the news at once from his network of informants, but he had a problem of his own: his entry was so lame it hadn't left Beckhampton. He told Billy Treen to send William Gregory's Papageno in place of his own horse. The two had similar conformation and colouring. As conspicuously as possible, Swindell marched into Weatherbys and slapped down two £100 notes, "For my match with Sir Joseph." The clerk, taken aback, said, "I heard your horse had broken down, Mr Swindell." "Did you, lad? I expect you hear many strange things hereabouts." No sooner had Swindell left the office than Hawley rushed in to ask if Mr Swindell's horse had arrived. "It must have, for he's just been in and posted his stake." "Then I pay forfeit," snapped Sir Joseph: "Mine can't run, that's certain." He handed over his £200 and stalked out. In no time the 'sting' was known all round Newmarket. Diamond cut diamond: Sir Joseph wasn't amused.

William Gregory's time at Beckhampton ended because of a piece of treachery. Gregory had a two year old called Damask, whom he thought too slow to be worth training. Treen insisted that Damask had some ability; Gregory sold him the horse. After an unpromising first season, Damask was entered for the following season's Ascot Stakes. He had a light weight, and Treen thought he had an excellent chance. For confirmation, Treen asked Gregory if he could find a horse to be used as trial tackle for Damask. Gregory provided the perfect tool: a horse of Lord Clifden's called Wanota, who was one of the early favourites for the Ascot race. Damask made short work of Wanota, with the result that Gregory and Clifden and their friends backed Damask heavily. To their surprise, its odds lengthened. Gregory traced the opposition to his horse to a small-time 'investor' called Glen – a baker by day – and a Turf Club member, Captain Vaughan. Gregory checked with Treen, who assured him that the horse 'Was well and sure to win,' but the more Damask was backed, the shakier he was in the betting. A perturbed Gregory questioned Treen again. He was appalled by what he was told. Treen confessed that he'd been short of money the previous winter and had sold Damask to Glen, who made him promise to keep the transaction secret. Treen said Glen had assured him that Damask would run. Gregory went off in search of Glen. The man admitted telling Treen the horse would run – but he'd changed his mind and he was going to scratch it. Only one thing could make the situation even worse, and sure enough it transpired: Wanota, the trial horse spat out by Damask on the Beckhampton gallops, won the Ascot Stakes easily.

"My anger burned hot within me," wrote William Gregory. "I and my fellow-sufferers cut the acquaintance of Captain Vaughan, and I determined to pay him back for his iniquity." It took Gregory a year. It was the Saturday after the 1851 Derby, and he was playing cards at the Turf Club when Vaughan appeared. Words were exchanged, and Gregory threw down his gauntlet in the fashion of the day: an insulting slap across Vaughan's face with his glove. That meant a duel, and by tradition, it would take place the following day, which couldn't happen, because it was Sunday. Gregory had over £10,000 to collect in winnings on the Derby on the Monday or Tuesday, 'and some large sums for friends.' Their winnings were in Gregory's name, which made them anxious. The result of the duel was seen as a foregone conclusion: Gregory counted pistol-shooting as 'a favourite amusement,' practised regularly and 'was a perfect master of the weapon.' Captain Vaughan wasn't. Nonetheless, good things do get beaten, and dead men don't collect winnings. It was agreed that Gregory would go to Tattersalls to collect the winnings before he faced Vaughan. The delay gave Gregory time to think that a life in exile, avoiding English justice, wasn't his preferred future. When they faced each other, Vaughan grabbed first shot. He missed. Gregory took careful aim between Vaughan's eyes, allowed the man a few terrifying moments – and fired in the air. This took place in the grounds of Lady Jersey's Osterley Park. She told Gregory that her children had been watching from the terrace, 'Highly delighted at having seen some gentlemen shooting at each other.'

Gregory looked back on, "A lovely spring morning, by no means one for leaving the world, especially with £10,000 in one's pocket." He emerged from the Damask affair a far greater winner than if he'd put a bullet through the forehead of the wretched Vaughan. The only sure loser was Treen. Gregory felt obliged to take his horses from Beckhampton, 'in deference to public opinion.' He never blamed Treen, whom he understood had got himself into a tangle which had no path through it. But too many people had lost too much over Damask for him to continue with Treen as if nothing had happened.

William Gregory's memoirs recalled a series of successful coups. One might wonder how it was that only two years after he took his horses from Beckhampton, he sold half his Galway estate, raising over £50,000 to pay off gambling and other debts. The likely explanation is selective editing. Gregory was a widower of 63 when he married the 28-year-old Lady Augusta Persse, the youngest daughter of another prominent west of Ireland family. She was one of the early champions of Irish literature and theatre, described by George Bernard Shaw as, "The greatest living Irishwoman." Unfortunately, her serious nature led her to 'improve' Gregory's posthumous autobiography before publication. In its preface she wrote, *"I have left out many passages that seemed too personal, or that might [have] slighted the memory of the dead."* Which may translate as, 'My husband's legacy isn't going to be tarnished with details of his disastrous betting.'

William Gregory's horses had been the mainstay of Beckhampton from the time of Fulwar Craven's retirement. Treen faced struggle and disappointments, in every aspect of his life. His wife Harriet died young, leaving him with four small children. His eldest son, the promising jockey William Jnr, died aged only 21. Meanwhile, the Beckhampton Inn was more trouble than it was worth. The failures of various tenants distracted Treen as he tried to train winners. A pair called William Toms and John Matthews went bankrupt in 1846, and the brewing equipment and the furniture and effects were back under the auctioneer's hammer the following January. The necessary local trade seems to have been in place: the Beaufort and Tedworth hunts and various private packs met at the Inn. The 'Autumnal Ploughing Match dinner' and similar events were held there until at least 1854. The surrounding downs were the venue for some of the best-attended coursing events in the south of England. But the coach routes that had paved the Bath road with gold had gone, and with them the Inn's profits.

Treen soldiered on as best he could. There was no shortage of owners who wanted to patronise Beckhampton, but the newcomers didn't pay their bills as fully or promptly as Craven and Gregory had done. He was forced to waste time and energy pursuing defaulters.

Fred Swindell rode to the rescue when Treen was foundering. Swindell came from modest beginnings in the north, where he saved enough money from meagre wages to give himself a treat: a visit to the races, where he backed every winner. He decided racing was more appealing than working in a factory. He set himself up as a backer and layer in Liverpool, and when he was established he moved to London. He took a pub, laid bets, gave decent odds, and if called on he paid promptly. Some of his customers were the servants of gentlemen who owned racehorses, so Swindell found out when their horses were fancied – and which of the owners knew when they were going to win. In time the masters brought their business to him. They found that if they wanted a proper bet, Swindell got the money on more efficiently than they could themselves. If necessary, he was the first man into Tattersalls and the last to leave. He built up a countrywide network of bookmakers who could be trusted to work a commission securely. Along the way to leaving £146,000 in his will, Swindell had fun with a horse or two.

One of them was a crocked Chester Cup winner. The brown horse Leamington – by Faugh-a-Ballagh out of an unnamed and unraced Pantaloon mare – was owned by Swindell in partnership with Fred Higgins, who raced the colt as a two year old in 1855, when he won at Warwick and Derby, trained by Edwin Parr. He didn't thrive the following year, and ran mostly at sprint distances. His reappearance the following season was in the two miles, two furlongs Chester Cup – the Tradesmen's Plate. As he hadn't won over further than a mile, it was a surprise to find Leamington only 14–1 when a market formed early in February. By the eve of the race in May, he was a rock-solid 9–2 favourite. His rider kept Leamington just behind the lead until the final straight, where two rivals hung away from each other at the distance, and Leamington sailed between them to win cosily.

Leamington's connections and supporters landed a huge gamble. *Bell's Life* wrote that, 'The big winners over Leamington included Fred Swindell. The lion's share – £30,000, it is reported – fell to Mr Swindell, who made no secret of his confidence throughout.'

In his next three outings, Leamington was out of the first six in the Gold Cup; won the Goodwood Stakes; and then flopped badly. Swindell transferred the horse to Billy Treen. Leamington ran just once as a five year old and broke down. Small wonder that in the spring of 1859, he was 50–1 in the opening shows for Chester. He was nibbled at in the betting during April, and then dropped suddenly to 9–1 favourite a fortnight before the Cup. Once his own money was 'on', Swindell spoke openly about his confidence. Leamington was 15–2 the night before the race. On Cup morning, he worked on the Roodee with both his forelegs bandaged. He sweated profusely, and his price drifted. Cometh the hour and the saddling, Treen took the bandages off and, 'exhibited Leamington's legs as hard and clean as a foal's.' That was the signal for a general public gamble, in which Fred Higgins was seen taking £500 to £100 just before the off. Half-way round the final circuit Leamington made rapid headway to pick up the leaders, went on at the entrance to the straight, and won even more easily than two years before. He was the first horse to win two Chester Cups.

"Today's performance stamps Leamington [as] one of the best horses of modern times," said *Bell's Life*: "Treen came in for his due share of congratulatory compliments." At stud, Leamington sired a number of minor winners before being bought for £1,575 by a Canadian breeder to stand in Kentucky. It was an inspired move: the unsound Leamington became one of America's most influential stallions in the late nineteenth century. He got Aristides, who won the first Kentucky Derby; Harold and Saunterer, who both won the Preakness Stakes – and Saunterer the Belmont Stakes; and the stallions Eolus and Longfellow. This side of the Atlantic, Leamington was represented by Iroquois, who in 1878 became the first American-bred and trained colt to win the Derby, and followed up in the St Leger.

Leamington's Chester success couldn't hide the reality that Treen wasn't making his stable pay. Two years later, his house and seven acres, "Delightfully situated adjoining the celebrated Beckhampton Downs," were advertised for sale by private treaty. No buyer came forward, and as the 1862 season began, Treen still had Fred Swindell as an owner, and despite the question marks hanging over the yard, had taken a few horses for another prominent bookmaker, James Smith. A year that started uncertainly would turn out remarkably well. The railways, which had ruined the Beckhampton Inn, now turned benefactor. Previously, a course like Newcastle might as well have been in Spain, so far as Beckhampton was concerned. Then a railway station opened in Marlborough, and any racecourse with a convenient rail link was brought within reach.

A week before the Northumberland Plate, the ante-post market had no mention of a Treen-trained horse. Then, havoc. A Beckhampton three year old called Montebello, winner of a five furlong seller in his first season and unsighted in a bad race at Bath on his reappearance, was introduced at 50–1 in the Plate betting, and plunged to 12–1 on the Monday before the race. The next day in London, 10–1 'was taken rather freely,' and by post time on the Friday, Montebello was 6–1 second favourite. The horse ran in the colours of a Mr Marshall, but he was known to have at least two co-owners. One of them was the formidable Fred Swindell. The arrival of his horse, from far beyond the footlights to centre stage in the betting, sent a shudder through the press tipsters.

Montebello's dismal form got him into the race with bottom weight of 5st 7lb. His jockey Jimmy Grimshaw took care to keep him close to the pacesetters for the first mile. He led soon after, and won by a length with something in hand. "The winner and [the] tiny rider were loudly cheered," reported *The Sporting Life:* "A copious supply of champagne was dispensed among the jockeys and officials there assembled." Other writers were less enthusiastic. Typical was the northern correspondent who fumed: "The success of Montebello was one of those clever pieces of racing tactics with which

Mr Treen every now and then favours us, but which he invariably does in his own quiet style. I may be pardoned for quoting the following, which [appeared] on Wednesday morning:

> "Tuesday night, 11 pm – From information which I have just received, I am led to the conclusion that MONTEBELLO will prove to be a most dangerous opponent to my selection for the Northumberland Plate. He is a brown gelding, and trained by Treen at Beckhampton. He appeared in public 11 times last year, but was a very indifferent performer. He is said to be so much improved that his trainer considers him a second Tim Whiffler.[1]
>
> "That his owner Mr Swindell took the racing world by surprise with him there is no doubt. The horse had only appeared in public once this season, when he cut up badly [at Bath], running among a lot of rank duffers. Time and money, however, work wonders, and 'Frederick the Great' can always afford to bide a wee [while]."

The improvement was explained after the prize and the bets were secure. Treen had been working Montebello with a horse of Lord Stamford's, Dusk, who'd already won at Ascot, Chester and Salisbury that season. One or two pundits like 'Our Detective' in *The Racing Times* admitted to having been, 'Informed early in the week of Montebello's trial with Dusk, but I admit that I thought it was too good to be true.' *The Morning Post* noted, "Montebello had no claims to be looked upon as the winner from his public running, which was not good enough to win a saddle. [He] had been tried very highly with Dusk, and the secret was preserved so well that the money was got on at a good price. Treen, the trainer, has won a 'stoater' as have all his friends."

1 Tim Whiffler was a three year old trained in Middleham. He was the top stayer of the 1862 season, winning nine times from 11 starts, including the Chester, Doncaster and Goodwood Cups, and the Ascot Gold Vase.

The word stoater has long since disappeared, but it implies enough in winnings to put food aplenty on Billy Treen's plate. He didn't have to wait long for the next helping. The galloping companion for Montebello and Dusk was a three year old maiden, Hartington, who belonged to James Smith. Hartington had failed to place in six outings as a two year old, but he blossomed in the spring and acquitted himself well in gallops against the other two, to the extent that Treen told Smith, 'He'll win the Cesarewitch.' Then Montebello won the Pitmen's Derby, Dusk won three more races, and in the autumn Hartington did a sensational piece of work which showed him to be Dusk's equal – and Hartington was in 'the long race' with just 5st 10lb. One or two rumours circulated, but they eluded the experts who assessed the race. One report noted, "Down in Beckhampton, William Treen and the touts think fondly of Hartington, but Mr James Smith is a funny fellow, and with [only] a couple of broken-downers to try a horse with, I think he is having a game this time." *The Racing Times* opined: "Hartington has been backed for some genuine money [but] the 'trying tackle' at Treen's command is not good enough to trust. His owner is a great favourite with all racegoers, but I am afraid all Treen's skills shall be found unavailing." The reasoning was obtuse; the stable housed the winner of the Northumberland Plate. What better trial tackle could there be for a long-distance handicap?

The ante-post move for Hartington wasn't as spectacular as Montebello's – he was backed from 33–1 to a starting price of 100–8, but it was a strong market. Treen was using the word 'certainty,' and Smith passed it on, verbatim. The finishing touch in the stable's preparations was to recruit Jimmy Grimshaw to ride Hartington. The youngster had already been booked to ride for George Payne, the best-known owner and losing punter of the time. Smith offered Payne a sweetener to release Grimshaw: £100 on Hartington at 25–1. Payne agreed to let Grimshaw change mounts, but, heroically foolish as ever, declined Smith's free bet and had £25 of his own money on, at a shorter price. The 1862 Cesarewitch had 37 runners, the largest field to that date. Nearing the Bushes, a group of seven horses had broken clear of their rivals, and there was still no sign of Hartington, but then he picked up his bit and scythed through in the last half furlong, drawing clear with an outsider. Grimshaw asked Hartington for one more surge in the shadow of the post, and he went a length up.

The bets said to have been landed were eye-watering. *The Sporting Life* reckoned that James Smith, 'a popular member of the Ring,' "Lands between £15,000 and £20,000" (£1.25 million to £1.65 million today). His bookmaker friend Mr Steele of Sheffield was credited with £7,000. "Among noble patrons of the sport we hear that Lord Stamford had one nice bet of £2,000 to £100" – no more than his due, after his horse Dusk's sterling work on the gallops; "and that Lord Westmorland was also 'well on…' Very few [bookmakers] can have escaped laying against Hartington, as he is backed for such an immense stake by his owner and party." Last but not least Billy Treen, "in addition to winning a nice stake on his own account, stood £1,000 to nothing with the owners." Small wonder that *Baily's Magazine* wrote, "Treen's luck brought us back to the [winners] he used to lead in before the fickle goddess went dead against him. It is pleasant to think that he has not only got in coals for the winter, but something to render him comfortable for the remainder of his days."

If only. In 1862 Treen took two three year olds, seemingly moderate, untried over the distances of their intended races. He got them handily weighted and produced them ready to run for their lives in two of the most coveted handicaps in the calendar, five months apart. The first Master of Beckhampton was obviously a trainer possessed of far above average skill. But the 'fickle goddess,' having beamed on him that summer, turned away again. The next few seasons spiralled downwards, and in May 1866 Beckhampton was back on the market, this time with no reprieve. The buyer was a fellow Wiltshire trainer, Harry Woolcott. Even the sale of Beckhampton failed to cover the debts Treen had accumulated because of defaulters among his owners. He filed for bankruptcy. Creditors were told Treen's assets were about £700, but that after payment of legal expenses it wasn't likely they'd see any of it.

Billy found a lifeline from Ceylon. Years after he'd taken his horses away from Beckhampton, Sir William Gregory gave Treen a reference. Gregory's career had reached its zenith with his appointment in 1872 to be Governor of Ceylon. He presided over a period of prosperity, in which coffee and tea planting played a big part. The smartest of the planters was an Okehampton man, Reginald Downall. He was so successful as an estate manager that he bought his own 250-acre holding in Ceylon's highlands, and was made superintendent of other estates. His meteoric rise caught Governor Gregory's eye, and Downall was appointed to the legislative council of Ceylon. He worked prodigiously hard, he had no family, and Sir William suggested an outside interest. It was racehorse ownership, and as there was little racing in Ceylon, Gregory encouraged Downall to look at the sport in India. If he needed a good trainer to get him going, the Governor knew just the man: Billy Treen.

Treen's brief sojourn in Bangalore and Madras provided him with stories that he shared around the paddock when he was home again: among them was a big coup with Downall's Dartmoor in the Mysore Maharajah's Cup. But mostly, his time in the sub-continent was blighted by illness. The few accounts that exist of his last years are based on a letter written by Sir William Gregory after Treen's death. Gregory told how Billy ended his days in Devon, happily looking after Reginald Downall's hunters, after Downall had returned from Ceylon. It was engaging, but it was inaccurate. Downall only repatriated when he was stricken by cancer and close to death. There was no stable of hunters in Devon, and no retirement for Treen. Billy had a couple of boxes in Lambourn to the end of his life, and he dreamed of winning one last marquee handicap. He died aged 70 in 1879. He was remembered by Sir William as, "A remarkably well-conducted and civil man, who never got drunk, never swore, and never took liberties with his employers. Few of his craft have gone before him to the silent land with a more satisfactory record."

Billy Treen took on the responsibility of the Beckhampton Inn in his twenties and developed a training yard in its outbuildings. He was decisive enough to shut the pub when it became a distraction. He had an Oaks winner, and was likely cheated out of a Derby winner. He turned out a series of winners of major handicaps, none of them unbacked. His voice calls to us from a far distance: in his time trainers weren't acknowledged, weren't interviewed or profiled, weren't even named in the *Racing Calendar.* There were no racecourse photographers to record Treen unsaddling his winners. But he established the nucleus of the Beckhampton stable that thrives today, 180 years on.

CHAPTER THREE

Formosa: four classics for Harry Woolcott

'As chubby as a cherub on a tombstone' was a contemporary's description of Harry Woolcott, the second Master of Beckhampton. Woolcott might've been rosy-cheeked and roly-poly, but in a short training career he showed he was an expert at his craft. He trained the first filly to win four English classics. He also took the hottest handicap in the calendar three times in a row, with three different horses. Woolcott could train a good 'un, and he could lay one out like a rose grower for Chelsea.

Harry Woolcott was born within sight of Stockbridge racecourse. Like Billy Treen before him, he was apprenticed to 'Honest John' Day. The salutation is a mystery, given that Day had the morals of a card sharp, but it usually appeared in inverted commas, and must've been intended as ironic. Woolcott spent 10 years at Danebury, the last four of them as head lad. He then joined his brother Isaac at the Druid's Head stable near Stonehenge. They were described as 'Guts and Gaiters'. When Beckhampton came on the market at the end of the 1866 season, Harry was invited to train there privately for a businessman, William Graham.

Racehorse ownership in the middle of the nineteenth century wasn't the democratic pastime it is today. Trade wasn't much represented in the paddock and the reserved enclosures. William Graham was an exception. He was a commoner from the provinces. He wasn't inclined to give his respect to any man who hadn't earned it. And with memories of the social evils of Gin Lane still fresh – *"Some find their death by sword and bullet, and some by fluids in the gullet"* – Graham's money came from an unfortunate source: the largest gin distillery of Victorian times, Nicholson's of Clerkenwell.

Graham first came to public attention as a wrestler. In 1827 he won the Cumberland and Westmorland Wrestling Society's annual championship. It was reported that, "He is only 19 years of age, but possesses a most athletic frame and wonderful strength. In vain did his opponents try every [trick] to throw him off his balance. He stood as if rooted to the earth." His success gave him great kudos around the northern towns where he represented Nicholson's. He had an interest in one or two horses in training in Malton. When his talent was rewarded with a promotion to Nicholson's head office, and then a partnership, Graham was able to extend his involvement in racing. His colours of 'green, black belt' were registered in 1865, and his first good horse was the filly Regalia, by Stockwell out of The Gem.

She was a big chestnut filly, owned and trained by William Harlock in Newmarket. She made her debut at the Houghton meeting, in a race which included a highly thought of French-bred colt, Gladiateur. Neither was placed. They went on to win their classics: Gladiateur the 2000 Guineas and Derby, Regalia the Oaks. At that point William Graham bought Regalia. He and Harlock fell out immediately, and Regalia was sent north to Malton, to be prepared for the St Leger. In the run-up to the race, Graham fastened onto the idea that Gladiateur was another old 'un, like Bloomsbury. Graham lodged an objection against Gladiateur, with a request that the Doncaster stewards should call for a veterinary examination of the horse's teeth. They refused, on the grounds that a certificate had been presented before the Derby to confirm Gladiateur's age.

The race was run, and beforehand Regalia struck *The Sporting Life* as, "One of the grandest mares ever seen on Town Moor, a perfect beauty." She ran gamely to finish three lengths second to Gladiateur. William Graham lodged another objection, this time at Weatherbys, to bar them from handing the prize money to Gladiateur's connections, 'until the horse's mouth had undergone examination.' Graham received some sympathy. *The Sporting Life* noted, "Mr Graham is comparatively [new to] the Turf. He is neither a blackleg [nor] a defaulter, nor a purloiner of stable secrets through the medium of touts and stable-boys." The writer added, 'I cannot see any reason why the stewards object to having the horse's mouth examined, and to hear the evidence of competent vets.' That opinion counted for as little as Graham's protests. Gladiateur was confirmed a triple crown winner, and one of the best horses of his century.

Harry Woolcott welcomed Regalia to Beckhampton early in 1867. He was on the proverbial hiding to nothing. She was over-raced and jaded: after running in three classics, she'd been asked to carry welter weights in the Cambridgeshire and the Cesarewitch. As a five year old with Woolcott, she ran 15 times and became practically unmanageable. She had a young jockey, Tom Heartfield, who understood her foibles. He found out she had to be left to her own devices. Any hint of persuasion, let alone insistence, from her rider and she'd pull herself up. She didn't even care for other horses around her getting a firm ride. Heartfield learned that at the stage of a race where the whips cracked, Regalia needed to be steered wide, into her own calm spaces. If everything went to plan and nothing upset her, the mare might put her best foot forward.

She won only twice from her 15 runs from Beckhampton, in part because so many jockeys knew how to get her beaten. This included a race in which the wily George Fordham kept his mount glued to Regalia, whipping unceasingly. Fordham was mostly hitting his own boot, but the machine-gun strikes were too much for Regalia, who ran up the white flag within sight of the post. Along came a Goodwood Cup that seemed to be Regalia's for the taking. Heartfield was readying himself when Harry Woolcott appeared, full of apologies. William Graham had been persuaded that Heartfield wasn't strong enough for Regalia. "You mustn't blame me for what I'm going to tell you," began Woolcott. He was followed by Graham himself, who as a consolation told Heartfield he was 'on Regalia for £200 to nothing.' Heartfield was advised by the weighing room elders to turn the other cheek. Everything went to script – 'young jockey shows stiff upper lip' – until the last seconds in the paddock, when Woolcott suggested to Heartfield that he might give his replacement a hint on how best to ride Regalia. It would've needed saintly qualities for Heartfield to pass up the chance for revenge. Never mind the £200, a green-eyed devil tugged at his sleeve. He told his stand-in that he should, "Take hold of her head, pull the bit through her mouth and be her master." Regalia moved smoothly into contention coming down the Goodwood straight, the substitute jockey tried to boss her, and the mare tossed her head and pulled herself up.

Regalia's decline was only a sideshow in Harry Woolcott's and William Graham's first season at Beckhampton. Graham had spent lavishly on yearlings the previous autumn, and among them was a dark chestnut filly by Buccaneer out of Eller, by Chanticleer. She was sent to the Doncaster sales from the stud of one of the best-known breeders in the north, James Cookson. She stood out as the pick of his consignment that year, and he agonised over whether to train her himself. He expected a high price, and 700 guineas wasn't enough, so he bought her in. The under-bidder was William Graham. Having slept on the matter, Cookson went looking for Graham the next morning, and found him at breakfast. Graham signed a cheque for 700 guineas and went back to his egg. The transaction took less than two minutes. The filly would be named Formosa and won him over £20,000 in prize money in her first two seasons.

Little in Formosa's first few runs hinted at the glory to come. On her fifth appearance she won a nursery handicap at Stockbridge by two lengths, getting 8lb from the placed horses, and then won the valuable Chesterfield Stakes at Newmarket's July meeting, at 20–1, followed by a tin-pot race at Abingdon. She finished off the season with an honourable fourth in the Middle Park. Over the winter, reports from Beckhampton consistently talked up Formosa: how well she looked, and how well she was working.

Nowadays, a good filly's early-season target would be the 1000 Guineas, racing against other fillies. Woolcott and Graham entered Formosa for the preceding 2000 Guineas as well. She came within a whisker of winning both. First she ran against the colts. A reappraisal of the previous autumn's Middle Park form caused Formosa to be a strong public fancy, receiving as she was a 5lb weight-for-sex allowance. The outcome of the previous October's race had been:

1.	Green Sleeve	8st 3lb	
2.	Rosicrucian	8st 9lb	head
3.	Lady Coventry	8st 3lb	2 lengths
4.	Formosa	8st 13lb	head
5.	Lady Elizabeth	8st 13lb	neck

Formosa had given weight to the colts Green Sleeve and Rosicrucian. In the 2000 Guineas she was 15lb and 9lb better off respectively with these two rivals. The betting just favoured Green Sleeve at 11–4 over Formosa at 3–1, with Rosicrucian 8–1. The 14 runners broke evenly, and before the end of the first furlong two horses had taken a clear lead: Formosa and an outsider, Moslem. The two raced side by side up the Rowley Mile and into the Dip, where they led their nearest pursuers by three lengths.

Moslem was narrowly in front as they climbed the rise to the post, but he swerved under pressure and Formosa's rider George Fordham was able to edge her into a half-length lead. Afterwards, some of the watchers thought Fordham became a shade complacent: at all events, Tom Chaloner on Moslem rode a furious finish and rejoined Formosa on the line. Amid great excitement and cheering, the judge called a dead heat – the only instance in the 200-plus years' history of the race. Formosa became only the third filly to win the colts' classic. As soon as the jockeys had weighed in, the stewards posted a notice saying Moslem and Formosa would run a match 15 minutes after the last race of the afternoon, to resolve their dead heat. Half an hour later the notice was taken down. "Everyone except the backers of Moslem was dissatisfied and disappointed," reported the *Morning Advertiser*. Harry Woolcott was keen to avoid his filly having another hard race, with the 1000 Guineas to follow two days later. Moslem's connections had no confidence that Moslem would beat Formosa in a run-off. The two parties agreed to divide the prize.

In reviewing the season's first classic, *The Sporting Chronicle* described Formosa as, "Brought out today by H. Woolcott in first-rate fettle." That evening, the call-overs for the 1000 Guineas quoted Formosa at even money, at which price she was backed to win some £20,000. The stable commission was handled by a leading bookmaker, John Stephenson, whom Graham had enlisted as his racing manager and confidant. Stephenson also laid £3,000 to £1,000 against the second favourite for the race, Lady Coventry. In contrast to the drama of the 2000 Guineas, the fillies' race was lacking in suspense. There were only eight runners, Formosa made all the running, and won in a canter by three lengths. One of the daily papers recorded the winner as, 'Mr Graham's Formosa.' Another gave her owner as 'Mr G Jones,' as does the 1868 *Racing Calendar.*

The conflicting details account for much of the controversy which plagued William Graham's few years as a noted racehorse owner. He'd barely been heard of when he raced horses with the Peck family in the north. Now, in his second season with Woolcott at Beckhampton, he had a filly who'd won both the Newmarket classics. But who was Mr G Jones? It was the alias of Graham, who had a whole posse of identities: Mr GG Keswick, Mr TG Hessey, Messrs Bertram, Brown, Winchester and Palmer were all William Graham in another guise. At the time, assumed names were both commonplace and legitimate. Sometimes the subterfuge had to do with a genuine desire for concealment: it was said of a member of the Hill-Wood family that he'd never have inherited the vast fortune of an elderly relative if she knew he was involved in betting and racing. So he ran his horses as 'Mr Eccles'. At other times, it was a necessary device: women were barred from ownership, so the dowager Duchess of Montrose raced as 'Mr Manton', though her presence in the racecourse paddock, booming instructions to her jockeys, left no doubt about her true position. The strange Alfred Cox raced as 'Mr Faerie', though again, there was no attempt to hide his identity. Sometimes the ruse was plain silly, as when Lord Somerset raced as 'Mr Somers.' Whatever the reason behind each individual's decision to run under an assumed name, the Jockey Club sanctioned it for a registration fee of £30 on the flat and £10 for National Hunt races.

William Graham felt awkward about his sudden and substantial investment in bloodstock. His senior partners at the distillers had no interest in racing until Graham became involved. When his horses became a constant talking point round the pubs and hotels which stocked their gin, they disliked the connection. Graham explained his partners' discomfort:

> "On the day of a great race, if I happen to have a favourite engaged, the whole of my [company] is disorganised, and the clerks are receiving telegrams every five minutes. Every man, too, who buys a drop of gin at the place thinks that he has the right to come and pester me about the horses. If they win they think I am a fine fellow, but if they lose they think something else."

So Graham ran his horses under a variety of names in an attempt to minimise the scale of his ownership. The subterfuge was made ridiculous by most of the horses which raced under his surrogate names carrying his colours – complemented by Harry Woolcott adopting a green and black cravat on race days. It was as if Picasso had taken to signing other names on his pictures of people with one eye and three arms; everyone would know they were by Picasso anyway. The betting public naturally thought that Graham was hatching plots. Their suspicions were reinforced because Graham was linked to the bookmaker Stephenson. The combination of multiple assumed names and a lurking bookie ensured that if a hostile interpretation could be put on the running of any of Graham's horses, it was. Graham saw himself as an injured innocent, and resented it.

No controversy attached itself to Formosa, and at Epsom, John Day provided a rod to draw away any passing lightning: a much-touted filly called Lady Elizabeth, owned by the reckless Marquis of Hastings. Her first season had been arduous. She ran 13 times and won all but one, her best performance coming in her sole defeat – the Middle Park. Formosa's fourth placing, conceding weight to the three finishers in front of her, staked her claim to be among the best of the two year olds. Almost alongside in fifth place was Lady Elizabeth, carrying the same weight as Formosa, and therefore with the same claims in the following year's big races. While Formosa was winning the 2000 and 1000 Guineas, Lady Elizabeth was kept back for an equally ambitious double: the Derby and Oaks. After Formosa's Newmarket success, the Middle Park form shone a bright light on Lady Elizabeth's prospects at Epsom. There were excitable reports of her brilliant work on the Danebury gallops. Come Derby day, she was 7–4 favourite to beat 18 rivals. She was unsighted behind a number of horses she'd beaten the previous season. An interval elapsed between the Derby principals passing the post and Lady Elizabeth appearing, to a storm of boos and whistles. Unabashed, Day announced that his filly would stick to the stable's plan, and run again two days later in the Oaks.

Some big bets were struck in the Castle Hotel in Bath on the eve of the Derby. William Graham's confederate John Stephenson was attending to a large group of sportsmen. Their focus was on the Derby. Stephenson surprised them by opening a book on the Oaks instead. He quoted *'An even £5,000, Formosa to beat Lady Elizabeth.'* When he'd taken that bet from a Lady Elizabeth supporter, he offered it to the room again. At the same time, he laid against Lady Elizabeth for both the Derby and the Oaks. It was said that, 'Something akin to a sensation was caused.' If only the fashionably-clad who rushed to Stephenson with their betting books open could've looked into the far future and read Damon Runyon's advice: 'If a stranger claims he can make the Jack of Spades jump from a sealed pack of cards and squirt cider in your ear, do not bet this man: *you are going to end up with an earful of cider.'* When a bookmaker connected with Formosa's owner offers to back her in a match against the hot favourite for the Oaks, only the sheep flock round. At the Castle Hotel that evening, they did, and they were fleeced.

The Oaks brought a cascade of praise for Beckhampton. *The Times* wrote that, "Formosa was brought to the post by Henry Woolcott in beautiful condition, altogether the best-looking mare in the race." The paper followed with a broadside at the connections of Lady Elizabeth. "[She was] a jaded, beaten, tucked-up animal, all the worse for her week's excitement, and worn to a scarecrow. [When she] appeared to take her preliminary canter, a cry almost of derision greeted the famous mare of last year. It is not too much to say she looked a bag of bones." The contrasting appearance of the two fillies resulted in Formosa hardening in the betting to 8–11, while Lady Elizabeth was 5–1. *Bell's Life* reported that the Beckhampton filly, "Looked the beau ideal of a thoroughbred, and H. Woolcott had trained her to perfection, as [her] muscle stood out as hard as nails, and her coat was bright and smooth as a piece of velvet."

After all the preceding dramas, the race, like the 1000 Guineas, was an anti-climax. Woolcott had entered a pacemaker, who made the running up the Epsom back straight to the top of the hill, where Formosa went past. Ridden by George Fordham, she gradually pulled away down the descent to Tattenham Corner, came into the straight several lengths clear, and kept on strongly to win by 10 lengths and five. When Fordham took Formosa into the winner's enclosure, Graham greeted him with a cheque for £500. He'd written it before he left London for Epsom, so confident was he of victory. As footnotes to the race, it was reported that, 'We believe Mr Stephenson wins a good stake,' which was putting it mildly; and Lady Elizabeth trailed in seventh of the Oaks' nine runners. The cheers that greeted Formosa changed to groans and hooting on Lady Elizabeth's return.

The week's uproar over Lady Elizabeth's failures obscured Formosa's brilliance in the Oaks. After the race, Graham and Woolcott ran her at Ascot, where she disappointed, and then gave her a long rest before the season's final classic at Doncaster in September. The St Leger was overshadowed by a brouhaha over yet another horse owned by the Marquis of Hastings and trained by 'Honest John' Day. It was the ante-post favourite, The Earl. The colt had solid form credentials for his place at the head of the St Leger betting. He was the only horse that season to have finished in front of the Derby winner Blue Gown. He won the Grand Prix de Paris at the start of June, and the St James's Palace Stakes. But after Lady Elizabeth, the betting public weren't inclined to repose their faith or cash in a horse trained by John Day. *Bell's Life* summed up: 'Ever since the ignominious exhibition of Lady Elizabeth in the Derby, [which] elicited a perfect storm of indignation, great curiosity has been felt as to the figure likely to be cut by her stable companion, The Earl, on the Town Moor. It is useless to deny [that] there has been a strong undercurrent of suspicion.'

As if to prove the doubters wrong, The Earl came in for fresh, heavy support 10 days before the race. His owner had come back to England from a holiday abroad in good time for the Doncaster meeting. He found a letter from Day, telling him that The Earl was very well. Hastings had another £1,000 on his colt, and his racing manager Henry Padwick staked £500. Hardly had their bets been struck than one of Day's sons appeared at Hastings' London house to tell him The Earl had broken down so badly that there was no chance of him running at Doncaster. To say this news was badly received wouldn't remotely convey the ensuing uproar. Padwick found that in some quarters he was assumed to be involved. He moved the Hastings horses from Danebury, and wrote an indignant open letter to the Jockey Club. He'd, "Been made the subject of much abuse, and imputations cast on me with reference to circumstances which occurred on the late Derby and the forthcoming St Leger." He ended by asking the Club to carry out a 'searching and complete' investigation into the scratching of The Earl.

Such was the climate of rumour and counter-rumour that Formosa, promoted to favouritism after The Earl's defection, was herself the subject of wild tittle-tattle. Her odds rose and fell with each passing whisper. The day before the race, she was having a steady canter on the course when Woolcott stopped her, thinking she might have picked up a stone. He lifted her leg to examine her foot. With nothing else to report, the touts said she was lame: out went her odds from 3–1 to 5–1. When the day of the race finally dawned, she was joint favourite at 100–30, looked in superb condition and paraded 'quiet as a sheep,' led by Woolcott, 'looking twice the dean he usually does.' The return journey was uneventful; Formosa travelled well at the back of the 12-runner field, was brought up behind the leaders at the entrance to the straight, led inside the final furlong, and won comfortably by two lengths, without her jockey Chaloner having to pick up his whip. William Graham 'Bore his victory very quietly, not indulging in any of those funny antics of throwing up his hat into the air or putting his foot through the roof. At the Albert Club, where his health was drunk in the most enthusiastic manner, he turned miracle-monger, for every liquid in the establishment was turned into champagne as if by a wave of the hand.'

Formosa became the first horse in racing history to win four classics. Sceptre repeated the achievement in 1902. As for the respective merits of Formosa and Sceptre, the palm must go to Sceptre. Not just because she won all her four classics outright and finished fourth in the Derby, but because she mixed it with the best. There's a sense from the form, and the race reports of the time, that Formosa hit on sub-standard classics in her year of glory. It's only possible to beat the opposition that lines up on the day, but there are contests and occasionally whole seasons when the competition is less demanding than on other days and in other years. Moslem's dead heat with Formosa in the 2000 Guineas was greeted with disbelief – "the biggest fluke ever known." As a two-year old, Moslem's best placing was when a remote third in a four-runner race. Another four-runner heat provided his only win prior to the Guineas. It was at Croxton Park, a venue seldom seen in a classic winner's CV. Then after the first fillies' classic, *Sporting Review* said of the runners, "Bar Formosa, a worse set of fillies never ran in the 1000 Guineas." A 10-length win at odds-on says all that's necessary about the Oaks. In the St Leger, Formosa was lucky not to meet the Derby first and third, and the last-minute absentee, The Earl. She picked a good year in which to be a three year old.

This isn't to disparage Formosa. Her run against the colts in the Middle Park, when she came out the best horse in the race at the weights, showed her to be high class. She was campaigned aggressively to take on the colts again in the 2000 Guineas, and she was managed judiciously, notably when given a three months' break before the St Leger. Harry Woolcott was singled out for praise for her appearance every time she ran. Formosa stayed in training for two more seasons, alternating between pot-hunting and tilts at the Cup races, which her pedigree suggested wouldn't suit her, as the offspring of Buccaneer generally didn't stay. When she was retired to stud she produced seven foals, none of which could run fast enough to scatter its own droppings.

William Graham attracted friendly comment through Formosa's classic year, for his modest acceptance of her successes and his generosity after each of her wins. Racing journalists looked forward to the cases of champagne he sent into the press room. It was a brief honeymoon.

CHAPTER FOUR

William Graham and a Gold Cup sulk

When William Graham liked a young horse, price seemed no object, so Woolcott could look forward each autumn to another draft of promising youngsters. During Formosa's record-setting year, the best was a colt called The Drummer. He made his three year old debut in the Lincoln, where he ran second in a big field. His next appearance was at Epsom in the City and Suburban Handicap, where he was heavily backed, from 100–8 a week before the race to 5–2 favourite on the day. He again finished second, and wasn't thought likely to run in the Great Metropolitan Handicap the following day. Nonetheless, he was led out to be saddled for the race, sparking a general plunge on him, from 7–1 to 3–1. He was held up at the back of the 11-runner field until the leaders were in line for home. Then he charged into the lead, forged ahead and won readily by three lengths and six. The win gave particular pleasure to William Graham, because prize money for the two miles, two furlongs Great Metropolitan was partly funded by subscriptions from the licensed trade. Many publicans took a keen interest in the race. The Drummer was the proverbial Group horse in a handicap; he went on to place third in the Derby and an unlucky second in the Grand Prix de Paris.

In the same season, William Graham had a posse of speedy two-year-olds. In little more than a week in mid-May, Woolcott sent out six juveniles to gain eight wins. The most successful among them was Gamos, a brown filly by Saunterer out of Bess Lyon. Graham bought her for 200 guineas as a yearling. She ran in eight races as a two year old, winning six times. One of Gamos's victories was greeted by a quip from a fellow racegoer who told Graham, "That's a game 'oss you have." The pun nonplussed the blunt northerner: "Yes, my lord, she seems a nice filly," he replied.

Gamos made her seasonal reappearance only eight days before the Derby and ten before the Oaks. She faced a colt called Macgregor, winner of the 2000 Guineas and hot favourite for the Derby. Macgregor's prep race at lowly Bath created tremendous excitement:

> "Macgregor was received at the station by a deputation of the nobility and gentry, several prominent bookmakers, a select body of touts, and the whole of young Bath. He was welcomed as if the Derby was over, and his number hoisted [in the frame]. The hotels, down to the humblest inn, were full."

Woolcott expected Gamos, 'To stretch the favourite's neck.' She didn't. Macgregor won, pulling up, by 12 lengths. *The Sportsman* claimed:

> "Gamos was so completely beaten that she could not make the necessary effort to get past the judge, who had quitted his box before she passed the winning post. From what I saw of the filly today I do not think that she can stay more than three-quarters of a mile. She can have no possible chance of winning the Oaks."

The race seemed to confirm that Macgregor was a good thing for the Derby, and he started at 4–9. The bubble burst: he finished only fourth. The result didn't bode well for Gamos's chance in the Oaks, 48 hours later. Two fillies dominated the betting. One was the even-money favourite and 1000 Guineas winner, Hester; the other was Sunshine, the winner of eight races as a two year old. Gamos was quoted at 100–8. As it played out, Hester never showed in the race. She'd been poisoned that morning, "So effectively that she was never worth sixpence afterwards." Sunshine seemed intent on pulling her jockey out of the saddle. She see-sawed from side to side until Gamos went by her easily in the last furlong. The win was greeted with disbelief. *The Sporting Review* summed up racing professionals' reaction:

> "No one paid her any attention. We never saw so many blank faces as there were after the race. It is patently hopeless to try to reconcile [her] Epsom victory with her miserable performance at Bath."

There were two plausible reasons to ignore the Bath form. Gamos had come into season before the race; and when Macgregor had quickened away, Fordham had heavily eased her. She might also have been affected by the hubbub surrounding Macgregor, who was followed to the start by a crowd of excited admirers. There the matter might have rested, had it not been for a letter published in the *Daily Telegraph* above a pseudonym:

> "Sir – Gamos. [The] word which heads this letter has been on a great many lips. A growing and widespread feeling pervades the community [that] some authoritative statement should be made by the owner of Gamos.
>
> "In the interest of Mr Graham, no less than that of the trainer and jockey, it seems to me very desirable that the world should be told why Gamos ran so badly at Bath and so well at Epsom."

The innuendo was manna for any journalist short of copy. Graham found himself on the back foot, reacting to headlines. He handled every turn in the tale clumsily. He told a journalist that he was the victim of 'poisoned pens', which prompted *Baily's Magazine* to ask if, 'More individuals are not likely to be poisoned with the liquor he distils than by writers in the press?'

He put up a £500 challenge to anyone who could show he'd done anything underhand. This was mocked – "*We want to touch the 'monkey'!*" cried *The Sporting Times*. The Epsom stewards hadn't called an enquiry into Gamos's running, so no official questions were ever tabled. Gamos won only twice more that season and the next. At stud she was a complete failure. Eventually she was sold for 10 guineas.

Graham had so much success on either side of Gamos's Oaks that one would've expected him to take criticism on the chin and be silent. Especially, he had a gelding called Sabinus, who ran twice – unsighted – as a two year old in the early spring of 1869. Between those April outings and his seasonal debut in the City and Suburban a year later, nothing was seen of Sabinus. As the months went by, though, Sabinus worked better and better, to the point where he was far ahead of the other Beckhampton two year olds. The following January, Woolcott decided to confirm Sabinus's ability. He arranged a trial gallop in full view, but no one saw it. The Beckhampton downs were host to a coursing meeting. The throng of country folk and bookmakers were intent on hares and hounds. Not far behind them the trial took place, unnoticed. It pitted the multiple classic-winner Formosa against the maiden Sabinus. At the weights, the outcome of the gallop was the equivalent of Formosa running in the City and Suburban with 6st 9lb.

The first odds on the race appeared at the beginning of February. Sabinus was briefly available at long odds. On the first Friday in February, bets of £1,000 to £25, £1,000 to £30 and £1,000 to £40 were struck (a take-out of almost £250,000 today). A week later the gelding was down to 14–1. Things went quiet for a month, and then the Beckhampton hope dropped through 100–8 and 10–1 down to 6–1. Once the money was all 'on', Woolcott told *The Sporting Times* about the gallop with Formosa. It produced some feverish copy:

> "I have heard even greater things of Sabinus. With a reasonable amount of luck it is hardly possible he can lose. His party assert that he is very

> nearly first class; his two miserable defeats of last year [count] for nothing. I anticipate an easy victory."

A reporter standing with Woolcott at Epsom told him Sabinus had a good berth coming down to Tattenham Corner, 'pulling double.' Woolcott left the stand at once, saying he was going to lead home the winner. His horse's success was met with loud and continuous cheering. It was evident that the public had followed the stable money. The following day Sabinus won the Great Metropolitan Handicap, carrying a 10lb penalty. Sabinus was 6–4 favourite. At the entrance to the straight, he shot clear to win by four lengths. Woolcott said his horse 'Had been tried to win ninety-nine Derbys out of a hundred.' Sadly, Sabinus showed temperament when he arrived at Beckhampton, with the result that he was gelded; his Derby potential could never be put to the test. But he was only the second horse to win Epsom's showpiece handicaps in the same year. Five weeks later, Woolcott sent him to Royal Ascot for the Gold Cup – and the most public of William Graham's tantrums.

He was in a tent behind the weighing room when the Gold Cup started. He seemed oblivious. There was a crescendo of cheering outside as the race was decided. People rushed in to tell him that Sabinus had won by four lengths. He responded, "Oh, that's all right. Shake hands," but didn't move the few yards from the tent to see his winner unsaddled. His jockey Richard Rowell arrived. Graham sighed and said, "Well, Dick, I suppose I must put some more money in the bank for you." An equerry appeared to ask Graham, would he join the Prince of Wales in his box, and receive his congratulations? For perhaps the only time in the gracious history of such invitations, the answer was, "Let the Prince come here." The startled equerry repeated his request. Graham replied that the Prince could be damned, for all he cared. The flunkey beat a precipitate retreat.

The image of Graham sitting sullenly in a tent on one of the biggest days of an owner's racing life suggests his conflicted feelings about racing. He liked horses, he liked to be a winner and he liked to bet. In two-and-a-half seasons' training with Woolcott at Beckhampton, Graham had won five classics, two Great Metropolitan Handicaps, a City and Suburban, a slew of two year old races, and now a Gold Cup. He could hardly have been luckier if he'd fallen off Beachy Head and landed in the arms of a beautiful and willing heiress. Yet he was morose. He resented being pestered for tips and information. His business partners were putting pressure on him to reduce his profile. It was becoming obvious that – like other rich men before him, and plenty still unborn – he was being run up at the sales. When he realised what was happening, he acted through third parties, but they were spotted in a trice, and their bids were pushed up too.

His use of assumed names for his horses' ownership generated suspicion and sometimes satire, as when *The Sporting Times* penned some 'Exclusive Intelligence from Beckhampton':

> "Mr G Jones was out early this morning to see his horses gallop. He was accompanied by his able trainer and by Mr GG Keswick. Mr W Graham joined them; and Mr JG Hessey watched the proceedings from his brougham. All the gentlemen expressed singularly unanimous approval of the appearance of the horses and the style in which they galloped."

No reader of the sporting press needed it explained that the four gentlemen were sure to express 'singular approval' – because they were the same man: William Graham.

Graham's snub to the Prince of Wales was the most visible expression of his northerner's dislike of 'airs and graces'. He seemed to go out of his way to be rude to the press and to any bar his close acquaintances. *Baily's Magazine* wrote that his, "Sensitive temperament compelled him violently to resent the ridicule and abuse which his own course of action brought down [on his] head; and he would querulously complain that the public misjudged him."

After the Gold Cup, Sabinus ran in the Goodwood Cup, was beaten half a mile from the finish, and ambled home in fourth place. The press wondered why, which prompted a further outburst from Graham. There'd been setbacks, too, alongside the prizes gathered in by Sabinus and Gamos. Two of the previous season's all-conquering two year olds, Astolfo and Captivator, were disappointments. Their failures were greeted with scorn. Even the Devizes paper joined in, the day after the Derby: "[Only] the other day Mr Graham's Astolfo was the crack. There was nothing like him for the Derby! Mr Graham had never before owned such a horse! There wasn't his equal in England! Where was he yesterday? Quietly eating his oats in the Beckhampton stable!" Fortunately, Captivator recovered all the losses and more at the start of the 1871 season, when he won the Great Metropolitan. It'd be hard to over-praise the skills of Harry Woolcott, who produced three different horses to win one of the most coveted and valuable handicaps in the calendar. The *Morning Advertiser* hailed the achievement, albeit in sarcastic terms:

"Fordham [brought] Captivator to the front before reaching the distance, and doing as he liked with his opponents, so contradicted [earlier] form that his success could hardly be believed in. There is no doubt that the shrewd Beckhampton division had laid themselves out for this particular race.

"To win once for his [customers] is a proof that Mr Graham intends practical good, not theoretical benefits. But when it is to be recorded that he has now won it three years in succession, with The Drummer, Sabinus and Captivator, congratulation and thankfulness must become elevated into the greatest veneration and confidence. Nothing less than knighthood should be conferred upon the eminent and wealthy distiller, in addition to an interview with Royalty."

After his behaviour at Ascot, it's unlikely that Graham would've been allowed over any Royal threshold, let alone knighted, but his popularity among hotel-keepers and landlords was secure. He served them up another big handicap at the end of the season with Sabinus, who won the Cambridgeshire under what was hailed as the greatest of George Fordham's rides, getting up in the last stride. And Graham had another pipeline of promising two year olds coming through. The best seemed to be Digby Grand, bought at Doncaster for 200 guineas. The colt won three times in his first season, and was beaten only a length and a half when fourth in the Middle Park. He ran well in the following year's Derby – a close fourth – but achieved little else as a three year old and seemed to be mulish. He caught at least one tipster's eye when he reappeared under 7st 8lb in the City and Suburban: 'I don't know why Digby Grand's chance is so universally neglected. He finished gamely enough in some of his two year old races and again in the Derby.'

Even at his starting price of 100–6, Digby Grand attracted public support. The Epsom crowd wasn't likely to overlook his connections' multiple course successes. Digby Grand was always up with leaders, hit the front well inside the last furlong, and ran on well, to loud cheering. The next day he followed up in the Prince of Wales's Stakes. A happy punter was moved to poetry:

> They may talk of some outsiders
> But if the bets you'll land
> Go in and back Beckhampton's black –
> Old Graham's Digby Grand!

It was Graham's last big-race winner. That December, he opened a letter from the senior partner at his distillery, William Nicholson. 'My dear William,' it began:

> "You are aware that the present partnership terminates this year and that we must have a new deed prepared. As there are one or two matters on which it is necessary to come [to] a clear understanding, I intended speaking to you today, but I think it better to write rather than to trust

to merely talking them over, when mistakes and misapprehensions are liable to occur.

"After our long partnership connection I feel very reluctant to mention the first point and you will believe, I am sure, that it is only a strong sense of its necessity that causes me to interfere with what is only an amusement to you, but the consequences of which reflect themselves not only on me, but on many persons in our employment. I mean, of course, the racing.

"Before we enter on a new partnership, I want you to give me your assurance that you will give up both the ownership of race horses and the habit of betting on them in the way in which you have done during the past few years.

"I feel that it is not for me to dictate in any way to you, but I have to say that I do not wish to be associated even indirectly with a sport [of which] I thoroughly disapprove.

"If you will kindly answer this, assenting to the views I have expressed, I will instruct [our solicitors] to prepare the new deed [of partnership]. I hope you will receive this in the spirit in which I have written it."

The letter was signed, 'Yours affectionately,' but its message could hardly have been blunter: 'The horses go, or your partnership goes.' As for the spirit in which it was written, it could be summed up as 'troubled'. Nicholson's copy of the letter contains repeated alterations and over-writing.

Graham's racehorse ownership was ended by those few paragraphs. His partnership agreement gave him a quarter of the 'gains and profits' of the distillery. At the time of William Nicholson's letter, the firm had a fully paid-up capital of £85,000. It owned a large freehold site close to the City of London. In the last three months of 1872, its profits were £407,000 in our money. There was a large credit balance at the bank. Nicholson left William Graham with no choice. Most of his horses left Beckhampton for the sales the following month.

A few of his string remained at Beckhampton. Two of them passed into the hands of a Jockey Club member, Sir George Chetwynd. He was only 24, but already had several years' experience of the Turf. At the time, his horses were trained by William Saunders at Hednesford, not far from Chetwynd's home, Grendon Hall in north Warwickshire. He had an estate of 6,000 acres, producing an income of £12,000 a year. Even so, Chetwynd's spendthrift lifestyle meant he needed more. His fortunes weren't improved by marriage to the Marquis of Hastings' widow, Florence. She was a great beauty – 'the pocket Venus' – but as her late husband lost everything gambling, she was a few noughts short of a decent dowry. The Newmarket trainer George Lambton described Sir George Chetwynd:

> "[He was] a tall, slight, distinguished-looking figure, with, when he chose to exert it, a considerable charm of manner… I don't think Sir George had ever been a rich man. He certainly was not one when I knew him. But he was determined to live as if money was no object, and in many ways he was the most extravagant man I have ever met. He was an extraordinarily fine judge of racing, and it was well known that the Turf had to supply the money to support his style of life."

Chetwynd aimed to clear £6,000 a year from his racing interests. Whatever instructions he gave to the small-time trainer Saunders, they failed to produce the results he expected. Meanwhile, Chetwynd noticed the fireworks sent up by Harry Woolcott from Beckhampton. The five classics were one thing. The cascade of handicap winners was another, was irresistible. It represented Chetwynd's dream of racehorse ownership.

Chetwynd became Woolcott's principal owner. He began with four horses in the yard, two of them bought from Graham's dispersal. One was the mare Lady Atholstone, whose wins in two minor handicaps at Shrewsbury encouraged Chetwynd to pay £1,000 for her, "But at first she was a very unlucky buy for me and I lost a lot of money on her." There were disappointments also from Cat's Eye, tried as a yearling on Chetwynd's first visit to Woolcott, and which Sir George thought was certain to develop into 'a flyer.' There were days when Cat's Eye flew, but they were hard to predict. In his three year old season the colt was heavily backed by Chetwynd for the Stewards' Cup: he was never sighted. Ten days later Cat's Eye met the winner of the race again, at the same weights, and beat him by 10 lengths. Chetwynd drily called this, "Not encouraging for those who, like myself, believe in public form."

In Sir George's second season at Beckhampton he bought several more horses in the yard. He told of going down to Beckhampton to try some hopefuls:

> "There had been a heavy fall of snow. Nevertheless, we tried the horses, but not on our ordinary ground. There were other horses in the trial, but Little Harry won it, and I bought him for £1,200 from Henry Woolcott, believing he would win the City and Suburban."

His confidence grew when one of the other horses in the trial won the Free Handicap. Alas:

> "We were doomed to disappointment [at Epsom], as Little Harry, although trained to the hour, was easily beaten by three lengths, and what is more, he went from bad to worse, never winning a race. The following year at Brighton, sick to death of a horse that had cost me so much money, I ordered Woolcott to shoot him that very night."

Chetwynd's shrewd placement of his horses meant that he usually made his investments pay. In 1876, his third year with Harry Woolcott, he wrote that, "Though my horses were moderate, by entering them carefully I found that up to the end of the Sussex fortnight [in August] I had cleared £10,000 on the year." His horses were mediocre across the five years in which he had horses at Beckhampton. Then at the end of the 1878 season, Sir George gave Harry Woolcott notice that he was moving his horses to Newmarket.

In the following January, several of Sir George's string left Marlborough station for the sales. Soon after, the remainder were sent to Joseph Dawson at Bedford Lodge in Newmarket. Woolcott could be forgiven for feeling bruised. He won over £20,000 in prize money for Chetwynd, who topped up the purses substantially by selective punting. Chetwynd has been pilloried for abandoning Woolcott, but in 1878 he was elected a Steward of the Jockey Club, which involved frequent visits to Newmarket. The neutral view would be that if his time was divided between London, Newmarket and his home in north Warwickshire, then Beckhampton simply wasn't a convenient place to train.

Sir George was responsible for the revival of George Fordham's career. The great jockey – not an inch behind Fred Archer in contemporaries' regard – had hung up his saddle to enjoy his investments. He spent a year drinking himself towards complete retirement when Chetwynd called on him and persuaded him to ride again. As a result, Fordham went to stay at Beckhampton with Harry Woolcott, rising early to ride work on the two year olds, gradually getting his confidence and fitness back.

Sir George's move to Newmarket was a disaster. His new trainer Dawson died, and his widow rented the yard to the capricious Duchess of Montrose. Dawson's head lad Richard Sherrard took over the trainer's licence. The stable jockey was Charles Wood, and he was the problem. He was an excellent jockey who had a shrewd head for investments, but his portfolio had been built up by betting, by selling information and by 'stopping' horses on an industrial scale. The running of Sherrard's horses was manipulated to the exclusive benefit of Chetwynd and Wood. The Duchess of Montrose suspected, with reason, that the news Sherrard gave her about her horses didn't always correspond to the true position. Volcanic rows were a staple of Bedford Lodge life. One of the properties that Wood owned in Newmarket was named Chetwynd House, in Sir

George's honour. It became clear that some of Chetwynd's horses were owned by Wood, contravening Jockey Club rules.

It was also obvious that they weren't being run on their merits. Wood and Chetwynd were acting so brazenly that they were bound to be challenged sooner or later, though not, as it turned out, by racecourse stewards. First came a damning accusation in the *Licensed Victuallers' Gazette*: "How about the running of Success at Lewes and Alexandra Park, where Charley Wood nearly pulled his head off on each occasion?" Wood sued for £5,000 damages. The case was heard in front of a judge whose asides suggested it was all rather a jape, and the jury responded by finding in Wood's favour, but awarding him a derisory farthing in damages. Not long afterwards, at the Gimcrack dinner in York, Lord Durham attacked:

> "A well known and aristocratic racing stable that has been conspicuous throughout the racing season for the constant and inexplicable in-and-out running of its horses."

Everyone in racing knew that Bedford Lodge and Chetwynd were Durham's targets. As George Lambton noted, "During the season there had been a great deal of talk about the running of horses from Sherrard's stable." For the avoidance of any doubt, Durham added: "I accuse Sir George Chetwynd of having connived at serious malpractices which are contrary to the rules of racing." Chetwynd challenged Durham to retract or to fight a duel. Durham refused to do either, leaving Sir George no option but to sue for libel. The parties agreed to be represented by barristers in front of a tribunal comprising three Stewards of the Jockey Club. Chetwynd 'won' but was also awarded just a farthing, and his costs were heavy. He resigned from the Jockey Club, cut his string back to a handful of horses, and gradually left racing altogether. He was often seen visiting Sam Lewis, the biggest money-lender in London.

The day came when Chetwynd entertained the notorious George Alexander Baird ['The Squire'] at his house in Curzon Street. Baird was champion amateur rider several times, and a substantial owner. He was also addicted to low life, prize-fighting and 'harlotry'. That evening, Baird expressed his delight at everything he saw in Chetwynd's home. He made a drunken offer for the building and every stick of furniture in it. Chetwynd accepted, handed over the keys and left. Baird staggered upstairs. Waking up in a strange bed, head throbbing, he had no recall of the previous evening. "Where am I?" he moaned. "At home, Squire," replied a hanger-on.

William Graham didn't outlive his racing interests by long. After his dispersal sale he disappeared from the racecourse, and died after a short illness three years later. Nicholson's was closed on the day of his funeral, and over 100 of the distillery staff were at the burial, decked out in hat-bands and gloves provided by his partners. *The Sporting Times* said, "Among the licensed victuallers of London he was a God." Yet none of the drinks trade newspapers carried an obituary of William Graham. Evidently he made as many enemies there as he did in the racing press. In his home county, the *Westmorland Gazette* headlined the *'Death of a once Famous Wrestler.'*

Harry Woolcott struggled after losing Chetwynd's horses. At the peak of his Mastership, Beckhampton employed 20 men and boys in the stables and a cook, housemaid and nursemaid in the house: a lot of mouths to feed, not forgetting his wife and four children. He wrote to a friend on *The Sportsman* saying he had many boxes and hardly a horse to fill them. The resulting mention was well meant, but not an ideal message: "Woolcott has plenty of room for either public horses or a private racing stud." He attracted new owners, but none of them raced on the scale of Chetwynd or Graham. One was the Duke of Hamilton. His brief spell at Beckhampton included the emergence of a promising two year colt, Lollypop. Woolcott kept it under wraps for an autumn debut at Newmarket. The moment the first prices on the Middle Park were quoted, Lollypop was the hot favourite. The Duke had probably been telling his friends about his star colt for weeks. He chose to blame Woolcott: "If a horse of mine trained in the wilds of Wiltshire can be a good thing before it has ever seen a racecourse, it is high time for me to find fresh quarters and a new trainer." Lollypop was beaten all ends up.

Woolcott struggled with poor health from the time of Chetwynd's departure. He was seldom seen on the racecourse, and the following year it was assumed that he'd given up training. In March 1882 he put Beckhampton up for auction. It failed to meet its reserve, but was sold privately a few days later. Harry Woolcott died of kidney failure that December, aged only 50. He was remembered as, "A man wonderfully well liked" in *The Sportsman*, and for his 'kindly disposition' in *The Sporting Life*: "He was one of the most intelligent and genial-hearted men that ever lived [and] a most excellent trainer."

CHAPTER FIVE

Sam Darling and Jack Gubbins

"No trainer in the history of racing was more respected, both for competence and character, than Sam Darling." So said *The Times*, almost 40 years after Darling bought Beckhampton from the ailing Harry Woolcott. Darling had a pedigree to match any of the horses that he trained. His grandfather, also Sam, was one of the best jockeys of the first half of the nineteenth century. In 1832 he rode in 174 races and won 73 of them: a 42 per cent strike rate. Among his successes was the valuable Tradesmen's Plate at Chester, which later became the Chester Cup. The following year he won it again – and twice more besides – and also rode his only classic winner, Rockingham, in the St Leger.

The win seems to have been the result of some trickery by the trainer, Dick Shepherd. He had two runners in the race for the same owner, Richard Watt. The owner's 'selected' was Belshazzar. Darling was booked to ride. He was in the weighing room, putting on Watt's 'harlequin' first colours, when the trainer appeared and told him, "Thee must ride in the white cap today. Thee'll win." Darling was taken aback, not least because he had £25 on Belshazzar. But Shepherd was persuasive: "Thee'll win," he repeated: "Have a glass of sherry for luck, and don't look so sulky." So Darling put on the white cap of Rockingham, held him up, hit the front inside the last furlong and won by a length. Belshazzar finished fourth. It was said that Shepherd sent Belshazzar's groom on an errand before the saddling, and in his absence gave the horse a bucket of water. His owner Watt believed it to his dying day. He must, though, have had a 'saver' on Rockingham, because he gave Darling a £200 present.

A two year old grey colt called Isaac made its unnoticed debut about that time. He was two years older and still a maiden when he caught Sam Darling's eye, finishing well in a little race at Liverpool. After a spell when he was used as a lead horse on a northern stable's gallops, he appeared at the sales, and there was Darling to buy him for 46 guineas. The horse hadn't been named, so Darling called him Isaac, after his previous trainer, Isaac Blades. The human Isaac was so upset that such a poor animal should be named after him that he 'cut' Darling, and swore never to speak to him again. Blades was made to look foolish. His reject, trained by Darling, went on to win a few races over hurdles and 46 on the flat – a win for every guinea of his purchase price, almost all of them ridden by Sam, shouting, "Come on, old 'un." Along the way, Darling sold him for an astonishing £2,000 to William Collins, an owner who was MP for Warwick. It became a priority for Darling to run Isaac in Collins' constituency. Darling retired in 1844. He used to visit Isaac in retirement. When the old horse became infirm and was put down, Darling had a chair covered in Isaac's hide, so that his later years were spent seated as he'd been for those winning rides.

Sam had two sons who became jockeys. His grandson Sam, Master of Beckhampton, had only this to say about his father: "[He] rode, but did not train, and died when I was quite young." Sam Darling was born at Bourton-on-the-Hill in 1852. When he was 16 he was apprenticed to a local man, Teddy Weever, who trained his own horses with notable success. Darling rode his first winner a year later, at Croydon. He didn't make much of a mark as a jockey: he struggled with his weight, and he partnered modest horses. After six years with Weever, he spent a year each with the trainers Tom Golby at Northleach and Tom Wadlow in Shropshire, "Assisting in stable management [and] gaining knowledge of the profession." By now his weight was up to 9st 6lb, and he was confined to riding over jumps. His opportunities were further reduced when his grandmother died and his grandfather became ill. He went back to Bourton: "I left Mr Wadlow's to go and live with him. I gave him two or three of the best years of my life, often taking my turn and sitting up for night duty." Not that Old Sam was alone or destitute. His successful riding career meant that, 30 years after retiring, he could still afford a housekeeper and two servants. Young Sam continued to ride over fences, including a single spin in the Grand National. His association with a string of alliterative 'chasers – Dainty, Debonnaire, Despair and Dewdrop – had a happy outcome. They were all home-breds owned by Stephen Davis of Pershore, they were trained by his son, and they all won races under Sam Darling. That could hardly fail to impress Davis's daughter Violetta, and a couple of years later, she and Sam married.

During the period when Sam was combining riding over fences with looking after his grandfather, he also took his first steps in training. He was a stockman without equal, able to see latent ability or lurking problems that others couldn't. His former employer Weever had a horse called Acrobat, who was useless and had a tendency to fly-jump when anything upset him. After a routinely awful run in a Worcester selling race, Weever accepted Darling's £25 offer for the horse. Darling had no gallops of his own, and thought Acrobat, "Was absolutely a bag of bones." He gradually built up the serial loser. In lieu of gallops he worked the horse along the verges of the local roads. He became convinced that Acrobat could run a bit. At the time, Weever had a horse who'd been winning handicaps under welter weights. Darling asked, could he try Acrobat against Weever's horse? Of course, replied Weever, who was astonished when Darling suggested that Acrobat should concede weight. Sure enough, Acrobat won the trial. Darling entered him on consecutive days at Sutton Park, a little course near Birmingham, and asked Weever to, 'Put me £10 on my horse, and do as you like for yourself.' Acrobat won at 6/1 and followed up the next day, despite jumping into the crowd, and briefly impaling his jaw on the paddock railings. Darling then rode him in a £125 handicap, a race in which no less a jockey than Fred Archer was riding a warm favourite. Darling made all the running to beat Archer a neck. The champion's mother was at the races that day; she plaintively asked Darling, "What made you beat our Fred?" In all, Darling won five races and £425 with Acrobat. As owner, groom, trainer, rider – and punter – he gathered in every possible reward from each of the wins, and then he sold the horse on for £320. It was a useful return on his £25 investment.

His first yard was Emblem Villa near Croome, where, he recalled, "I bought horses for jumping and schooled them, and won races with many of them." One was Uncle Tom, a neglected horse whose previous owner had fed him badly or not at all. Darling bought Uncle Tom for £60, spent several months building him up, and then won a couple of hurdle races with him, before selling the rejuvenated horse on for £180. By many small steps, Darling built a reputation and the beginnings of a fortune. He moved next to Lord Coventry's Sandford House at Severn Stoke. His first ride for Teddy Weever had been in Coventry's colours, and he'd ridden a number of winners for his Lordship. He started at Sandford training his own horses, but "Soon afterwards I had several clients." Small wonder, because he continued to find diamonds in the dust: he saw a mare pulling a baker's cart, bought her for £20, got some muscle on her, hunted her – and won a hurdle race on her at Worcester.

Four years later and newly married, Sam Darling moved again. He took a yard at Heddington in Wiltshire, seven miles west of Beckhampton. He'd hardly settled in when Harry Woolcott's yard was auctioned in March 1882. It failed to reach its reserve. Nonetheless, Woolcott and the auctioneer Charles Parry were negotiating with a potential buyer soon after. On the day scheduled for completion, Darling took a chance and went to Parry's offices. He found Parry and Woolcott twiddling their thumbs: the purchaser hadn't turned up. Darling asked, had they completed? Woolcott said 'No.' Parry took the initiative and suggested, "Why not deal with Mr Darling, and no humbug?" He asked Darling if he was prepared to put down a deposit.

Darling's reply was to write out a cheque for £500. Beckhampton was his. The full amount that he paid for the yard was £3,000. The sale particulars described what he'd bought:

> "A capital and conveniently-arranged dwelling-house, in perfect condition, with pleasure and kitchen gardens. [It] is commodious, substantially and well built, and in first-rate condition [with] large dining, drawing and breakfast rooms, excellent kitchen, larder, 12 bedrooms, WC, scullery, brewhouse, laundry, large and well-ventilated servants' dining room, capital underground wine and beer cellars, etc.
>
> "There are extensive and well-arranged yards around which are 36 roomy and well-ventilated loose boxes and stalls, fitted with all the necessary requirements, and over which is a large loft where 200 quarters of oats and 10 tons of straw can be secured. [There is a] feeding room, two extensive saddle and harness rooms, boys' room, double carriage house and an extensive supply of both hard and soft water. Adjoining are two rich paddocks, well fenced."

Darling had spent 14 years preparing for the moment. If he was daunted by the vault to Beckhampton and its classic-winning history, it never showed for an instant. Portraits of Darling from the end of the 1880s show a face of great strength: not overweening, simply a handsome man in his pomp, with a direct gaze that would've commanded confidence in any walk of life. He developed the Beckhampton that thrives today, 100 years after his retirement.

He had a formidable neighbour looming over him: Alec Taylor at Manton. Taylor had built his yard in a fold of the Marlborough Downs a dozen years before. He was bank-rolled by wealthy owners. He had all the gallops he could wish for: Sam Darling had none. Billy Treen and Harry Woolcott had worked their horses on common land on the downs, or on a gallop on the adjacent farm. That wouldn't do for Darling. He persuaded the farmer, a Colonel Holford, to sell. "To make quite sure of having the use of [the] gallop, my only course was to become its purchaser." The elders of the village shook their heads: "The buildings were in a deplorable condition and the land was very foul. In fact it was in such a state that the neighbouring farmers thought I was very plucky to tackle it at all."

Darling said, "It was never my intention to farm and train at the same time," but having acquired one farm, he decided to do the job on a larger scale. Over time, he bought several other farms, creating an estate that took in the villages of Beckhampton and the adjoining Avebury, with its circle of giant standing stones – one of the largest prehistoric temples in Europe. His land extended eastwards to surround the mysterious cone of Silbury Hill. In all, he assembled between 1,200 and 1,300 acres of his own land, divided between cash crops and pasture for his pedigree Hampshire Downs sheep. He took as much pride in winning at a farmers' show as he did on the racecourse. An inside wall of his tack room was covered with prize cards from all the local agricultural shows, and from further afield; he even sent a pen of his sheep to New York to win a prize. Not far behind the sheep in his affections came his Shorthorn cattle. They too were regularly best-in-class. To store his animals' feeds, he built a colossal Dutch barn. It was fully 100 yards long, and said to be the largest in the country. Another barn was used as a granary, doubling as a concert, film and party venue.

Like Rome, all this wasn't created overnight. Darling talked of, 'Incessant attention for 14 or 15 years,' adding without false modesty, "I think I may claim to have made a success of it, having won over 200 prizes with cattle, sheep, cart-horses, swedes, [beets] and turnips. My carters have taken the first prizes for ploughing. I can also boast of [harvesting] 46lb weight of winter oats to the bushel." A writer in *The Bloodstock Breeders' Review* said Darling's farm, "Was renowned throughout the countryside as a model of excellence in every respect. Everything was in its proper place and in perfect order. There was no litter to be seen. He loathed untidiness. The same principles were applied to his racing stable. Thoroughness was the mainspring of his life, and to it he owed [the] conspicuous success he enjoyed as a trainer and an employer."

Darling himself said that from the day he moved into Beckhampton in the late summer of 1882, he never ceased to invest in new buildings and improvements – "Bringing everything up to date in every way." He introduced gas lighting, spent heavily on drainage, and built a new range of stabling, extending Woolcott's 36 boxes to over 60. Each was lined with pitch pine and strapped with galvanised iron. He built a wash-house and laundry and greenhouses. The house was modernised, too, to accommodate a rapidly-increasing family. The only development that was purely ornamental was the addition of a large porch, an imposing crenelated structure with a patterned floor of black and white tiles. It looks like the sentry box of a Gothic folly, out of place stuck onto a red-brick Georgian house, but Darling was delighted with it. He invariably posed there for photographs, looking proud and proprietorial. The investment that Darling made in Beckhampton would, he thought, have built "A very good country mansion. It's an expensive business when you come to pull an old place apart."

He needed winners to pay all the bills, and it was to be seven years before he won a major race on the flat. Meantime, he had plenty of success over jumps and in minor flat races. In his early years at Beckhampton, it was a dual-purpose yard, with the jumpers taking precedence. Any owner of a half-decent point-to-pointer today could be forgiven for drooling over the numerous races staged for hunters in the latter years of the nineteenth century. Quite apart from hunter chases, there were hunters' hurdle races, hunters' flat races ('bumpers'), even hunters' selling chases. Darling made hay in what were often uncompetitive, small-field heats. His first multiple winner was Valjean, who won 17 races over four seasons, two of them in hunters' hurdles, all the rest in hunters' bumpers. Next came Bloodstone, who won 14 races – all of them hunters' flat races.

Sam Darling's two best jumps horses were Ballot Box and Coronet. Ballot Box won three minor races as a four year old before his connections unwisely put him in a race where any horse could be claimed for £80. In stepped one of Darling's owners, Patterson Nickalls. He was a notable all-round horseman. While at Oxford he was awarded a Blue for polo, acted as whipper-in for the University Drag Hounds, and rode three winners in a day at the Oxford v Cambridge point-to-point – all on the same horse. He had tremendous sport with Ballot Box over a couple of seasons, training him 'around my cabbage patch,' and riding him to several successes at country meetings. Darling told Nickalls that his horse was being wasted. So Ballot Box was sent to Beckhampton, the first result being a hunter chase win over proper fences at Sandown Park. It was noticeable that the horse took Sandown's trappy railway fences on a perfect stride. Ballot Box was gaining lengths at each obstacle. Darling at once put him aside for the big autumn races of the following season. He ran first in Croydon's showpiece, the four-mile Great Metropolitan Steeplechase, won that, and went back to Sandown a week later with a 14lb penalty for the Great Sandown Steeplechase. He won again, in an eventful race; of the six runners, the odds-on favourite and two others fell, but Ballot Box still emerged with huge credit, because his rider Arthur Nightingall rode the race with only one iron. A stirrup leather broke at the first fence. It was a remarkable effort by the jockey, who rode into the winner's enclosure expecting praise and congratulations. What he actually heard was, 'You've won by too far,' and that as a result his mount would go up in the Grand National weights. "And that after my riding three miles over a big country with one iron!" protested Nightingall.

The following season, Ballot Box underlined his liking for Sandown by winning the Grand International Steeplechase. Before that, he ran a mighty race at Aintree under the huge weight of 12st 4lb. He was third, beaten 10 lengths by a horse to whom he conceded 25lb and a further four lengths by the second, giving him 16lb. On any reading of the result, Ballot Box was the best horse in the race, and he might have been even better. The Beckhampton gallops had been under a foot of snow for two weeks, and although Darling was able to harrow it, Ballot Box was a gallop or two short of his peak.

Coronet ran in the colours of J Gardiner Muir. In the 1888 season he ran in six hunter chases, winning five of them. Ordinarily that wouldn't cause undue excitement, but the five included two huge pay-days. First, a whopping £1,485 (£220,000 today) in Sandown's Mammoth Hunter Chase: the Grand National that year was worth £310 less. Then Coronet carried off another £624 at Liverpool in the forerunner to the Foxhunters'. In 1889 he won another five hunters' races before, at the end of the year, he fell heavily at Sandown and broke a shoulder. Where today there'd be screens raised and a swift, humane ending, instead there was a crowd of gawpers round the fence and a prolonged effort to get the unfortunate Coronet into a horse ambulance. It upset Darling so much that he decided to stop training jumpers. Ballot Box went back to Pat Nickalls' cabbage patch, and to point-to-pointing. Nickalls gave Darling a gold watch inscribed simply, 'Ballot Box.'

Darling would look back and say that he had the two best 'chasers in training, Coronet at up to three miles and Ballot Box over longer trips. As his jumpers and their owners left Beckhampton, new faces replaced them. Among them was Charles Lea, son of one of the founders of the Worcestershire Sauce firm Lea & Perrins. The Perrins family spent their money on collections of rare books and Worcester porcelain, which they gave to museums. Lea had fun instead. He owned the first winner that Darling sent out from Beckhampton: Assay, in a little race at Manchester. Darling won up to 10 races a year for Lea over the next few seasons, regularly showing his sure hand. At the end of one May, Lord Portsmouth was unwise enough to run a promising two year old in a Bath selling race. It won by six lengths. The form was unfathomable, but Darling had seen enough to buy the colt, Gules, for 610 guineas – a huge price for the winner of a Bath seller. Running in Charles Lea's colours, Gules won seven races over the next three seasons. At the start of 1889 he was dropped into a valuable seller at Kempton, won by four lengths and was sold – for 610 guineas. He ended up costing nothing, provided Lea with a lot of entertainment, and won over £1,500 in prize money.

All the while, Darling was training moderate horses and placing them to win at minor courses. He was alert to opportunities as far afield as Redcar, taking two of Charles Lea's horses to the north-east course, and winning three races with them at the meeting. Darling's breakthrough year was 1889. He trained close to 50 winners on the flat, beginning on the second day of the season with a double at Lincoln and continuing deep into November. The biggest win came at Epsom in April with Noel Fenwick's Tissaphernes. The horse had won the Great Metropolitan the previous year for another owner and trainer, but then disappointed. Fenwick bought the colt for £800, with a hurdles career in mind. The outcome was unnerving. Darling told how, "The first time he was put at a hurdle he stopped dead and seized the top bar with his teeth," pulling the obstacle clean out of the ground. Darling asked Fenwick to think about a return to flat racing: specifically, to let him train Tissaphernes for another visit to Epsom and the Great Metropolitan. Tissaphernes won, recouping £695 of his purchase price. *The Sporting Life* thought the colt was much more forward in condition than he'd been the year before: "Very hard and full of muscle. That he had the confidence of his owner and trainer on the score of well-being was soon shown in the race, as he went to the front almost at once and [jockey] George Barratt, making the pace pretty good all the way, had half his field beaten round Tattenham Corner. In the straight [he] won comfortably by a length. The victory was popular, as Mr Fenwick is a good young sportsman and the genial trainer Darling is liked by everyone."

After the successes of 1888 and 1889, Darling had a series of quiet seasons, but he'd already achieved enough to ensure that new owners were keen to patronise Beckhampton. Two were from Ireland: Harry Greer and Jack Gubbins. Greer was a product of Wellington College and Sandhurst; like William Gregory in Billy Treen's time, he was an inheritor of the 'ascendancy' – the distribution of Irish land and status to Protestant incomers from England and Scotland. Jack Gubbins was a Munster man through and through. Two unrelated events in 1893 led Gubbins to Beckhampton. The first was the closure of a small yard in Sussex. Gubbins had a few horses in training there with his friend Tommy Lushington, who decided to go back to Ireland.

The other reason for Gubbins' impulse to race his horses in England was resentment in County Limerick over his behaviour as a landowner and landlord. His wealth came from fortuitous inheritance. His elder brother died in a fall, so Jack stepped in for an estate and stud farm at Knockany. Then an uncle in the spirits business in Cork died childless, dividing his estate between his nephews and nieces. They were numerous, but as the uncle left close on a million pounds, Gubbins had £100,000 to come. He bought the big house in the village of Bruree, knocked it down and spent lavishly on rebuilding and on horses. He rode in high-weight races and won at Punchestown, Cork and Down Royal – at 15st 8lb. And he was a passionate huntsman, Master and financier of the Limerick Foxhounds. In the final years of the nineteenth century there was bitter combat between landlords and Irish Nationalists – notably the Land League. Hunting was one of the dividing lines between campaigners and landowners. Jack Gubbins was native Irish, but he pursued the ascendancy pastime of hunting and, worse, he was an unsympathetic landlord. A number of tenants on his lands were behind with their rents. He threatened eviction. It was his misfortune that a new parish priest arrived in Bruree at that time, and that it should be Eugene Sheehy, a firebrand who became known as 'the Land League priest.' His arrival in Jack Gubbins' parish spelt trouble, although it seems Sheehy was a conciliator at first. Many of his parishioners wanted the Limerick hunt stopped at once, and for Gubbins to be called to account for unwarranted evictions. Sheehy argued for patience: Gubbins, he said, provided local jobs on his estate and with the hunt. Nonetheless, Gubbins was bent on punitive action against six of his tenants. Together they owed him £189. He was in the process of spending £40,000 on Bruree and the hunt kennels. Now, he pressed the hapless tenants to pay him, or go to an arbitration which required a £1 deposit. Some didn't have a pound to their name. Gubbins and the hunt set off for a meet. Fr Sheehy was waiting, with a crowd estimated at a thousand: Nationalists, local farmers, tenants and mischief-makers. Sam Darling told in his memoirs how Gubbins was:

"Met with a large party of hooligans, who started throwing sticks and stones at the hounds, scattering them in all directions. Mr Gubbins then said: 'For God's sake leave the hounds alone. I'd rather you threw your stones at me!'"

The only possible source for Darling's account was Gubbins himself, whose quote must've read well in the London clubs: '*Good sort, this Gubbins.*' The *Cork Examiner* had a reporter on the spot. Gubbins didn't come out so well from his version. It began with a recap: Gubbins had been spared the anti-hunting pressure which was common elsewhere in Ireland; yet he hadn't generated the jobs that he'd promised; and he'd broken off talks with his tenants by sending lawyers' letters. The news report began, "Father Sheehy [was] at the head of the people. When Mr Gubbins and his party rode up, Father Sheehy asked Mr Gubbins for an interview, which after some hesitation he granted. The huntsmen and people gathered close around." Sheehy asked Gubbins to delay action against his tenants. Gubbins replied that they had, "Paid me no rent since I came into possession [of Bruree]." Sheehy contradicted him. Gubbins referred insultingly to, "Mister Sheehy." After which, Fr Sheehy raised his voice:

"With regret and reluctance I have now to deliver the ultimatum of the people of this district. You shall not hunt over their lands today, nor at any time in the future."

Gubbins, furious, replied: "Very good, Mr Sheehy, you are doing me great service; you save me several hundreds of pounds a year." The hunt staff tried to open a passage through the demonstrators, but several of the hounds were beaten: "A stout country girl felled a dog with a blow, and seemed to make [Gubbins] realise the situation."

Gubbins disbanded the hunt at once. The horses were sold. A few weeks later, he evicted his tenants. The district coroner was responsible for the evictions. He'd been elected to his post as a staunch Nationalist. It was assumed by the *Cork Examiner* that he "Would forthwith resign and do anything rather than be the instrument of ruin to these poor families." Alas, Coroner Ambrose took the silver. He was jeered and pelted, but Gubbins' tenants were thrown out regardless. One of them, the widow Murnane, had lost her husband in a railway accident and was left homeless with three small children. The English newspapers who later hailed Gubbins as, "A sportsman of the truest old Irish type," and declared that a man, "More generous or open-hearted was seldom met," can't have troubled themselves to ask what people in his home county thought of him, and why. The widow Murnane would've provided an alternative view of his generous, open heart. However, all through racing history the possession of a good horse has had a redemptive effect on a man's reputation. Even a heartless landlord needs only a classic winner to join the ranks of jolly good fellows. So it was with Jack Gubbins. He had one brilliant horse with Sam Darling at Beckhampton, and then an even better one.

CHAPTER SIX

The first Irish winner of the Derby

Vindication of Gubbins' decision to move his horses to Sam Darling came in their first season together. One of the least promising of Darling's new charges was a maiden called Blairfinde, home-bred by Gubbins at Bruree. Blairfinde's performances as a two year old in 1893 were abysmal. He ran twice, finishing out of the first three in a maiden race at Portsmouth and again unplaced in a field of six at Warwick. These weren't the credentials of a future star, but Darling found some ability that the horse's previous trainer had overlooked, and he and Gubbins decided to enter Blairfinde for the Irish Derby at the end of June. The race didn't offer remotely the same prestige or value that it does nowadays. The London sporting papers paid it almost no attention. Nonetheless, it was an event that any Irish owner would want to win. When Gubbins' colt left Beckhampton for the boat train, without a preliminary run as a three year old, the local tout predicted that, "[He] should about win the Irish Derby at the Curragh."

Darling was at Euston to catch an early train when he was greeted by the Lord Chief Justice, who was travelling to Dublin to accept the freedom of the city. He seemed more interested in the Derby than the ceremony, and arranged to meet Darling at the races. There, Harry Linde, who trained on the Curragh, sized up Blairfinde, described him as a 'damned coach-horse,' and swore that, "If he wins our Irish Derby, I'll eat him!" The Lord Chief

Justice arrived with his freedom box and asked Darling, "What will win?" "I think I shall." By this time the stable money was down, and Blairfinde had been backed from 3–1 to 6–4. His Lordship thought his new status in Dublin entitled him to better than that. He told the commissioner, "I'll have £5 on with the stable." Blairfinde jumped off in front, stayed on strongly, and beat nine rivals by 10 lengths and more. Harry Linde was man enough to congratulate Darling on, 'A divil of a fine horse,' but peeved that Gubbins, who stayed with him for the meeting, hadn't told him he was expecting to win. The Lord Chief Justice was delighted with his £15-£5. Almost the only mention of the race in London was a dismissive paragraph in *The Sportsman*: "[Blairfinde] won in a canter, but the conditions of the race gave it very much the complexion of a handicap, and the winner was receiving a stone from some of the competitors." The colt was difficult to keep sound, and never ran again. He was of no account at stud.

When Jack Gubbins looked east from Bruree towards Tipperary, he saw the Galtee mountains and their pinnacle, the steep-sided Galtee More. Any horse named after 'the big hill' would've been singled out by Gubbins' stud staff. They were spot on with their assessment of the bay colt by Kendal out of Morganette. The sire and dam had markedly different profiles. Kendal was bred and raced by the Duke of Westminster. He won five contested races in his first season but broke down, and never raced at three. He had, however, a reputation beyond that of a precocious two year old. He'd worked with another of Westminster's youngsters, Ormonde. They were equal in merit. Ormonde went on to win the triple crown – the 2000 Guineas, Derby and St Leger. The grateful Duke gave Kendal as a present to his trainer John Porter, and Porter accepted Gubbins' offer of £3,000 for the young colt. Morganette had no back-story to compete. She only ran once, attracting the verdict that she was no better than a selling plater. Gubbins noted that she came from a good family, took a chance, bought her, and sent her to his stud. Her second covering by Kendal produced Blairfinde; her fifth resulted in the bay colt that was named Galtee More. When Darling saw him at Knockany as a yearling, there were others that he preferred. Gubbins' stud manager begged to differ. For him, Galtee More was the pick. The colt was sent to Beckhampton in the autumn of 1895. He made his debut the following season in the Hurstbourne Stakes at Stockbridge, a race that always included some good two year olds. One of the touts wired that Galtee More, "Is smart, and if intended for this event will certainly be worth support, as he has done a most satisfactory preparation." On the first afternoon of the meeting, Darling found Bob Sievier next to him on the Stockbridge grandstand. Sievier was a man of many parts, all of them colourful; he was a heavy backer and layer. Sievier told how Darling tried to put him off:

> "[I was] chatting with Sam Darling and casually asked him if he was running anything in the Hurstbourne the following day. He replied that he was bringing out a niceish sort of colt called Galtee More – *but rather backward*. Looking the youngster over before the race, he took [my] fancy immensely. Despite the fact that he was ridden by a little-known jockey [I was] compelled to back him at the tempting odds of 6–1. He won in great style and at once stamped himself a good horse."

The jockey was one of Darling's work-riders; senior jockeys took over for Galtee More's remaining first-season outings. He was narrowly beaten at Liverpool – "A result I have never attempted to understand," rued Sievier – but won all his other starts. The headline-maker was the Middle Park, in which he faced Lord Rosebery's Velasquez, unbeaten winner of four races, including the July Stakes at Newmarket and the Champagne Stakes at Doncaster. Velasquez had created such a stir that he was backed to 1–5 for the Middle Park. The race was run in a downpour, on ground heavier than anyone could remember at Newmarket. Galtee More ran clean away from his rival, winning hard held by six lengths. One newspaperman somehow interpreted the result as inconclusive, telling Darling he'd never beat Velasquez again. The colts were joint favourites for the Derby over the winter.

The following spring was wet and miserable. A week before the 2000 Guineas, Darling told *The Sportsman* that, "The heavy rains have been a great source of trouble. The going on the downs has [made] it almost impossible to get horses forward in condition." The reporter drew his own conclusion: "I should therefore judge that although Galtee More is very well in himself he cannot be sufficiently wound up to give him a chance of repeating his Middle Park defeat of Velasquez, who will go to post very clean and fit." Those who'd laid long odds on Velasquez the previous autumn came back for more, taking 4–7 for the Guineas. The Marlborough tout wrote that Galtee More, "Acquitted himself most satisfactorily in a stripped gallop over a mile. There is no horse in training that has made more improvement than him. I think he will win."

He did. When the last of the gallops reports had been digested, Galtee More was backed from 2–1 to 5–4. He arrived in Newmarket on the Monday, was stabled at Mrs Aldcroft's livery yard in the High Street, and worked over six furlongs on Racecourse Side the following morning. *The Sporting Life* described a 'perfectly-trained weight-carrying thoroughbred.' On the morning of the race he did two more bits of half-speed work. After he'd finished the second of them, a watcher noticed that there were broken bottles in the grass where Galtee More had galloped. Darling was aghast. Galtee More was praised to the skies when he appeared on the course before the Guineas. "To the whole crowd of spectators his grand size, power and quality [were] a revelation. I doubt if a more perfectly trained horse was ever sent to the post. From all sides Darling was congratulated as if the race was over. He smiled confidently." Despite the throng around him, 'the big horse walked round as soberly as an old hunter.' The only caveat was that the most critical onlookers thought Darling had left a little to work on for the Derby. In the betting ring, supporters of Velasquez wouldn't abandon their champion, with the result that he and Galtee More were almost inseparable: 5–4 Galtee More, 6–4 Velasquez and 20–1 bar two, in a field of eight. The odds suggested there'd be little between the two colts, but anyone who expected a contest that day was disappointed. Galtee More was ridden by Charles Wood, relicensed after a long suspension. Wood took a lead from one of the outsiders, hugging the stands-side rail. Velasquez was alongside. Galtee More was pulling double as Wood moved him out to share the lead at the Bushes, and 'In the Dip it was all over bar the shouting, as the Irish colt, shaken up, simply left his opponents for dead, and defeated Velasquez as easily as he had in the Middle Park, the verdict being four lengths.' It was a day of firsts: the first classic winner for both Sam Darling and Jack Gubbins; a record time for the race, on ground eased by heavy overnight rain; and a first 2000 Guineas for Charles Wood, to add to his five previous classic wins. Among those congratulating Wood was Lord Durham, who'd done more than most to send him on his nine-year 'holiday'.

During the final moments before the Guineas, a bet of £1,500 to £1,000 was laid against Galtee More for the Derby. After the race, backers wanted 4–6, but no bookmaker would accommodate them. *The Sporting Life* concluded that, "With Galtee More's speed seemingly equal to his endurance, the Derby seems to depend only on his health, and escaping incident in the race." Within a few days of the Guineas, Galtee More was 1–2 for Epsom. Darling had decided on a prep race, the Newmarket Stakes over 10 furlongs. It was noticeable – in an era when horses were worked hard and often – that during the two weeks between the Newmarket races, Galtee More was worked mostly at a canter, usually at five furlongs, and never more than seven. He started at 6–100 in the Newmarket Stakes and won hard held.

In the fortnight to Derby Day, Sam Darling gave his colt just one piece of work over the full 12 furlongs of the Epsom race. It was a steady gallop, with an old-fashioned 'twicing' – a good handicapper led for six furlongs, and another horse jumped in for the last six. "The crack moved out well," exulted the local tout. Otherwise, Galtee More's work again comprised short sprints. There were whispers that there'd be an attempt to nobble the horse, so Darling borrowed an enormous cross-bred dog which slept every night on a mat outside Galtee More's box. When the colt was taken to Marlborough station on the Monday before the Derby, the dog shadowed him all the way to the train. Darling had a trying journey. First the train was shunted into a siding in south London and left stationary on a boiling hot afternoon, to let other services through, while Darling furiously pointed out they were mostly empty. When Galtee More and Beckhampton's other runners for the meeting eventually arrived at Epsom station, Darling found a huge crowd waiting to see the favourite. He recruited two policemen, and set off for one of the Epsom yards with one PC at the head of his string, followed by his horses and their lads, followed by the second policeman, Darling, and finally the crowd.

On raceday, Darling had a set-to with a gateman who tried to bar his and Galtee More's way onto the racecourse. For a while, Galtee More was kept walking about in a crowd of vehicles and onlookers. The race could've been lost in those few minutes, if the colt had been excitable or nervous. Thereafter, everything went as Darling had hoped. Jack Gubbins had given his stud team a treat, and brought over his vet, his manager Mike Burns and the stud groom who had helped Morganette to foal. The evening before he'd been interviewed, conveying supreme confidence:

> "I think that he'll win and win easily. No man could have taken more pains with his preparation than my trainer, Darling. All through, he has told me what a great colt he believes my colt to be, and his performances this year have shown that the merits of the colt have not been over-estimated. [Galtee More] is as well as he ever was in his life, if not better. I have secured to ride him one of the best jockeys that ever wore silk, and I am glad to think it may be through [me] that Wood will ride the winner of the triple crown."

Paddock critics insisted that Gubbins' hope was a shade fitter than before the Guineas, though the same was said of Velasquez, who took Galtee More on for a third time. There were 11 runners, and after £375 had been laid on several times to win £100, the final betting was 1–4 Galtee More, 10–1 Velasquez and 25–1 and upwards the others. Gubbins gave Wood a simple instruction: 'Don't be afraid of him [handling] Tattenham Corner, and come home as soon as you can.' Wood kept Galtee More close behind the early pace, got onto the rails early in the straight, hit the front two furlongs from the finish, and when Velasquez challenged, the Irish colt lengthened well and won comfortably by two lengths. Wood was asked what it took to win a Derby: "A saddle, a bridle and a good horse."

Before the race, a local paper told how, "All the villagers of Beckhampton hope and expect Sam Darling to win the Derby with Galtee More. Sam is noted for his generosity to the inhabitants of the village, especially when he sends a winner out. He has promised them a treat should 'Galtee' secure the Blue Riband." In Ireland, the celebrations were uninhibited. In the towns and villages around Bruree, night was turned into day. Tar barrels blazed on top of the ruins of King John's Castle in Kilmallock. Brass, fife and drum bands paraded in the streets below, followed by a cheering crowd. In Charleville, the Race Committee had made preparations for the Irish victory: the town 'was illuminated from end to end.' Repeated cheers were given for Galtee More. High above the revelry, a huge fire burned on the summit of the Galtee mountains. *Baily's Magazine* told its readers that the locals, "[Lit] bonfires on the range, and so confident were they of the result of the great race that they collected faggots and other materials long before the evening." It was a nice story, but it was Jack Gubbins himself who'd arranged for wood to be hauled up the mountain.

Darling was reminded of the heroic status of Galtee More's win whenever he visited Gubbins' studs. At Limerick station a porter asked him, was he Sam Darling? The man gathered a number of his fellow porters, and said: "Your honour, we're delighted to meet you. You trained Galtee More when he won the first English Derby for Ireland, and shure we will never forget the whiskey flying about that night. The mountains were alight with it!" As

Darling's train moved off, his new friend appeared at the carriage window, and told him, "Your honour, we can tell you that if you'd only [stand for] Limerick we'd return you for Parliament."

It was a pretty compliment – and Darling would've outshone many honourable members, past and present; but of more value to the trainer was an accolade from *The Sporting Life*: "Sam Darling quite excelled himself as a master of the training art. [To] win three races in six weeks and bring out a colt in the fettle that Galtee More was in yesterday bespeaks patience and skill of the highest order." Galtee More also brought about the rehabilitation of Jack Gubbins. The *Limerick Chronicle* called him, "One of the most popular country gentlemen to be found within the ocean-fringed shores of Ireland. Nowhere are his excellent and manly qualities more appreciated than in the county of Limerick, and in the vicinity of Bruree House."

In what remained of June, Galtee More mopped up two valuable stakes races from which he scared off all serious competition. At Ascot he was made 1–33 to beat three others in the Prince of Wales's Stakes. He gave them each 16lb and won hard held. That collected £1,775 for Gubbins: £1,300 more came from the Sandringham Cup at Sandown Park, where Galtee More was made 1–9 to beat a solitary opponent, giving 17lb. After that, Sam Darling put the colt aside for the St Leger at the start of September. The 10 weeks were marked by temptation and health scares. The temptation was a stream of offers to buy Galtee More. One came from Marcus Daly, the 'Montana copper king.' He pledged $125,000, equal then to £25,000. It represented only part of the proceeds of a huge plunge in the previous year's Futurity Stakes at Belmont Park. Daly had an English-bred two year old called Ogden, which won at country meetings in Montana before being shipped to New York, where it was trained in secret on Saratoga racecourse. Ogden arrived at Belmont, apparently from the boondocks, with an unknown jockey, and was backed from long odds to 'no offers'. A New York paper wrote after the race that, "Never in this country has a great coup been so successfully manipulated, nor so successfully carried [off]." It would've been appropriate for

Daly's winnings to be invested in a potential champion stallion, but Gubbins ignored his offer.

In the run-up to the St Leger, rumours about health problems became more persistent. They had nothing to do with Galtee More, who was going about his work at Beckhampton as willingly as ever. The concerns were for Gubbins, and they arose because at the time, a horse's race entries were voided by an owner's death. Jack Gubbins was an overweight man who suffered generally poor health and specifically from gout, the affliction cartooned as a demon sinking its teeth into a grossly swollen big toe. Today an attack of gout can be swept aside by an over-the-counter pill within hours. In Gubbins' day it could be so painful that its victim was unable to walk. At the end of August, Gubbins was at Leopardstown, 'became unwell,' and retreated to Bruree. Then he was cruising on his yacht when it had to return to port for him, again, to be taken home. The grapevine suggested he wouldn't live long enough for Galtee More to meet his engagement at Doncaster. Gubbins sent a telegram to *The Sportsman*: "I am thankful for your kind enquiry. I am now nearly quite well." It was left to *The Graphic* to put the hysterics into context:

> "If Mr Gubbins did not happen to be somewhat of a martyr to gout, we should have had no excitement at all [over the St Leger]. But, whenever Mr Gubbins experienced an extra twinge in his toe and felt it expedient to retire to his house in Limerick, sensation-mongers got to work to magnify the evil into a serious illness. Mr Gubbins has not yet had the experience of reading his own obituary, but he has learned, to his surprise, how exceedingly ill he is."

The St Leger was an exciting race, but farcical. Most of Galtee More's usual rivals had abandoned any hope of beating him, and he faced just four rivals. He was 1–10. The interesting contender was a filly, Chelàndry, who won the 1000 Guineas but disappointed twice afterwards. She represented Velasquez's owner Lord Rosebery. When the starter let the field go, none of the five runners wanted to make the pace. They barely cantered for the first quarter of a mile. Then, tightly grouped, they moved up to a half-speed gallop, only accelerating three furlongs from the finish, where Galtee More took a narrow lead. The inevitable result was a bunch finish. With the other runners snapping at his heels, Charles Wood shook up his mount 200 yards from the post, and he 'shot out to win very easily by three parts of a length' from Chelàndry with the American-bred St Cloud II a neck behind in third. It was only a head back to the fourth. It wasn't the outcome that the pre-race betting suggested. No one who saw the race was fooled: *The Sporting Life* called it the worst-run contest ever seen. Nonetheless, the bookmakers took an immediate negative view of Galtee More's prospects for his last target of the season, the Cambridgeshire. From having been as short as 11–2, he was at once shunted out to 10–1. It wasn't hard to see why. St Cloud II was only a length behind Galtee More at Doncaster, at level weights. In the Cambridgeshire, St Cloud II was set to receive 31lb. There were any number of horses entered for Newmarket whose form tied in with Galtee More, and unless Darling conjured vast improvement from his horse – which was unlikely, at the end of a busy season – he had no realistic prospect of winning. Darling picked up another useful pot – £2,042 – for Gubbins in the 10-furlong Sandown Foal Stakes, six days before the Cambridgeshire. He won easily, but in doing so he simply advertised the chance of the horse in second place, Cortegar. At Sandown, Galtee More beat Cortegar by three lengths, conceding 7lb. The following week he was set to give away 32lb. Such was the public faith in Galtee More that despite all the evidence in the form book, he was restored to favouritism on race day: 9–2, despite giving away from 14lb to 48lb to his 19 rivals.

Charles Wood had sized up the form and got off Galtee More to ride one of the placed horses from the Eclipse. Jack Watts took over on Galtee More. Afterwards, Watts would tell Darling that Galtee More flinched slightly running down into the Dip. The trainer thought perhaps his favourite was 'A trifle sore from his continuous work,' and that otherwise he might just about have won, so fast was he finishing. Darling was adamant that the outcome was Galtee More placed fifth, not more than a length behind the winner, to whom he was giving 44lb. St Cloud II was beaten a head in second. Cortegar was two further heads behind in fourth. If Darling had judged his horse's placing correctly, it was an astonishing weight-carrying performance to run the first four so close. However, there were dissenting voices. The experienced race-reader Bob Sievier said Galtee More was out of the first six; other accounts put him tenth.

Surprisingly, the result caused a downward revision of the horse's reputation. The gist of his critics' views was that he was no more than the best horse in a sub-standard year. *Truth*, whose racing writer became agitated whenever Galtee More was her topic, claimed after the Cambridgeshire it was, "All nonsense and rubbish to pretend that Galtee More was set [a] hard task last week." For good measure, 'If it is true that an offer of £27,000 for Galtee More was refused before [Newmarket] by Mr Gubbins, it is certain there are at least two exceedingly foolish persons in this world.' If there were any lingering doubts about her position, she wrote that Galtee More's merits, "Have been preposterously overrated." Fortunately for her blood pressure, the Newmarket race was the last of Galtee More's career. Darling was worried that the colt wouldn't stand another season's training, and he had only one entry for the following season, but Galtee More was still at Beckhampton when a Russian bloodstock agent arrived at the yard the following spring, looking for a stallion. His budget was 10,000 guineas. He'd been sent to see Galtee More's regular galloping companion, Kilcock. The recommendation came from William Allison, a close friend of Sam Darling who ran his own bloodstock agency, though he was best known as an author and journalist – the 'Special Commissioner' of *The Sportsman.*

The Russian visitor liked Kilcock, but when he saw Galtee More his affections were transferred. "I should prefer to buy that horse!" Darling congratulated him on his good judgement, but told him the price would be rather higher: 20,000 guineas. The Russian reported back to his superiors. In the middle of May, he came back with two companions. The decision-maker was General Arapoff, representing the Russian Horse Breeding Board. William Allison accompanied them. He hadn't met anyone quite like 'the wild Russian general' before. Arapoff, who owned a large vodka distillery, insisted the journey to Beckhampton should be broken at a hotel in Marlborough, where he downed a large tumbler of neat whisky. Darling and Gubbins greeted the General, who adored Galtee More at first sight, and confirmed the purchase immediately, subject to the colt's soundness for stud duties. He begged for Darling to let him see Galtee More work, 'as he wouldn't be doing any galloping in Russia.' Darling had by now written off any thought of Galtee More racing again, because of a questionable leg, but Gubbins agreed, so Darling teamed his triple crown winner with a moderate handicapper and supervised a gingerly uphill gallop over three furlongs. "The Russians were in ecstasies," said Darling – indeed so excited that as they left, Arapoff took down a painting of Galtee More from Darling's smoking room wall and carried it off. The picture was quickly returned, but there was one more obstacle to the sale: a dinner in London. Jack Gubbins and William Allison sat down with Arapoff and his fellow Russians to celebrate the deal. Arapoff spied an attractive lady at a nearby table and became coltish. Allison persuaded him, with difficulty, not to approach her. As a diversion, he suggested an establishment where the General, "Might speak to ladies without getting into trouble – at least not immediately." After Arapoff's enthusiastic departure, Gubbins became morose and declared he wouldn't sell Galtee More, after all. Allison saw a large commission disappearing. He told his underling not to move from Gubbins' side until he had a receipt for the Russians' payment, and by hook and by crook the deal went through.

Galtee More was shipped to Russia in June 1888. He was a notably successful sire there, before being re-sold 10 years later to the German government for £14,000. He sired the winners of 310 races in Germany before being fatally injured in an accident on the way to a stud at Hoppegarten. When he went to Russia, *Truth* gave him a sour send-off:

> "A better sold horse never left this country. Twenty thousand guineas is a truly exorbitant price. [Gubbins] has been so prodigiously favoured by fortune in connection with last year's Derby winner – both in his turf career and his sale for such a monstrous price, that he will do well to take leave of the turf, lest he should experience the lean time which is certain to [follow] such a flood tide of good luck."

The paper proved to be hopelessly wide of the mark, as much in its forecast of a lean time for Jack Gubbins as in its assessment of Galtee More's ability.

CHAPTER SEVEN

An owner shown the door

Captain Harry Greer was a racehorse owner, proprietor of a stud on the Curragh, a member of the Irish Turf Club and Steward of the Jockey Club. Along the way, he became Sam Darling's patron, business partner and friend. The connection began when Greer suggested to Darling that the two of them might go into partnership together. Each would put in a small number of mares, they'd agree the matings, and decide ownership of the foals on a case-by-case basis. The timing was perfect. Darling had cash to invest from another good bloodstock deal. He paid £1,000 for a yearling filly called Bird Of Passage, and trained her to win on her two year old debut, and then at Newmarket. Several offers were made for her, and Darling accepted £4,000, after which he went back to Bird Of Passage's breeder and spent half the proceeds on two mares to send to Greer. They were Bonnie Morn, and Bird Of Passage's dam, Hirondelle. Bonnie Morn was a particular success. She was carrying Kilcock, who became the best handicapper up to a mile that Darling trained, and Galtee More's regular galloping companion. She then produced Break Of Day, who won a £1,000 race at Epsom, and a fast two-year-old, Good Morning, who won the Coventry Stakes in Harry Greer's colours, but then caused nothing but trouble.

The woes began on Good Morning's debut over five furlongs at Kempton. He went to post with a stable-companion, Jack Gubbins' Revenue. The two colts had worked together: Good Morning gave Revenue 18lb and beat him. What followed was recalled by Darling as, "An awful catastrophe." It was a problem from the start of his training career that bookmakers took no chances with his runners. The journalist Sidney Galtrey wrote that Darling's runners were over-bet: " He would prefer that his judgement in fancying one of his horses to win was not so highly estimated. The result of the public following a Beckhampton lead in favour of one of [its] horses invariably means that the horse starts at a false price." Good Morning was backed from 4–5 to a ludicrously short 4–7, while Revenue was 10–1. Good Morning led inside the last furlong, apparently winning easily, but ran green. The vigorously-ridden Revenue caught him and won going away. Darling wrote, "I can't find words to describe my feelings. I had a very bad race." Good Morning then disgraced himself when refusing to start at Epsom. The colt made small amends by winning the Coventry Stakes, but showed more temperament when down the field in the July Stakes. An attempt to restart his career as a three year old was abandoned after he bit through a leading rein on the gallops and disappeared over the downs. Darling recorded grimly that, "He was sold to go abroad, where he turned [into] an absolute savage."

At the start of Darling's and Greer's stud partnership, it seemed that Sam's mares were producing the results. When the balance shifted it was thanks to Greer's £900 purchase of a potential stallion, Gallinule, by Isonomy out of Moorhen, a daughter of the Derby winner Hermit. Gallinule was a big, handsome chestnut with a lot of white about him. He won three times as a two year old for Lord Savernake, a friend of 'the Squire,' Abingdon Baird. Savernake inherited the Ailesbury title and became the fourth Marquess, which didn't prevent him from being warned off after running a flagrant non-trier at York. His horses were sold, including Gallinule, knocked down to Baird for 5,100 guineas. Ailesbury raised his hat to Mr Tattersall and said, 'Thank you, now I have some money for cards tonight.' It was a high price for a colt who hadn't won a race as a three year old, and in his first season for Baird he ran seven more times without success. However, Gallinule worked well at the start of the following year, including winning a trial easily from a stablemate with strong handicap form, and as a result Baird and his coterie backed him down to favouritism for the Lincoln. The colt burst a blood vessel, and bled again in his next race. For all his dissipation, Baird was clear-headed where horseflesh was concerned, and he told his trainer to find a buyer at around £1,500. By chance, it happened to be when Harry Greer was looking for a stallion. He liked Gallinule's looks and he liked his breeding. He seemed to be prepared to accept the colt's infirmity; the dam's sire Hermit was a notorious 'bleeder' but it hadn't stopped him winning the Derby. Greer might have balked if he knew that Gallinule had also developed a breathing problem, but Baird's trainer Charles Morton kept that to himself. Greer had negotiated the price down to £1,000 when Morton closed the sale by offering to take £900. A vet was sent to look Gallinule over, and failed to check his wind, so the deal went through. Baird asked, 'Who's the mug? I hope he's got the money.'

The postscript was, said Charles Morton, that "Gallinule, who by all the canons of breeding should have turned out a complete failure at the stud, instead became one of the most successful sires of his time." It didn't become apparent overnight. The twin stigma of bleeder and roarer didn't attract many breeders, and Greer, who'd pitched Gallinule's fee low at £25, was forced to offer free services. Prospects took another turn for the worse when Gallinule was sub-fertile. A gloomy Greer tried and failed to sell Gallinule on for £300. Gradually, the tide turned. One of his sons won the 1895 Irish Derby, and he sired the winners of five of the next six renewals. His greatest offspring was to be Pretty Polly (out of Admiration), one of the best race mares of all time. Before that, he produced a colt named Wildfowler, out of Tragedy, owned jointly by Greer and Sam Darling. Wildfowler was an above-average two year old, winning three times before coming up short against the best of his peers in the Middle Park, finishing third, beaten three lengths and a head. Darling struggled to get him fit at the start of the 1889 season; a pipe-opener at Derby in March resulted in an embarrassing defeat at 1–10 in a match.

He was still backward when finishing in midfield in the 2000 Guineas. Wildfowler came back from Newmarket a sick horse, and couldn't be prepared for the Derby, which was won by a 100–1 shot, Jeddah, who'd been miles behind in the 2000 Guineas. Even so, Jeddah followed up his Derby win in the Prince of Wales's Stakes at Ascot, and approached the St Leger as a warm favourite.

Meanwhile, Darling was at last getting a tune out of Wildfowler on the Beckhampton gallops. At the end of August, the Marlborough tout told *Sporting Luck* that, "Our St Leger candidate is doing a real good preparation," and chanced his arm by adding, "I don't think he is good enough to prove successful." He followed with a report which read, "Wildfowler was sent over to the Ogbourne Downs to be tried with Lytton and Northallerton. The result I don't know, in fact no one saw the spin but the trainers. My opinion still is Wildfowler is not good enough." This reads like a suicide note: the tout who failed to watch a vital piece of work. Among the questions he left unanswered was, why these galloping companions? One was a moderate handicapper, the other a selling plater.

It was a dry summer. The ground everywhere was firm, at best. At one meeting, Darling was asked what he thought of the going. He pointed to his shoes, which were covered in dust, and said he'd 'grown corns walking across the course.' At Doncaster the surface was made harder still by the use of the home straight as a public footpath: "The pattering of a million feet had rendered Town Moor as hard as iron by the time the St Leger was run." Ante-post betting had been subdued. Jeddah was a shade of odds on, with nothing else quoted at under 10–1. Come the day, Greer and Darling told their commission agent to put £500 to win on Wildfowler and £300 to place. From 10–1, the Beckhampton colt dropped briefly to 6–1, which the commissioner declined. Wildfowler then eased back to 10–1, and 4–5 a place, but for whatever reason, only half the money was 'on'. It was a boiling hot day, and most of the 12 runners were sweating copiously. The outsiders set a good pace all down the back straight, over Rose Hill and round the long turn towards home. A vast cheer went up as Jeddah took the lead at the top of the straight. He saw off his nearest pursuers readily enough, but when Charles Wood sent Wildfowler to challenge, Jeddah couldn't respond. Wood waited until well inside the last furlong before asking his mount for maximum effort, and Wildfowler quickly drew four lengths clear. The third horse was another six lengths back. After the race, Darling was much praised for having brought back Wildfowler at peak fitness from a four-month absence. He rated his winner 21lb inferior to Galtee More. Harry Greer presented the Beckhampton lads with a piano for their hostel. *Sporting Luck* sacked its tout.

Wildfowler didn't stand further training. Greer bought Darling's share and took the colt back to his stud, where he stood for nine years, siring only the winners of an Irish Derby and an Eclipse. Greer sold him to France for £5,000. He did little better there, and was later sold for £15.

After Wildfowler's St Leger, it was announced that a wealthy American, James Keene, planned to increase his family's involvement in English racing. His son Foxhall Keene already had his colours registered here, and the father enjoyed immediate success when he sent a handful of American-bred horses to Sam Darling. Four of them won in 1900, headed by Disguise II, who was third in the Derby before winning a big pot, £7,190, in the Jockey Club Stakes. At the time only the Eclipse carried a larger prize. It was no surprise that at the beginning of November, 10 more of Keene's horses arrived at Beckhampton from the United States. One of them was a two year old filly, Cap and Bells II, by Domino out of Ben-My-Chree. Cap and Bells II had won two of her three first-season races in America, her only defeat coming when she ran too freely from the front, but she quickly showed Darling above-average ability. One of her working companions was Noonday II, rated by Darling as 'a very smart filly.' Noonday II was second in a valuable all-aged handicap at Kempton at the beginning of May, and she then joined Cap and Bells II in a 10-furlong trial for the Oaks. Cap and Bells II was set to give away 21lb and won the gallop easily. Despite never having run in public over more than six furlongs, or in this country, she went to Epsom with maximum confidence behind her. Noonday II was entered to make the running and set a strong enough pace for Cap and Bells II to settle behind. On the day of the race, Cap and Bells II was offered on course at 5–1. The money poured onto her, with the result that she started at 9–4.

Among the crowd were numerous show business personalities. The association of caps and bells with jesters was irresistible to a notably superstitious profession. Most of the music hall comedians of the day were in the grandstand. They were given plenty to laugh about. Noonday II set a good clip from flag fall to the end of the back straight, with her stable companion never worse than third. Coming down the hill, Cap and Bells II moved into second, and as soon as she turned to face the straight, her American jockey Milton Henry sent her clear. She won by six lengths. One of the comics, who'd been 'resting' for a while, won so much over Cap and Bells II that for months afterwards it was a matter of indifference whether he worked or not.

Darling won 14 races and £10,800 in prize money for the Keenes that year, following eight races and £9,049 the year before. Yet it became known in December that the Keene horses would be leaving Beckhampton, to be trained by Felix Leach at Newmarket. It was said Darling had been ill from overwork, and had been ordered by his doctor to take a holiday. That was true, but the deductions drawn from it weren't. One was, Darling had decided to reduce his number of horses; if so, how likely was it that an Oaks winner would be included in the cull? Another suggested that James Keene was unsure about Darling's return date, and took pre-emptive action, rather than find himself without a trainer as the 1902 flat season started. Darling's other owners were in the same position as Keene; why weren't they moving their horses? William Allison, wearing his journalist's hat, made an asinine contribution in *The Sportsman*:

> "I learn that [Sam] Darling finds the claims of his older clients likely to tax his energies to the utmost next season. For that reason, he has been obliged, very reluctantly, to cease acting as trainer for Mr James R Keene,

> whose horses will leave Beckhampton tomorrow for Newmarket, where they will be entrusted to Felix Leach, than whom a better selection could not have been made."

Allison was conflicted. His bloodstock agency sold English broodmares to Keene's stud. He worked with Darling on high-profile deals like the sale of Galtee More to Russia. Not least, he was Sam's friend and travelling companion. The paragraph quoted is an early example of a PR hand-out: 'Everything between Darling and Keene is sweetness and light, and there's a happy ending.' Hogwash. The simplest explanation was the right one: Darling and Keene didn't get along. Keene, though English-born, was typical of the American robber barons who made immense fortunes in the second half of the nineteenth century. He accumulated millions manipulating the stock markets, lost everything, and clawed his way back to even more millions. He pursued relentless vendettas. On his daily commute, the train conductor asked him to show his ticket. Keene couldn't find it. 'That'll be $1.25, mister.' Keene, like many rich men, had no money on him. He protested that he made the journey regularly and would pay the next day. 'Pay now or you must leave the train,' said the conductor, and Keene was ejected at the next station. He complained to the superintendent of the line, and got short shrift. He contacted the rail company's president and was ignored. He began buying the rail company's stock and continued until he was its largest shareholder. He saw to it that the conductor, the superintendent and the president were fired. Then he sold the stock. All over $1.25. Such a man expected a 'your wish is my command' response from those he employed, including racehorse trainers.

He hadn't done due diligence on Sam Darling. No owner told Sam how to train his horses, or what their targets should be, or who rode them. Darling and Keene fell out on most things. One was jockeys. Keene wanted to put up American riders; Sam knew most of them had queues of punters longer than a January sale. Another was the horses' programmes. Keene thought his colt

THE HAZARDS of the downs. The coaching services needed shelter and regular stops for their horses and passengers. Inns on isolated stretches of road like Beckhampton were provided with a continuous flow of visitors.

THE CRAVEN. Fulwar Craven was a famous dandy, a racehorse owner and a hellraiser. He owned the filly Deception, trained by Billy Treen to win Beckhampton's first classic, the 1839 Oaks.

VANITY FAIR. Dec. 30, 1871.

National Portrait Gallery

Opposite: WILLIAM GREGORY acquired an expensive addiction to racing while an Oxford undergraduate. He was one of Billy Treen's major patrons at Beckhampton, and later found Treen a job training in India.

SIR GEORGE CHETWYND was a spendthrift who topped up his income with shrewd and successful betting. His horses' removal from Beckhampton was unrelated to their performances, but left Harry Woolcott struggling.

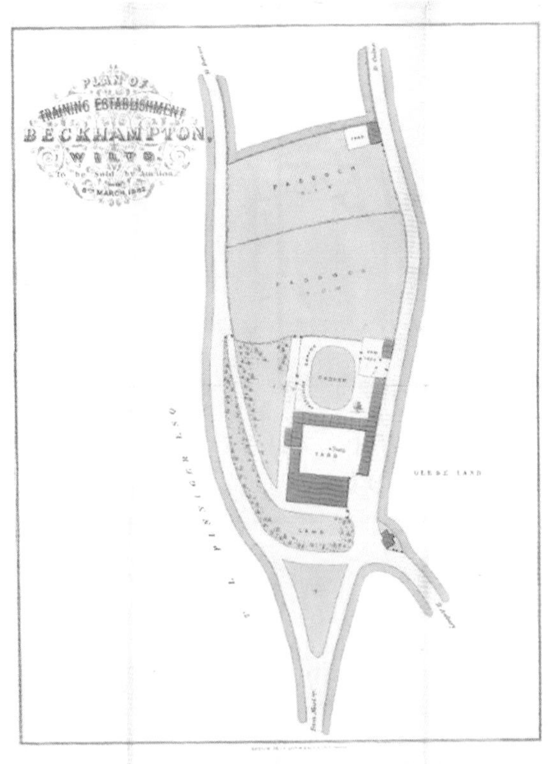

SMALL BEGINNINGS. The yard that Harry Woolcott sold to Sam Darling in 1882 comprised only the former Beckhampton Inn, its stabling and two small paddocks. Darling built an estate of over 1,200 acres.

SAM DARLING laid the foundations for the trainers who followed him at Beckhampton. He rebuilt and modernised the yard, bought land, nurtured the gallops and farmed on a large scale.

CROSSROADS. Beckhampton House circa 1900. Sam Darling's porch stands out. The foreman's house on the right, alongside the Calne Road, has long since been demolished.

Roger and Clare Charlton

JACK GUBBINS provided Ireland with its first Derby winner, Galtee More in 1897, and soon after a second, Ard Patrick. However, he was remembered with qualified enthusiasm in his home parish.

PARTNER. Harry Greer was Sam Darling's friend and business partner. The two men had a successful stud in Ireland, where the colt Slieve Gallion was bred: he was trained by Darling to win the 2000 Guineas in Greer's colours.

DERBY DAY. Galtee More, ridden by Charles Wood and led by Sam Darling, is paraded on the course before the 1897 Derby. Jack Gubbins' colt had already won the 2000 Guineas and went on to triple crown glory.

The Rouch Wilmot Thoroughbred Racing Library

UNSUNG HERO: Sam Darling oversees the exercise of his and Jack Gubbins' second Derby winner, Ard Patrick, described as 'the greatest unsung hero in British flat racing.'

WILLONYX won the Chester Cup, the Ascot Stakes, the Ascot Gold Cup, the Jockey Club Cup and the Cesarewitch – under a record weight – in 1911. The colt's grateful owner presented Sam Darling with the Gold Cup.

THE VALUE of Willonyx's wins to Sam Darling is hinted at in his acquisition of a large dwelling the other side of the Devizes road from his Beckhampton stable. He named it Willonyx House.

DYNASTY. Besides managing a large training yard and several farms, Sam Darling (at right) found time to sire eight children. His eldest son Sam became a successful trainer at Newmarket. His second son Fred (at left) inherited Beckhampton, where Douglas (centre) worked for a time.

Olympian would win the Derby. Darling said he didn't think Olympian would stay the trip. 'He runs in the Derby,' was Keene's response. The colt broke fast, careered up Epsom's hill, freewheeled down and came to a halt. Keene insisted that Olympian should next travel to Paris for the Grand Prix, over a mile and seven. Darling noted gleefully that Olympian was tailed off last; he rubbed it in by running the horse at Ascot over five furlongs the following Thursday. It was touch and go: Olympian only arrived at the racecourse stables at midnight on Wednesday. Darling gave him some stout to perk him up, and did the same in the morning. Olympian won, ridden by Milton Henry, over the minimum trip, after Keene's insistence on a campaign over middle to long distances. A final straw was Keene's failure to consult Darling about a yearling purchase. It was at Doncaster sales, and Darling wanted to buy a full brother to Wildfowler for Harry Greer. His friend William Allison bid vigorously against him. Eventually Allison went beyond Greer's limit, signed for the colt, and then told Sam that he'd been bidding for James Keene. Darling was outraged, even though the horse was sent to him to train. He waited until the end of the season and told Keene to go. Nothing leaked out until Allison's communiqué was published in December. In this as in many ways, Sam Darling was the *pater familias* of Beckhampton. He set a precedent to be followed enthusiastically by his son Fred, and more diplomatically by Jeremy Tree: if the owner didn't fit, the owner went.

Of course, it was easier for Sam and his successors to show an owner the door than it would be for the great majority of trainers. The Darlings and Tree were offered more horses than they had boxes to accommodate them. The luxury of indulging a dislike isn't an option for a small stable with empty boxes. Even so, Darling's ejection of Keene was a magisterial statement. Keene was worth around $15 million, had a sizeable stud in Kentucky, and had stated his intention to race in England 'on a large scale.' Darling had taken his 10 horses the previous autumn and made eight of them winners. Apart from the Oaks with Caps and Bells II, he won four from four with Sinopi, including the Ascot Stakes. There were a couple of two year old winners who promised much for the following season. But Darling could shrug all that aside. He had an ace in his hand: a two year old colt called Ard Patrick, who turned out to be perhaps the best middle-distance horse trained at Beckhampton.

Ard Patrick, by St Florian out of Morganette, was a dark brown colt, foaled at Jack Gubbins' Bruree stud and named after a village a few miles away. He was big, backward and slow to come to hand, with the result that his three runs as a two year old were promising, but no more than that. He made his debut in mid-October in Kempton's Imperial Produce Stakes. As a half-brother to Galtee More, he was the focus of all eyes around the paddock. He struck one watcher as, 'On an even bigger scale than his famous relative: it's some time since I saw such a powerful and massive two year old.' Ard Patrick towered over his rivals in the paddock, and was made a warm favourite. In the event, it was only in the last couple of strides that he overhauled a colt, Royal Lancer, who was conceding 13lb. Darling was keen to get as much experience as possible into Ard Patrick, and he sent him to Newmarket four days later. Royal Lancer was again among his opponents, and the weight concession was now 3lb. A 10lb 'pull' for a neck made Royal Lancer the probable winner. Ard Patrick showed clear improvement in winning stylishly, with Royal Lancer a neck and two lengths away in third. Ard Patrick's third run was in the Dewhurst, where his wins meant that he was now the horse giving the weight away. He finished second, beaten a neck by a filly, Game Chick. Royal Lancer received 1lb from Ard Patrick and finished unplaced, beaten some way. Measured against that colt, Ard Patrick had improved by 14lb and several lengths in the space of 20 days. After each of his runs, the racing press noted his infinite potential for improvement: after his run in the Dewhurst, *The Sportsman* wrote that Ard Patrick, "Appears to be capable of so much improvement that Game Chick may never finish in front of him again."

Sam Darling came back from a break in South Africa at the end of February. His travelling companion William Allison said that before the outbound voyage was half completed, Darling was 'as fresh as a lark,' and 'will return to England a 10 years younger man.' The two of them spent much of their time on the Cape visiting racing stables and stud farms. On the day that Darling sailed home, Allison's wire to *The Sportsman* included the note: "The change has done him an immense amount of good, and if he lands in England as fit as he is now, it will be good business to follow the Beckhampton horses throughout the coming season." His head lad had supervised the yard in his absence, and he was able to tell Darling that all had gone well with Ard Patrick – but, as he'd been as a two year old, he was slow to bring to anything like full fitness. He needed the race when he reappeared in the 2000 Guineas. He shared second favouritism at 9–2, behind the 4–1 co-favourites Duke of Westminster and Sceptre, both of whom were at one time owned by Bob Sievier. The great rascal had paid a record 10,000 guineas to buy Sceptre and 5,600 guineas for Duke of Westminster. When Sievier was financially embarrassed, he was forced to put the two horses up for sale. A wealthy owner, George Faber, was interested. Sievier played a nerveless bluff by putting a much higher price on Duke of Westminster than on Sceptre – even though he thought the filly was stones better than the colt. Faber was duped. He assumed that there must be something wrong with Sceptre, so he bought Duke of Westminster – for £22,000. Sievier made a healthy profit on the two horses, regained his solvency, and kept his beloved Sceptre. She became the second horse in English racing history to win four classics, after Beckhampton's Formosa, and the 2000 Guineas was the first in the sequence. She won comfortably by two lengths and three, with the backward Ard Patrick in third.

In the rear was James Keene's Kearsage, whom Darling had trained to win twice at Newmarket the previous season. Kearsage ran seven times for Keene's new trainer, Felix Leach, without a further win. The Ascot winner Sinopi ran six times for Leach, unsighted. As for Keene's one-time Derby contender, Olympian, he ran 10 times in the 1902 season, mostly in sprint handicaps, without even placing. After his two years of prodigious success with Sam Darling, Keene had three winners of £688. It must've been grisly for Leach, who was a good trainer: it was also a powerful endorsement of Sam Darling.

Sceptre won the 1000 Guineas two days after the colts' classic. Ard Patrick ran next in the Newmarket Stakes and was first past the post, but had rolled about and bumped the second-placed horse, and he was disqualified. It was a big prize to lose – over £3,000 – but as far as Darling was concerned it was a satisfactory prep for what had been the plan from the day he first set eyes on Ard Patrick: the Derby. When he left South Africa, he told William Allison, 'Don't bet on the Derby yet. I certainly shan't.' It was canny advice, because after the two Guineas had been run and won by Sceptre, Bob Sievier revealed that his filly would take in the Derby as part of an attempt to win all five classics. The ante-post betting was turned upside down, with Sceptre introduced as the warm favourite. On the weekend before the race, she was 13–8, while from the clouds dropped a mystery outsider, Pekin. On his two year old form, Pekin couldn't possibly win a Derby; his last three runs were in nursery handicaps, and he failed to place in any of them. However, he represented one of the most feared gambling yards, Percy Bewicke's Grateley. Bewicke and his associate GA Prentice had pulled off a number of high-profile coups, and when the Grateley money appeared, bookmakers tended to take evasive action. From 20–1, Pekin fell to 6–1. There was a single bet of £8,000 to £1,000 and in all, the Grateley connections were said to have backed their colt to win £100,000. Bob Sievier spoke openly of supporting Sceptre for £33,000. All of which caused Ard Patrick to fluctuate between 7–1 and 8–1. The signals from the gallops were positive: Darling said that, 'He came to hand nicely' and, 'was set practically the same work as Galtee More.' The only concerns were over the stable's overall form, and the stable's bets. Beckhampton's runners in the weeks before the Derby had hardly shone. Jack Gubbins' Revenue – the colt who upset Good Morning on his debut – was punted for the Great Jubilee at Kempton, and finished only third. The yard's other runners at the meeting were well supported but ran badly. Another gamble went awry at Newmarket, and the disqualification of Ard Patrick rubbed it in. As for the bets, Darling told Gubbins he was 'very pleased' with Ard Patrick. He'd written to Gubbins telling him he ought to back Ard Patrick. He hadn't received a reply, so he'd asked a commission agent to put £1,000 on for Gubbins. 'You can have as much or as little as you like of the bet,' Darling told Gubbins, who replied he already had £2,000 on for himself, thanks. "I suppose that means I've got to stand [the bet]," said a surprised Sam. Pressed by Gubbins, he conceded that he thought Ard Patrick would win. "How about Sceptre?" "Well, I saw Sceptre out this morning. She was looking light and fretting. I think we are sure to beat her."

So it transpired. A wave of public support forced Sceptre to even money; the 'dark' Pekin was 6–1 and Ard Patrick 100–14. Jack Gubbins' colt was ridden by JH 'Skeets' Martin, an American jockey who'd arrived in Britain three years earlier. Unlike the rest of the 'Yankees,' who came, conquered and left, he remained in England until he retired. His instructions were to keep Ard Patrick handy, and he did that to perfection. Chasing a pace set by an outsider, he was a place behind Sceptre in fourth or fifth for the first half of the race, moved up to the leaders coming down the hill, and turned into the straight alongside Sceptre. There was no commentary, but those in the crowd with binoculars and a clear view shouted "Sceptre!" to those around them, and a vast cheer went up. It was silenced within a furlong: Martin gave Ard Patrick one slap, one kick and away he went. Sceptre buckled and was passed for the place money. "[Ard Patrick] strode clean away to win in as easy a style as we ever recorded in a Derby," wrote *Sporting Luck*: 'He's a horse of the highest class, who has simply never been fully wound up before.'

The judge's verdict was three lengths. The race-readers' verdict was that if the jockey had called for it, Gubbins' colt could have won by 10. The owner, propped on his sticks, struggled in the tightly-packed crowd, and Darling led the winner in, his face one broad smile. His colt's reception was muted: most of the crowd wanted Sceptre to win, and were deflated. Not as much as the Grateley stable. *Sporting Luck* accused its principals of, "A gigantic mistake with Pekin, who soon fell into the rear group and never progressed. Captain Bewicke and his confederates bet as if defeat was impossible, and lost considerable sums of money." The spoils of the 1902 Derby went to Bruree and to Beckhampton. Darling said that he won £6,000 (£580,000 now) over the race, though the racing press put his winnings at three times as much.

> "Good luck to him. He is a master of his craft – no finer proof than the [way] in which he has managed Ard Patrick. One point stands out in great distinction in the Beckhampton policy. Comparatively few races are contested but the proportion of wins is large. And it is a fine betting stable. When there is a supposed good thing the money is put down not by the hundred, but in 'monkeys.'"

The London *Evening Standard* joined in the praise: "The most admired in the paddock was Ard Patrick, who seemed capable of carrying any one of his rivals. He is the best looking colt [seen on] Epsom Downs for many years. Darling, in his long and honourable career, has never sent a horse to post more fitted for the serious struggle, and clearly from the time he returned from South Africa he has timed the preparation of Ard Patrick [to perfection]. He won with 10lb in hand, and something extraordinary will have to happen to prevent his success in the St Leger."

Something did happen: Ard Patrick went lame at Ascot in the Prince of Wales's Stakes and missed the Eclipse and the St Leger, at which point Darling rated him behind Jack Gubbins' previous Derby winner, Galtee More. He revised that opinion the following year, when Ard Patrick featured in one of those hypothetical contenders for 'race of the century.' The racing authors Tony Morris and John Randall take a decided view in their book *A Century of Champions*: they rate Ard Patrick as, "The greatest unsung hero of British flat racing." To earn that accolade he was required to beat a dual classic winner, and Sceptre at the top of her game, and he did.

CHAPTER EIGHT

Unreliable memoirs

The first half of the 1903 flat season was dominated by a colt called Rock Sand, winner of the 2000 Guineas, Derby and St James's Palace Stakes. When he lined up for the Eclipse Stakes, he had the enticing profile of 10 wins from 11 starts. What they amounted to was unclear. After his Guineas win he was made odds-on for the Derby, but in a field of only seven runners he did no more than again beat the Guineas second and third. At Ascot he was 1–14 to beat three rivals. Here he was at Sandown, in the traditional first clash of the generations, facing the two horses who'd won all five classics in 1902, yet he was made 5–4 favourite. After finishing fourth behind Ard Patrick in the previous year's Derby, Sceptre had won the Oaks and St Leger. She was 7–4 and Ard Patrick 5–1 in a field of five. Sam Darling was confident about Ard Patrick's chance. On the Beckhampton gallops he set his Derby winner to give 42lb to a filly called Caravel, winner of four of her five runs as a two year old. Ard Patrick beat Caravel in the gallop. Darling worked him over the full 10 furlongs of the Eclipse course to accustom him to the long right-handed bend. Darling was, as always, focused on detail. He noted that the ground was 'frightfully hard.' He fretted at the danger of a slip when navigating the turn at racing speed. He told his blacksmith to build up the outside of Ard Patrick's near-side racing plates, including with larger-headed nails. In effect, Ard Patrick ran with his own camber.

All racing's roads led to Sandown Park on Eclipse day. What was estimated to be the course's record crowd 'packed the enclosures to suffocation.' Sceptre was described as, 'The darling of the multitude. Nine people out of every 10 longed to see her win.' Round the long turn to the straight, Rock Sand went on from Ard Patrick, just ahead of Sceptre. When they were in line for home, Ard Patrick and Sceptre quickly joined Rock Sand, and the three of them raced line abreast. 'Men noted for their coolness and nerve trembled with excitement.' Then, suddenly, two furlongs from home, Rock Sand folded and dropped behind his elders, who continued to race head to head to the furlong pole. There, Sceptre seemed to be marginally ahead, and a huge roar went up. Moments later it died away as Ard Patrick recovered the lost margin. In the final 100 yards he inched ahead to win by a neck. Rock Sand was officially placed third. The judge gave the distance back to him as three lengths: photographs suggest it was nearer 10. Sam Darling said, "You could have heard a pin drop during the last part of the race and everybody seemed to be holding their breath." The crowd were deflated. Even though Rock Sand was favourite, Sceptre was their darling. Ard Patrick returned to a muted reception. Jack Gubbins was nowhere to be seen. He was barely able to move from gout, and watched the race from a car on the far side of the racecourse.

That was Ard Patrick's last race. He was sold to a German stud owner, Count Georg von Lehndorff, for £20,000. He was a successful sire, producing four sons who won German classics, and daughters who foaled eight more. Sam Darling told a friend, the evening after Ard Patrick's Derby, he was inclined to think that Galtee More was the best horse he'd trained. After the Eclipse and the defeat of Sceptre, he shifted to Ard Patrick. Rock Sand, pulverised at Sandown, went on to complete his triple crown in the St Leger. Darling later acknowledged Ard Patrick's Eclipse as the zenith of his training career. It capped a decade of extraordinary achievements. The next 10 years, leading to his retirement, were quieter, but he had two more headline horses to come: Slieve Gallion and Willonyx.

Before then and to no great surprise, Jack Gubbins retired from the turf. His 27 horses in training were sold at Tattersalls in July 1904. He won Ireland its first Derby, followed swiftly by its second. It was a pity he sold Galtee More and Ard Patrick overseas. They were two of the best Derby winners in a quarter of a century, and they would've had stronger books of mares if they'd stood in England or Ireland, and greater opportunities to prove their merit as stallions. Meanwhile, Gubbins had earned a measure of redemption. After his harsh treatment of defenceless tenants and his confrontation with the Land League, Gubbins spent most of his time in England. When Ard Patrick had scaled the heights, he threw a sop to public opinion in Limerick: his tenants around Bruree were given extended rent 'holidays'.

The year after Gubbins' dispersal sale, Harry Greer sent Darling a yearling by Gallinule out of Reclusion. He was called Slieve Gallion, after a mountain in County Londonderry. He was an imposing black colt with a defect in his conformation: he was ewe-necked, with the top line of his neck concave, and the underneath more heavily muscled. The most obvious result was a high head carriage, with the potential to make it harder for his rider to control him. It made it difficult to break Slieve Gallion in:

> "It was less natural for him to bend to the bridle tackle [on] the long lunging rein. It was six weeks before I thought it advisable to put a jockey on him, though with ordinary yearlings this may be done in three or four weeks. When a jockey was put on him he was led straight after the other horses until I considered he could go loose with the jockey. For this preliminary training I did not use any ordinary jockey, but the best available."

The jockey assigned to Slieve Gallion was Billy 'Farmer' Higgs, who became Beckhampton's first retained rider at the start of the 1905 season. Meyrick Good of *The Sporting Life* described Higgs as, "One of the strongest jockeys I have ever known. He had shoulders and thighs that would have done credit to any prize-fighter." With Beckhampton behind him, Higgs was champion jockey in 1906 and 1907.

Once Darling had brought Slieve Gallion close to full fitness, he worked him with a horse with recent winning form, 'in order to see what he was like.' The outcome was that Slieve Gallion was fully 'expected' when he won on his debut at Sandown Park, followed by the New Stakes at Ascot and the Champagne Stakes at Doncaster. His starting prices for these races were 8–13, 1–5 and 1–4, prompting *Baily's Magazine* to note that, "Darling gave up all idea of getting a price about any runner of his before most of us began racing." Slieve Gallion met his only defeat as a two year old in the Middle Park, when again long odds-on, but went down by half a length to another three-time winner. Afterwards it was revealed that Slieve Gallion hadn't recovered from a multiple tooth extraction the previous week. His mouth was sore, he was reluctant to take hold of his bit, and Higgs had to handle him 'very tenderly indeed.'

Harry Greer's colt began his classic season in the Craven Stakes. He took a quick lead when Higgs asked him to go forward, and made all the running to win by five lengths. *The Sporting Life* called it a striking victory: "It is hard to say where his Derby conqueror is to come from; his present condition reflects great credit on Sam Darling, who was visibly delighted with the colt's handsome victory." The paper went on to report that most of Slieve Gallion's potential rivals for the 2000 Guineas were planning to avoid him: "The first of the season's classic races appears to be merely a question of [his] health."

So it proved, but not before Slieve Gallion acted up badly in the paddock and went to the start pulling Higgs' arms out, his head cocked towards the Suffolk coast. Nonetheless, Higgs got his mount away smartly and he never saw another horse, winning the Guineas by three lengths. The performance told nothing new about the Beckhampton colt: he beat a colt called Bezonian by three lengths, and had done the same in the Champagne Stakes as a two year old. Sam Darling nominated Bezonian as Slieve Gallion's main danger in the Derby – which implied that he saw no danger at all. Darling welcomed a visitor a few days before the Derby, and purred with excitement as he approached Slieve Gallion's box. "Listen to him! Listen to him!" he exclaimed, his smile broadening: "He's having a roll, and isn't he enjoying himself!" As ever, Darling left nothing to chance: he hired a special constable to patrol the yard. The visitor noted, as so many did, Darling's eye for detail. While showing off a pen of lambs, he saw a pitchfork on the ground and immediately scolded his shepherd: "Fancy if Slieve Gallion got loose and struck his leg into that."

On the Saturday before the Derby, Slieve Gallion's owner Harry Greer joined Darling at Beckhampton to watch his colt's final gallop. The Marlborough tout reported that the Derby favourite, 'Went a good striding gallop of nearly one mile and a quarter, the colt going in splendid style and pulling up sound and well.' Having been even money for the Derby, Slieve Gallion hardened to 8–13. Following him in the betting were Galvani – who'd beaten him in the Middle Park – at 4–1, his repeat victim Bezonian at 8–1, and an Irish-trained American-bred, Orby at 9–1. A certain amount of hubris was apparent in the predictions for the Derby:

> There is a black colt called Slieve Gallion
> Who at racing can beat a battalion
> When racing is done
> He'll have some rare fun
> For he goes to the stud as a stallion

As so often, hubris was followed by nemesis. Opposition to Slieve Gallion melted away in the preliminaries at Epsom. Galvani drifted to 7–1, Bezonian to 9–1 and Orby shared 100–9 with Wool Finder. Darling sent Slieve Gallion to the races with a travelling companion to calm him, a solid brown cob, and at the saddling Slieve Gallion was 'as cool as a cucumber,' nuzzling his friend. Orby looked notably well: many of the paddock judges backed him for a 'saver.' There were only nine runners, but they produced a stirring renewal of the Derby. Slieve Gallion went to post with his head high in the air, and pulled his way into the lead after a quarter of a mile. He led Bezonian by two lengths along the back and down the hill. On the descent, the American jockey Johnny Reiff made ground into third on Orby. As the field reached the bottom of Tattenham Corner, Slieve Gallion hung away from the rails. Bezonian followed him. Up their inside moved Orby. Spectators on the bend said that Reiff was grinning broadly, and well he might. He went clear, Bezonian faded, Slieve Gallion swerved up the camber to the centre of the course, finishing third.

Even in defeat, Slieve Gallion provided a testimonial to Sam Darling's training skills. Some would've looked at Harry Greer's ungainly colt and thought him untrainable. Others might have ruined him by demanding that he comply with the same preparation as their other yearlings. From the first day, Darling gave patient, individual, time-consuming attention to Slieve Gallion. On the day, the colt's faulty make-up and the gradients of Epsom proved insurmountable. Billy Higgs simply couldn't steer him. Slieve Gallion ran next in the St James's Palace Stakes, where he beat two opponents at 1–20. Afterwards he was sold to the Hungarian National Stud for 15,000 guineas. Bizarrely, Slieve Gallion's stock were either early two year olds who didn't train on, or staying 'chasers, with little in between.

One small incident concerning Slieve Gallion shows how forward-looking Darling was. He worked out, uniquely in his own time and decades before racehorse trainers as a collective, that good relationships with the press weren't specially difficult to maintain – and that the outcomes would be to his benefit. He treated even the local touts civilly. In the few days before the 1907 Derby, Darling allowed a film crew, the Palace Electric Bioscope, to look in at Beckhampton. The resulting footage was shown in cinemas all over the country. It showed Darling superintending the gallops, the downs and the stable yard.

Sam Darling came by his last champion because a yearling colt by the Gold Cup winner William The Third out of Tribonyx failed to meet his reserve at the Doncaster yearling sales. The consignor was Sir John Robinson. He wanted £800 for his yearling, but the bidding fell short. Afterwards, Darling asked Sir John if he'd take less for the colt: "Yes. To you, seven hundred," was the answer, and they shook hands. Darling had an owner asking him to find a horse, a builder called Charles Howard. His colt, named Willonyx, made an early two year old debut at Kempton and finished last. More than a year passed before his next race, and that was his first win: a one-mile £130 maiden plate at Kempton Park. He had a hectic second season campaign, running 12 times in all and winning five. In his second race as a four year old he won the Chester Cup – dashing into the lead five furlongs out and comfortably holding off a strong-finishing outsider.

A few weeks later in the Ascot Stakes, Willonyx won by a comfortable four lengths, his huge ears pricked as he went past the post. Darling had no qualms about saddling him again two days later in the Gold Cup. There, he met proper Group horses for the first time: the previous year's Derby second and third, Greenback and Charles O'Malley. They were joined by Yellow Slave, winner of the Park Hill Stakes, and by another Ascot Stakes winner, Declare. The first three in the betting represented the three dominant Wiltshire stables: Willonyx from Beckhampton, Declare from Manton, and Charles O'Malley from Druid's Lodge. They filled the first three places in the Gold Cup, with plenty of drama along the way. It began at the start, when Charles O'Malley threw his head up, catching his jockey, Steve Donoghue, in the face. Donoghue was knocked out of the saddle, and after getting to his feet he fell again. When he was finally legged up, he fought to control Charles O'Malley for the first third of the race. The colt 'Came past the stands for the first time yawing about all over the place, like a helmless ship in the trough of the waves.' Down towards Swinley Bottom, Charles O'Malley led by six lengths from Declare, Yellow Slave and Willonyx. The pursuers closed up on the incline to the home turn, with Willonyx twice seeming to slip on the hard ground. Notwithstanding, Higgs sent his mount into the lead as they turned in. Charles O'Malley buckled down gamely to a sustained struggle in the last three furlongs. Close home, Declare broke down and dropped away, while Higgs forced Willonyx to a neck advantage on the line. Steve Donoghue caused surprise when he rode into the unsaddling area and asked, "When do we start?"

Willonyx was lauded for racing four and a half miles round Ascot in the space of 48 hours, on bone-hard ground, to win a top handicap and the greatest staying race in the calendar. Higgs said after the Gold Cup, "It was sheer pluck that got him home" after losing his action twice in the last six furlongs. The race readers' enthusiasm was muted. *Truth* spelt out the caveats: Lemberg, who won the 1910 Derby from Greenback and Charles O'Malley, was a non-runner because of the ground. Likewise the first two in the 1910 St Leger. The top French stayer, Basse Pointe, had arrived at Ascot with many a *turfiste* to support him, but he too was taken out because of the ground. As for the six runners who did turn up, Greenback didn't stay and Declare finished on three legs. The only item absent from the paper's charge sheet was that Steve Donoghue was in action, but concussed.

Sam Darling gave Willonyx almost four months off before his next race, the Cesarewitch. To Darling's horror, almost every animal in his stable and around his farms was coughing that autumn. He hardly had a horse able to gallop with Willonyx. One useful side-effect was that Charles Howard's colt was easy to back. Ten days before the Cesarewitch, Willonyx was 100–8. With two days to go, and Darling satisfied that Willonyx had escaped the stable's bug, the commission was launched in the London offices: "A big move was made for Willonyx, when 10–1 was laid to over 200 sovs. Then came wagers of £900 to £100 and £800 to £100, besides many others at £100 to £11 and £100 to £12, and [at the close] it was difficult to get 8–1." On the day, Willonyx was backed in from 7–1 to 9–2 co-favourite. Bob Sievier wrote in *The Winning Post* that, "His condition was a fine advertisement [for] what Sam Darling can do with a racehorse when that horse has legs sound enough to carry him through a Beckhampton preparation. Tight as a drum with muscle standing up hard all over him, and each rib clearly defined under a surface of satin, it is not often that one sees such a perfect sample of the trainer's art."

Willonyx was asked to carry more weight than any horse had ever done to win a Cesarewitch, but he succeeded, and more easily than the result suggested. Higgs held onto him until reaching the Bushes, where he took up the running and rode Willonyx right out, without picking up his whip, to win by three quarters of a length and five from Martingale II, to whom he was giving 29lb, with the same concession to the third. His burden of 9st 5lb was a weight-carrying record for the race. It wasn't surpassed for 30 years. The victory was greeted by wave upon wave of cheering: "Those who witnessed the remarkable victory of Willonyx are never likely to forget the scene of enthusiasm that it evoked. Winners and losers seemed equally to appreciate the success of a really good and thoroughly exposed horse."

The racing career of a brave, consistent and high-class racehorse ended in a low-key Jockey Club Cup. It was a match against Martingale II, second to Willonyx in the Cesarewitch, with Willonyx better off at the weights. He won in a canter by 20 lengths. "It was known that this was Willonyx's last race," reported *Baily's Magazine,* and as he passed the post, "A storm of cheering arose, which was taken up in all the enclosures. A crowd surrounded the horse in the paddock, and it was with a touch of sadness that one saw him led away [from] the last time he would ever carry silk." Willonyx was walked across Newmarket Heath to the Egerton stud. Watching him go, Darling said sadly, "If I could train him again next season I'd improve him by another 7lb." Charles Howard took a bold risk in standing Willonyx at his own stud, at a 300 guineas fee. The Duke of Westminster offered £40,000 for Willonyx – 'I have the cheque here in my pocket,' said his representative. A French syndicate asked if £50,000 might be accepted? Howard's answer was no. His loyalty to his colt was ill-rewarded: Willonyx was a failure as a sire.

Quite suddenly at the end of the 1913 season, Sam Darling was gone. "It may be asked why I have decided to retire from the practice of a profession to which I have devoted so many years with profit and success," he wrote.

"I can only reply that I was beginning to feel the strain of it, and prudence suggested that I should not go on too long. It is surely better to [go] before you begin to fail." He admitted that it was a choice between his farms and his stable: "The two responsibilities combined seemed rather too much; and as my son Fred was available to take over the stable, I thought it best for all concerned to arrange that he should do so. [The] continuous pressure of training and racing is now relaxed." He emphasised that the management of 1,200 acres and 23 farm staff was quite enough to occupy him. But, he added, "Since giving up the stable and devoting myself to the farm, I feel twenty years younger than I did." So he sat down to write his memoirs.

Sam Darling's Reminiscences was published in 1914. It chronicles the achievements of one of the giants of the trainers' ranks. It's also the primary source for information about Darling's life. Many of the details are fascinating, and wouldn't otherwise be in the public domain. Unfortunately, there's much that a curious reader would want to ask Darling that remains unanswered. The admission, "I have not kept a diary or notes of any description" in the book's first sentence isn't encouraging. The biography suffers from too many travelogues. Fully a third of its pages are devoted to his overseas journeys, and many of them merely reprint the newspaper columns written by his friend William Allison. They show that Darling had a much wider hinterland than his contemporaries: he was inquisitive, always on the look-out for a farming, breeding or veterinary advance, and as prepared to find it on another continent as in the next parish. But the pages devoted to foreign jaunts are at the expense of a number of episodes in his life that he chose not to address. Two or three of the gambles that went astray are mentioned, but the name 'Ravensdale' is absent.

Darling made few mistakes when the money was down. Ravensdale was the worst of those mistakes, and evidently the thought of it was still painful when he wrote his book, long after the Lincoln of 1898. Ravensdale was the darkest of dark horses, an animal who'd only run once each season. As a two year old he ran unplaced on his debut. The following year he bolted up by eight lengths in an all-aged race at Warwick. Twelve months on, and Ravensdale again put in a solitary appearance, finishing a modest third. Of all the horses in training, Ravensdale might appear to any sane person to be the last possible conveyance for a life-changing gamble. But in the early weeks of 1898, Ravensdale was lighting up the Beckhampton gallops. He had a Lincoln entry, and he stood at a super-cautious 14–1 in the ante-post betting. Rumours spread about a gallop which pitted Ravensdale against Kilcock. It was said the gallop put Kilcock in the Lincoln at around 8st 11lb, and that Ravensdale with 6st 11lb was a penalty kick. The following day he was cut to 12–1, and then a flood of money the day after saw him the new favourite for the Lincoln, at 5–1. 'Vigilant' pointed out in *The Sportsman* that Ravensdale's record 'Is not an imposing one,' but added, "Assuming [the] trial to be correct, however, Ravensdale should not only win the Lincolnshire Handicap very easily indeed, but [it's unlikely] that the penalty incurred would stop him in the Jubilee Stakes." The gamble continued on course from 5–2 down to 11–8, the shortest price there'd ever been in a Lincoln. 'Vigilant' was unimpressed when he saw the favourite: 'very plain, common-looking, terribly light.' The jockey was a tiny apprentice, and the first omens of trouble came when he struggled to get Ravensdale onto the course. However, he started well enough, and held a good position all through the race. The finish was decided by the strength of the respective jockeys. Less than a length covered the first three, and Ravensdale was third, his rider "powerless to render his mount much assistance."

Also missing from Darling's memoirs is a case in which he sued one of his owners for an unpaid bill. A dispute arose when John Rutherford queried his £254 annual account; specifically, the inclusion of fees for jockeys riding in trials. Rutherford was annoyed because his horses had been tried with those belonging to other owners. He argued that Darling had no right to do that without the prior consent of all the owners concerned. He added that, once all permissions had been given and the trial had taken place, each owner was entitled to receive a detailed report of the gallop, including the weights carried.

Rutherford refused to settle his bill until Darling had conceded on these points of principle. Darling replied that he was doing his best for every horse in his care, and he should be free to work them how, when and in what combinations he saw fit. After 18 months of legal wrangling, the matter ended in the High Court. Its resolution was swift: Darling was paid the £254 and both sides paid their own costs. One of his lawyers gave a statement which had been agreed between the two men. What he read out endorsed Rutherford's views:

> "Mr Darling regrets that with regard to the trial of [horses owned by] Mr Rutherford he took a mistaken view of his position. Mr Rutherford, in accepting this statement of Mr Darling, desired to say that in defending this action he intended only to establish a principle which he considered important [and] made no reflection on Mr Darling."

At once, a new duty of care was imposed, not just on Darling, but on all public trainers. It would've been interesting for Darling's readers to know what he thought of the concession he made, and to what extent he acted on it. He must've hated the implication of negligence towards an owner's interests. Yet the only mention of Rutherford in his book is the man's name in the list of his owners.

The worst omission from *Sam Darling's Reminiscences* is the near-total absence of judgement on the jockeys he knew. Beyond describing Tod Sloan as a good rider – about as insightful as saying he was American – Darling offered no worthwhile comment on the champions of his time. As a young man he rode against Fred Archer and George Fordham. As a trainer he used Sloan, Charles Wood, the Cannon brothers, Billy Higgs, Danny Maher, the Reiff brothers and the other Americans. Few people were better placed or qualified to analyse their respective talents, strengths and weaknesses. It's a pity he neglected to.

Cavils about Sam Darling's autobiography are nothing when set against his achievements. He expanded Beckhampton from Harry Woolcott's two paddocks to 1,200 acres and model farms. He saddled the winners of seven classics and endless other races which today are Group or Listed. He bet boldly and mostly successfully. With his neighbours Alec Taylor at Manton and John Porter at Kingsclere, he accelerated the emergence of the modern racehorse trainer. They were called Masters for good reason. Darling was also, notwithstanding his disagreement with John Rutherford, attentive to his owners' interests. In March 1913, at the start of his last season's training, he opened a letter from Victor Cavendish, the ninth Duke of Devonshire. The Duke had decided to give up racing and breeding. At the time, he had 10 horses at Beckhampton. The following day, Darling went to Devonshire House in Piccadilly. The Duke wrote to his wife that evening:

> "Though [Darling] was naturally sorry he quite understood the position. He thinks the horses in training will sell far better at the July sales than any other time. All the buyers come then. The [brood] mares sell better in December and he thinks I would be better to keep them till then."

Darling must've been disappointed that he wouldn't be passing on to his son the patronage of a top owner-breeder. Yet he focused on how the Duke could maximise the proceeds of his dispersal. Four months later, the Duke was able to tell his wife, "The horses in training were sold on Tuesday [for] £12,920. Taslett [a close second in the 1,000 Guineas] made over five thousand. The four yearlings were sold yesterday for £3,670." At the start of December, Devonshire's 10 broodmares and four foals realised a further £26,600. He'd exactly followed Darling's advice.

Among all the valedictory messages, Darling most valued the one from Harry Greer:

> "Such an event as your retirement from active training could not take place without being also an event of great importance to me. We have worked together on the Turf for so many years. They have been marked

> by such unremitting care and attention to my interests on your part, and such marked success, considering the few horses I've [owned], that I can look back on every incident connected with my racing career, not only with pleasure, but with the knowledge that I owe most of that pleasure to you."

Darling left reminders of his achievements around his yard and land. Colonel Holford's farmhouse was renamed Galtee More. Some accommodation for the lads became Wildfowler Cottages. A large house that he bought, the other side of the Devizes road, was called Willonyx. Whatever might be missing from his autobiography, it isn't photographs, especially ones which communicate his status and prosperity. A view of Willonyx House – with another eye-catching porch – includes four domestic and garden staff, standing to attention. If it was a conceit, he'd earned it. He told the writer Sidney Galtrey, "I was just an ordinary countryman to begin with, and I've been making my own way ever since." "Right from the beginning?" "Yes, right from the start."

CHAPTER NINE

Fred Darling, Lillie Langtry and a first classic winner

Fred Darling's training career began with a spell working for Alfred Sadler in Newmarket. Sadler was private trainer to Lord Rosebery before opening a public yard at Freemason Lodge. He was able, hard-working and popular – the ideal mentor. In 1907 Darling moved a short distance from the town to train Lillie Langtry's horses at Regal Lodge, Kentford. She was his principal patron, but he had other owners too; the first time the words, 'winner trained by F Darling' appeared after a race was when Li Hung won a little race for Edgar Cohen at Sandown Park's Eclipse meeting in July. His second winner followed half an hour later, again for Cohen. Nonetheless, Langtry provided him with most of his stable strength, and – by his association with her – a great deal of prominence. She was then in her mid-fifties, but still known to a generation of socialites and racegoers as 'The Jersey Lily,' the erstwhile mistress of the Prince of Wales and many other men of influence or wealth. When she made her debut in London society she was an immediate sensation, a fresh beauty whom no one had ever heard of, because until early adulthood she'd lived, unnoticed, on the island of Jersey. She'd unwisely married a widower who she thought had money. He didn't, and as she became a star of London's salons, staterooms and stage, he was swiftly set aside.

It was the time of the so-called 'professional beauties,' with their wasp waists, piled-up hair and dreamy expressions. Langtry slept, if not exclusively with the first XI, certainly the wealthiest players she could attract. Her affairs more than once involved figures connected to Beckhampton. Riding with Lord Lonsdale in Hyde Park, she stopped to exchange pleasantries with Sir George Chetwynd. Lonsdale was affronted. Words were exchanged between the men, followed by a vigorous set-to, much to the delight of passing society. On another day and as publicly, Chetwynd punched an acquaintance who said something disrespectful about his beloved Lillie. Alas, he introduced her to his house-buyer, the deep-pocketed rake George 'Abingdon' Baird. Baird had a tumultuous affair with Lillie. He was obsessively jealous, and violent with it. She seemed unable to escape from a relationship in which the only, marginal consolation was that each instance of physical abuse was followed by a lavish cash gift. After one dreadful beating in Paris, Baird was so consumed with guilt that he gave Lillie a cheque for £50,000 and a three-masted yacht, *The Whyte Lady*. The wags dubbed it 'The Black Eye.'

Lillie was sailing in the Mediterranean when news arrived that Baird had died in America, wrecked by drink. She hurried back to London for news of the wealth he'd promised to leave her, to find his final betrayal: she received nothing. Unabashed, she set about finding other admirers to keep her in her accustomed style, until she retired from the fun and frolics and married, aged 40, an unremarkable younger man, Hugo de Bathe. He succeeded to a Baronetcy in 1907, so that Fred Darling's first owner was Lady de Bathe. By then she was described, ungallantly, as, 'An old tart of a girl with reddish hair and a flamboyant manner.' A photograph of her with Darling at Newbury in 1909 suggests otherwise: she was still a strikingly handsome woman, likely to attract and keep attention in any company. She was also intelligent and confident, more than able to talk business or world affairs with the powerful men whose company she sought. As a result, her affairs with 'Bertie' and others became friendships and lasted long after their physical element had waned. She acquired considerable knowledge of racing along the way. Gifts of racehorses and broodmares were a regular feature of her relationships.

In his second season training for Lady de Bathe, Darling laid down the sort of marker that every young trainer needs. He trained 28 winners, the equivalent of perhaps 100 today, given the lower number of races then; more importantly, he won a top handicap with a heavily-punted horse. In effect, he called, 'I'm here. I can get them ready, and I know the time of day.' Lillie had been taken aback at her first sight of Fred Darling:

> "His father, Sam Darling, brought him to discuss business with me at Sandown Park one race day. I must confess when I saw him I felt rather doubtful. He was about twenty-one [but] being rather small of build, he looked about sixteen. Still, if his father recommended him, I knew he must be clever. And how he proved it."

The horse was the colt Yentoi, bought by Lillie for 1,000 guineas in 1907. The following year, Darling trained Yentoi to win a two-mile handicap at Doncaster; the colt made most of the running to win by two lengths from the easy Chester Cup winner Glacis, who conceded 19lb. The pair were at once made prominent in the betting for the Cesarewitch, where Glacis would be 4lb better off at the weights. A torrent of bets went onto Yentoi at 6–1 and 7–1. The support evaporated when the Newmarket touts reported a gallop which included Yentoi and another Cesarewitch hopeful, the colt All Black, representing another stable. The touts were adamant: All Black had won the trial by 15 lengths, and Yentoi had weakened dramatically in the closing stages. 'A non-stayer,' cried the knowing ones. The racing press tipsters were inclined to favour racecourse form over home gallops, and kept Yentoi on their short lists. It was noted that the stable confidence behind the colt didn't seem to have wavered. At the call-overs, though, there were periods when Yentoi could hardly be given away. Two days before the race, support resurfaced briefly with sizeable bets at 10–1 and 9–1, but the following day and then on course, the odds lengthened to 16–1, the stable commission having been worked at much shorter prices.

Yentoi had a presumed 'graveyard' draw in the Cesarewitch, just one away from the rail, but under an apprentice rider, Freddie Fox, he quickly took a prominent position, was never out of the leading group, and went clear from the Bushes. He won by three lengths, with three-quarters of a length back to Glacis in third. Darling had coaxed 4lb and almost four lengths' improvement from Yentoi since his run against Glacis at Doncaster. *The Sporting Life* complimented, "Young Fred Darling on scoring so signal a success so early in his career as a trainer." Bob Sievier praised Freddie Fox in *The Winning Post*: "The winner was splendidly ridden by Fox, who never lost an inch or his head. He has the makings of a real good jockey." It was a prescient forecast: the day would come when Darling and Fox combined for much bigger prizes than a Cesarewitch. At Kentford in October 1908, it was enough that Lady de Bathe had won £11,000 in bets over Yentoi, and that Darling, not for the last time, had shown that races are won on the racecourse, not on the gallops. Sievier thought it was hilarious:

> 'The result was a dual triumph for public form and Lady de Bathe. It was said that in a gallop All Black had beaten Yentoi by fifteen lengths, and that this was authentic. All Black's owners were confident. They lost their money, for in the race Yentoi beat All Black by fifteen lengths!'

It would've been an obvious move for Fred Darling to capitalise on Yentoi's win and move into his own yard in Newmarket, assured of patronage from a wider circle of owners. Instead, he set out to get broader experience on the continent, accepting an offer to be the private trainer for the industrialists Arthur and Carl Weinberg. Their Gestüt Waldfried stable near Frankfurt was one of the largest racing yards in Germany. As well as its own gallops, the stable had the use of Frankfurt racecourse to exercise its 35 horses. Darling was given a two-year contract. Without reference to him, the Weinberg brothers also recruited a top English rider, Joe Childs. After a successful apprenticeship, Childs had found his rides dwindling away with his claim, and he moved to France. In the two seasons before joining Darling and the Weinbergs, he rode 75 and 90 winners there. It was a surprise that he should turn his back on Paris; he explained the move in terms of his well-being. "I had to do a great deal of wasting [which] was undoubtedly affecting my health. My new contract did not specify any riding weight, which I felt would be beneficial to my health and strength."

Childs was a good and experienced rider, but also stubborn, touchy, and alert to any opportunity to take offence. He and Darling frequently argued, but they won the German Oaks and over 30 other races, placing the Weinbergs second only to the German National Stud among winning owners. In the following season Darling and Childs won the local equivalent of the 2000 Guineas. Despite their victories, the trainer and jockey were at loggerheads. According to Childs, "Although [we] were having a fairly successful season, I wasn't always able to see eye to eye with Fred Darling. We often had our differences, and towards the end of the racing season, matters ended in a clash between us in which Dr [Arthur] Weinberg intervened. The upshot of this was that Dr Weinberg informed me they were not renewing Fred Darling's contact." Childs went back to France; Darling was invited to train for Prince Hohenlohe in Austria, and it was from there at the end of the 1913 season that he was called back to England by his father Sam. He was to be the next Master of Beckhampton.

It would've been hard to follow Sam Darling's achievements at Beckhampton under any circumstances. In the event, Fred Darling's first season was overshadowed by the assassination of Archduke Franz Ferdinand at the end of June, which triggered, a month later, the outbreak of the first world war. The effect on racing in this country was immediate. The Government took over the railways and commandeered all rolling stock, meaning that for a while there was no transport available to take horses to their races. In August, three weeks went by without a single race meeting taking place. The fixture list for the rest of the year was decimated by abandonments. Trainers lost their staff and horses to the national cause.

Thousands of stable staff signed up, leaving their yards to be staffed by the older married lads, and young boys. The War Department sent its agents out to round up horses – 'remounts' – for service in northern France. The agents were sympathetic towards the bloodstock industry; no blue-blooded colts or valuable broodmares were taken away. But a sound gelding or hunter faced an unpleasant and probably short working life in the mud at the front. Trainers and stable staff soon found themselves without any suitable hacks. Animal feeds were diverted to the remounts; prize money was lost along with race meetings. It was inevitable that the racehorse population would shrink rapidly, even without what *The Bloodstock Breeders' Review* called:

> "A rather pronounced feeling in certain Turf circles that at a time when the country was engaged in a life and death struggle, the pleasures of [our] sport were somewhat out of place."

It was as gloomy a backdrop as the inheritor of a large stable could have faced. Yet, unknown to him, the fates were smiling kindly on Beckhampton's new Master. Newmarket's July sales were held between the murder in Sarajevo and the multiple declarations of war that followed. From 140 or so yearlings on offer, Fred Darling had paid 500 guineas for 'a big, gawky, overgrown' colt by Marcovil out of Toute Suite. It wasn't, on the face of it, a promising pairing. Marcovil had terrible forelegs; his best performance in four seasons' racing was winning the Cambridgeshire with 7st 11lb. Toute Suite had been through the sales ring for a modest 105 guineas as a yearling. She was hardly bigger than a pony, and never considered for training. Improbably, she produced a huge foal. Fred Darling saw something he liked, or decided that the breeding was worth a risk. Toute Suite was tiny, but she was by a Derby winner, Sanfoin, out of a smart mare called Star, twice a winner at Newmarket and beaten only a head in the Park Hill Stakes. As for Marcovil, he had some significance as one of the last representatives of the bloodlines tracing to the Godolphin Arabian. Darling backed his judgement, bought the golden chestnut yearling, and passed him on to the whisky magnate James Buchanan. The colt was named Hurry On, which was the precise opposite of the course that Darling took with him. It was apparent that Hurry On was far too backward to be trained as a two year old, so his trainer, despite not knowing how much racing there'd be the following season, sat out the whole of 1915 with his, by now, enormous colt.

Hurry On was hard work. As he filled out and strengthened in proportion to his size, he became boisterous to a fault, and bossy. One of his party tricks was to rear up without warning on his hind legs: an intimidating prospect for a stable lad, confronted with a 17 hands colt measuring almost seven feet round his girth. He carted Joe Childs off the gallops one morning, to Childs' fury, and for good measure ran off with Darling himself the following day. Darling liked to show that he could do any job in the yard as well as any of his employees, and he took it on himself to ride much of the work on Hurry On. It was admirable, because no one else was volunteering. No matter how much exercise the colt was given, it was hard to get him to relax in slow, steady work, and despite being the equine alpha male in the yard, he spooked at the slightest surprise. A sparrow flying into his box was enough to set him off. But, he had a huge stride, a superb action, and nothing on the Beckhampton gallops could live with him. He made his debut in a one-mile maiden race at Lingfield in June 1916, where he was second favourite in a field of 15. He was as green as grass at the start and in the early stages, and then pulled clear under Joe Childs' brother Charlie to win by two lengths and eight. He was stepped up to a mile and a half to win equally easily from a small field at Newmarket, and then took on stronger opposition in the Newbury Stakes. Here he beat a recent dual winner, Blackadder, by three lengths and the 1000 Guineas winner Canyon by eight lengths.

In the few column inches that were devoted to racing in the national press in the third year of war, it was suggested that Hurry On had put down a bold claim for the substitute St Leger, the 14-furlong September Stakes. It was so named because while the other four wartime Classics carried the prefix 'new', as in 'New Derby', Doncaster Corporation had taken umbrage at Town Moor losing all its fixtures. Most of the big arms factories were based in the north – as far as possible from the reach of Zeppelin bombing raids – and the authorities were apparently determined to deny munitions workers the temptation to take a day off work. So the Corporation refused to license the description, 'New St Leger'. Hurry On faced only five opponents, but they included Clarissimus, the winner of the 2000 Guineas; Canyon, who re-opposed on 4lb better terms from the Newbury Stakes; and Atheling, the unbeaten winner of the previous season's Dewhurst. The betting was 11–10 Hurry On, 5–2 Clarissimus and 4–1 Atheling, and the three colts finished in that order, Hurry On winning easily. Some breeding pundits wondered if a son of Marcovil would stay the St Leger distance, but Toute Suite's dam had won over two miles. Darling had no hesitation in telling Charlie Childs to make plenty of use of Hurry On. His confidence was based on a trial over the full September Stakes trip at Beckhampton a few days before. The horses involved were:

Hurry On (aged 3)	9st 12lb	
Brownii (4)	6st 12lb	(51lb better than weight for age with Hurry On)
Ferox (3)	7st 12lb	
Gay Lally (4)	8st 4lb	(31lb better)

The stablemates finished in that order. It was as decisive a trial as Darling and James Buchanan could've wished for. The key horse was Brownii, who'd won a 15-furlong handicap at Lingfield before finishing a head second under 6st 9lb in the Newbury Autumn Cup. Nor were the other two galloping companions there to make up the numbers. Gay Lally was fresh from a mile and a half conditions race win; Ferox had been Darling's fact-finder in the New Derby, running unplaced but giving lines to the classic form. Darling's instructions were that Hurry On should give the other three horses a start of six to eight lengths. He made a mockery of his weight by sailing past Brownii and the others after 10 furlongs and won the trial running away.

At Newmarket, Hurry On set a nice swinging pace and was in the lead with his four opponents bunched behind as they came into view. With half a mile to run, his jockey took a long look behind him, and sent his mount clear going down into the Dip, with Clarissimus in vain pursuit. Hurry On beat the Guineas winner by three lengths, with five more lengths back to Atheling. It was so easy that some asked what the form was worth. The racing correspondent of *The Times* gave his view that Hurry On "Was lucky in having had the way cleared for him by the absences of [the New Derby winner Fifinella and others]. The success does not therefore amount to much, especially as it is doubtful whether Clarissimus has really got over his severe race in [the 2000 Guineas]".

A form student would've replied that Canyon had beaten Fifinella in the 1000 Guineas before herself being mauled twice by Hurry On. James Buchanan chose to reply with a cheque book. Irked by the claim that his colt had won the replacement St Leger by default, he issued a £5,000-a-side challenge: Hurry On to run a match over a mile and a half. If he won, Buchanan would donate his winnings to the Red Cross. For Hurry On's intended match, Buchanan made a point of ignoring his colt's three year old peers. Instead, he issued the challenge to the previous year's Triple Crown winner, Pommern. Nothing was heard back from Pommern's owner. Hurry On ended his season with two more facile wins from small fields, with odds of 1–25 and 1–40 laid on him.

Shortly afterwards, Fred Darling went from presiding over a slimmed-down Beckhampton, to no stable at all. He'd enjoyed a temporary exemption from military service, which expired at the end of 1916. He was called up, joined the 9th Lancers, and in the New Year he closed Beckhampton indefinitely. By then, most of his lads had signed up with the Army or gone to work in munitions factories. His owners' horses went to the sales, James Buchanan's among them. Hurry On was one of the few to be kept in training.

He was sent to Peter Purcell Gilpin at Newmarket, with the aim of mopping up the 1917 Cup races, but he didn't stand further training, and was retired to Buchanan's stud at Lavington in Sussex. Remarkably, he sired a Derby winner with his first ever covering, and over a long career at Lavington he produced the winners of eight classics, three Derbys among them. Darling visited Hurry On at stud and found him taking charge of his groom, just as he had the work riders at Beckhampton. "Does he still get on his hind legs?" Darling asked the groom; "He was always trying it with me and always without warning." The answer came, yes.

If there's truth in the saying that a horse's merit isn't fully established until it's beaten, it's difficult to be confident about Hurry On's place in the pantheon. He only raced for one season, only ran six times, mostly in small fields, and was never off the bridle. However, he met two of his year's other classic winners and beat them comfortably. Fred Darling had no doubts: "The best horse I have ever seen, the best I am ever likely to see." Over time, mindful of his owners' commercial interests, he'd now and then hail a new 'best ever' in the unsaddling enclosure at Newmarket or Epsom, but he always came back to Hurry On. At the end of his training career he was asked to rank his multiple classic winners from the decades past: "I should say Hurry On was the best."

His father Sam died in 1921, after a long illness. He had time to make all the arrangements for his own funeral, and they were meticulous, like everything else he did in his life. He specified the colours in which the cart carrying his coffin should be painted: the roads were to be tidied, and sprinkled with sand. If it was a surprise to some that his funeral cortege went along the Marlborough road to East Kennett, rather than to the parish church in Avebury, there was a reason. Sam had offered, some years before, to pay for the church's roof repairs. A prelate who was politically correct, generations before the term was coined, waved the gift away, *shocked*: he couldn't *possibly* accept a donation from gambling winnings. Darling said nothing, but he was buried at East Kennett.

He would've been saddened that his son immediately set about selling the farms that he'd worked so many years to acquire and so fruitfully to develop. The first dispersal was the whole of the Galtee More farm, across the Devizes road from the yard, its land extending west to encircle Silbury Hill. It went on the market in 1922. The economy still hadn't recovered from the first world war, and it wasn't until 1925 that Galtee More was sold. The buyers were the Hues family, who've farmed there ever since.

Darling's motive for selling the Galtee More estate was straightforward. He was completely focused on horses and training. He had no interest in farming. He used the proceeds of the farm sale to buy a 100-acre stud near Calne. It was the Blacklands stud, established by his father's stable jockey 'Farmer' Higgs. Darling bred over 140 winners there, and one of the last crop provided him with a farewell that he couldn't have dared to script.

CHAPTER TEN

'M' is for Martinet

Many of the words used to describe Fred Darling begin with the letter 'M.' Several of his obituary writers arrived at 'martinet' – 'A man who maintains strict discipline.' Sir Peter O'Sullevan remembered Darling as, "Misery guts, intimidating. He was forbidding and not very engaging." Peter Willett, the doyen of bloodstock writers and co-author of *The Biographical Encyclopaedia of British Flat Racing* says, "Darling was a monster."

The charge sheet against Fred Darling is extensive. It begins with his treatment of his nephew Marcus Marsh, who worked as his assistant during two years – 1925 and 1926 – in which Beckhampton won back-to-back Derbys. One morning, he asked Marsh for the daily list. Marsh fished in his pocket and handed Darling a piece of paper: the wrong piece. Instead of details on each horse's feeding or ailment or intended work, the 22 year old Marcus had given his uncle a long list of bets. "What the hell's this?" demanded Darling. "Oh, that's just a few bets I've had." "You know it's a stable rule that all bets have to be made through me." Marsh said sometimes he wanted to back horses that Darling might not fancy, and surely that was reasonable? He had a point; one afternoon when the yard had four runners, Marsh had asked Darling to put £5 on each of them. They all won. When Darling paid him the winnings, they were short by £25. Marsh asked why. "Oh, I didn't fancy one of them, so you weren't on," his uncle replied.

From that day, Marsh decided not to rely on Darling. But Marsh had been warned before. Darling sacked him on the spot: "If you can't do what I tell you, you'd better go somewhere else." After serving two weeks' notice, he was out.

Where the jockey Freddie Fox was concerned, Darling was merely unfeeling, in a particularly brutal way. The two men had combined at the start of their careers to win the 1908 Cesarewitch with Yentoi. Almost 20 years on, Darling retained Fox at the start of the 1930 season as Beckhampton's first jockey. It was an open secret that Darling had wanted the rising star, Gordon Richards, but Richards had signed a £6,000 retainer with Lord Glanely.

Fox's first season at Beckhampton could hardly have gone better. He was champion jockey. After which, Darling asked Fox if he'd consider an arrangement whereby Gordon Richards rode for the yard when he could, and Fox took the leftovers? Fox was the mildest-tempered of men, but even to him, the scope for humiliation was obvious. His answer was, no. The season began badly for him when he had to choose between two Beckhampton runners in both the 1000 and 2000 Guineas – and in each race picked the wrong one. But he bounced back by winning the Derby and the St James's Palace Stakes. Then at the beginning of October he picked up *The Sporting Life* to read the headline: "Gordon Richards' retainer – first jockey for Beckhampton next year." In the story below, it was reported that, "Fred Fox, who is the first jockey to Beckhampton, was completely taken by surprise by the announcement." 'Shock' was nearer the mark. Darling made no attempt to warn Fox. The distinction between 'business' and 'personal' didn't exist for Darling: there was only business.

When Gordon Richards came to write his memoirs, he could look back on the British Turf's greatest flat-race riding career. The retainer from Fred Darling, which began in 1932, continued uninterrupted for 16 seasons. Few men knew the trainer better than Gordon Richards, and his assessment was blunt: "I don't think he ever understood friendship at all."

> "[He] was ruthless with horses and with men. If he thought a horse was not absolutely first class, he had no use for that horse, and out it went. If he thought one of his men was not absolutely first class, he had no use for him, and out he went."

One incident influenced his opinion more than any other. It followed from Darling's enthusiastic involvement in the Home Guard in the second world war. Among the men in the Marlborough area who volunteered to join 'Dad's Army' were a couple of dozen from Beckhampton, working for Darling or at Galtee More farm. The Beckhampton Platoon was created, within the Marlborough Battalion of the Home Guard. Darling announced that he would be its commanding officer. One of his men, in the Home Guard and in the yard, was Pat Templeton. Templeton was 42. He'd spent his whole working life at Beckhampton, from apprentice to paid lad and then head lad. He was always immaculately turned out, a strict disciplinarian in the mould of his master, and brilliant with horses. It was said when he was in the yard, there was never any need to send for a vet.

The platoon had a night exercise. Battalion officers made a surprise visit, and Darling took them round his platoon's posts. Templeton's post was unmanned: Pat was in a local pub. He was dismissed at once from the platoon – and from his job at Beckhampton, even though his offence had no bearing on his work in the yard. "He's made a complete fool of me," was Darling's snarled justification. In vain did Gordon Richards plead with Darling to change his mind, on the grounds Templeton was the best head man that he was ever likely to employ. Darling was unmoved. Templeton and his family were evicted from their tied cottage. He found work at the local RAF station, and was dead six months later. Darling can't realistically be blamed for the onset of his former employee's cancer, but Templeton's family believed that it was brought about by shock at the brutality of his treatment. Gordon Richards said the man, "Lived only for Beckhampton and its horses."

Few who came into contact with Fred Darling were completely unbruised. The racing historian and journalist Roger Mortimer called him, "Hard, ruthless and uncompromising."

> "Small, spare and neat, he could never be accused of wearing his heart on his sleeve. In fact he was taciturn, secretive and quick-tempered. He never tired himself out by laborious efforts to tolerate bores and fools. Far from courting the approval of the racing press, he treated them [with] a brusqueness that bordered on hostility and contempt. [He was] ruthless to achieve his ends [and] rarely came off second best in a clash of wills [with] a difficult owner or a recalcitrant horse."

Darling's younger brother Douglas worked for 10 years as assistant to Fred. Even he remembered Fred as a man who, 'Ruled with a rod of iron.' "He was terribly strict with the lads, the jockeys and me – and we all called him Guv'nor." The older Darling brother, Sam, seems to have had the kindness and generosity which were so lacking in Fred. Although he ran his own yard in Newmarket, Sam was always prepared to help out when ill-health forced his brother to seek treatment or rest. On the eve of his last season as a trainer, Fred was forced by a recurrence of tuberculosis to spend much of the winter resting in Switzerland. Sam was enlisted to look after the yard, in particular Tudor Minstrel, favourite for the following spring's 2000 Guineas. The day the Guv'nor returned, he looked into Tudor Minstrel's box and called out for everyone in the yard to hear, "What horse is this?" He feigned amazement at being told, 'Tudor Minstrel,' and called louder still, "What have you been doing with it? Fetch some oats and hay. I've got to build this horse up again." Sam cringed and walked away without a word.

Darling seldom resisted the compulsion to have a dig at another professional, whether it was his own brother or the artist Alfred Munnings. Munnings was the twentieth century's greatest painter of horses. That meant nothing to Darling. When Beckhampton horses were the subject of Munnings' brushstrokes, Darling seemed set on making life as difficult for the artist as possible. First, when Munnings was asked to paint one of Beckhampton's Derby winners. Munnings had donated a blank canvas to a charity auction, with the pledge, 'To paint a horse on it, for whoever buys it.' The winning bid was from Arthur Dewar, whose colt Cameronian had won that year's Derby.

> "I went to Beckhampton, meaning to do more than my best for this well-deserving bidder. My zeal and my hopes were somewhat dashed when, full of enthusiasm, I tried to carry out my object – the best painting I could do. Fred Darling, my host, [did] not want him to stand out of doors."
>
> "You must paint him in his box," he said. "But the boxes are so dark," Munnings protested: "The walls are the same colour as the horse." "That can't be helped," said Fred: "He's not going to be held out of doors." Munnings bewailed, "His word was law. I made the best of the irritating and difficult conditions, standing in the passage-way.
>
> "I painted what I saw. When hung, such a picture is bound to appear a dark spot on a wall, [a] dark-brown horse in a dark-brown box, painted under stress, for even in the box the lad was afraid to take the sheet off the horse. It was turned back from his shoulders while I painted the fore half, and lifted off his quarters as I painted the rear half."

A dozen years passed, and Munnings had forgotten or forgiven: "It was refreshing to get back [to] Beckhampton downs [with] Silbury Hill nearby, and the great Sarsen Stones standing about." He had a commission from the King to paint Sun Chariot, the resulting artwork to be a gift from His Majesty to Darling. It was October and Sun Chariot had run her last race, so Darling was less inclined to interfere, but Munnings had to compensate for the mare's long, thick coat and the low sunlight of late autumn. Darling later provided a dismissive critique of Munnings and his painting: "He's made her look like a bloody didicoy's pony."

'He never married,' reads one of Fred Darling's obituaries. He did. He met a girl when he was training for the Weinbergs in Frankfurt in 1912. She was called Gretel, and they married, and nothing more is known of her, or of their relationship. She came to England with Darling but didn't stay. Perhaps their marriage didn't take; or she didn't like her new home, and was lonely; or, her homeland was at war with England and she felt it impossible to remain here. She disappeared from Fred Darling's life. There were stories about him keeping her picture hanging at Beckhampton, 'forever after.' No one who worked for Darling in his later years recalls any photograph or painting. There's only a tantalising glimpse of what might have been – or perhaps what Fred Darling hoped might be. After the war, his chauffeur drove him up to London one evening. He took Darling to the Mayfair Hotel. Darling came out of the hotel with a woman that the chauffeur recognised as his wife. They parted, and the chauffeur told one of the stable lads that Darling was in tears on the drive back to Beckhampton.

There's no saying why Fred Darling never married again. He was an enthusiastic and indiscriminate womaniser. He kept an eye out for the WAAF girls at nearby RAF Yatesbury. He had a relationship with a London brewery heiress, and he also liked to finish evening stables and then summon his driver to take him up to the West End and the nightclubs. Sometimes he had company on the return journey, and the housekeeping staff would know to take breakfast upstairs to the young woman, help her pack, and take her down the back stairs, where the chauffeur waited to drop her off at Marlborough station. None of that got in the way of the yard's business, but Darling showed himself in a poor light at a stable party when a classic win was being celebrated. One of the Marlborough hotels was booked, a band played, and Darling spotted the pretty girlfriend of one of his stable lads. He monopolised her for the whole evening. Before long his car was spotted outside the girl's home in a nearby village, and then, to the irritation of the staff, her bicycle would be brazenly propped in the porch at Beckhampton while Darling trysted with her upstairs. Their affair proved surprisingly long-lasting; the humiliated stable lad left the yard soon after it began.

Not many recruits to Darling's Beckhampton lasted long. His standards were impossibly high, discipline was strict, compliance was non-negotiable. He also hired from the fringes of society, often Borstal boys on probation, or lads from the meaner city streets with few options. They were cheap and they were desperate for work. Even so, there was a high turnover. It was enough to be found standing around: 'Nothing to do? Get your cards.' One teenager said that, "Mr Darling was the strictest man I've ever known with man or horse. You didn't have to look sideways to get a clout round the ear." He and his ilk fought like cats, and for the most part their employment was measured in days and weeks rather than months or years. One of Beckhampton's longest-serving men, Dai Rees, began as an apprentice under Darling. He remembered 15 new lads being hired; after a month, only two of them remained. Even so, a few stayed the course, and those that did developed a surprising fondness for their uncompromising Guv'nor. Gordon Richards explained:

> "He had no friendships with his men [but] strangely enough he inspired immense affection, even love, on the part of those he employed, as well as fear. His incredible ability and his immense craftsmanship were things which created a burning admiration. And, if you did your stuff, he looked after you. All his men knew that, although they knew also that one mistake might mean their instant dismissal."

The other side of the coin was that, for the men who reached Darling's demanding standards, and stayed the course, he shared the proceeds from the yard's successes. After a two-day Salisbury meeting that produced six winners for Beckhampton, all the lads were given a bonus of two weeks' wages. And while Darling reserved the right to treat his lads badly, woe betide any outsider who tried the same. Harry Wragg rode for the yard one season when Gordon Richards was injured. The convention of the time was that a winning horse's lad was rewarded with a £1 present from the jockey. One of the lads didn't receive a present after his horse had been ridden to victory by Wragg. He approached the jockey: 'Excuse me, Mr Wragg, but will you be giving me that 'drink'? Wragg pointed to the pump in the corner of the yard: "You can have as much to drink as you like over there, son." The lad told Darling: "Oh, he said that, did he? Leave it to me." The next time Wragg was in the yard, the lad got his £1.

Darling was hard on his men, and he was intransigent with his owners. He could afford to be. His reputation was so high that he enjoyed the luxury of selecting them. Many called. Few were chosen. As Gordon Richards said, no owner ever objected to Darling's plans for his horse: he was the Guv'nor to his patrons, as much as to his staff and his riders. He kept a surprise for any owner who outstayed his welcome, or perhaps wasn't welcome in the first place. He, who usually went up to the gallops in an Austin van, would make a show of riding up on an old hunter. The owner was offered a similar mount. On the way back to the yard was a high, unyielding hedge. Without warning, Fred gave his horse a kick in the belly. Off it bounded, joyously, to jump the hedge. The owner's mount, who'd also done the same a hundred times, followed without bidding. Not a few visitors were left sprawling on the other side.

Dorothy Paget was the obvious candidate for 'the owner who was told to go.' A thousand stories have been told about her; many of them are true. She was the Croesus-rich daughter of English aristocracy and American money, an accomplished and slim horsewoman in her youth who ate herself to a vast bulk wrapped in a tent-sized overcoat. She wasn't inclined towards male company, and she grew to find almost any human contact painful. She had a phalanx of female secretaries and gofers to shield her. She inverted the clock, sleeping most of the daytime and filling the night with large meals. Her chosen passion was racing, with adrenalin added by planetary-sized bets. She contributed much to racing, not least through her ownership of

Golden Miller, the winner of five Cheltenham Gold Cups. She had innumerable other good horses, but mostly she was known for extreme wilfulness and eccentricity. Her nocturnal lifestyle meant that she was starting to take an interest in each day's racing long after anyone with a racing stable to run had retired to bed. Paget would pick up the phone to her trainers in the small hours, to find out how her horses were; what were their running plans; and should she have a bet? This stretched her trainers' tolerance to breaking point, as did her unrealistic expectations. Fulke Walwyn trained the first five winners for her one afternoon at Folkestone and was then the target of furious criticism because her horse in the last race was beaten.

It's surprising that the autocratic Darling took Dorothy Paget's horses in the first place. They arrived from a top Newmarket yard – only the most recent of a number of stopping-off points for Paget's string. But, it seemed to him that among them was a ready-made Royal Ascot winner. It was Captain Payne, half-brother to a 2000 Guineas winner, who cost Paget 15,000 guineas as a yearling but failed to win a race of any description during two seasons in Newmarket. That was incentive enough for Darling. He 'tried' Captain Payne as a certainty for the Cork and Orrery, and unwisely told Miss Paget to help herself. Her first bet was £10,000 to win, and she fired similar salvoes round the Ring, up to post time. Captain Payne declined to exert himself. For a big woman, Dorothy Paget could move quite quickly when she wanted, and she arrived at her horse's unsaddling far ahead of her retinue. "Where's Mr Darling?" she snapped at Gordon Richards, repeating the question several times. The jockey took a chance: "I wouldn't be quite sure, Miss Paget, but I've a pretty shrewd idea he's up on the stand, cutting his throat." To her credit, Paget responded with a roar of laughter.

A difficult owner-trainer relationship limped on for four seasons, and if that was three more than might've been expected, it was wartime, and even Darling had to compromise. From a full yard of 60 horses in 1939 his numbers had fallen to 22 by 1944. Darling told Paget's secretaries that he was on no account to be phoned after 6 pm. When she ignored the rule, or forgot it, Darling responded by taking his phone off the hook when he went to bed. One of Paget's staff motored to Beckhampton after midnight, to bang on the yard door and ask why the line was always engaged? Darling told his head lad Norman Bertie to, 'Prepare Miss Paget's horses. They're leaving tomorrow. If they haven't been collected by 10 am, turn them loose on the downs.' With five minutes to spare, a convoy of boxes appeared, and away the Paget horses went.

The Earl of Carnarvon was another owner who tried Darling's patience to snapping point. 'Porchey' may be best remembered nowadays for his libido: his *Daily Telegraph* obituary described him as an, "Uncompromisingly direct ladies' man." He was also an accomplished horseman. He established the Highclere stud, and he was a keen and competitive rider, betting like no amateur since Captain Percy Bewicke a generation earlier. Porchey's notes show that in his pomp, the years between 1924 and 1930, riding and punting his own horses, he was £22,141 ahead. In 1929 alone, he won £8,424 (almost £450,000 today). Over the next few years and until injury forced his retirement from the saddle, he broke even. Only a tiny number of owner-riders have taken on the opposition and the bookmakers and come out far ahead, as Porchey did: Bewicke was one, 'The Squire' Abingdon Baird was another. Porchey trained with Dick Dawson at Whatcombe before moving his horses to Beckhampton in 1936, at about the time he stopped riding. He and his friends compiled a 'trainers' handicap'. Fred Darling topped it every season, with 12st 7lb.

On the face of it, Porchey had attributes which any trainer would prize in an owner, among them extensive race-riding experience and his own stud. Unfortunately, he was prone to self-importance: he subscribed to a news cuttings service, to monitor his press coverage. He possessed boundless self-confidence, and never suffered from a moment's doubt about his judgement. And he was a punter. He and Darling clashed regularly. Porchey peered into a box: "When's this one going to run, Fred?" "That's none of your business: your horse is in the box over there," was the trainer's reply. Up on the gallops, Darling used the traditional signals to his work riders, holding a handkerchief, and waving it high above his head if he wanted them to quicken up, or dropping his hand for them to ease up. There he stood one morning, intent on the gallop, his hands still. He sensed movement behind him, and looked round to see Porchey on tiptoes, waving his arms above him like a cheerleader at a football match. Porchey was told to remove himself and his horses from Beckhampton at once. The Earl had charm to spare, and uniquely among those who crossed Fred Darling, he negotiated a reprieve.

Insofar as he could, Darling discouraged his owners' involvement, and he was an expert discourager. His focus was entirely on their horses, and just as he did from his lads, he expected them to give him hard work and complete obedience. The targets for the two year olds were decided before each season had started. The earlier sorts were earmarked for Royal Ascot, and usually made their debuts at the first Salisbury meeting. The bigger, backward types would be set aside for Goodwood. The youngsters who failed to qualify for either group were likely to be on their way back to their owners by mid-season. If a horse's work went as anticipated, then Darling would start preparing it for its race three weeks beforehand. He paid little attention to other trainers' horses. If in February he'd written 'Queen Mary Stakes' alongside a filly's name, that's where she went, irrespective of the reputations ranged against her. There were a few rival trainers with whom Darling was friendly. They included his neighbour Joe Lawson at Manton, Cecil Boyd-Rochfort, and Jack Colling at West Ilsley. If asked, Darling would tell them where his horses were running. Lawson used to reciprocate with a list of his Ascot 'intendeds.'

Noel Murless, who succeeded Darling at Beckhampton, described his predecessor as, "A marvellous trainer, particularly brilliant at preparing a horse for a specific race. But he was a very tough man and I don't think he had much affection for his animals. He was very hard on them." 'Hard' included that when they were being groomed in their box, or shown at evening stables, his horses were held fast by three rack chains. Sue Colling, the wife of

Darling's friend Jack, described Beckhampton's evening stables as, 'Like a troop review.' "He carried a little short cosh which he rattled down the side of the boxes and the horses would stand to attention like Grenadiers." If they moved about while Darling was inspecting them, he hit them. They learned to stand still when the Master was about. They were also held in the rack chains while they were 'whisked' – vigorously brushed with balled straw – for an hour or more at a time, to put on muscle. The regime could hardly have been better designed to produce bad-tempered animals. Not that it was exclusive to Darling's yard; horses then were handled less sympathetically at every stage in their development.

One morning on the gallops, a horse attacked an apprentice without warning. As Gordon Richards described the scene, 'Everyone was standing back, undecided and frankly frightened.' Not Darling: he ran over to the horse and the trapped boy, and hit the horse as hard as he could. It let go and bolted. Richards and a couple of the lads jumped into Darling's van; together they cornered the horse near the stable yard. Without hesitation, Darling walked over to the savage and hit him across the knees to bring him down. Then he got onto the horse's head and beat it. 'It was the only thing to do,' said Richards: 'although at that moment it seemed almost cruel. But that horse had savaged a lad and he had to be taught. The Guv'nor got off him and led him into the stable himself, and the horse never put a foot wrong afterwards.'

It's a hundred years since Fred Darling took over Beckhampton from his father. In his time he was regarded as a progressive trainer, but in truth he was among the last of the old timers, not a trailblazer for a new generation. If a trainer from 1815 could've been transported to Beckhampton in 1915, he would've marvelled at fittings like Sam Darling's acetylene lights. But most aspects of Fred Darling's horse management would've been entirely familiar. And it probably wouldn't have occurred to either the time-traveller or his host that a savage horse was likely to be so because it had been badly handled by humans – not because it had an inherently nasty nature.

By chance, three senior trainers touched on the subject within a few weeks in 2013:

> John Gosden: "You think of the term 'breaking' and that's exactly what people thought you had to do, the idea being that you would break their spirit, as though their spirit was somehow designed to do the opposite of what you wanted them to do. Some of the techniques were complete insanity, designed to draw the evil out of the horse, but all you did was completely terrify it."
>
> Barry Hills: "I remember when horses would come in from the field wild and be sent [straight] off to the sales... A lot of things used to be done that drove horses mad."
>
> Sir Mark Prescott: "Horses are better [treated] at their studs now and that has transformed the breaking-in process. How we didn't all get killed in the old days, I'll never know."

Fred Darling didn't set out to produce wild beasts or savages, but the regime of his and other yards had that effect, in a few cases. If any commentator had been rash enough to suggest the possibility, Darling could point to 14 horses who he trained to win 19 Classics. His runners were noted on the racecourse for their air of well-being, for the silky sheen of their coats. It was called, 'the Beckhampton Bloom.' But that was nothing to do with training or grooming. It was the result of him feeding them arsenic.

CHAPTER ELEVEN

"Buy me the best yearling"

One February during Sam Darling's time, arsenic poisoning affected 22 of the lads, several of them seriously. The culprit was contaminated beer. High levels of arsenic in beer, in the home (in paint, wallpaper and flypaper) and in quack medicines were a public health scandal of late Victorian times. Arsenic occurs naturally in water and soil, so traces of it are sure to be present in a product like beer which is mostly water, and which uses an ingredient like rice. In the lax environment of late nineteenth century brewing, other factors turned a hazard into a killer. Thousands of beer drinkers were poisoned. Several hundred died. No one spotted that the pub customers who stuck to spirits were symptom and illness-free. An awful episode gave birth to a pub greeting: 'What's your poison?'

The Beckhampton lads were lucky to drink only a one-off batch of bad beer, and to respond to prompt treatment. It was ironic that stable staff should be victims, because the role that arsenic could play in the preparation of horses had been known for decades. It started in central Europe:

> "Grooms and especially coachmen that are employed by persons of high rank feed their horses with arsenic. [It] is the cause of the shining and beautiful appearance of most refined coach horses."

Fred Darling trained in Austria for two years before his return to Beckhampton. He could hardly have failed to notice that other trainers fed small quantities of arsenic to their horses. The 'tonic' was administered either by wrapping a pea-sized dose in a cloth and tying it to the bit, so that the horse's saliva dissolved the arsenic; or by scattering arsenic powder among the oats.

The racing writer Tim Fitzgeorge-Parker put the question to Fred Darling's successor Noel Murless:

> "I asked him why Fred Darling's horses stood out in the paddock [so] that you could not mistake that incredible sheen on their coats. Noel answered simply, 'He always used arsenic.'"

Peter O'Sullevan's first trainer was Charlie Bell. Bell had been a stable lad with Fred Darling.

> "One day I said to Charlie how well a leading trainer's horses always looked. I was surprised when he told me, 'I'll bet you he gives them arsenic. I could prove it: if you pull a hair out of a horse that's been fed arsenic, there'll be a little brown globule on the end of it. Darling topped his horses up with arsenic to give their skins that wonderful silkiness.'"

Sue Colling, widow of the trainer Jack Colling, wrote:

> "It was quite a well-known fact, I think, that a certain brand of 'solution' always arrived with Fred's runners when they came to stay at Newmarket. It was permissible then. It came in large stone jars."

The only explanation for Darling's action is that he was looking for any competitive edge that he could find. After his call-up in 1916 and the closure of the yard, he was posted to Ireland and spent the rest of the war there, finding and bringing on horses for his regiment. When the war ended Beckhampton housed only three horses. Darling's name was missing from the list of the top dozen trainers between 1919 and 1921. He didn't have any horses of merit in his string, but he could at least ensure they looked well.

Gradually, Darling built his numbers back up. James Buchanan, who owned Fred Darling's wartime classic winner Hurry On, returned to the stable after selling his horses in 1916. His was an extraordinary story. He was already 30 when a Glasgow whisky firm sent him as its representative to London. He quickly outgrew the role, started his own business and created, among its brands, Black & White. In time he built a vast commercial empire. Luckily for British bloodstock, his pastime was racing, and he established a stud at Lavington Park near Petworth in Sussex. He was knighted in 1920 and elevated to the peerage as Lord Woolavington two years later. It was rumoured that he paid tens of thousands to Lloyd George's Liberal party for his title. If so, he wasn't alone, and he took a precaution against any 'welshing'. He dated his cheque for the day after the New Year honours, and he signed it 'Woolavington,' so that if his name was missing from the list, the cheque would bounce.

Hurry On stood at Lavington, and the first mare brought to him was Bellavista, by the Gold Cup winner Cyllene out of a mare tracing back to the Derby winner Hermit. When Woolavington bought her she was already a successful broodmare, the dam of eight foals, all of whom had won races. She was the first mare covered by Hurry On, and there was only one service. The following January she produced a big chestnut colt foal with plenty of white about him: he was named Captain Cuttle and sent to Beckhampton. Just as Fred Darling made no attempt to get the huge, uncoordinated Hurry On to the races as a two year old, so he left it until the September of Captain Cuttle's first season before giving the colt an outing. He ran well to be second at Doncaster to a fast two year old, looking backward and running green.

Captain Cuttle evidently adored his trainer. He was as placid a thoroughbred as could be imagined. He was happy to stand and watch Darling's string walk or canter by. He gave a buck and a kick when it was his turn to work, especially if there was a new rider on his back, and he pulled hard, but for the rest of the time he was calm and cooperative. Darling used to lead Captain Cuttle himself, and the colt would take his coat sleeve between his teeth and follow him happily up to the gallops and back to his box. He came to hand quickly at the start of his three year old year and made mincemeat of his opponents in the Wood Ditton Stakes, winning by six lengths. He was made favourite for the 2000 Guineas, but not a pronounced one: it was a year in which few of the top stables had played their cards. Most of those prominent in the betting had run only once. Typical was St Louis, a colt trained by PP Gilpin to run sixth at Royal Ascot. He'd been prominent in the Newmarket touts' reports. It rained heavily during the night before the Guineas, and into the morning of the race. Soft ground evidently pleased St Louis's connections; in the last hour before the race he was backed from 100–6 to 6–1. The paddock critics thought Captain Cuttle 'big and burly.'

There was a reason, which only emerged after the race; Lord Woolavington's colt had missed a week's work. In the circumstances, his jockey Victor Smyth asked a lot of Captain Cuttle by keeping him up with the pace all through the first six furlongs. As the no-hopers dropped away, the favourite led briefly at the Bushes, but along came St Louis and another, and Captain Cuttle was readily left behind. Smyth reported that his mount didn't stay.

Darling tried his colt over the full mile-and-a-half trip 11 days before the Derby against a useful handicapper, Willonya, and the previous season's St Leger third, Westward Ho. Captain Cuttle was 'wrong' 40lb and 17 lb with the other two, and did all Darling could've hoped for in the gallop. Four days later Victor Smyth came down to partner Captain Cuttle in a similar work-out. Expectation turned to concern: this time Captain Cuttle finished behind. If there was a variable that could be improved, it was the man on top. So began the annual musical chairs of Steve Donoghue's Derby ride. In the years since Donoghue's pomp in the 1920s, only Lester Piggott has occupied such a central role in Derby deliberations, and for the same reason: each was supreme around Epsom. Piggott won the Derby nine times, Donoghue six.

Over time, the statistics become self-fulfilling: the best rides get offered to the elite riders. So it was with Captain Cuttle. Darling had taken the decision to replace Smyth: an Irish jockey, Tommy Burns, had been offered a £500 fee to take the Derby ride. Burns had ridden six Irish classic winners, but he was powerless in the face of the Donoghue bandwagon. Steve had been offered three rides in the race. He didn't regard any of them with enthusiasm. He and a friend, the financier Jimmy White, talked it over on the Friday before the race. "What about Captain Cuttle?" asked White. "Ring up Lord Woolavington and tell him you're free to ride. He'll jump at the chance of getting you. Go on! If you don't, I will." Donoghue had a conceit; no matter how badly he wanted a ride, he hated to ask for it. While he hesitated, White called Woolavington. When he'd finished his call, he passed the phone to Steve. Woolavington asked Donoghue to go to Beckhampton the following morning to get to know Captain Cuttle.

Donoghue hired a plane to take him from Croydon aerodrome at dawn the next day. When they found out where he was going, the ground crew and maintenance staff begged him for a tip. He flew first to Lambourn and Shrewton to ride work and then on to Beckhampton, where the pilot landed on the downs. "What are you doing here?" asked Fred Darling. "Didn't Lord Woolavington telephone you?" "About what?" "He wants me to ride Captain Cuttle in the Derby and to sit on his back today," explained Donoghue. "I haven't heard a word about it. Tommy Burns has come down to ride him in a gallop. He's here now. He expects to ride him in the Derby."

It was an awkward moment: one horse and two jockeys, each of them retained to ride it at Epsom. Darling sent them away and rode the work on Captain Cuttle himself. Donoghue flew back to Croydon and told the staff: 'Captain Cuttle went splendidly. I'll win on him.' Darling asked Donoghue to go back to Beckhampton on the Monday morning to get a feel of his colt. There were no mishaps. Darling said Captain Cuttle went better than he'd ever done before. It seemed that every question had been answered, every arrangement completed. As it turned out, there were still two alarms to overcome. The first came when Captain Cuttle was being boxed up for Epsom. For a few moments he broke loose, ran into the adjacent yard, and set his sights on the gate opening out onto the road. Fred Darling bellowed the colt's name. Captain Cuttle hesitated, stopped, turned and trotted over to his trainer. All the hours that Darling had spent with his colt paid off: disaster was averted.

In the pre-race betting, the 2000 Guineas winner St Louis was always favourite at around 4–1. Optimistic reports from Beckhampton kept Captain Cuttle second favourite at 8–1. Then a few minutes before the start, Darling suffered his second, far worse scare. Donoghue was about to ride onto the course when he felt something amiss. He looked down and saw the edge of Captain Cuttle's off-fore plate sticking out. Darling had left the paddock. His head lad Norman Bertie frantically looked for a farrier, and for Darling. Eventually the Epsom blacksmith was found. He looked doubtfully at Captain Cuttle's twisted shoe: 'I haven't got one as large as that.' As a compromise, he beat the twisted plate back into shape and refitted it. Captain Cuttle limped forward. Donoghue told Darling it was hopeless: "He's dead lame." No, said Darling, 'It's just that he's been standing on three legs.' Darling told his jockey to make plenty of use of Captain Cuttle on the way to the start, in the hope of loosening his stiffness. By the time Donoghue rode onto the course, most of his rivals were nearing the starting gate. The crowd reacted to its first sight of Steve with an enthusiastic roar. Not all the watchers were convinced. The King had asked his trainer Richard Marsh what would win the Derby? Marsh suggested Captain Cuttle, each way. Neither man was encouraged by what he saw. His Majesty thought his fancy 'went rather short.' Marsh said that at first glance Donoghue's mount 'Was the lamest horse I ever saw go to post.' In the betting ring, the horse was pushed out to 10–1. But Donoghue followed Darling's instructions to the letter:

"As I went out on to the course I sent him along in a sharp burst for a few hundred yards. Then I took a slight pull at him and gently swung his head this way and that way, making him look at the crowds first on one side of the course and then on the other, and after a moment he strode out as sound as possible."

By the time Captain Cuttle reached the start he was moving freely. Steve Donoghue had a firm and fixed idea about riding a horse in the Derby. First, he said, it was vital to get away quickly and take a position on the inside rail. Then, be handy, just behind the pace. And once Tattenham Corner had been safely navigated, head for the winning post as fast as possible. He followed his script to perfection on Captain Cuttle, whose draw, 28 out of 30 runners, put the colt almost in the trees on the far side of the course. Fortunately he broke quickly, Donoghue tacked across, and before the end of the first two furlongs he was on the rails.

In the haze of a boiling hot afternoon, it was impossible from the stands to pick out the horses at the start and during the early stages of the races, but as they left the back straight Darling was heard to mutter, "If he acts down the hill he should win." As the field made its final turn for home, Donoghue was stationed exactly where he wanted, in a share of second place, a length or so behind an outsider. "I could feel that he was sensitive to the hard going, but he was a courageous horse, and when I sent him up to the front he drew away easily and passed the post four lengths to the good." Captain Cuttle's extended starting price delighted tens, possibly hundreds of thousands of small punters who put their shillings and half-crowns on Steve in the Derby each year, irrespective of his mount. Jimmy White, who helped to broker the ride for Donoghue, won £30,000. Croydon aerodrome was a happy place. One of the biggest beneficiaries was Steve himself. It was reported before the race that he was on £500 for the ride, with a £1,000 present for victory. Even this paled alongside the winnings of Miss Jennie Thomas of Wallasey.

To open an eve-of-Derby newspaper from the years surrounding Captain Cuttle's win is to step into a golden age of enthusiasm for 'the Sport of Kings'. The race dominated the news as well as the sports pages. Saturation coverage was devoted to the popular sweepstakes of the day. The grand-daddy among them was the Calcutta, a lottery-sized pot with a twist to horrify our data-protective times: every ticket-holder was named. This had its consequences. A big winner was likely to acquire, overnight, legions of new friends, not all of them welcome. But for someone with a ticket for one of the favourites, there'd be numerous offers to buy all or part of it. The press were given a couple of days during which they could hunt down the ticket-holders and prepare their post-race human-interest stories. The sums involved were staggering. The Calcutta Sweepstake in 1922 had a first prize of £116,720 (£5.7 million today); £58,310 went to the second; £29,155 to the holder of the third-placed horse. Every ticket with a runner won several thousands. The ticket for Captain Cuttle was found to be held by Jennie Thomas, "A comely young lady under 30 years of age, of quiet disposition, employed at the Royal Insurance company's offices [in] Liverpool." The day before the race, she parted with a half-share of the ticket to a speculator in India, who offered 'several thousand pounds if Donoghue rode Captain Cuttle, and £1,000 less if he did not.' She rebuffed an offer for a further quarter share: "I'm hedging no more."

Captain Cuttle added little to his honours board after the Derby. He was slightly jarred by the firm ground at Epsom, but met his engagement in the St James's Palace Stakes, beating five moderate opponents at long odds on. The ground at Ascot was again firm, and although he was sent to Goodwood with a choice of targets, a racecourse gallop left him visibly lame. Woolavington announced that his colt had been scratched from the St Leger on veterinary advice, and that he'd be rested before any decision was taken about keeping him in training. At the start of the following season he won a stakes race at Kempton over 10 furlongs, but his forelegs were sore again afterwards. He was retired to Lavington. *The Bloodstock Breeders' Review* called Captain Cuttle 'The best-looking horse seen on the British Turf for generations,' but in five years he got only a 1,000 Guineas winner and a Derby second, despite being well patronised. Woolavington had other young stallions coming through – and Hurry On was still going strong – so Captain Cuttle was sold for 50,000 guineas to Italy. He was killed in an exercise accident about the time that his first offspring were reaching the racecourse.

The instruction was simple enough: "Buy me the best yearling in the [Doncaster sales] catalogue." The cable came from Henry Morriss, a financier based in Shanghai. Darling picked out an Irish-bred bay colt by the sound, weight-carrying sprinter Phalaris out of a tiny, unraced mare called Waffles. The colt had the most perfect conformation, and Darling was pushed to 6,300 guineas to buy him. It was soon evident that the money was well spent. Named Manna, the colt ran five times as a two year old, usually in the best company and invariably giving a good account of himself. He won the Richmond Stakes in a canter, and then had the first of two encounters with the Manton-trained Picaroon; he was beaten a length by Picaroon, conceding 6lb, the pair clear. Ten days later he re-opposed Picaroon at level weights in the Middle Park, and went down by one and a half lengths and a neck, the second-placed horse being Sir John Rutherford's Solario.

In the Free Handicap, Manna was rated the third-best colt, 9lb behind Picaroon and 2lb below Solario. Manna was a handful to train, equally prone to escaping and to kicking. One of his adventures involved throwing his lad, jumping a five-foot hedge and rolling down a steep bank onto the main road. Another flirtation with freedom resulted in bad cuts from a fence. As for kicking, Marcus Marsh said, "One of his alarming habits was his playful way of kicking, quite deliberately, anyone whom apparently he had a fancy for. He had a great fancy for Fred." 'Playful' wasn't the assessment of those on the business end. Manna did once succeed in kicking his trainer, but saved his star turn for a visit by his owner's wife. Darling told her, "You'll see the best mover you've ever seen in your life." In a way, she did. Manna bucked like a rodeo pony, threw his boy high in the air and caught him with both hind hooves as he came down.

The spring of 1925 was wet and the Beckhampton gallops were heavy. Steve Donoghue rode Manna before the Guineas, and told Darling that the colt had, "Blown like a steam engine; he's only half fit." "Don't let that bother you," Darling told the jockey: "I've got it all worked out. You won't know him in a week or two." But the truth was, Darling had taken a view that over a mile, Picaroon would probably beat Manna again, and he'd be better employed preparing Manna for a summer campaign, beginning with the Derby. Picaroon had enjoyed a perfect prep race in the Craven Stakes, beating Solario by three and a half lengths; the other notable Guineas trial was Zionist giving weight to 23 rivals in a Newbury handicap. He was beaten only half a length in third, immediately behind Beckhampton's Warden Of The Marches, conceding that horse 16lb. It was common knowledge that Warden Of The Marches was one of Manna's regular galloping companions, and not, said the touts, at anything like 16lb difference. The inference was that Zionist was superior to Manna. Then came a bombshell: Picaroon was declared a non-runner. A minor cut had become infected, an abscess appeared and burst, and Taylor was forced to abandon any hope of training his colt for the Guineas or Derby. The news meant that Darling and other trainers rushed to get one or two extra gallops into their colts before the Guineas. At the end of April at Newmarket, when the field of 13 faced the starter, Zionist was a strong favourite at 5–4, Solario next best at 7–1, and Manna was 100–8. In the parade, Manna appeared to be the smallest of the field and among the most backward. It made no difference. Steve Donoghue allowed his mount an early share of the lead, the pair went two lengths clear at half way, and with the advantage maintained all the way to the line, Manna barely saw another horse.

As Manna had shown his superiority to every horse set against him in the Guineas, it would've been logical for him to be favourite for the Derby, but various breeding pundits claimed he wouldn't stay the trip. His sire Phalaris had shown his best form at sprint distances. Manna drifted out to 9–1. Darling determined to test his stamina. He borrowed a good staying handicapper from a Lambourn trainer, set Manna to give the horse 21lb, and watched him trot up over the full Derby trip. The only remaining worry was a persistent rumour that Manna would be 'got at'. Darling asked Jack Blake to guard Manna's box every night in the two weeks before the race. Blake made himself as comfortable as he could, propped up against the door of Manna's box, with a shotgun across his lap and Darling's dog by his side.

The Derby lunch was held at the Press Club two days before the race. Edgar Wallace presided, and the leading connections gave light-hearted assessments of their chances. Henry Morriss told the guests, "The reason why the Israelites found themselves in the rich and fertile plains of the Jordan is that they followed Manna. My advice to you is to do the same." Steve Donoghue jumped on a chair to be seen and heard: "You can take a straight tip. Whatever beats me will win the Derby. Manna is a handy little horse, not a big one, but genuine and game. The other morning he did a wonderfully good gallop; no horse could have gone better." Morriss took Donoghue at his word. He tracked down the winner of Manna's ticket in the Stock Exchange sweepstake and bought a half share.

Meanwhile, as a snapshot of Derby Day in 1925, the good people of Devizes had all sorts of goings-on to entertain them. The BBC had announced plans to broadcast 'impressions of the race' from a car on Epsom Downs. An enterprising tradesman had arranged a link and set up a loudspeaker outside his shop. A throng waited in tense anticipation. Alas, after three perfect trials of the BBC's transmission, a short circuit on the racecourse meant the race was run without so much as a crackle or hiss outside Mr Willis's shop. Elsewhere in the town, choreographed by the police for maximum impact, there was a raid on the local bookmaker. The Devizes paper reported that:

> "The excitement in the Market Place [to listen to the broadcast] was mild compared to that in New Park Street, where something unusual was expected. A large crowd gathered and [treated] the matter in a jocular vein – a sort of embroidery to the great Derby Day. Presently a body of police arrived. The excitement reached the crest of a wave."

An inspector and four constables, including the ill-matched PC Bullock and PC Balls, arrived at the premises of Herbert Bean, a commission agent. They showed a warrant, went into the house, and waited. A number of punters arrived to place bets. An honour guard of grinning onlookers might've given them a hint that something was up, but no, they walked into the trap and were detained. A dozen or so were taken to the police station and remanded. When the case came to court, Bean the bookie was fined £10. His clients were bound over to keep the peace. One of them told the magistrate that, "I have always had a gamble on the Derby, as every Englishman and Englishwoman does, and I always shall. The police might have chosen some other occasion. They were not very sporting." He was loudly cheered.

About the time that Bean's punters were detained, Steve Donoghue was riding out of the Epsom paddock with a writ in his hand. A money-lender had thrust it on him when his attention was on other matters. The writ was for money owed by a third party, but guaranteed by Steve. So he stuffed it into his breeches and rode Manna off to the start: it was a shambles, even by the standards of the day. The starter released the tapes without warning. Some of the horses were caught up; the worst affected were those drawn on the far side from the stands, which included Solario. His jockey expected a recall and hesitated for a few moments. When he set off, he'd lost 15 to 20 lengths. By contrast, Manna was drawn low and started quickly. Donoghue could ride the same race as he had on Captain Cuttle, except that he was going so well that he didn't wait until the straight before launching Manna. He took up the running at half way, went clear with ears pricked coming down to Tattenham Corner and maintained the gallop to the finishing line, ridden out hands and heels to win by eight lengths. Solario ran on into a remote fourth after his mishap at the start. He had his revenge when beating Manna by two lengths in the Ascot Derby, in receipt of 10lb. They went to the St Leger as co-favourites, where triumph waited for one and disaster for the other. The triumph was Solario's. Hobbling behind him in tenth place was Manna. On the way to post, another horse suddenly crossed him, and

Donoghue had to check his mount sharply. The manoeuvre seemed to cause a sprain, which was aggravated on the firm ground in the race. Later, Manna was hardly able to hobble into the horse ambulance, but he recovered with rest and treatment, and was retired to stud. Morriss founded the Banstead Manor Stud to house his champion.

Fred Darling booked Marlborough Town Hall for a post-race party for his staff and their families. As for the wider impact of Manna's success around the parish, a senior resident of Avebury recalled that there and in Beckhampton village, 'Everyone was drunk for a week.' One of Harry Morriss' gestures before the Derby was to give his employees £5 each with which to back Manna. After the race, he had £11,095 to come in prize money, £25,000 from his half-share in the winning sweepstake ticket, and who knows how much more in bets. Morriss thanked Darling by building him a new yard, the other side of the Calne road from the main stable block. It was constructed to the highest specifications, including central heating. Each of its 11 boxes was said to have cost Morriss £1,000 (a total of £570,000 today). Darling found the heating caused his horses to cough continuously; the boiler was dispensed with the following spring.

Meanwhile, Darling assured Jack Blake that his sleepless nights outside Manna's box would be generously rewarded. A package arrived. It contained a clock – an ugly clock, but prominent on the Blake mantelpiece because of its associations. Jack died, years passed, and eventually his son Ron took it to a jeweller. "I haven't seen one of those for a while," the man said. He explained that in the 1920s, one of the tea brands had a promotion: 'Buy a packet and collect a coupon.' A hundred coupons earned a clock. Some reward.

CHAPTER TWELVE

James Buchanan, Lord Woolavington

James Buchanan was one of the leading businessmen, art collectors and racehorse owners of his time. Having moved from a humdrum job in the whisky trade in Glasgow to take his chance in London, he lived in a bedsit, and he was his firm's manager, salesman and clerk, rolled into one. He often worked 16 hour days. When he was 35, one of the many contacts he'd made was sufficiently impressed by his grit and perseverance to suggest he should start his own business, and offered to finance him. Later, Buchanan said that it never occurred to him that he might fail. He set up a sales and distribution agency, persuading a distiller to sell to him on credit. His genius lay in marketing in its broadest sense. The external symbols were the horse-drawn carriages that delivered his whisky – and the carthorses themselves, carefully chosen and beautifully turned out. Even the sternest of teetotallers took pleasure from the sight of Buchanan's horses. Later, Buchanan introduced the pair of terriers on the packaging and advertising of his Black & White whisky.

Buchanan set out to find what his potential customers wanted, and then directed his supplier to produce it. When he arrived in London, 'whisky' meant malts: an acquired taste, too harsh for many, and lacking any widely-known brands. Buchanan asked his customers to try blended samples, then he had the blends changed to respond to their reactions, and if need be, tweaked again. Eventually he arrived at a product that was smoother to drink and more consistent than anything before it. His Glasgow partner produced it to strict specifications, and Buchanan sold it with prodigious energy. His earliest and greatest success was getting it accepted by the House of Commons. He was a patient and brilliant salesman. For 18 months he called on a man who owned a number of thriving pubs and hotels, without taking an order. The man was a widower with two single daughters. Buchanan asked them to a Burns Night dance. He then organised his bachelor friends and gave them instructions; the girls' cards were filled all evening, and they were danced off their feet. Back they went to Papa in delight. Soon after, the man invited Buchanan over, telling him there hadn't been such happiness in the household since before his wife's death. His first order was for five thousand gallons of Buchanan's whisky.

Buchanan seems to have had an interest in racing and horses from an early age. He was 15 when he had his first bet, 2/6d on Blair Athol, who won the Derby of 1864 on his racecourse debut, at 14–1. Buchanan took a close interest in the selection and welfare of his firm's horses; among his favourite trophies was the challenge cup for the London Carthorse Parade. As he won it three times in a row, he kept it. On a visit to Argentina he met a man called Kincaid who showed him round the local racing scene, and gave him an introduction to a Newmarket vet, William Livock. With a nod to his introducer, Buchanan registered the racing name of T Kincaid and the colours of 'white, violet sleeves, red cap.' Livock bought him a sprinter called Little Red Rat out of a Brighton auction plate in 1899; it cost Buchanan 250 guineas and won six races. It was followed by two more inspired purchases by Livock; one was Black Sand, also bought out of a seller, who won the Cesarewitch. Best of all Buchanan's early ventures was the acquisition of Epsom Lad, a cull from Lord Rosebery's stable. Livock bought Epsom Lad for 1,050 guineas at Tattersalls' October sales in 1900, and he earned almost twenty times his purchase price.

The most surprising aspect of Buchanan's entry into racing was his import of an Argentinian trainer and jockey, Luis Alvarez and Santiago Gomez. They were based at the Queensbury House stables in Newmarket High Street. It's not easy to imagine how the racing community took to the pair, or how they adjusted to Newmarket in winter. At any event, they knew what they were doing. Epsom Lad made his debut for Buchanan in the Princess of Wales's Stakes at Newmarket. The previous year's triple crown winner Diamond Jubilee was one of Epsom Lad's opponents; receiving 8lb. Buchanan's apparent no-hoper beat the classic winner by half a length, earning £7,185. He then went to Sandown and won a memorable Eclipse and another £9,952. Diamond Jubilee re-opposed on 5lb better terms. The fact that Epsom Lad won from two outsiders by a head and the same, with Diamond Jubilee close up in fourth, suggests a thrilling finish; the reality was nearer to sensation. Epsom Lad's saddle slipped. In the final furlong it was disappearing under his belly, whereupon Gomez grabbed the saddle and weight cloth and tucked them under one arm, riding a finish with the other. Never was the phrase 'clung on to win' more exact.

After Epsom Lad, Buchanan had a few quiet years on the racecourse. His exotic trainer and rider went home, and he spread his horses among a number of English yards until 1908, when he sent most of them to Sam Darling at Beckhampton. He stayed with the stable during the transition to Sam's son and was rewarded when Fred made his inspired 500 guineas investment in Hurry On, followed by the Derby win of Hurry On's first son, Captain Cuttle. By this time, much had changed in Buchanan's life. The sales of his blended whisky had swollen to an amber Niagara. He was advised one day that a London site which he'd long hankered for – the Black Swan Distillery in Holborn – was for sale. Within 24 hours he'd shaken hands on a purchase price of £87,000. "Where the money was coming from I had no idea, but I was quite satisfied with what I had done." Such was his reputation that he was over-subscribed with offers of finance. When his producer in Glasgow ran into financial trouble, Buchanan bought the firm, to ensure continuity of supply. He diversified into cooperage and bottling businesses; he even took over some of the malt distilleries which he'd driven out of the London market. As he made his fortune, he spent it: he bought the Lavington Park estate in Sussex and established a large stud there, while filling the house with sporting art. By the time of Captain Cuttle's Derby victory he was Lord Woolavington, and he'd changed his racing colours to 'white, black hoop.' He never passed up an opportunity to remind people of his whisky.

Sam Darling's former stable jockey Billy Higgs was training in a small way at Blewbury after the first world war, and he kept a few broodmares. Among them was Wet Kiss, bought for 140 guineas to share with one of his owners. She won two nurseries and placed fourth in a wartime Oaks, after which Higgs bought out his partner for 1,000 guineas; he took a nice profit by selling her to Woolavington for £3,000. She was put to Hurry On, and after losing one foal, she produced the image of his sire: a big, powerfully built chestnut colt who was named Coronach after a Scottish mourning song. When Fred Darling divided his two year olds, Coronach was in the group earmarked for Goodwood. He made his debut in a 22-runner field at Salisbury's Bibury Club meeting, and won comfortably. Then he went to Goodwood and won the Rous Memorial, even more easily. The manner of his wins suggested that Beckhampton had another good colt.

Nothing happened to dispel the impression when Coronach travelled to Doncaster for the Champagne Stakes. The winners of most of the important two year old races lined up; the only notable absentee was Lord Derby's Colorado, facile winner of the Coventry Stakes. Coronach beat his opponents on a tight rein. One reporter wrote, 'He did his work in the manner of a really high-class colt. It seemed certain that he would go through the rest of the season without defeat.' His next race was the Middle Park, and he frightened off all bar two opponents, one of whom, Lex, had been four lengths behind him at Doncaster. Odds of 15–100 were laid on Coronach, but Lex harried the favourite out of the Dip and on the rise to the winning post, and beat him by a neck. There seemed no possible explanation other than that Coronach was in some way unwell. Darling would have none of it: the horse had done a good piece of work the previous day, and all concerned had been brimful of confidence. However, no sooner had Coronach arrived home than he was found to be running a temperature, and he missed his feed for a couple of days. He recovered quickly, and the official handicapper wasn't alone in putting a line through the Middle Park; the Free Handicap had Coronach on 9st 0lb, Lex on 8st 10lb and Colorado on 8st 6lb.

Coronach was ridden in his first-season races by the American jockey George Archibald. Any neutral observer would concede that his performances had been satisfactory, yet Woolavington was unhappy with the defeat in the Middle Park. He asked Darling to find another jockey for the following season, and that was a complication. After Captain Cuttle's Derby win, Woolavington not only wrote a cheque to Steve Donoghue; he signed Donoghue on a £2,000-a-season personal retainer. Woolavington could hardly be expected to know that for the charming but feckless Steve, a contract was no more than the prelude to a multi-part drama. Woolavington wanted Donoghue to ride one of his horses in a Newmarket stable. Steve, who probably hadn't looked at the paperwork before signing it, argued that the retainer only covered the owner's Beckhampton horses, and accepted an outside ride. Woolavington, whose word or handshake meant absolute commitment, was outraged. Donoghue's retainer was torn up, and Darling was told that under no circumstances was Steve to ride Woolavington's horses, after which Joe Childs was offered the seat on Coronach.

The colt's seasonal debut in 1926 gave him another look at Newmarket; he won a stakes race convincingly, with odds laid on: "He looked the picture of a fine big colt, with most of the attributes associated with classic winners." He was made 5–4 favourite in a 19-runner field for the 2,000 Guineas; the Middle Park winner Lex was 100–8, along with Colorado. Lord Derby's colt had won his prep race at Liverpool by eight lengths, but then, it was rumoured, could finish only fourth in a home gallop. Coronach dwelt at the start of the Guineas, but Joe Childs made up the lost ground quickly, and took Coronach to the outside of the field to be sure of a clear run. Nearing the Bushes, Childs sent him into the lead, travelling strongly, but just when he looked sure to win, Colorado came alongside, gathered momentum going down into the Dip, and fairly sprinted away to beat Coronach by five lengths. The connections of both horses were astonished. Derby said he'd always thought Colorado was a good horse but, "After the trial I couldn't feel any particular confidence." Fred Darling said, 'Although he'd done plenty of work, and pleased me at home, he's naturally rather a backward horse, and I consider this effort exhausted him; he never had a chance to take a breather.'

The verdict of the betting markets was simple: Coronach was a non-stayer. After their early-season wins, Coronach was 7–2 for the Derby and Colorado 10–1. The Guineas result turned the Epsom betting on its head. Colorado was as low as 6–4 and Coronach was pushed out to 7–1. In the run-up to the Derby, the press focus was on Colorado: 'In gallop after gallop he showed to advantage with older horses of proved stamina, and more than held his own when tested with others for speed. All Newmarket seemed supremely confident.' Fred Darling, free from onlookers on the Beckhampton downs, made a game-changing discovery. His top work rider Billy Wells rode Coronach in his work, and Wells suspected that Darling's gallops routine – 'The slowest horse at the front, the best at the back, move up at the end of the gallop but don't go past' – didn't suit Coronach. He persuaded Darling to let Coronach loose, and suddenly his full ability was revealed. When he was allowed to bowl along in front, his tendency to keenness was reduced, and he put all the Beckhampton trial tackle to the sword.

Front-running was anathema to Joe Childs. He was a high-class jockey, but one-dimensional. In that generation of jockeys, Harry Wragg was known as 'the head waiter' because of his passion for hold-up rides: the nickname applied equally to Childs. He liked to ride considerately and he was recognised as a good partner for two year olds, because he never beat them up. Marcus Marsh recalled the trial of wills between his uncle Fred and Joe Childs, and how Joe muttered and sulked his way up to the gallops; Marsh said asking Childs to make the running was, "A bit like asking [the Conservative prime minister] Stanley Baldwin to sing *The Red Flag* at a May Day rally." Although Coronach went like a dream for Joe, he complained, "It's all wrong. I still don't like it. Never will." Derby Day arrived in what the *Daily Telegraph* called 'The most appalling conditions of weather':

> "Ordinary language is altogether inadequate to describe the miseries and utter wretchedness of this day of incessant heavy rain… [which] would not concede even a moment's respite, and always more and more mud."

The *Daily Express* reported in similar vein:

> "Thousands of men and women sat in motor-omnibuses or in their cars, not venturing out on the grass. [They] played bridge and waited to hear the results. The refreshment tents were so crowded with people seeking shelter that would-be customers went away."

Woolavington was among the many who stayed at home, dry. He had a weak constitution from childhood. Many of his long-distance travels were as much for clean sea air as to find new outlets for his whisky. The photographs show a thin, frail-looking man, though they date mostly from his fifties and later, when the scale of his business success had become recognised. He was 77 at the time of Coronach's Derby, and he left it to his daughter to represent him at Epsom.

At the saddling, Darling reminded Childs of his instruction to make the running. As the truculent jockey took Coronach to post, a steady stream of bets forced the colt from a high of 8–1 down to 11–2 second favourite to Colorado. The previous evening, Darling had dined in the West End and, as he occasionally did when his own bets had been placed, he spoke freely about his hopes for Coronach. One of the colt's last bits of work had been with Harry Greer's Warden Of The Marches, who'd won the City and Suburban under top weight. The gallop, Darling told his companions, would've meant Coronach winning that competitive handicap under 10st 7lb. For good measure, Greer had that day accepted an offer of £20,000 for Warden Of The Marches. As his fellow diners and the waiters started looking around for an off-duty bookmaker, Darling warmed to his theme: 'Colorado?' he was asked. "Colorado needs to be a world-beater to beat Coronach – and he's not a world-beater. Whatever the price is it doesn't matter. There's nothing to fear."

News of his confidence rippled out across club and theatre-land, and lapped up on the steps of Fleet Street. The racing correspondent of the *Daily Express* changed his Derby tip at the last moment:

> "I have just heard from an unimpeachable source that we must expect to see a greatly improved Coronach tomorrow. Bearing in mind the origin of my information I have no alternative but to select Coronach."

At the Derby start, Coronach played up and backed away, as he had before the Guineas. Childs, still indignant at the part he'd been asked to play, gave him an almighty whack at the moment the starter pulled his lever. Up went the tapes, Coronach was level with the leaders after a furlong, kept company with an outsider to the top of the hill and down the descent to the straight, and took a clear lead soon after, seemingly revelling in the going. Colorado went in pursuit – his tail plaited up like an Irish steeplechaser's – but his move petered out, and he was overhauled for second place close home. Coronach powered on to win by five lengths, with Woolavington's silks the only ones in the field to come back clean. Few of the other colours could be seen through their coatings of mud. Reactions after the race were varied. Woolavington's daughter Catharine beamed as she became the first woman to lead in a Derby winner. A shipping broker called Robert Bishop held Coronach's ticket in the Calcutta Sweep; he'd sold a half-share for £7,000, but the remaining half was worth £60,000. Fleet Street's finest called at his office. He wasn't happy: "I am much too busy to talk about the matter," he snapped: "I am going on with my work." Joe Childs was also somewhat lacking in joy. As *The Sporting Life* pointed out, "It is quite unusual for Childs to be first off and first home," and it was evident that as far as Joe was concerned, the end hadn't justified the means. The paper reported that:

> "Fred Darling and Joe Childs supplied a remarkable study in contrasts when Coronach had been led in. Darling was beaming, but it would take more than the riding of a Derby winner to cause Childs to lose that old-fashioned, set expression which seems inseparable from him."

Childs threw down his saddle after weighing in and spat, "What a bloody way to ride a horse." He settled the score when he published his memoirs, *My Racing Reminiscences*, shortly before Darling's death. Coronach was a coward, wrote Childs. Before those days were reached, he'd ridden Coronach to an armchair eight-length win over Lex at 1–6 in the St James's Palace Stakes, followed by a six-length stroll in the Eclipse, again long odds on. Coronach ended his season by winning the St Leger at 8–15. The newspaper headline, "Coronach Doddles The St Leger" was sufficient description of the race. Childs' only exertions in the Doncaster straight were taking repeated pulls on his mount's reins, and looking round at his toiling opponents. The second-place horse was allowed to get to within two lengths of Coronach at the finish. One of the northern trainers exclaimed that on the day, 'Coronach could have won the Portland Plate [a sprint] as well as the St Leger.' The *Daily Express* reported that:

> "The only unexpected feature of the race was that Childs actually smiled when he unsaddled Coronach. Then he made himself scarce for over half an hour."

During his second season, Coronach won £39,624 in win prize-money, breaking the £38,666 record set by the Duke of Portland's Donovan in 1889. He propelled Lord Woolavington to the head of the winning owners' list, as Captain Cuttle had done in 1922. And for the first time, Fred Darling was the leading trainer, by a wide margin from Alec Taylor and George Lambton.

The colt's four year old season was an anti-climax. Even in his triumphal progress the previous season, there were critics who wondered how clean-winded Coronach was. They pointed out that he had 'roarers' on both sides of his pedigree. Nothing seemed amiss on his seasonal debut, when 30–100 was laid on him to beat two rivals in the Coronation Cup. Coronach followed up by beating another small field in the Hardwicke Stakes, 'cantering by 12 lengths.' His next engagement was in Newmarket's Princess of Wales's Stakes and another win was expected, but there'd been a mishap at Beckhampton which, uniquely, Fred Darling didn't know about. He was away when Coronach unshipped his rider during routine work and galloped off as fast as he could go. He was led back to the yard panting, in distress. The lads who'd seen the incident swore each other to silence.

When Darling arrived at Newmarket, it was to discover that, unexpectedly, Colorado had been declared to run against his colt. The Beckhampton colt was 2–7, Colorado 4–1. The race mirrored the previous year's 2,000 Guineas; Coronach made the running, with Colorado tracking him before coming alongside at the two-furlong marker. Then, as in the Guineas, Colorado sailed away, winning by eight lengths. A fortnight later at Sandown, the pair met again in the Eclipse. Between them the two colts had scared off all but one rival. The betting was 10–11 Colorado, 11–10 Coronach and 25–1 the other. In the parade, Coronach looked jaded and edgy. Coronach started a little after the other two, but quickly went to the front, and led Colorado by two lengths into the straight, after which it became a repeat of Newmarket: Colorado challenged, led two furlongs out and sprinted six lengths clear. Behind him Coronach almost came to a standstill and in the last few yards he was even run out of second place by the outsider. *The Bloodstock Breeders' Review* summed up:

"It will be impossible to dissuade most people from the belief that Coronach was a great horse when at the height of his fame. Allusion has been made to his wind infirmity. Hints concerning this had been heard for some time, even last year, but the rumours did not take shape until Colorado beat him at Newmarket. A qualified expert who met Coronach when he was returning after the Eclipse Stakes came definitely to the conclusion that the horse made a noise. Others who could not be classed as experts remarked that he was 'blowing hard.'"

The Derby and St Leger winner was retired at once to his owner's stud at Lavington. The magazine suggested that breeders who were thinking of patronising Coronach, "Will appreciate the importance of selecting mares free from [a wind] defect." No one was put off by his ignominious final appearances: his fee was set at 400 guineas and his book filled up at once for his first two covering seasons. Woolavington invited Alfred Munnings to paint his colt. The artist stayed several days at Lavington, with its ballroom hung with paintings by Stubbs and Fernley and Marshall – a challenging reminder of the standard expected. Woolavington had asked Munnings, 'How much do you charge?' When Munnings replied – his usual fee was around £500 – Woolavington said, "That seems a great deal of money for painting a racehorse." At the time, the two men were standing by a table on which stood the Coronation Cup. Munnings thought fleetingly of His Lordship's Derby winners and the amounts he'd paid at public auction for his Ben Marshalls.

Woolavington's lifelong respiratory problems had settled in old age into a 'chronic, wheezy cough.' Munnings thought it was simple to find his client whenever he needed to; he followed the cough. But Woolavington kept an old grey parrot which was a master mimic: Munnings heard, "A prolonged fit of very bad coughing. I went through into the hall." It was empty. "There sat the parrot in his cage: he gave a shrill whistle of derision."

Coronach presented Munnings with another set of problems: "[He] was a big, forceful, unruly individual. This masterful horse was led out into the open. I have heard horses snort, but Coronach's snort was like the trumpet on the Day of Judgement. With head erect, dilated nostrils, he snorted three times. I was watching one of the finest displays of horse agility, power and strength that anyone would ever see." The horse's groom found it difficult to get Coronach to settle and stand, so Munnings began his commission by painting the groom. Over the following sunny afternoons, Coronach 'grew placid, full of contentment and peace,' and Munnings completed his portrait. Woolavington was as thrilled with the result as he was with any of his Fernleys.

Despite extensive patronage, Coronach was a failure at stud in England. From Marcel Boussac's mare Zariba he got one of the best French fillies of the twentieth century – the dual Prix de l'Arc de Triomphe winner Corrida; but in 16 seasons at Lavington he didn't sire an English classic winner. Woolavington's daughter gave the horse to New Zealand's breeding industry, and he was sent there in 1940, becoming the first Derby winner to stand in New Zealand. In the nine years to his death he got the winners of four local classics.

CHAPTER THIRTEEN

An Edgar Wallace thriller and a doping mystery

The two classics won by Coronach meant Fred Darling had won five in five years, three Derbys among them. There was a pause before Beckhampton was again on the honours board, but then came the *annus mirabilis* of 1931 – with some help from Lady Luck. She'd shown her hand two years earlier, in a courtroom, at the instigation of the thriller writer and racing enthusiast Edgar Wallace.

The cause that Wallace represented was the repeal of the Jockey Club rule by which a horse's entries were voided if its owner died. The rule had a number of outcomes, all of them bad, especially for the connections of a colt with classic aspirations. The horse lost most of its value the moment its entries were cancelled; the deceased's inheritors were deprived of that value. The essence of racing and the improvement of the breed – the best competing against the best – was undermined if a top-class horse was scratched for reasons other than its ability or soundness. At times an ante-post market was moved more by rumours about an owner's health than his horse's. Sam Darling had seen the market strength of Ard Patrick shaken every time Jack Gubbins had an attack of gout.

The stewards of the Jockey Club were unhappy with their rule, as well they might be. The description, 'past the prime of life' fitted many of them too closely for comfort. Their problem was the Gaming Act of 1845, the origin of the principle that betting transactions weren't enforceable by law. Insofar as a horse's entries were contracts, they were 'gaming or wagering' contracts, without legal sanction. The contracts were voided by a death, so a horse's entries were void too. In an attempt to unravel the legal tangle, the Jockey Club got together with Edgar Wallace. They agreed that Wallace would make entries for two of his horses; they wouldn't run – and Wallace would decline to pay the forfeit. The Club sued him in a 'friendly action', intending to lose. To general dismay, the action succeeded: the provisions of the Gaming Act were upheld. The Jockey Club and Weatherbys were obliged to appeal against a 'victory' they didn't want. Wallace's costs were underwritten by the Jockey Club. The appeal was successful and the rule was changed: a horse's engagements were no longer lost by the death of the person who'd made its entries.

The first man to benefit from the change was one of Beckhampton's long-serving owners, Thomas Dewar. It was Fred Darling's good fortune that his stable should be patronised by the two great whisky barons of the time. Dewar took a small enterprise begun by his father and turned it into a global business. His marketing flair matched James Buchanan's. When his company's booth was squeezed into a remote corner at a trade show, he hired a piper, in full regalia, to play the bagpipes. A crowd gathered. Before long, a piper had been co-opted into Dewar's advertising and packaging, much like Buchanan's black and white dogs.

Dewar bought and bred racehorses for over 30 years. Immediately after the first world war he combined with Fred Darling to win six races with Abbots Trace, a colt who made most of the running in the 1920 Derby before tiring and being knocked over by another runner. He later beat the winner, Spion Kop, and was second in the Doncaster Cup and Coronation Cup. In 1928 Dewar bred a colt by the multiple race-winning Pharos out of a Gainsborough mare, Una Cameron. The colt was a medium-sized bay of eye-catching quality, and Thomas Dewar accompanied him the day he was sent to Beckhampton, arriving to tell Fred Darling and all within earshot,

"I've brought you a Derby winner." He was right, but he was fated not to see it. He died not long after. Thanks to Edgar Wallace, he was able to leave Cameronian's classic engagements to his nephew.

There's no sign of Arthur Dewar having any interest in racing until his uncle died, unmarried and childless. Arthur was the nearest male heir, and his inheritance was colossal: £1 million in ready money, a two-thirds interest in a £2.5 million trust, and a string of racehorses and the Homestall Stud in Sussex. Fred Darling seldom entertained an angel unawares, and Cameronian soon showed him plenty of ability. He was given just one run as a two year old, in a maiden race at Salisbury. It was over five furlongs, which was unlikely to suit Cameronian on breeding. He faced 16 opponents and was only third in the betting at 8–1, but won comfortably by three lengths. When the time came for the season's two year olds to be ranked, he was pretty well impossible to assess. The second and third-placed horses from his Salisbury bow had both won next time – only in modest little races, but enough to show that Cameronian hadn't been galloping past trees. Nonetheless, he didn't appear in the top 50 in the Free Handicap. Darling had two of the top 10, the colt Lemnarchus and the filly Four Course. Lemnarchus had won five of his last six starts, including the Coventry Stakes. The filly Four Course won the July, Richmond and Gimcrack stakes. Lemnarchus and Four Course must have been uppermost in the mind of Fred Darling's bookmaker Ted Heathorn when the trainer asked him for a playful bet on the following season's classics – £5 against him winning all five. Heathorn laid £10,000 to Darling's fiver, saying he'd be happy to pay out if the bet came off.

At the start of the 1931 season, Cameronian was only third in the Craven Stakes. That seemed to answer any questions about the Beckhampton pecking order, and at the start of the 2000 Guineas the betting was 4–1 Lemnarchus and 100–8 Cameronian. The favourite at 5–2 was Portlaw – conqueror of Lemnarchus in the Champagne Stakes. When they did their final work together at Beckhampton, Lemnarchus was ridden by the stable jockey Freddie Fox, and held off Cameronian decisively. Fox had long told his friends that Dewar's colt wouldn't be ready for Newmarket; now he added that the Guineas was a 'certainty' for Lemnarchus. Darling turned to Joe Childs to partner Cameronian. What followed at Newmarket was uneventful, especially in a field of 24; the first and third from the Champagne Stakes, Portlaw and Lemnarchus, blazed off together with Cameronian prominent in the group just behind. Soon after the Bushes their stamina faded, and they dropped away; Cameronian came through and readily held off the late challenges, winning by two lengths and three. Had he been foaled a year earlier, Cameronian would have fallen foul of the void nominations rule, and wouldn't even have run at Newmarket. Thanks to the repeal of that rule, Darling trained and Arthur Dewar owned a classic winner. If that wasn't sufficient good fortune, Lady Luck provided a rich topping two days later in the 1,000 Guineas.

As he had in the colts' classic, Fred Darling sent two runners to post in the fillies' race. One was Four Course, owned by coal magnate Lord Ellesmere. The other, Lord Woolavington's Windybrae, was rated 6lb behind Four Course in the Free Handicap. The two fillies made their seasonal debuts in the Guineas, so there was nothing to add to their two year old form, other than rumours of their home work. It was notable that Freddie Fox seemed to be unsure which to ride. Darling, who'd booked the French-based former champion jockey Charlie Elliott to ride whichever horse Fox didn't, became exasperated. Poor Freddie simply couldn't make up his mind. Fox was a worthy man, and a good jockey, but he had a number of irritating traits, one of which was the telling of long, inconsequential stories. The only sure way of spotting their endings was that Freddie would chuckle contentedly – and then as like as not begin on another. Darling had zero tolerance for faffing and waffling, and at length he snapped, gave Fox a coin, and told him to toss for the Guineas ride with Elliott. The coin fell Elliott's way, and he chose Four Course.

The favourite for the 1000 Guineas was Gordon Richards' mount Lady Marjorie, recent winner of a seven-furlong Epsom handicap. She was assumed to be likely to stay the Newmarket mile – an important consideration in a race where several of the principals were daughters of Tetratema, a colt by The Tetrarch who'd won the Guineas but was really a sprinter, like his sire. The second favourite was a Manton filly who'd scrambled home by a neck in her only win from three races. Four Course, who was the pick on form, languished at 100–9. The betting public was prejudiced against her because she was by Tetratema and she was brown. The popular view was that the best descendants of The Tetrarch were greys. The race was incident-free until its last few yards; Lady Marjorie was always with the leaders, as was Windybrae. Only as they approached the Bushes did Four Course appear on the scene. Going down into the Dip she hit the front. Lady Marjorie was close behind, and she ran on to lead with a hundred yards to go. At that moment Gordon Richards made one of his few mistakes. To keep Lady Marjorie focused and make sure of victory, he hit her once with his whip. She instantly jinked sideways and lost perhaps two lengths. Richards had her straightened up in another stride, and she flew home up the hill – but failed by a head to catch Four Course at the line. Windybrae was back in eighth. After the race it transpired that Lady Marjorie had never been touched with a whip before. Gordon Richards said, "I ought to have won [by] a length. If only I hadn't hit her!" No one got a quote from Lady Marjorie's trainer, Martin Hartigan; he'd been promised a new Rolls-Royce if his filly won.

Fred Darling, who'd held few hopes for the first classics, had won them both. Freddie Fox was the picture of misery. He'd chosen the wrong horse from his retained stable in both races. Arthur Dewar smilingly deflected congratulations after Cameronian's win, saying, "Congratulate my jockey, for I had a splendid man in the saddle." Joe Childs was, naturally, cock-a-hoop. He rode work at Beckhampton soon after, and told Cameronian's boy to, "Look after him, son. If I ride him in the Derby, you're 'on' for £500."

To the lad's disappointment, Childs had a retainer elsewhere, and he was claimed to ride another horse at Epsom. Fox, with his £3,000 retainer from the Beckhampton owners, was assured of his Derby ride. Ever the pessimist, he told Fred Darling that he wasn't convinced Cameronian would stay a mile and a half, but any doubts were allayed during the colt's strong, uninterrupted work during May. Its culmination was four days before Epsom, when Darling set up a trial over the full distance for Cameronian and his Oaks filly, Four Course:

Cameronian (aged 3)	8st 9lb	
Parenthesis (4)	9st 3lb	(13lb better than weight for age with Cameronian)
Brother-In-Law (4)	7st 12lb	(31lb better)
Rallye II (5)	7st 1lb	(45lb better)
Four Course (3)	8st 3lb	

It was a stern task for the three year olds at the weights. Cameronian conceded the older horses far more than the weight-for-age scale required – and they were serious rivals. Woolavington's Parenthesis had been second when favourite for the previous season's St Leger. Brother-In-Law was second in the Gold Vase. Rallye II had been bought as a lead horse after winning a Lingfield handicap for another yard. Cameronian won the trial easily. Two days later, his owner and trainer were at the Derby Press lunch. Dewar said – hardly in the spirit of the traditional banter: "My horse is fit and well. My trainer, to whom I owe so much, is fit and well. Fox is fit and well." Darling added that, "It's difficult to be optimistic, but Cameronian has given every satisfaction in his work." His riding instructions to Freddie Fox on the day of the race were simple: "Be in front at Tattenham Corner." Fox kept closely enough to his script, and it was as well that he did, in what was a notably rough running of the Derby. Cameronian was the clear favourite at 7–2. The stable were said to have backed him at 20–1 over the winter, but he was still available at 100–6 after his third place in the Craven Stakes. *The Winning Post* could claim credit for spotting and tipping him there and then. Its race reader described Cameronian as, "Nicely balanced and an Epsom colt all over." The paper urged its readers to, "Back Cameronian for the Derby, [he] is Fred Darling's best. Back him now." Someone did: £1,000 to £60 (£60,000 to £3,500) was taken just before the 2000 Guineas. After the race he was 6–1, and he was a steady favourite in the four weeks to Epsom. On course, he shortened to 7–2, with 8–1 bar one.

Cameronian was quickly away at the start, 'Into his bridle with the dash of a sprinter,' according to the *Daily Telegraph*, and in a share of the lead after half a mile, when Fox checked him to get some cover. After that manoeuvre he continued on the heels of the leaders down the descent, and it was as well that he did; a number of the 25 runners got themselves into a terrible scrimmage. One jockey joked afterwards that for a long way his horse didn't touch the ground: he was carried aloft by the press of horses around him. A particular sufferer was the second favourite, Lord Rosebery's Sandwich – aptly named, as it turned out. It was a bad race for Harry Wragg to ride one of his trademark waiting races. His mount had been a massive 'springer' in the betting, from 66–1 a week earlier to 8–1 second favourite. After interference at the start, Sandwich was perhaps 20 lengths off the lead. Coming down the hill on the rails, Wragg said, "I found so many others so constantly changed their positions that I was completely blocked, and horses I had already passed, repassed me. I had to sit and suffer until a clear course came eventually in the straight." By then, the fat lady had sung. Fox produced Cameronian three furlongs from home, and a vast roar rose from the crowd: the Derby favourite in front, apparently on a tight rein. The 2000 Guineas third, Orpen, laid down a determined challenge, but after one flick from Fox's whip, Cameronian had him in safe keeping, and he maintained a three-quarter length advantage through the last furlong. Behind them, Sandwich came from out of the clouds to be beaten the same margin in third. Harry Wragg admitted, "It's possible I was an unlucky loser."

Cameronian's win was greeted with joy. He was the form horse; there'd never been a moment's adverse rumour about him; the public had latched on to a Derby favourite at an attractive price. The papers were filled with the annual parade of winners of the big sweepstakes: the father of eight from County Kerry who won his £15,000 Irish Sweeps ticket in a card game; the blind basket-maker from Stepney who'd seen Sanfoin win in 1890, before losing his sight; he had an order for 300 round baskets and didn't plan to let anybody down, despite winning £30,000. A widower from Limehouse thought he'd move to a nice suburb and find a new wife. The best story concerned Caspar Berther, the head waiter of a hotel in Birmingham. One of the regular customers gave him a half-share in the Calcutta ticket for Cameronian. The share won him £55,000 (£3.3 million). Berther was pleased to see the 18 of his fellow hotel staff who turned up that night at his house; he invited them in for a drink. The celebration went quiet when their spokesman put it to Berther that the ticket was really a tip, given in appreciation of the services of the entire staff. The man suggested the winnings should be shared among all the waiters. Berther didn't see it that way. He showed them the door; there was enraged talk of legal action. Cameronian's lad was crestfallen. Childs had promised him a £500 present; Freddie Fox gave him a tenner.

The next day at Epsom, Beckhampton's Parenthesis won the Coronation Cup. The trial he'd run with Cameronian and Four Course on the Saturday before the Derby could hardly have read more favourably for Four Course in the Oaks the day after. Well might Ted Heathorn look at his £10,000 liability on Fred Darling's optimistic wager. Darling was already a useful winner over the filly. He'd bought her as a foal at Newmarket for 910 guineas, took her back to his stud, built her up, and returned her to Newmarket a year later, where she was sold to Lord Ellesmere for £3,150. Ellesmere entrusted her to Darling to train, so he had the filly as well as the profit. After her fortunate win in the 1,000 Guineas she continued to thrive: one paddock critic at Epsom for the Oaks wrote, "Perhaps of the whole field the one which came in for most admiration in the matter of appearance and fitness was Four

Course. She was typical of the perfectly-trained Beckhampton candidate for a classic race."

She was only third favourite for the Oaks, behind Lady Marjorie and a French filly, Brulette. Both were heavily backed at 7–2; Four Course was 6–1. In contrast to the Derby, the fancied horses were all held up. Lady Marjorie never progressed from the rear group, but Fox made up ground coming down the hill and sent Four Course for home soon after coming into the straight, closely attended by Brulette and a Manton filly, Links Tor. At a mile or 10 furlongs, Four Course would have been a decisive winner, but her sprinter's breeding found her out. Gamely as she stuck her neck out, she couldn't hold off the late-challenging Brulette, who beat her by a length.

It would seem that with three out of the four classics to his credit, Fred Darling would be sure to finish the 1931 season as leading trainer. Over the downs, though, Manton's Joe Lawson was clinging on tenaciously. By September, it was apparent that to be sure of heading the table, Darling needed Cameronian to win the St Leger. Not that there seemed much concern on that count; Dewar's colt had shown no sign of stopping at the end of the Derby, had hacked up in the St James's Palace Stakes before being given a long rest, and faced only the usual suspects who he'd beaten before. He was a shade of odds-on to win. It wasn't to be: Cameronian's presumed victory parade went badly wrong, in odd circumstances. After the race, it was said the signs were there at morning exercise; Cameronian worked with a two year old, who was entered for a race after the St Leger. In no sense was it a trial, but the watchers were surprised that the younger horse hung onto Cameronian as they worked. That afternoon, when he was saddled, the Derby winner sweated and lashed out. As before, Freddie Fox had been told, 'Hold him up until the straight and then come through.' Fox had no chance of riding to his orders. He confessed later to being frightened by his mount's antics:

"It was obvious when I got Cameronian to the starting post that something was very wrong with him. He was upset and kicked Orpen. He then

> literally went mad, ran himself right out and was completely done with after turning into the straight."

Fox had taken Cameronian to the wide outside, away from the other runners, in an attempt to get him to settle. It had no effect. By the time he negotiated the bend into the straight, the horse was a spent force. He stopped to nothing and trailed in last, a hundred yards or more behind the winner. That evening he was found to have a temperature of 103°, against the norm of 99° to 100.5°. Unbelievably, the Doncaster stewards took no action; they ordered no test or enquiry. Darling was besieged with questions, including for his comment on the possibility that Cameronian might have been 'got at'. His response was surprising: "There are various causes for horses going wrong in this way and I put no sinister construction whatever of the horse being 'got at' or anything like that." Sidney Galtrey, one of the most respected racing writers of the time, wrote:

> "What on earth had happened? This could not be the horse that had won at Epsom and Ascot and then [been] judiciously rested for the last of the season's classic races. Here was a dead horse; not a horse that is sent out from Beckhampton perfectly trained and having satisfied his exacting trainer. I cannot say that he was 'got at'. It is so easy to use those words, impossible to prove them. [And yet] having eliminated all possibilities and explored every avenue, one is left with no alternative explanation."

Darling couldn't have been pleased by this and similar commentaries, directly contradicting his strangely passive reaction after the St Leger. However, the Jockey Club's draconian rules on doping were still in place; where doping was proved, the horse's trainer was held responsible, and his licence withdrawn. Darling had so many well-connected owners that it's possible a fudge of some sort would've been cobbled together, but the risks involved were hardly worth provoking by crying 'Foul'. It was an ugly episode, whose most likely explanations were that Cameronian was indeed doped, at the racecourse, and Darling saw only trouble in store if he took the matter any further.

He was also nursing a financial headache. The journalist Sidney Galtrey – who if not a friend of Fred Darling, was a little closer to him than the rest of the detested press – believed that the two biggest bets of Darling's life were Manna and Cameronian in their respective St Legers. Both lost. If Galtrey was right, that was another reason for Darling to want to put Cameronian behind him. Jack Colling placed some of Darling's bets; his widow Sue reckoned, "Darling was pretty hopeless at [betting]. Brilliant trainer though he was, he seldom studied the form book."

The season that had begun so well ended with disappointment. Beckhampton had nothing competitive for the big prizes at the back end, and Joe Lawson sailed by to take the trainers' title with a prize-money haul that broke a record going back 42 years. Darling looked around for a scapegoat; he found it in Freddie Fox, who learned about his dismissal from a newspaper. Gordon Richards was the jockey to take Beckhampton forward. Neither he nor Darling could have imagined that the retainer would last for 21 years, or that Richards would one day be titled Sir Gordon, and train from Beckhampton himself.

CHAPTER FOURTEEN

Released from a powerful catapult

Fred Darling had won four Derbys in 10 years, two of them for Lord Woolavington. He had to wait another seven years before his next classic success, and he was lucky to live to see it. After the St Leger meeting, he and Gordon Richards drove to nearby Armthorpe Aerodrome to meet the 10-seater aircraft taking them back to London. Among the other passengers was Darling's neighbour and fellow trainer, Herbert Blagrave. As their plane took off, it failed to gain altitude and crashed into a hedge. The pilot was killed: Freddie Fox and others on a second flight, waiting to take off, ran to help, and pulled Darling and the others from the wreckage. Gordon Richards barely had a scratch – and rode a winner at Alexandra Park the following day. Darling had the worst injuries: a lacerated knee and his nose broken. He needed an operation to remove splinters of bone from his face. He spent two weeks in hospital.

There were other reminders that every race has an ending: in the space of 12 months, two of Beckhampton's greatest supporters died. The first was Harry Greer, Sam Darling's friend and stud partner, and owner of the classic winners Slieve Gallion and Wildfowler. In 1908 Greer was elected a steward of the Jockey Club, and dissolved his partnership with Darling to preclude any conflict of interest. Greer was an obvious choice to take charge of the National Stud when it was established at the end of 1915.

Once he was satisfied that it was running smoothly, he took over the management of the Aga Khan's breeding interests in Ireland. His services were rewarded by Ireland – he was appointed to the first Senate of the Irish Free State in 1922; and by England, in the shape of a knighthood.

James Buchanan overcame a weak constitution to build a huge business, and then extend it all round the world. From his commercial success came vast riches, a knighthood, and then a baronetcy. His wealth enabled him to donate large sums to good causes. The largest single gift was of £125,000 (£6.5 million today) to the Middlesex Hospital, to build a ward in memory of his wife. They met on one of the sea journeys which he took to clear his lungs. She was a nurse, and died at the end of the first world war, it was said as a result of overwork as a hospital volunteer. He also gave £50,000 to St George's Chapel at Windsor, for the refurbishment of its nave. His generosity extended to licensed trade charities, to further hospitals in London and Edinburgh, and to veterinary research.

In the last year or two of his life, Woolavington was increasingly infirm; at the races, he would watch from his car, parked by the stands. With doctors hovering, Woolavington insisted on being moved from his Berkeley Square house to Lavington, so that he could host his customary party for Glorious Goodwood. He died a few days later. His funeral was almost on the scale of a state occasion. The highest-born in the land mixed with the drinks trade and the racing world, and for possibly the only time the extent of his philanthropy was revealed, in the shape of representatives from any number of institutions and charities which he supported. The tipster Ras Prince Monolulu left a bouquet of lilies, with a card: "Your name will always be spoken well of." So it was. One obituary called Woolavington, 'The most generous man in the world.' His legacy to racing continues. One of the few regrets in his long life was that his only son died at birth. However, his daughter married Reginald Macdonald, who joined their two names. To date, the Macdonald-Buchanan family has produced two senior stewards of the Jockey Club.

The Lavington Park Stud continues, 125 years after James Buchanan founded it.

Fred Darling lost a great owner-breeder with the passing of Lord Woolavington, but if a box was empty at Beckhampton, there was never a shortage of aspirants to fill it. Unfortunately for him, in the middle years of the 1930s the horses coming in weren't as good as the ones they replaced. From heading the trainers' list in 1933, he dropped to seventh place in the next two seasons, followed by twelfth in 1936 and ninth in 1937. Then, as swiftly as the tide had ebbed, it flowed back, and brought with it the greatest five years of his training career. It began with a good old-fashioned dark 'un, the subject of knowing winks and whispers long before his racecourse debut. It was a colt called Pasch, and the circumstances of his breeding meant his owner Henry Morriss was already a winner. Dick Dawson, the owner and former trainer of the champion sire Blandford, wanted to send a mare to Morriss' Manna. In place of Manna's £198 fee, Morriss sent his mare Pasca to Blandford. That mating produced Pasch: Dawson's mare went home empty.

Pasch didn't run as a two year old, but over the winter and into the spring of 1938, the rumour was that Darling had found another good colt. Long before the jumping season's climax at Aintree, Pasch had been backed at 33–1 for the Derby. Darling took him to Newmarket for the Craven meeting, but decided not to risk him on the prevailing hard ground. He ran instead in a Kempton conditions race where as a maiden he received weight from most of his 11 rivals, who included the fourth, fifth and sixth in the official ranking of the previous season's two year olds. On the morning of the race, Pasch was already as low as 10–1 for the 2000 Guineas and 14–1 for the Derby. At Kempton, despite greenness, he showed a good turn of foot to win by two lengths from the Aga Khan's Tahir, receiving 15lb. The outcome suggested that Tahir ought to reverse the result at level weights in the first classic, but the bookmakers' immediate reaction was to make Pasch 5–1 for Newmarket and 10–1 for the Derby. They took the view that Pasch would make the greater progress from the race. And there was a pigeon-catching gallops story. Meyrick Good of *The Sporting Life* wrote:

> "The trial Pasch was set with a 'stranger' before his first race was a particularly high one, and had he been [a runner] in the Free Handicap he would, on that spin, have won with over 9st 7lb in the saddle."

The 'stranger' was a Royal Ascot winner lent by Joe Lawson. After the trial, Darling put £1,000 on Pasch for the Derby at 20–1. Meyrick Good napped Pasch on the morning of the 2000 Guineas, and emphasised the strength of his information: "[He's] sure to win if [the] Beckhampton trial was true." Morriss' colt, available at 9–2 the day before the race, was the subject of sustained support and started a strong 5–2 favourite. He was drawn on the outside of the 18 runners, and Gordon Richards had him away from the tapes in a flash, taking a clear lead before steadying him at the end of the first two furlongs. At the Bushes he led again, going easily, and won by two lengths from the strong-finishing Scottish Union, representing the prominent miller James Rank and the Druid's Lodge trainer Noel Cannon. It was a race of 'firsts' – Gordon Richards' first win in the 2000 Guineas, the first visit by King George VI to Newmarket, and the first classic on the course to be accompanied by a commentary. Richards quickly nominated Pasch as his Derby ride. Scottish Union's trainer left the course delighted with his colt's run, saying, "Never mind – it'll be first next time!"

For Pasch, Scottish Union and the Guineas third and fourth, Mirza II and Portmarnock, 'next time' was the Derby. Pasch advanced to 9–4 favourite, with Scottish Union and Portmarnock at 8–1. The pundits who supported Pasch at Newmarket were even more confident: "There's no Derby problem for Pasch," crowed Meyrick Good. Here at last, it seemed, was the colt to give Gordon Richards his long-awaited first Derby winner. The great jockey was irritated by a suggestion that he had 'an inferiority complex' about the race: "It's the horses that have been inferior," he said.

The Honourable Peter Beatty was a young man with a silver spoon. His father was the distinguished naval commander and First Sea Lord, David Beatty; his mother Ethel was heiress to the American mail order magnate Marshall Field. He was 28, and had been an owner for three or four years with his uncle Vandy Beatty at Newmarket. He hadn't paid more than 800 guineas for a horse, but the day came when he decided to buy something ready-made, to win him a major race. He asked his friend Prince Aly Khan to buy him a horse. Prince Aly found an unraced three year old colt in France, owned by the theatrical impresario Leon Volterra. It was Bois Roussel, by Vatout out of Lucky Liège, by Spearmint. The colt had an engagement in the Prix Juigné, for unraced three year olds. Beatty asked Fred Darling to go with him to Longchamp to watch the race. The result was inconclusive: Bois Roussel started slowly, met interference, and won only narrowly. Darling told Beatty the horse was too fat to be got ready for the Derby. Beatty was undeterred: he told Darling, "Don't tell me you don't know how to deal with him: I'm going to have him". He bought Bois Roussel for £8,000.

Bois Roussel arrived at Beckhampton less than a fortnight before Pasch won the 2000 Guineas. Darling had almost no time to prepare Bois Roussel for Epsom, and no option but to forget about acclimatisation and work him hard – which meant, alongside Pasch. In Darling's words at the time, "While it is not the case that Pasch and Bois Roussel have been formally tried against each other, it is true that they have done a great deal of work together." Bois Roussel worked lazily; there came a morning when Darling decided to wake him up. An apprentice called Tommy Seed rode Bois Roussel right out, with his whip handy. He beat Pasch so easily that Darling chided the Guineas winner's rider for dropping his hands.

His actions spoke louder than his words: he followed his £20,000 to £1,000 bet on Pasch with £33,000 to £1,000 about Bois Roussel. He arranged a re-run of the gallop on the Saturday before the Derby. The veteran jockey

Charlie Elliott had been booked to get to know Bois Roussel, but fog prevented his plane from reaching Beckhampton. Tommy Seed was told, "You're not to gallop today. You'll come at half-speed, with no whip." Lo and behold, Pasch dominated the work. In just six weeks and two key bits of work, Darling had divined the key to Bois Roussel: he needed to be bossed. The two colts were driven to Epsom the day before their race. By chance, the next horsebox at the racecourse stables carried Noel Cannon's runners from Druid's Lodge. Its lads were full of chaff: Scottish Union would take his revenge on Pasch, they crowed. Darling's box driver smiled at them: "Don't forget I've got two in here, lads." On the morning of the Derby, Darling sent his two colts round the course at half-speed. It was as well that they worked so early that none of the shrewdies saw them, because, Darling recalled, "Pasch came down the hill damned awful." In the paddock, he told Charlie Elliott, who was seeing Bois Roussel for the first time, "Don't forget: when you really get at him he'll find a bit."

On the morning of the race, a string of hefty bets forced Pasch from 3–1 down to 9–4. He showed signs of temperament in the preliminaries, refusing to go into a saddling box and sweating in the parade, but he broke well enough at the start, and raced in the leading group to the highest point of the course. Anchored at the other end of the field, Bois Roussel had started slowly and was making no progress from among the backmarkers. His jockey Elliott was resigned to a lost cause. In those days he was retained to ride in France; he'd seen Bois Roussel's debut win, hadn't been impressed, and thought he had little or no chance. After half a mile, he mentally deleted 'little':

> "When the tapes went up he took so long to find his stride that I was last of all, straight away. As we went up the hill I niggled at him a little to see if he could take up a better position. He couldn't. I was still last when we got to the top of the hill. Up to then he hadn't given me a 'feel' at all. When I put some pressure on him as we started the descent there was no noticeable improvement.

> "I had a look at the leaders and found I'd gained practically nothing on them. Half way down the hill I had not the slightest hope of winning. The leaders were well ahead. It was about 50 yards before we got to Tattenham Corner that I gave Bois Roussel a hearty crack. It was a last [resort] and you can imagine my surprise when we bounded forward. Then I remembered what Fred Darling had said."

Far in front of his stablemate, Pasch became unbalanced on the descent to Tattenham Corner. Gordon Richards lost several places, but picked up momentum again as soon as he reached the straight. At that point, a 100–1 outsider led, with Scottish Union and Pasch in pursuit – and Bois Roussel still out of sight, with most of the field in front of him. Scottish Union took the lead three furlongs out, going easily, but Pasch drew up to him, and the crowd was treated to the spectacle of the favourite and second favourite battling head to head. Gradually, though, Scottish Union outstayed Pasch, and pulled a couple of lengths ahead. Most of the crowd and the serious punters would've been on one or other of the two horses, and what happened at the furlong pole took them all by surprise. The modern-era equivalent would be Arazi's astonishing performance in the 1991 Breeders' Cup Juvenile. One race-reader noted Bois Roussel reeling in horse after horse from the entrance to the Epsom straight, 'As if he'd been released from some powerful catapult.'

> "I was something like 12 lengths behind the leaders, but that touch with the whip had transformed him," said Charlie Elliott: "Along the straight he tore at a much faster pace than anything else. One after another I passed them as if they were standing still."

With a furlong to go, Bois Roussel had caught and passed his stable companion Pasch. That left only Scottish Union, whose jockey 'Brownie' Carslake was heading confidently to his first Derby victory – with, he felt, a length or two in reserve. To his horror, out of the corner of his eye, he suddenly saw,

"Something in a white jacket dash by, and it was goodbye to a life's ambition. I've never been on a good horse who was beaten so quickly." Bois Roussel put four lengths between himself and Scottish Union in the last furlong, with two further lengths back to Pasch. Elliott said that if the race had been over a furlong further, he'd have won by 100 yards.

Bois Roussel was only the second horse that Elliott had ridden for Fred Darling; the first was Four Course, on whom he won the 1000 Guineas. He acted with exemplary generosity after his win, handing Bois Roussel's lad Tommy Seed £100. He said, "Fred Darling has worked wonders with the colt since I last saw him." Peter Beatty was reported to have won £40,000 over the Derby, starting with a modest bet at 50–1 and pressing up at starting price. He commissioned a handsome present for his trainer. It was a gold Cartier cigarette box, inscribed in his handwriting on the inside of the lid, *"To Fred with grateful thanks from Peter Beatty."* The box's lid was decorated with an outline of the Epsom course, framing five figures of horses, representing Darling's Derby winners to that date. Bois Roussel took pride of place in the centre. Happiness spread as far as the village school in Avebury, where Henry Blake was a pupil. He'd heard all about Bois Roussel at home. He and two of his friends pooled their pocket money and persuaded the village baker to place their bet. One of the trio had just left the school and gone to work. It was arranged that if the horse won, he'd come at once and stand outside the classroom. Henry was fidgeting at his desk as the afternoon passed. Then his friend appeared at the window, grinning broadly. Cue pandemonium in the class. When the teacher restored order and asked what was going on, Blake revealed all. Some teachers might've reached for the cane: Mrs Still said, "That's brilliant. Well done!"

After the achievement of winning that year's 2000 Guineas and Derby with colts who'd each run only once before, Fred Darling quickly added further classics to Beckhampton's honours board. The racing season of 1939 was cut short by the declaration of war. Most of the autumn racing calendar, including the St Leger, was abandoned so that transport and other resources could be diverted to the national cause. Overall it was a moderate season for Darling – he finished only sixth in the trainers' prize-money list; but providing the major races were staged in 1940, Darling could look forward to it with the best two year old of 1939: Tant Mieux. The first person to greet Peter Beatty after Bois Roussel's Derby was the Aly Khan – "I did say I'd keep half of him, didn't I?" he joked, and the two friends were joint owners of the neat bay colt Tant Mieux. He won them four of the main stakes races, among them the Norfolk, Woodcote and Gimcrack.

Darling and his neighbours reacted quickly to the outbreak of the second world war. He told his distraught stud groom at Blacklands, "We can't keep the horses because we won't have any food for them." Two broodmares were shot, along with the unraced two year olds. Their carcasses were sent to the kennels of the local hunt. Everyone did whatever they could to get round wartime restrictions. Darling's neighbour Herbert Blagrave planted a potato patch, thereby qualifying for farming status and extra rations for his lads. The Hues at Galtee More farm grew a large patch of clover for Darling, hidden in the middle of a field of oats. Darling himself kept some Jersey cows, enabling him to be classified as a farmer, while providing butter for his married lads.

Tant Mieux headed the two year old Free Handicap. No account was taken of a colt bought as a yearling in France for 1,000 guineas by 'Manna' Morriss: it didn't feature in the top 40 in the handicap. It was Pont l'Eveque, by the Grand Prix de Paris winner Barneveldt, out of Ponteba. Darling was unimpressed by Pont l'Eveque when he arrived at Beckhampton. While Tant Mieux laid down markers for the following season, Pont l'Eveque finished unplaced on his debut and then second in a minor maiden race at Newmarket. Over the winter, with uncertainty about the following season's racing, the Morriss family began to fret. Henry Morriss was in Shanghai; his wife and son in England had to take decisions about his bloodstock interests. The first was to cut back, and they told Fred Darling to get rid of Pont l'Eveque. "Wait," Darling told them: "I've had many a bad two year old through my hands and then seen it turn out good." This ought to have served as a warning to the Morrisses, but they knew best. They asked Darling to sell Pont l'Eveque for £500. He offered it to several of his other owners. No one was interested. So despite Pont l'Eveque having no classic entries, Darling bought the colt: "Surely I can't go wrong at the price?"

He was right. Pont l'Eveque was a beneficiary of the Jockey Club's support for the French breeders in an hour of need. English owners with horses trained in France had repatriated them, and a number of French colts had been sent to England. The Jockey Club re-opened entries to the 1940 classics. Pont l'Eveque won a big-field maiden at Newbury on his first run as a three year old and a little race at Salisbury, with odds from 4–9 to 1–4 laid on lustily. In between, he ran in a valuable stakes race at Newmarket. Darling sent a cable to Morriss in Shanghai beforehand: "You can have [a] half-share Pont l'Eveque [for] £2,500 if he wins at Newmarket." The contingency never arose: Pont l'Eveque was routed by a horse called Lighthouse II, who'd placed sixth in the 2000 Guineas, where Beckhampton's Tant Mieux was in third.

The Morriss family went quiet after Pont l'Eveque's defeat. They never replied to Darling's offer of a half-share. Meanwhile, anyone with a form book and a moment to spare could see Tant Mieux had finished three places in front of Lighthouse II in the 2000 Guineas, and that colt had brushed aside Pont l'Eveque at Newmarket. What could be plainer than Tant Mieux's superiority to Pont l'Eveque? Not to mention, Gordon Richards was booked to ride Tant Mieux. In truth, the jockey booking had no significance. Richards was retained to ride for the Beckhampton owners; Fred Darling wasn't part of the owners' pool, so Richards was obliged to ride Tant Mieux. The 'New Derby' was run at Newmarket, not without its critics. One of them was the journalist and author Roger Mortimer:

"The extraordinary thing about the 1940 Derby was the fact that it took place at all, coinciding as it did with the [collapse] of French resistance and the evacuation of the British Expeditionary Force from Dunkirk. Yet at this moment of national peril, some thousands of people had the time and the inclination to go racing. A tribute to national imperturbability in the face of crisis – or a deplorable example of lack of imagination, combined with a refusal to face unpleasant facts."

Lighthouse II was the 85–40 favourite with Tant Mieux at 11–2 and Pont l'Eveque, ridden by Sam Wragg, at 10–1. The race turned out 'dull and colourless' for most observers: meaning, anyone who hadn't backed Pont l'Eveque. The colt took up the running at half way, was never threatened, and extended in the last furlong to win by three lengths. Despite training and owning the winner, Fred Darling showed no emotion at all. Just before the start, unable to get onto the crowded grandstand, he asked the journalist Quintin Gilbey if he could join him on the press balcony. Gilbey was on sick leave from his regiment, having broken his jaw in a motor accident. As the horses cantered to post, Darling said that a Newmarket Derby was nothing like the real thing, and he 'Couldn't get worked up' about it. He sympathised with Gilbey's forthcoming dental repairs, described at length the discomfort and loss of his own teeth, and as he left Gilbey to lead in his winner, uppermost in his mind was, "I hope your false teeth are better than mine." Pont l'Eveque ran only once after the New Derby, finishing third after being outpaced in the Champion Stakes. He was retired to stud and soon afterwards sold to Argentina.

There's a tendency to look back at the substitute classics of both wars with the assumption that they were inferior. It was true that the number of horses in training was much reduced. But with fewer race meetings and far less prize money, the horses that were taken out of training were the slow and the moderate. The owners who left the sport weren't the sort who trained with Fred Darling. The best horses stayed in training. *The Bloodstock Breeders' Review* concluded that Pont l'Eveque, "Was probably as good a Derby winner as would be seen over any group of average years, without perhaps the class of a Hyperion or a Bahram." Those are exalted benchmarks. Pont l'Eveque beat all the best home-trained horses at Newmarket, though he did avoid the French winner of the 2000 Guineas, Djebel, who was later to win an Arc and become an important sire. Djebel's connections unwisely took him back to France after the Guineas, and then couldn't travel him back for the New Derby. He and Pont l'Eveque hadn't been among the original entries for the classics: the reopening of the Guineas and Derby handed the races to two French-breds.

Darling followed up by saddling first and second in the New Derby the following year. He approached the race with a fleet of entries, and eventually declared four, two of them owned by Catharine Macdonald-Buchanan. Her father had bought, shortly before his death, a broodmare from France: Mary Tudor II, winner of several races as a two year old, and then the French 1000 Guineas. The mare was put to Hyperion, and the resulting colt foal was named Owen Tudor. He ran three times as a two year old, winning a little race at Salisbury on his debut. He won again on his 1941 seasonal debut in the Column Stakes at Newmarket, but was overshadowed by his stablemate Morogoro, who won the New Craven Stakes over the same distance, in an appreciably faster time. Morogoro and Owen Tudor were close in the betting for the 2000 Guineas, finishing second and fourth respectively. Owen Tudor was then beaten at Salisbury with odds laid on him, in a race he should've won. As a result, a prejudice set in against the Beckhampton horses *en bloc* for the New Derby. If Darling was running four, it seemed he lacked confidence in any of them. Owen Tudor started at 25–1, the outsider of the quartet. One significant voice went unheard; it was that of Gordon Richards, hospitalised with a broken leg. If he'd been fit to ride, Gordon said, he would've chosen Owen Tudor, who tore up the form book, winning with a long run down the centre of the Newmarket straight. His nearest pursuer at a length and a half was Morogoro. Owen Tudor's northern jockey Billy Nevett was ecstatic after the race: "I've never had such a lovely ride in my life. After we'd gone five furlongs I felt very happy and at the mile [post] I knew I could take him to the front whenever I liked and go on to win." Fred Darling told the press he was "Pleased, but surprised."

The following day, Darling saddled Arthur Dewar's filly Commotion, by Mieuxce out of Riot, to win the New Oaks. She was ridden by 'the head waiter,' Harry Wragg. There was a question about Commotion's stamina, but the race developed perfectly for her and her rider. Coming down into the Dip, a bunch of half-a-dozen horses were scrimmaging for position, Commotion seemingly boxed in behind them. At the last moment they parted like the Red Sea, and Commotion, her stamina conserved, raced through the gap to win comfortably. It was described as, "One of Harry Wragg's brilliant runs." He liked to ride every race that way. It wouldn't have looked at all brilliant had the gap not come. Commotion ran once more, winning the Falmouth Stakes.

The flat season of 1941 showed there was nothing inferior about wartime racing. The classics were strongly contested. The two year olds had special significance, because among them were a filly and a colt who were owned by the National Stud, trained at Beckhampton, and leased to King George VI. His Majesty's involvement made wartime racing not only tolerated but a focus of keen press and public attention; and his filly turned out to be one of the best of her sex in generations. As for Owen Tudor, he continued somewhat in-and-out on the racecourse. He flopped in the New St Leger, run at Manchester. Form students were left bewildered when he won the Newmarket St Leger, reversing placings with five of those in front of him at Manchester. As a four year old he won the Newmarket version of the Gold Cup, becoming the first horse since Persimmon in 1903 to win that race and the Derby. When he was retired to stud at Lavington, he established himself as the most potent son of Hyperion, and an influence on breeding all over the world. In his first six years at stud, he sired two colts, both of them trained at Beckhampton, who were among the best at their respective distances who ever raced in this country.

CHAPTER FIFTEEN

All the King's horses – and the tanks on the lawn

A cow. A minx. Those were the milder descriptions of the brown filly who arrived at Beckhampton in the autumn of 1940. She was bred at the National Stud at Tully in Kildare, she was called Sun Chariot, and she made her attitude to stable routine clear from the start. She bit, she kicked, and if she was upset she threw herself down and refused to move. Breaking her in was difficult, drawn out and dangerous. Jack Blake, who handled all Fred Darling's Derby winners, had his ankle broken by Sun Chariot; his brother Tom had a thumb smashed, and the head lad Norman Bertie a wrist. There was a pressing reason for Darling to persist with Sun Chariot, and to give her every chance to transform herself into a racehorse, but the day came when he'd had enough. He blamed her dam, who'd herself been sent away from Beckhampton without seeing a racecourse. Darling declared of her daughter, "She's bloody useless. Why they wasted a good stallion like Hyperion on a mare like Clarence I'll never know." The National Stud's manager was told that Sun Chariot was on her way back. It proved difficult to find transport across the Irish Sea. The delay turned out to be miraculous. One morning when she should've been back in Ireland, Sun Chariot was messing around at the back of the string. The apprentice Stan Warren remembered her:

> "Playing hell, kicking and squealing and setting the whole lot off. If anything got behind her she let them have it with both barrels. Mr Darling could do nothing with her. He'd set about her with a Long Tom and chase after her in his van, leaning out of the window and slapping the side of the door with his hand, but he couldn't get her to go on the gallops. The more he tried the more temperamental she became.
>
> "She was playing up as usual at the bottom of the gallops one day when Pat Templeton told her rider to try and quieten her down and jump her in 12 or 15 lengths behind three year olds who were about to do a bit of work. It was fantastic. She suddenly took it into her head to go, and after two furlongs she went flying by them."

The relief and the excitement were felt all the way to Windsor Castle. Darling had good reason to try everything he could to tame the wayward Sun Chariot. One of his owners, Lord Lonsdale, had an agreement with the National Stud to lease its yearlings for their racing careers. Lonsdale had an inspiration. Racing in England was under threat in wartime; what better way to cement its place in the national heart than to have a couple of horses running for His Majesty? So Lonsdale arranged that a filly and a colt should be leased to King George. He suggested that the pair should be trained by Fred Darling. There must have been a sleepless night or two when word came back that the King's filly 'Behaved like a neurotic film star in search of an analyst.' Then, joy: Beckhampton had found a key to Sun Chariot. One was the work rider, 'Speedy' Holloway, a big, heavy lad with good hands. Another was a tiny apprentice, Dai Rees. His first job was to look after Sun Chariot. Perhaps she thought him hardly worth savaging; at all events, he was the only human who could safely go into her box.

She made her racecourse debut at Newbury. She disgraced herself by lying down in the paddock and had to be led riderless to the start by Jack Blake. Nonetheless, she won the race stylishly from three previous winners. The Royal win was greeted with prolonged cheers. Then Sun Chariot received a colossal compliment from one of the three year olds who she'd scooted past in her first piece of work. It was Commotion, and a fortnight after Sun Chariot's debut, Commotion won the New Oaks. When word got out, Sun Chariot was made a warm favourite to beat 11 opponents in the Queen Mary Stakes, one of a number of Royal Ascot races staged that year at Newmarket. She was fractious at the start, lost ground by jumping sideways, and appeared not to handle the course, becoming unbalanced, and really only getting going on the final rise. She then finished to good effect, winning by a head from a filly who later won the Cheveley Park. On her next outing, at Salisbury, she again misbehaved. She played up so badly in the paddock that Harry Wragg could hardly get into the saddle, she lashed out, and once on the course she pointed herself in every direction except to the start.

Darling was accompanied at Salisbury by the King's racing manager, Captain Charles Moore. As the two men watched Wragg struggling with Sun Chariot, Darling took a decision. He had a commission to back Sun Chariot from Sir Ulick Alexander in the Royal household. He told Moore it seemed unwise to place the bet; Moore agreed. After prolonged mulishness at the start, Sun Chariot lost a length or two. Wragg took a nice lead to the distance, gave Sun Chariot one nudge, and she cleared away in spectacular style to win by 10 lengths. It was a smashing performance, but left the racing correspondents with a dilemma: how to address the filly's waywardness when she had such august connections? Meyrick Good produced a masterpiece of understatement in *The Sporting Life*: "She was somewhat light-hearted in the preliminaries and used her tail a lot." Fred Darling wrote to the Keeper of the Privy Purse:

> "As Sun Chariot was odds on, and she was misbehaving rather badly going to post, I declared with Captain Moore that I was not betting for you. I hope this was right. She was not much trouble when she got to post [and] won at her ease... She is certainly a good one."

'THE JERSEY LILY'. Lady de Bathe's wild days were behind her when Fred Darling began his training career at her yard near Newmarket. The pair – seen at Newbury in 1909 – landed a big gamble with Yentoi in the previous year's Cesarewitch.

BLACK AND WHITE.
James Buchanan, later Lord Woolavington, was one of the greatest business-men and philanthropists of his time. Fred Darling trained three colts to win four classics for the whisky magnate.

GOING, GONE.
Fred Darling had no interest in farming. His first dispersal of land after his father's death was the Galtee More estate, named after the 1897 triple crown winner. It was bought by the Hues family, who farm it to this day.

David Hues

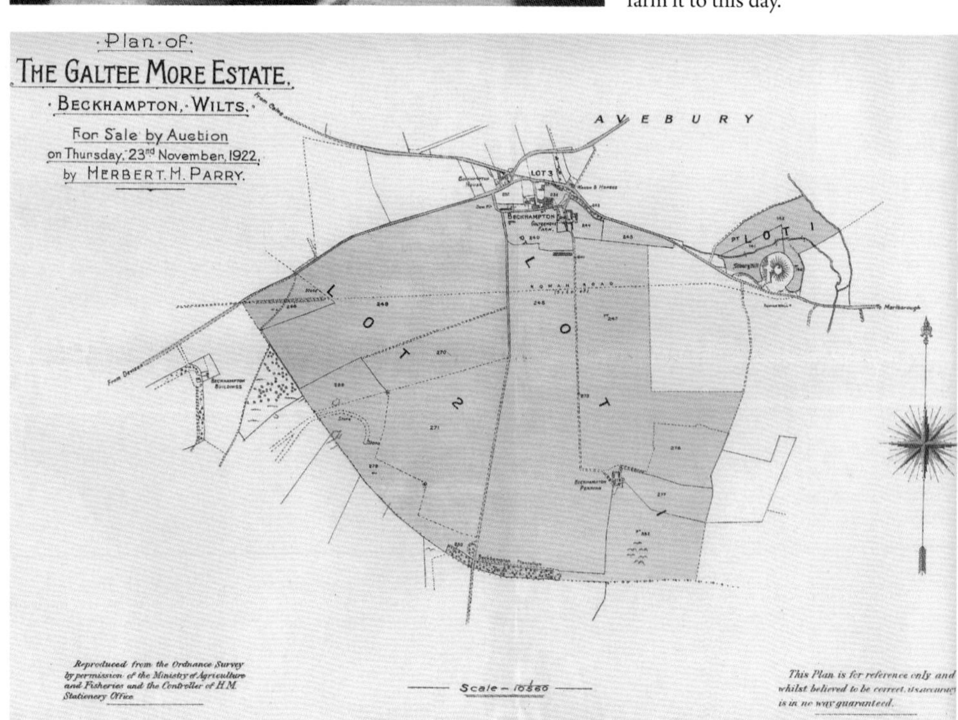

FRED'S ARMY. Darling ran the Beckhampton platoon of the Home Guard as he did his stable yard – autocratically. He's seated in the middle of the front row, with his head lad Norman Bertie second from left. The front two rows in the photograph are mostly Beckhampton lads and apprentices; the back two rows are Galtee More farm hands.

GOT AT. Fred Darling may've had reasons for denying that any questions attached to Cameronian's abysmal run in the 1931 St Leger. He was in a minority of one. As this Daily Mail cartoon shows, the public verdict was: doped.

HATS OFF. The involvement of King George VI was key to the survival of racing in the war years. Fred Darling's handling of the wayward Sun Chariot to win three classics – here, the New Oaks – cemented the Royal connection. Gordon Richards rides: Norman Bertie looks on anxiously.

TWO CLASSICS. On a Newmarket morning in June 1941, Fred Darling stands between Reginald Macdonald-Buchanan (left) and Arthur Dewar. His owners won the New Derby and New Oaks, with Owen Tudor and Commotion.

© Christie's

GOLD STANDARD. Fred Darling's will included six gold cigarette boxes given to him by grateful owners. This was commissioned from Cartier by Peter Beatty after his Bois Roussel had won the 1938 Derby.

SIMPLY THE BEST horse trained at Beckhampton and – at distances up to a mile – one of the best ever to race in Britain. That was Tudor Minstrel, the last of Fred Darling's 19 classic winners, pictured spread-eagling the 2000 Guineas of 1947.

Central Press Photos

Sport and General

SADDLING UP. The care taken by Noel Murless – such as carrying his runners' saddles himself – drew him to the attention of Gordon Richards and Fred Darling, and so to the Mastership of Beckhampton.

Opposite top: HOUSE PARTY. Noel Murless (standing at right) welcomes Sir Gordon Richards (left), the jockey Michael Beary and the American champion rider Johnny Longsden (third and fourth left), and his neighbour Fulke Johnson-Houghton (at right) to Beckhampton.

"A LITTLE RAT". Abernant survived Fred Darling's verdict to be, trained by Noel Murless, one of the greatest sprinters of all time, rated the best horse in training as a two, three and four year old.

Opposite bottom: BIG MAN. Gordon Richards watches Fred Darling's string in May 1942. In time he would train at Beckhampton himself, but his tenancy was short-lived.

Alastair Macdonald-Buchanan

DISAPPEARING ACT. The former SOE officer Dick Warden was a blend of The Scarlet Pimpernel and Macavity: daring, but mostly absent. Training racehorses came a distant second to his passion for hunting.

John Walsh Bloodstock

DICK WARDEN accepts the congratulations of Timeform founder Phil Bull after Bull's equine namesake Felipe Toro had won the 1986 Portland Handicap, owned by Warden and trained by Peter Easterby.

John Walsh: Bloodstock

Sir Ulick was forgiving:

> "I, of course, understand about the bet on Sun Chariot, and you were perfectly right not to transact the commission. I was delighted to hear Sun Chariot won so easily. This looks as though she must be the best two year old filly in this country, and should turn out a useful three year old, and stay. It is unfortunate she should give so much trouble going down to the post, and one can only hope that you will be able to get her to overcome this."

Sun Chariot's final run as a two year old was against the colts in the Middle Park; no filly had won it for 20 years. There were only four runners, but the other three had won good races. Sun Chariot laughed at them. She sat behind the leader, pulling double, and Harry Wragg let her stride on some way from the finish. She cantered home three lengths clear. When the official handicapper published the two year old Free Handicap of 1941, Sun Chariot was top-weighted with 9st 7lb. The colts she'd beaten in the Middle Park, receiving 3lb from each of them, were ranked third [Watling Street, 9st 4lb], fifth [Ujiji 9st 1lb] and eighth [Gold Nib, 8st 13lb]. They were to have their say in the next year's classics. However, ranked ahead of them in second place in the handicap was another colt, also trained at Beckhampton and racing in the King's colours: Big Game [9st 6lb], a son of the Aga Khan's triple crown winner Bahram.

The smartest bloodstock agent or pin-hooker who ever lived could only stand and applaud Lord Lonsdale's handiwork. The filly and colt he picked out at the National Stud as yearlings for King George were each unbeaten after four races, and ranked first and second in their generation.

Big Game's first season with Darling closely matched that of Sun Chariot. His debut was at Salisbury in mid-April, when, ridden by Gordon Richards, he won a 20-runner maiden. Three weeks later, again at Salisbury, Richards was due to ride Big Game, but before an earlier race that afternoon he was kicked and had a leg broken; he missed the rest of the season.

Harry Wragg deputised for him on Big Game and enjoyed an armchair ride to win.

Darling sent Big Game to win the Coventry Stakes by four lengths from Watling Street. He beat Watling Street again in the Champagne Stakes, run at Newbury, this time by only a short head. It was enough, though, to place him at the forefront of the season's two year old colts. The breeding experts who looked at his chances for the 1942 classics were dubious. His dam Myrobella was one of the best sprinters that Fred Darling had trained. She in turn was a daughter of The Tetrarch, the great juvenile sprinter. The omens for Big Game's stamina prospects weren't promising. No such doubts surrounded Sun Chariot, so Fred Darling could look towards 1942 with satisfaction and optimism. He'd saddled Owen Tudor and Commotion to win the replacement Derby and Oaks, and he had the top-rated two year old colt and filly to dream about over the winter.

Gordon Richards surrendered the jockeys' championship that season, as a result of his injury. It was the first time in his 11-year association with Beckhampton that he hadn't been champion. At the start of the 1942 season, by way of a welcome back, Sun Chariot provided him with one of the most unsatisfactory of his thousands of rides. It was only with much cajoling that she could be persuaded to leave the paddock. Then she planted herself. When she eventually consented to race, one of the other runners bumped her onto the rails, at which point she lost interest, dead-heating for third place, three lengths and half a length behind Ujiji, whom she'd readily beaten in the Middle Park. *The Times* reporter said her behaviour was that of 'a naughty little girl.'

Sun Chariot continued to alarm and vex Fred Darling at home. The King and Queen and the Princesses Elizabeth and Margaret visited Beckhampton to see her and Big Game. The colt was his usual amenable self; Sun Chariot wouldn't jump off at the start of her intended work, reacted with fury when Gordon Richards tapped her with his whip, bolted into a ploughed field, sank to her knees and tore at the ground, roaring like a bull. There was much trepidation when Sun Chariot went back to Salisbury to complete her preparation for the 1000 Guineas. She again attracted the description 'flighty' in the form book; *The Sporting Life* tried to assure its readers that, "Her habit of twirling her tail is just a mannerism." Racegoers allowed her to start at odds against, for the only time in her career. Gordon Richards held her up, led at the distance and won without asking the filly any sort of question. An hour later Big Game won equally easily. The King's horses had put down markers for the first two classics, and they were backed for their respective Guineas; Sun Chariot was made 2–1 favourite for the 1000, Big Game 6–4 favourite for the colts' race.

Just for once in racing, a fairy tale came true. Big Game was a brilliant winner of the New 2000 Guineas. He stood out in the paddock for size and quality, and was backed at odds from 10–11 to 8–11. Gordon Richards allowed an outsider to give him a lead for the first half of the race on the stands side, before Big Game pulled himself to the front over two furlongs out. He was pursued by Watling Street, Ujiji and Gold Nib, but as soon as he met the incline to the winning post, he stretched away comfortably to win by four lengths and two. He was made 6–4 favourite for the New Derby, notwithstanding all the sprinting influence on his dam's side of his pedigree.

Sun Chariot completed the King's Guineas double the following afternoon, with two surprises: her good behaviour and her starting price. The 2000 Guineas had given her form a tremendous boost, with the three colts who she'd beaten easily in the Middle Park finishing second, third and fourth to Big Game. The only explanation for her starting at evens was that the heavy hitters had decided her temperament made backing her too risky. The previous morning she'd treated work-watchers on the heath to a prolonged show of obstinacy; it took over a quarter of an hour to induce her to move. To Fred Darling's relief, there was no repeat on the racecourse. Gordon Richards took a firm hold of the filly as she left the paddock; on arriving at the start she whipped round twice, but jumped off on terms and allowed herself to be restrained a few lengths behind the leaders. At half-way it was obvious that she was pulling over the other 17 runners, and Richards let her go – sooner than he would've liked, but, it seemed to him, a lesser risk than checking and disappointing her. The crowd began cheering as she took the lead, and the celebrations grew in volume as she pulled away, winning in a canter by four lengths.

The two horses' wins provided a timely boost for racing. As in the first world war, there were plenty of critics in Parliament and the press who argued that to continue with racing was a frivolity when Britain was struggling to contain Nazi Germany. They believed the war effort was reduced by every bushel of oats and gallon of petrol diverted to racehorses and their transport. The pleadings of racing's supporters – that servicemen on leave were enthusiastic attendees at every race meeting, and that competitive racing was the only way to maintain the breed – didn't have the emotive force of the 'antis'. Then along came the King to the rescue. He and Queen Elizabeth were tireless in their work to support Britain's morale, engaging on every possible visit to the armed forces, to bomb-damaged towns, to factories, farms and hospitals. To the glee of the racing press, they made it unpatriotic to question the principle of wartime racing. "Stimulating effect of Royal double" and "Nation shares in great classic successes" were the headlines in *The Sporting Life*:

> "Our pleasure in the fact that the King won both races is enhanced by the knowledge that the winners are products of the National Stud. Although leased by His Majesty the Guineas winners are in fact the Nation's property, and we can each claim to own a hair of them and to be a trifle better off as a result of their enhanced value. Perhaps the Parliamentary critics of racing will be a little less severe, now they are part-owners of classic winners!"

To Fred Darling's irritation, the build-up of expectation in the four weeks to the New Derby and Oaks meant he had to cooperate with the sort of media intrusion which he'd spent the previous 30 years repelling. Reporters and photographers appeared at Beckhampton and had to be made welcome. His visitors went away with numerous photographs of men, horses and stable routine, but little in the way of stirring quotes from the Master: "I have never been a super-optimist. All I can say is that I am very hopeful," was as far as he went.

On the morning of the New Oaks, Sun Chariot was as low as 2–5 in the betting. She was re-opposed by five fillies from the 1000 Guineas, the pick of them Afterthought, who'd finished fourth, beaten six lengths. The other quartet had been tail-enders, none of them having any realistic chance of reversing the form. When the crowd had seen Sun Chariot behave perfectly in the paddock and on the way to post, the odds were laid on her with infectious confidence. She started at 1–4, the shortest-ever Oaks favourite. Her supporters continued in good humour when she could be seen quiet and amenable at the start. But when the tapes went up, she dived left, losing as much as six lengths. When Richards wrestled her round behind the other runners, she was plumb last. Then she missed the right-hand turn into the straight and continued her leftward drift. Richards didn't try to stop her. "You have to be very careful and not upset her. I took her in a little to get something to follow, but she soon went outside everything again." She was racing so keenly that with half a mile still to travel she'd passed every filly apart from Afterthought, and went past that rival at the distance. Having done so, she thought her afternoon's work was done: Richards had to ride her out vigorously, without daring to use his whip. She beat Afterthought by a length, to the relief of the many in the stands who'd decided to buy money. Richards said after the race:

> "She's a brilliant but erratic filly. It's a relief now it's over. Nobody knows the anxious time I've had with her on the downs. You simply don't know what she'll do."

The King had won the season's first three classics. The day was made better by his being on hand, in khaki, to lead in his filly. An hour before the Oaks, the crowd in the Silver Ring and down the course had suddenly cheered wildly. As those in the stands craned their necks to see what was happening, it was realised that a motorcade had driven up the course, stopped, and the King and Queen were walking the short distance to the enclosures. It was their first visit to the races since the start of the war, and there was a tumultuous reception for the King as he led in his winner. His visit had been kept secret to the last moment. Next day, the crowd was on full alert, and the cheering began as soon as the first police car was spotted, far down the course. Alas, Big Game couldn't deliver the result that the country wished for, and for the reason that some had forecast: he didn't stay.

Big Game pulled furiously for the first half mile of the New Derby. Gordon Richards managed to settle him, but after seven furlongs a horse charged up on either side of him, and Big Game took off again. He carried himself into the lead two furlongs out, but his stride shortened. Watling Street and Hyperides swallowed him up, followed soon enough by Ujiji, and when Richards dropped his hands, Big Game faded into sixth.

There was lively rivalry between the Beckhampton lads over the respective merits of their charges. Big Game's devoted lad always called his horse 'Champion'. He pinned up a magazine photo of Big Game in the tack room. It was captioned, *The Head of a Great Horse*. After the New Derby and Oaks, someone added a photo of Sun Chariot, taken from behind her, with the message, *The Arse of a Better One*. Inelegant, but accurate; Darling never worked the two together, but he always felt the filly had the edge. The Newmarket races gave him a clear focus for the rest of the season. He dropped Big Game back to 10 furlongs for the Champion Stakes, and his colt beat Afterthought, Ujiji and Hyperides. Sun Chariot stepped up to one mile and six furlongs for her last race, the New St Leger. Nothing had been left to chance in her preparation. The King's racing manager Charles Moore asked Joe Lawson for a favour, and the upshot was that Lawson's owner Alfred Allnatt agreed to lend Ujiji and Shahpoor to be trial companions for Sun Chariot. She was, at last, calming down and working enthusiastically for a new work rider, Stan

Warren, and for the only time in her two seasons in training, she was a good, honest, straightforward doer. When Allnatt's colts came over from Manton, she made short work of them, and she did again in the substitute St Leger. She delighted Gordon Richards by taking the preliminaries, the parade, the canter down and the start without missing a beat.

> "She was a bit keen when we jumped off, but I got her nicely in hand before long, and dropped her back last as I had planned. When we turned into the straight I was still last of all, but even at this stage Sun Chariot was giving me a rare feel."

Watling Street's rider Harry Wragg made first run three furlongs out. Gordon Richards realised then:

> "It was all over. I gave the filly a bit of rein. She drew up to Watling Street without any trouble and was past him in a flash. From that point I had merely to keep her going with the hands to run out a comfortable winner. She never put a foot wrong and did all I asked her in a manner which satisfied me she is the best I have ever ridden."

Sun Chariot won the New St Leger by three lengths, with a further five back to Hyperides in third; Alfred Allnatt's Shahpoor and Ujiji were fourth and sixth. She was unquestionably the best horse of the year, despite her temperament. Somehow and after much pain and frustration, Fred Darling and the Beckhampton yardmen and lads cajoled Sun Chariot into a frame of mind where she produced racecourse performances that place her in the pantheon of the greats. Before her, the only other winners of the fillies' triple crown of 1000 Guineas, Oaks and St Leger were Beckhampton's Formosa in 1868; Hannah in 1871; Apology in 1874; La Flèche in 1892; Sceptre in 1902 and Pretty Polly in 1904. Only Meld in 1955 and Oh So Sharp in 1985 have managed the feat since. Inclusion in that list suggests that Sun Chariot was one of the best half-dozen fillies ever to race in England, the more so as she mostly raced against colts.

The connections of Sun Chariot and Big Game exchanged commemorative gifts. The King asked Alfred Munnings to paint two versions of a portrait of Sun Chariot. One was presented to Gordon Richards, the other to Darling, who reciprocated by having two racing plates mounted by Asprey: Sun Chariot's for the King, Big Game's for the Queen. After the New St Leger, it was planned to keep Sun Chariot in training as a four year old, to win the Gold Cup. Charles Moore asked the National Stud to extend the King's lease for another season. After second thoughts, she was retired. Without the pressure of training, she relaxed. She was a docile, model broodmare, without producing a foal half as good as herself.

The immediate consequence of her retirement for her lad Dai Rees was that his call-up papers arrived. For the preceding six months, he was on the 'deferred' list – probably the only man in England to have his national service postponed so he could look after a horse. Fred Darling had written to the authorities to say that Rees was indispensable to the training of the King's 'unmanageable' filly. Many years later, Rees visited Ireland. On a whim and a wet day, he looked round the National Stud, and was delighted to find it had a Sun Chariot yard. His daughter told the Stud staff of the part her father had played in Sun Chariot's racing career. Everyone wanted to hear his stories; a group of American visitors asked about her personality. "Am I allowed to say this?" he asked: "She was a bitch."

Fred Darling's incomparable season extended to winning the replacement Gold Cup with Owen Tudor. He ended the season as champion trainer once more. The feast was followed by famine. With his big guns retired, Darling won only 17 races from 7 horses the following year, and dropped to eighth place in the trainers' prize money list. He fared little better in 1944, saddling 23 winners and finishing fifth in the trainers' table.

During this period, he was busy protecting Beckhampton from a threat he could never have envisaged: the US Army. For months before the return of Allied troops to France on D-Day, the south of England was home to tens of thousands of US troops, training intensively and assembling materiel for the invasion. Salisbury Plain has long been home to tank and artillery exercises; Beckhampton's downs were added to the area for tank manoeuvres. Compensation was paid to farmers and landowners for damage. The Galtee More Farm accounts books for March and April 1944 include the entries:

> March 19 and 20: "Five men filling in tank ruts and large holes on 13 acres [of] oats: £5/10/0"
> March 22 and 23: "Two men repairing fences and hanging new gates: £2/4/0"
> March 27: "One man repairing hedges damaged by tanks: £0/11/0"
> April 3 to 8: "Five men each day filling in tank marks on 115 acres of wheat: £16/10/0"
> April 10 to 15: "Two tractors each day rolling and harrowing the above wheat: £24/0/0"

The Hues family's records hint at the extent of the compensation paid out in Wiltshire and neighbouring counties. This was a single farm, submitting its 'Claims for American Damage' for £87/14/0 (about £3,500 today) in only two months. The details also highlight the threat to Beckhampton. A hedge can be repaired and a gate replaced. Crops will grow again next year. But Darling's horses were trained on downs which had never been disturbed. His father Sam had spent years nurturing the gallops to perfection. A few minutes' incursion by a Sherman tank would've wrecked decades of hard work and husbandry. Darling lobbied furiously for his gallops to be an exclusion zone. He had an ally in 'Porchey' Carnarvon, who was appointed assistant director of claims for Southern Command. In that role, he had direct access to senior British and American army officers. Even so, the preservation of the Beckhampton gallops wasn't guaranteed. Porchey recalled a confrontation with an unnamed American tank colonel: "Together with my American liaison officer, I had explained that we had marked off the gallops so that his men could easily avoid them." He got short shrift. The officer said he and his troops had come across the Atlantic to beat the Germans:

> "If it means my tanks having to go across your God-damned gallops – well – they'll just go across 'em! I'm not aiming to hold back my men for a bunch of racehorse owners."

Porchey set diplomacy aside:

> "Those gallops have probably been in existence a good deal longer than your country. They are part of our heritage and we need to protect them. There are thousands of acres on either side [on] which your tanks are free to train. Surely your troops can be made to avoid these gallops? Good day to you, Colonel."

The matter escalated. It seems that behind the scenes, Darling sought intervention from a power greater even than a feisty Earl. Darling had mounted a charm offensive, inviting locally-stationed American officers, showing them round Beckhampton and giving them dinner. At the end of January 1944, he was visited by the armoured division General, Holmes Ely Dager. Darling's account of the meeting was sent to the stewards of the Jockey Club and to Windsor Castle. It read:

> "This morning I [showed] General Holmes Ely Dager… over the gallops, and explained all there was to explain… He was most sympathetic, and gave me his assurance that the tanks would not go on the gallops, which was, as you can imagine, a great relief."

Sir Ulick Alexander wrote back to say he was delighted, and hoped 'This question has now been satisfactorily and definitely settled.' It was. The gallops were preserved. Beckhampton had in any case done its bit for the war effort. Darling had formed a Home Guard platoon. The Royal Artillery commandeered the top yard from 1940 onwards. Other outbuildings and cottages housed British and American servicemen for shorter periods. Among the visitors were two dozen special forces men. No one saw them; they trained only at night. One day their officer asked if the men's wives and sweethearts could be accommodated. They had a last night with their menfolk, who left the next day for their undisclosed mission. It was said none of them came back.

Darling was exhausted at the end of the war. Besides the strain of keeping the yard going, and intact, his tuberculosis had returned. The 1945 season was another disappointment; no good horses, and only eleventh in the trainers' list. But the autumn brought the annual rebirth of a new contingent of yearlings. They included the best horse ever trained at Beckhampton: Tudor Minstrel.

CHAPTER SIXTEEN

Tudor Minstrel: England's horse

When strangers meet and discover a shared interest in racing, the chances are their talk will turn to the 'Best horse you ever saw?' question. The combination of deep expertise and a long life are useful attributes for weighing up different generations. Sir Peter O'Sullevan answered the question without a second's hesitation: "Frankel". Peter Willett also replied "Frankel," but continued without a pause, "and Tudor Minstrel."

It's 70 years since Arthur Dewar's home-bred brown colt, by Owen Tudor out of Sansonnet, by Sansovino, arrived as a yearling at Beckhampton. Few following racing today will have seen Tudor Minstrel, but those who did can testify that the level of excitement and expectation surrounding the colt at least equalled that attached to Frankel. Probably exceeded it, as racing then had a far wider public following and media coverage.

Gordon Richards told a friend before Tudor Minstrel ever ran that he'd never be beaten, barring mishaps. When he made his debut at Bath at the end of April 1946, one of the most influential form students in the history of British racing was watching, and he noted: "Very nice colt, strong, made all, impressive." After Tudor Minstrel's next run, in the Salisbury Foal Stakes, the watcher used the phrase 'common canter.' He had no truck with the official winning distance of four lengths. It was eight lengths, he asserted, and as he was Phil Bull, a pioneer of race timing and the founder of Timeform, he was probably right. Then came an electrifying performance in the Coventry Stakes. Bull recorded that Tudor Minstrel 'quickly went clear, sailing along on the bridle.' The remarkable feature of the performance was the time of Tudor Minstrel's win: Phil Bull rated it as '**1.25** fast'.

Bull created, and published between 1942 and 1947, his own speed figures in *The Best Horses Of...* annuals. They were based on his definition of standard time: 'The average merit of winning performances at Newmarket.' The times were adjusted for the conformation of other courses, the going, the wind and weather, the age of the horse and the weight it carried. Any figures faster than standard were notable; Bull printed them in bold. He linked his figures to weight, the basis of every handicap. His equivalent of 1lb was four-tenths of a second. By dividing Tudor Minstrel's **1.25** fast by four, he arrived at a performance equivalent to over 31lb better than standard. This might sound faintly Heath Robinson, but it worked. In 1944 Bull clocked a two year old maiden race at lowly Stockton. He was astounded: the winner ran to a time value of **1.41** fast. It next appeared at Royal Ascot in the Coventry Stakes. Thanks in part to Bull's trumpeting, it started at 11–8 joint favourite, but because its Stockton time made it, in his eyes, "More like a 1–10 shot," he "Had to have a splash." He had another 'splash' in the following season's 2000 Guineas, which the colt lost, a shade unluckily. Bull went in again for the Derby, winning back his Guineas losses and more. The colt was Dante, who had run to **1.24** fast in the Coventry Stakes. At that time Bull had clocked only four horses at better than **1.20** fast. They included Beckhampton's Sun Chariot at **1.35** fast (comfortably) and Big Game at **1.22** fast (when all out).

Now, he'd found another, and a month later, Tudor Minstrel stepped up to a different level. In the National Breeders' Produce Stakes at Ascot, he gave weight all round, set a strong gallop, and 'drew away without having to be pressed.' The time value figure was **1.70** fast. Bull's essay on Tudor Minstrel in *Best Horses of 1946* bubbled with excitement:

> "A figure of **1.25** fast is of top classic quality, but **1.70** fast represents an astonishing performance! What sort of racehorse must Tudor Minstrel be, with a figure [which] is more than 8lb superior to the best recorded by either Sun Chariot or Dante in their first seasons? And, let it be remembered, with Tudor Minstrel hardly off the bridle to do it! It is a phenomenal time performance, and the conclusion from which I have tried to escape, but cannot, is that Tudor Minstrel *must be one of the fastest two year olds ever seen.*"

Bull forecast that in the following season's 2000 Guineas:

> "Tudor Minstrel has only one horse to beat – Petition. I think he will beat him, and beat him comfortably." He added, "When the Derby comes along [colts] such as Migoli, Blue Train and Sayajirao will no doubt be making more progress [but] I doubt if the other horses will be able to get him off the bridle without killing themselves."

Petition was trained in Newmarket by Frank Butters, Fred Darling's regular challenger for the trainers' championship. Tudor Minstrel mopped up the good two year old heats in the first half of the season, Petition those in the second half. In the Gimcrack, Petition summoned Phil Bull's keen interest with a blistering **1.38** fast speed figure. That made Petition a probable classic winner, but still inferior to Tudor Minstrel. Since they ran nine times between them, it was surprising that only one horse ran against each of them: Migoli. He was eight lengths behind Petition and – in Bull's notes – 10 behind Tudor Minstrel. It wasn't decisive collateral form, but it gave a pointer.

Among the Derby candidates named by Bull, Blue Train was Tudor Minstrel's stablemate, and the product of two champions, the 1939 Derby winner Blue Peter and Sun Chariot. Like his dam, he was leased by the King from the National Stud, and at the end of his two year old season, he had a perfect record: ran once, won once. It wasn't a race from which many conclusions could be drawn; an end-of-season Ascot maiden with moderate opposition. The time Bull clocked was unremarkable. He concluded that, "Blue Train did what good horses frequently do: he [won] convincingly in undistinguished company when half fit. I certainly expect him to turn out a first-class racehorse."

Tudor Minstrel ended his season early. Arthur Dewar was said to have decided not to over-face his colt. There was another reason: his trainer's absence. Fred Darling had spent much of his life in the shadow of tuberculosis. He phoned Gordon Richards and told him he'd suffered a haemorrhage. Richards called a specialist, and Darling was sent to a sanatorium in Sussex. He spent three months there. His older brother Sam stepped in to oversee Beckhampton. He and Richards paid regular visits to Fred, and came away with his instructions: "The Guv'nor was still very much the Guv'nor!" recalled Richards. Then Darling returned to Beckhampton, and reminded everyone who was in charge by suggesting that his brother hadn't properly looked after Tudor Minstrel.

The 1947 renewal of the 2000 Guineas was expected to be a match between Tudor Minstrel and Petition. Each had a prep race, more accurately an exercise canter. When they met at Newmarket, Tudor Minstrel was 11–8, Petition 5–2. The next best was 100–7. What followed was beyond superlatives. It was one of Darling's supreme training feats that after one of the coldest winters for decades, and before all-weather gallops, he produced Tudor Minstrel ready to run for his life at Newmarket. His colt blew apart the 2000 Guineas of 1947 in the same fashion that Frankel did in 2011. At half way, he led, hard held, by a couple of lengths from the scrubbed-along Petition, with three or four lengths more to a flat-out group headed by Sayajirao. Then he routed them, seeming to sprint faster and faster, while the rest toiled in his wake along the Rowley Mile. The racing correspondent of *The Times* wrote:

> "I shall never forget the sight of this colt as he gathered himself together three furlongs from home and with enormous power and energy strode

> away from his field, making them look like hunters at the end of a six-mile [run] in November. At once the thought sprang to mind, is this the horse of the century?"

There were many similar effusions; that of Phil Bull can summarise for the rest:

> "The memory of Tudor Minstrel strolling home the length of a street in front of everything else will remain with me for the rest of my life. I don't expect to see such a thing in a classic race again".

Gordon Richards said that he'd given Tudor Minstrel a 'breather' after five furlongs:

> "I went on cantering further ahead of them all. How far he could have won is impossible to say. [It was] the easiest race I have ever had – and am likely to have."

The official distance was eight lengths; photographs suggest it was at least 10. The outsiders Saravan and Sayajirao were second and third, separated by a short head. Petition was far in arrears; it transpired that he'd charged the starting tape and fallen to his haunches. At the time it was said this hadn't affected him physically, but he didn't run again for two months, and never matched his two year old form. Phil Bull and other 'clockers' weren't concerned with the placings and distances. On Bull's scale, Tudor Minstrel had run **1.74** fast: 43½lb better than standard. It was the highest speed figure Bull ever recorded.

A few moments before the 2000 Guineas, the bookmaker William Hill laid a bet of £25,000 to £3,000 against Tudor Minstrel for the Derby. The equivalent today would be £105,000 to win £875,000. Hill was happy to lay the bet. He knew something that most didn't: Tudor Minstrel wasn't

Darling's intended Derby horse. That role was filled by Blue Train. After the Guineas, Tudor Minstrel was made 6–4 favourite for Epsom, and people fell over themselves to take the price. Few paid heed to Darling's having two colts in the Derby, or to the absence of any guidance as to which would be Gordon Richards' ride. Blue Train made his seasonal reappearance at Sandown, three days after the Guineas. He was backward, but still beat a small field at his leisure, at which point Darling put £1,000 on him for the Derby. Blue Train was difficult to get race-fit; Darling ran him again only 11 days later in the Newmarket Stakes over 10 furlongs. The colt looked fitter, was long odds-on, and won easily, doing all his best work in the last furlong. Darling told Gordon Richards this was his Derby mount. The trainer believed Blue Train was certain to stay the Derby trip, and he had a doubt about Tudor Minstrel.

The most obvious question was his style of running; if Tudor Minstrel tore off as he had in the Guineas, he'd be unlikely to maintain the gallop over a mile and a half. Then there was his breeding: the bottom half of his pedigree was inclined to speed. His dam Sansonnet had already produced a good filly and an outstanding one, both trained by Darling, but neither of them had attempted more than a mile. Darling knew the family well, and it was significant that he aimed the less-experienced Blue Train at the Derby, as insurance against Tudor Minstrel's stamina. William Hill had taken a strong view: on breeding, he said, Tudor Minstrel had no chance in the Derby.

A week before the race, Darling's cover disappeared. After Blue Train's final piece of work, he was found to have a swollen leg. 'He won't stand another gallop,' advised the vet. Blue Train was retired at once. His scratching was hardly noticed by the once-a-year army of 'Come on Gordon!' punters and race-goers. They were sure Tudor Minstrel was going to provide Richards with the Derby win which had eluded him for so long. They didn't know Tudor Minstrel had worked badly. A replica Derby course had been prepared on the downs, and Tudor Minstrel had been following a lead horse quietly round it, twice a week. The morning arrived when Darling stepped up the tempo, and Richards was in the saddle. He was horrified: "On pulling up I went straight to the Guv'nor and said to him, 'This fellow's action is all *right*. He can't get on his other leg. If he does, he's all at sea.'"

Most of the press had abandoned rational analysis of the Derby. It was reported that the jockey Michael Beary had bought the boots worn by Steve Donoghue when he won the Derby on Manna. He presented them to Gordon Richards 'to bring him extra luck.' Donoghue was large for a jockey; Richards was tiny. Surprise: the boots didn't fit and Richards didn't wear them. Clive Graham of the *Daily Express* walked the Derby course and was told of a plot to nobble Tudor Minstrel. The favourite would be leading in the closing stages, where persons unknown would be waiting to drop some dogs over the rails to impede him. This and similar piffle suggested that the press had decided the silly season should start early. Clive Graham redeemed himself with a piece on the pedigree of the Derby hopefuls: "Students of breeding will side with Migoli and [a French colt] Pearl Diver." Mostly, though, the racing professionals like Meyrick Good envisaged only one result:

> "Today's Derby is going to be won by the best horse I have ever seen, who will be steered by the best jockey of my time."

On the first two days of the Epsom meeting, French invaders won the Oaks and the Coronation Cup. Tudor Minstrel carried the extra burden of being 'England's horse'. The 1947 Derby was the first to be run on a Saturday; the Government told the Jockey Club to switch the race from Wednesday. The economy was so shattered by war that the last thing the country needed was a day's production lost, to an event that would empty factories and offices. A huge crowd gathered on Epsom Downs. A torrent of money poured into the bookmakers' satchels. Half went on Gordon Richards, the other half on Tudor Minstrel. He was returned at 4–7; next best was the Guineas third, Sayajirao, at 13–2. The longer shots included Migoli at 20–1. The betting reporter Geoffrey Hamlyn of *The Sporting Life* said, "By far the biggest gamble during my 60 years racing was on Tudor Minstrel. Had there been betting shops [in those days] then it would undoubtedly have been the biggest plunge in racing history." The last big bet that Hamlyn noted at Epsom was £14,000 to win £7,000 (£490,000 to win £245,000). William Hill stood impervious: he backed his judgement of breeding and laid Tudor Minstrel to lose £175,000 [over £6 million today].

Tudor Minstrel did as might've been predicted after the Guineas: he lit his own touch-paper and fired himself at the horizon. There was nothing Richards could do.

> "I have never in the whole of my life had such an uncomfortable ride at Epsom. If I held him up he fought me. If I let him down to go, he shot off to the right. Either way, he was making certain that he lost the race. It was a nightmare."

Mouth agape, on the wrong leg, head pulling away to the right: it was a surprise Tudor Minstrel stayed in contention as long as he did. One of his closest attenders was a French outsider, Pearl Diver. When they spilled off Tattenham Corner and into the straight, Richards had no option but to press on, with Pearl Diver to his right and Sayajirao on the rails. The portion of the crowd who could see that part of the race began cheering. Excitement spread across the downs. Below them, Tudor Minstrel's run had stopped. Sayajirao and Migoli ran past him. But the unconsidered Pearl Diver had made the first run and wasn't for catching. He won by four lengths at 40–1, from Migoli who was three-quarters of a length ahead of Sayajirao, with an unimaginable eight further lengths back to Tudor Minstrel in fourth place. Tudor Minstrel's defeat was painful and expensive, for all but William Hill and the other bookmakers: Hill admitted to a relative that if the result had gone against him, he wouldn't have been able to settle.

'Porchey' Carnarvon wrote to a friend that he'd finished the Epsom meeting with a winning day, "Which is a very slight compensation for the horrors which occurred to me on Derby day!" To make the result more agonising for Tudor Minstrel's supporters, Arthur Dewar's colours were similar to those of Pearl Diver. When racecourse commentaries were introduced, the Jockey Club decreed they should end before the closing stages of a race, so the 'race cast' didn't influence the judge. The commentator Raymond Glendenning mixed up the colours. He called Tudor Minstrel the leader up to the moment when his words were silenced. Radio listeners around the country celebrated. On course, Peter O'Sullevan couldn't believe he was watching the same race. He'd seen the early spring gallops at Chantilly and been told Pearl Diver, "Is a good 'orse." He invested, as he did so often and so profitably. His eyes were on Pearl Diver, his ears were hearing Tudor Minstrel, and he remembered thinking, 'He must be wrong.' Worse for the tens of thousands on the course and the downs, mostly relying on surges of rumour around them, not only were Pearl Diver's and Tudor Minstrel's colours alike: their respective race card numbers were 8 and 18. When the number 8 was hoisted, many thought from a distance it was 18: relief and enthusiasm were redoubled. Arthur Dewar had his disappointment made worse when people around him in the grandstand grabbed his hand and congratulated him.

The result was greeted with dismay. Richards was notably downcast, muttering only, "He didn't stay." The newspapers, so full of the Derby 'good thing' before the race, descended into gloom. French horses had won the 1000 Guineas and all three big races at Epsom. The *Daily Mail* ran a cartoon showing an angry-looking judge peering across his court. In the dock stood an assortment of contemporary 'British sporting failures': a cricketer, a boxer, a footballer, a golfer and a horse. No one needed telling who that was.

Fred Darling dropped Tudor Minstrel back in distance to a mile for the St James's Palace Stakes. Then he was tried at 10 furlongs in the Eclipse, where he re-met Migoli, who'd finished eight lengths ahead of him at Epsom. He led into the straight, pulling hard, but Migoli joined him two furlongs out and quickly went a couple of lengths clear. The race proved that Tudor Minstrel didn't stay a yard beyond a mile. Darling was on the point of retiring him when

Ascot announced a valuable new one-mile race at the end of September, to attract not only Tudor Minstrel, but one of the best sprinters seen for years, The Bug. Darling took the bait. The forgotten horse Petition joined in with two French raiders, one from the all-conquering Marcel Boussac yard, the other no more than a handicapper. Ascot's enterprise was rewarded with a big crowd. Tudor Minstrel made the running and quickened at the entrance to the straight. In a few strides The Bug, Petition and the Boussac horse were all floundering. As the crowd roared home Tudor Minstrel for the last time, Gordon Richards looked round at the furlong pole, saw no danger, and stopped riding. The unconsidered 33–1 outsider, a seven year old handicapper, ran on strongly and got to within two lengths. Its rider Rae Johnstone swore he would've won in another furlong. Johnstone was a heavy-betting Australian jockey. One day he was walking from the weighing room to the paddock, saw Peter O'Sullevan, tapped him with his whip and said, "Put me a monkey on this one." O'Sullevan was talking to two stewards at the time.

Phil Bull's assessment of Tudor Minstrel's last two races was that the colt had become the victim of over-keenness. By the Ascot race, Bull concluded, 'His optimum distance was no more than seven furlongs'.

> "But do not let anyone underestimate him on that account, nor be misled by the fact that his failures in the Derby and the Eclipse Stakes robbed him of his 'glamour'. At his distance, from five to seven furlongs, he was a really brilliant horse. So far as I know I have never yet described any horse [as] a world-beater, but, with this reservation about distance, I think I am prepared so to describe Tudor Minstrel".

Quintin Gilbey wrote a similar valedictory in *The Sporting Chronicle*: "I shall always remember Tudor Minstrel as the most brilliant horse of my time."

The longer-range view of Tudor Minstrel can be found in *A Century of Champions*, by the bloodstock expert Tony Morris and the racing historian John Randall. Their scope is the horses and trainers of the twentieth century; of Britain and Europe and worldwide. They take as their basis the end-of-season rating figure which Timeform introduced in its *Racehorses of 1948* annual [the successor to Bull's *Best Horses*] and which continues to the present day. Randall and Morris assess the form of all the prominent horses that ran between 1900 and 1999, in effect stretching Timeform ratings back to 1900. Their best-of-the-best list is:

Sea Bird [FR] (three year old in 1965)	145
Secretariat [USA] (1973)	144
Ribot [IT] (1955)	143
Brigadier Gerard (1971)	143
Citation [USA] (1948)	142
Hyperion (1933)	142
Tudor Minstrel (1947)	142
Mill Reef (1971)	141
Spectacular Bid [USA] (1979)	141
Bayardo (1909)	141

On Randall's and Morris's assessment, Tudor Minstrel was: "[The] third greatest [UK trained] flat champion of the century. [He] ranks even higher based on his devastating victories in the 1946 Coventry Stakes and National Breeders' Produce Stakes. His Derby failure should not overshadow his brilliant successes."

A new century has brought a new champion, Frankel. His Timeform rating of 147 is the highest the organisation has given to a horse. The work of Morris and Randall in weighing up horses from 1900 onwards – including those who never ran in Britain – indicates that Frankel would also have been the highest-rated horse of the whole of the last century. It's entertaining to speculate how the best horses from separate eras and countries would fare against each other. There can't ever be an answer, and some of the top horses probably wouldn't have met even if they'd been foaled in the same week in adjacent studs. Frankel raced only up to 10 furlongs and only in this country; Sea Bird ran all but one of his races in France, and was rated on his performances at a mile and a half. Either of them would've made mincemeat of Tudor Minstrel at distances beyond a mile. But would he have cleared away from them at that trip? The most enticing prospect would be, up there in the field of dreams, a challenge over a mile between Brigadier Gerard, Frankel and Tudor Minstrel, ideally at Newmarket, where each of them was such a brilliant winner of the 2000 Guineas.

When they review the fillies of the period, Morris and Randall nominate Pretty Polly as the best of the best, with a rating of 137. They place the French-trained Arc winner Allez France with Sun Chariot on 136, followed by 'the peerless' Sceptre on 135. The three English-trained fillies in that exclusive list all won their triple crown of 1000 Guineas, Oaks and St Leger; Sceptre won the 2000 Guineas as well. By placing Sun Chariot between Pretty Polly and Sceptre, Morris and Randall assert that in the space of five years, Beckhampton housed one of the best three fillies to race in England in the twentieth century – and one of the top three English-trained colts as well.

Finally, the authors weigh up the trainers. They write of Fred Darling, "In the Human Hall of Fame, [he] ranks second only to Vincent O'Brien among Trainers of the Century." To place Darling behind only the quiet genius from Tipperary is an extraordinary tribute. Fortunately, the writers make no attempt at a league table of twentieth century trainers' humanity, generosity or decency. Had they done so, Darling might not even be in the book's footnotes. He was a brilliant horse master but a cold, withdrawn, unlovely man.

Tudor Minstrel was the book-end to Fred Darling's long career. The horse was syndicated by Arthur Dewar as a stallion for £100,000. He wasn't an outstanding sire, but he did get a Kentucky Derby winner, Tomy Lee, in 1959, after which he was exported to stand in America. He sired a variety of Group-class sons in Europe, most of them an influence for speed.

Darling had nothing left to give. He was ill and exhausted. He'd talked often to Gordon Richards about the future of Beckhampton. Richards wanted to train from the yard. He told Darling he had a friend who'd put up the capital. Darling sensed Gordon wasn't ready to stop riding: he was still hungry, and there was unfinished business – including the small matter of a Derby winner. Darling asked his jockey: 'If not you, then who?' Richards, after much prompting, came up with a shortlist. One was a young north-country trainer about whom Darling knew almost nothing. Richards told him to look out for the man at Ascot. Darling was at the meeting for the last time as a trainer – a glorious adieu, with five winners, including Tudor Minstrel in the St James's Palace Stakes. He introduced himself to the stranger. Noel Murless had saddled the first two in the Britannia Stakes, the winner ridden by Gordon Richards:

> "I was in the weighing room waiting for Gordon to pass the scales when I felt a tug on my sleeve. I looked down and saw a face I knew well, although I'd never met [the man]. 'I'm Fred Darling,' he said. 'I'd like a word with you.' 'Certainly, sir,' I said, and we met after the next race.
>
> "He told me he was going to give up and asked whether I would consider moving to Beckhampton to take over from him. He said he thought that if I did, [Arthur] Dewar would buy the place and lease it to me."

It sounds a perfunctory way to recruit your successor, especially at one of the most successful yards in England. Darling had, though, every confidence in Gordon Richards' judgement, and Richards was riding all Murless' runners in the south of England when he was available. Darling watched Murless closely. He liked what he saw, including the man's attention to detail: he carried his runners' saddles himself, rather than delegate. Their talks moved to a swift conclusion. The first inkling came when Quintin Gilbey gave a nudge and a wink in *The Sporting Chronicle*: "[Noel] Murless' rise to fame has been one of the features of post-war racing. His brilliant training of horses has caused him to be referred to as the Fred Darling of the north." Ten days later, *The Sporting Life* caught up:

"A Newmarket report in circulation yesterday that Noel Murless [will] succeed Fred Darling at Beckhampton has not been confirmed. Mr Darling said, 'Nothing can happen about Beckhampton until I have given my word and that has not been done yet. When some arrangement is come to, I will make a prompt announcement.'"

The paper was able to flesh out its original report a week later. Fred Darling would be leaving Beckhampton in October, for health reasons. Arthur Dewar had signed a contract to buy the yard. Noel Murless was to be the fifth Master of Beckhampton. The yard's other owners, including the King, were happy with the arrangement and would support Murless. Gordon Richards would continue as stable jockey. The only detail missing was the price paid by Dewar: it was £60,000. Darling said, "I am grateful to all my patrons. Everything will go on exactly as before." He hoped, he added, "If my health permits, to take up residence at Beckhampton once more on my return from Kenya next summer." He had the satisfaction of ending the season as champion trainer for the sixth and last time, sending out 26 winners of 56 races, with his best-ever prize-money tally – £65,313 (£2,286,000 today).

'Porchey' had been asked by a friend, 'Is Fred Darling going to write his memoirs; can you encourage him?' He wrote back, at the time when Darling was in a sanatorium, "I do not think he is well enough to suggest anything to him of this sort at the moment, but I will do so when he gives up training in the middle of October." One Saturday that month, Porchey phoned Beckhampton to wish Darling well, only to find to his surprise that 'The bird had flown and I never had the opportunity.' He wrote that when his former trainer Dick Dawson retired from training, "I thought it dubious that I should have any fun racing in the future. I was quite wrong: I had 12 years during which I had the good fortune to be associated with Beckhampton." Fred Darling didn't write his memoirs, and he was never likely to. Communication was low on his 'to do' list. As Carnarvon's account shows, he didn't even make time for courtesy 'goodbyes' to his owners.

Darling threw a farewell party for his staff and set sail for South Africa, followed by an overland journey to stay with his younger brother Douglas in the Kenya highlands. There, it was hoped, his lungs would clear. He left a door ajar, telling *The Sporting Life* that he planned occasional return trips to supervise his Blacklands stud, and if he felt well enough after a couple of years away, he might even resume training. That was in the future: for now, the baton had been passed to Noel Murless.

CHAPTER SEVENTEEN

Noel Murless: first-season champion

A great trainer succeeded two others at Beckhampton in October 1947. Noel Murless arrived with his lads and his horses while Fred Darling was packing for Kenya. The handover wasn't entirely comfortable: Murless' northerners clashed with Darling's hardened scrappers. The incoming trainer admitted that while the Beckhampton lads were good stable men, "They were in general not the type that I like very much." The trainers joined forces to take Darling's star two year old, The Cobbler, to Newmarket for the Middle Park. Darling wasn't well enough to leave his car; Murless saddled the colt, who beat a small field, all out.

A few days later, Darling was on a boat to Cape Town and Murless was the Master of Beckhampton. His love of horses extended back to the first world war, and his early childhood in Cheshire. His father was away, serving in the Army and his mother worked full-time. His constant companion was a pony which he doted on. He hunted from the age of six. By his mid-teens he was riding work and schooling for small-time jumps trainers. His parents' friends the Peel family took an interest in his progress. Noel's first visit to a racecourse was the day in 1919 when Mrs Peel's horse Poethlyn won his second Grand National. The Peels offered to arrange for him to join Frank Hartigan at Weyhill, near Andover. Murless jumped at the opportunity; he was 18.

For all that he later called it a good life, Murless didn't unpack his suitcase in his first six months at Weyhill. As the yard's pupil-assistant and amateur rider, he had a little cottage, and was spared the primitive conditions of the apprentices, who slept two to a bed on straw mattresses. If they didn't react quickly enough when the head man appeared to rouse them in the mornings, he threw their clothes out of the window, regardless of the weather, and invited them to go fetch. Not that life under Hartigan varied much from other stables in the 1920s – including its emphasis on betting. Murless' education at Weyhill included watching his employer get one ready for a gamble: only Hartigan knew what weight each horse was carrying in a gallop:

> "The work riders would be weighed out beforehand so that Frank could make exact calculations. In his car he had weight cloths looking identical, but loaded with differing amounts of lead; only he knew how much. On the gallops Frank would allow no one else to handle those cloths. He alone would re-saddle each horse, placing the lead underneath and fastening the girth. Immediately the work was over he would whip off the weight cloths and drive away, leaving the lads guessing. Secrecy was of paramount importance. At Weyhill a lad would frequently look after a horse for several months without knowing its real name, so there was no chance of him talking about the horse outside the yard."

Murless' time with Frank Hartigan ended after he'd taken a heavy fall over fences. The next day, as he was weighing out to ride, the clerk of the scales asked him, 'Are you feeling all right?' 'No', replied Murless, he felt awful. The clerk stood him down and called for the trainer, who was unimpressed. Hartigan's brother Hubert was at the racecourse, and told Murless, "You come back to Ireland with me." Hubert Hartigan had about 60 horses in training, and Murless acted as a combination of secretary, head lad, assistant trainer and horse-breaker. His time in Ireland was shorter than he'd have wished, but Hartigan decided to move. At the time, duty was payable on

Irish livestock shipped to England; it was levied on the declared value of the horse or cow. Horse dealers being naturally cute, there were instances of valuable racehorses slipped through in the guise of moderate hunters. Scrutiny was tightened. Bringing on horses for sale was an important part of Hartigan's business, so he moved to England, with Murless in tow.

Their base was Penrith, and the gallops were in the grounds of Lowther Castle. Murless brought with him a horse called Eagle Hill, schooled him over fences, and was rewarded with some steeplechase wins – the most important being at Kelso, when another race on the card went to a young Scottish owner called Gwen Carlow. The pair met at a party after racing. It was at a turning-point for Murless; he'd made up his mind to take the plunge and apply for a training licence. Hubert Hartigan gave his blessing, and at the start of July 1935, aged 25, Murless moved with five horses to his first yard, Hambleton Lodge on the North Yorkshire moors. He had a windfall when he sent Eagle Hill to the sales and his horse was knocked down to Lord Derby for 800 guineas, having cost Murless £47. Then the new trainer received a bigger boost: Derby sent Eagle Hill back to him to train. In his first months with a licence, Noel Murless was patronised by the most famous name in racing.

In that first year, Murless trained one winner on the flat and his first jumps winner in December. There were several more jumping successes over the winter, and again one flat-race winner in 1936. The following season there were four winners, and then seven in 1938; these 11 comprised a seller, two lowly stakes races and eight handicaps. It was a slow, painstaking start, but the handicaps won in his fourth campaign included the Cecil Frail at Haydock and the Carlisle Bell. Murless was on his way. In 1939 he trained his first winner for Miss G Carlow, and four for Sir Alfred McAlpine, out of a total of nine. Murless' final winner of the season was ridden by a jockey with whom he'd become friendly during his time at Weyhill: Gordon Richards. Two days later, war was declared. Hambleton's peat gallops were requisitioned, and turned into a dummy airfield for German bombers to attack. Murless' staff and the younger among his owners joined the Army. He was turned down, the legacy of an injury from one of his rides for Frank Hartigan. He caught a foot in the wing of a hurdle: it was left pointing backwards. The doctors wired it up, but he had trouble with the foot for the rest of his life.

It was a difficult time for Murless. His yard had been closed. He had the chagrin of exclusion from military service with his friends and contemporaries. Racing was curtailed by the war, and National Hunt pretty well closed down. He moved with a few horses to Middleham, and after the 1940 season, in which he saddled just one winner, he married Gwen Carlow. She was an accomplished horsewoman, well known in the show ring for her success with her ponies and later her hunters. She arranged her summer holiday so that it coincided with a race meeting in Denmark which featured a ladies' Cup race. She won the race once and was placed in other years. It would've been difficult to draw up a better template for a trainer's wife. The two spent the next three years planning and hoping for the best. Murless reinvented himself as a Middleham farmer. He and Gwen invested in a few broodmares. In 1944 they signed a lease on The Cliff, a North Yorkshire stud farm. It was a punt not only on themselves but on a swift end to the war and the return of a full racing programme. Murless returned to training in 1943 with a couple of winners and edged up to five in 1944 and nine in 1945.

The next two seasons were eye-opening. The canny owners of the north of England sent him almost 30 horses. He responded by winning 34 races. Among them were his first winner in the south of England – at Epsom during the Derby meeting, and two at Newmarket. He finished in tenth place in that season's trainers' prize-money list. Inevitably that attracted new owners and more horses; he began the 1947 season with 41 in training. Three winners at York's May meeting were followed by his first success at Royal Ascot and his meeting with Fred Darling. During the season, Murless trained 32 winners, including the Stewards' Cup with Closeburn, home-bred at The Cliff. He was sixth among that year's trainers. If he felt any trepidation about the move to take over a major yard from one of the most successful trainers in history, he didn't show it. Luckily for him, his predecessor was far out of sight; not always out of mind, because the lads were inclined to mutter, 'Mr Darling wouldn't have done it that way.' Half a dozen of the animals he inherited from Darling were savage. When they were being groomed, they were held by three rack chains. If it occurred to anyone that being tied up while they were strapped and whisked might make them worse-tempered than they already were, no one had acted. Murless did. Two of the rack chains in each box were taken out; the worst of the savages were off-loaded. Life for the lads and the remaining horses at once became easier.

One or two problems didn't have easy answers. Murless' owners at Hambleton were local folk. It didn't matter that they liked and admired him, and wanted him to train their horses: Beckhampton was 250 miles away. The opportunity to visit their trainer's yard, to watch the gallops and to see their horses was reduced when Murless moved. There were also space constraints at Beckhampton. At the end of each flat season, yearlings would arrive from Arthur Dewar, from the Macdonald-Buchanans, from the National Stud to be trained for the King, from other owner-breeders. They had space set aside for them as if they were 13 year olds arriving at Eton. There weren't many boxes available for Murless' incomers. It was possible to make mistakes. A couple of yearlings arrived from one of Darling's owners and were led to empty boxes, only to have their way barred by a Murless lad who insisted, 'These are for us.' The horses were re-directed to Kingsclere: one of them turned out to be top class. The result of the coming-together of the two yards was that of the 41 horses Murless had in training in Yorkshire in 1947, and his two dozen owners, only seven horses and their owners followed him to Beckhampton.

The horses which Murless took with him provided ample testament to his skills. In the 1948 season six of the seven won races – eight wins in all, from 31 runs, a strike rate of better than one in four. However, their wins were mostly in little races, short on value or prestige. Darling had lured Murless south with the promise of wealthy owners, champion bloodlines and a posse of promising three year olds. He delivered in spades. At the end of his last season, Darling had an unbeaten two year old, The Cobbler, ranked second in the Free Handicap. He also passed on Queenpot, a brown filly by Big Game out of Poker Chip, a three-race winner whose best performance was beating most of the other good fillies by six lengths and more in the Lavant Stakes at Goodwood. Murless was at the meeting to win the Stewards' Cup with Closeburn; Darling saddled Queenpot and two other winners. The two men were invited to visit the Lavington Stud for a first look at the Macdonald-Buchanan yearlings. Three colts were brought out. Murless was drawn to a grey by Owen Tudor. Darling scoffed: "You don't want him. He's just a little rat." Murless asked for the colts to be turned out in a paddock, to watch them move. "Away they went, and it was then that I saw [a] wonderful action. I said to Fred, 'We couldn't possibly leave him behind!' He agreed." The little grey colt was Abernant.

Murless' first season at Beckhampton must've surpassed anything he could've hoped for. His classic hopes came to hand early. Queenpot won her prep race for the 1000 Guineas, beating fillies she'd been rated below in the Free Handicap. In the 2000 Guineas, The Cobbler disputed favouritism with My Babu, winner of the previous autumn's Champagne Stakes from Pride Of India and Queenpot. My Babu was 2–1 with The Cobbler at 100–30. That was how they finished, with Pride Of India in third.

Any disappointment Murless felt was set aside when Queenpot contested the 1000 Guineas two days later. Like her stablemate, she seemed to have one horse to beat – the Aga Khan's Masaka, who finished much closer to My Babu as a two year old than Queenpot, and had won a better trial race. Masaka was 9–4, Queenpot 6–1 – the proverbial each-way 'steal', given the running of My Babu and Pride Of India in the 2000 Guineas. The fillies' classic was decided at the start; Masaka dug her heels in and gave away several lengths. Gordon Richards kept Queenpot close up for the first half mile, and then set sail for home. In the last half furlong Queenpot's stride was shortening and two outsiders ran on to within a head and a length and a half of her. 'Another classic to Beckhampton,' headlined *The Sporting Life.* The Cobbler was dropped to five and six furlongs for his last three races that year, winning two. The remainder of Murless' first season at Beckhampton was headlined by his two year olds. The late Jeremy Hindley was Murless' pupil-assistant before training successfully himself. He said:

> "A great part of Noel's secret was that he could identify a classic horse incredibly quickly, far earlier in its life than anyone else. As a result, he would point it in that direction and start training it with the classics in mind at an early stage... It was quite obvious at evening stables which animals the Guv'nor fancied. I thought [one filly] was an appalling mover with very little class about her. But long before she'd done any work, Noel was high on her. Of course, he was right; she turned out very good indeed. If you have this sort of intuition, you can be like a schoolmaster and place the horse in the right stream."

Abernant made his debut at Lingfield. He was slowly away, green as grass, finished fast to be beaten a head, and went into the form book as, 'improved rapidly, unlucky.' He was unbeaten in five subsequent races, including the Chesham Stakes by five lengths, the Champagne Stakes and the Middle Park. The only time Murless tried Abernant properly at home was before the Champagne Stakes, to make sure he was ready to step up to six furlongs. Murless worked him with a three year old sprinter, Gold Mist. Abernant conceded 32lb worse than weight for age. Murless said, "Abernant won that gallop as he liked. He trotted up." So he did in the Champagne Stakes, beating a colt called Nimbus by six lengths. The gallop at Beckhampton had been one of those bits of work that dreams are made of: two days later, Gold Mist won the Portland handicap under 7st 12lb, suggesting the two year old Abernant would've won carrying over 10st.

As the back-end races approached and Abernant mowed down all comers, it became known that Murless had a Derby horse in mind: Royal Forest. He too came from the Lavington Stud's 1947 yearlings. He made his debut in a

Salisbury maiden at the end of May, clearly backward, but beat a decent field by three lengths and the same. He appeared next in the Coventry Stakes and beat Nimbus by a head, providing an obvious collateral form comparison with Abernant. Then he ran a shocker back at Ascot, and no one, Murless included, had any idea why, but he bounced back in the Dewhurst Stakes.

Abernant and Royal Forest were placed first and third respectively when the Free Handicap was published. Murless' success in most of 1948's top two year old races attracted a charming compliment from Atty Persse, one of the best exponents of a debut gamble – responsible, among many juvenile flyers, for The Tetrarch. Persse, by now in his 80s, leaning on sticks, approached Murless, peered over his half-glasses, eyes twinkling and said, "Young man, I like to win with my two year olds first time out. I don't want to run up against any of your hotpots. You'd better give me plenty of warning – tip me off!"

Noel Murless had a daunting role to fill at Beckhampton and he did so with aplomb. Fred Darling's last year ended as leading trainer, with 56 races won and £65,313 in prize-money. Murless surpassed both figures, with his own trainers' title, 64 races won and £67,046 in prize-money. The owners could be well satisfied, including the most challenging of them, Fred Darling himself. Darling left two fillies with Murless. One was a two year old, Feu Follet, who spread-eagled a field of 29 in a Windsor maiden plate. The other was Goblet, a three year old with just a minor-race dead-heat to show for her first season in training. Darling saw something in Goblet, because he passed her to Murless with some ambitious engagements. She won a nine-furlong stakes race at Newmarket before the Falmouth Stakes and the Nassau Stakes, both Group 1 events nowadays.

A few weeks after picking Abernant from among the yearlings at Lavington, Murless was at the Doncaster sales, where he bought a brown Bois Roussel colt for 4,000 guineas. Named Ridge Wood (out of Hanging Fall, by Solario), he ran only three times as a two year old in 1948, in minor races, twice placed. *Racehorses of 1948* had no time for Ridge Wood: "Will stay well and win races but is just a fair handicapper."

Murless' second season at Beckhampton was expected to revolve around Abernant. Phil Bull joined the official handicapper in rating Abernant as the best two year old of 1948. He timed Abernant at **1.32** fast: 'Very nice colt, has terrific speed. May stay the Guineas mile but is not certain to do so: top-class racehorse.' 'The little grey' lived up to almost every expectation, beginning in the 2000 Guineas. Asked, 'Will he stay a mile?' by Meyrick Good, Murless replied, "I wish I knew!" The interest and the betting revolved around Abernant, Star King and Nimbus. All three confirmed their well-being in trial races. The conclusions seemed favourable to Abernant; he'd beaten both his rivals as a two year old, and had clearly trained on. The betting was 5–4 Abernant, 9–2 Star King, and 10–1 Nimbus. What followed was a pulsating classic and a ride of brilliance – in defeat. Abernant was quickly away, speeding up the stands' side rails. He was never as far clear of his rivals as Tudor Minstrel had been two years earlier, but everything else was set on replay – the stable, the running style, the still figure in the saddle, the rivals floundering before half-way. The only horse within hailing distance of Abernant was Nimbus. Going down into the Dip, Abernant was still three lengths ahead. As they met the rising ground, his stride began to shorten. Charlie Elliott on Nimbus gathered in a length, then another. Richards sat quietly. Not once did he pick up his whip. Abernant, Nimbus and the line converged. It was the first time the photo-finish had been used in a Newmarket classic, and it showed that in the last yard, Nimbus had caught Abernant. Murless was as good a loser as he was a trainer:

> "Gordon rode the most wonderful race. He dared not move on the horse and he sat still until the last stride. Nimbus just collared him … If anyone but Gordon had been on him it would have been four or five lengths. It was yet another education in race-riding by a great champion."

Nimbus went on to win the Derby. Abernant never again ran beyond six furlongs. Thanks to Gordon Richards, he didn't receive the thrashing in the

Guineas that many a lesser jockey would've handed out, in a desperate attempt to win. Abernant had a hard race, but not a bad experience, and he repaid his tender handling from Richards in spectacular style. He ran four more times that season, and won each time. First in the King's Stand Stakes, when the form book's remark alongside the second horse – 'struggled on gamely' – tells everything about Abernant's four-length win. Then the July Cup, in which Abernant handed a merciless demolition to Star King, beaten 11 lengths. This race was the first to highlight a subplot to Abernant's appearances: many of the professional punters had taken the view that he wasn't for beating. No matter how short the odds were, Abernant was better than money in a deposit account. Odds of 1–2 equated to a 50 per cent return in a little over a minute. Abernant was backed from 1–3 to 2–11 in the July Cup. At Goodwood in the King George Stakes he was supported from 4–7 to 3–10, made all, and came home unextended. He ended his season in the Nunthorpe, where *The Sporting Life* betting report read, "Odds from 2–9 to 2–11 were heavily laid on Abernant," and he won in effortless style by five lengths. Timeform's *Racehorses of 1949* assessed Abernant as, "Without question the fastest horse in training, and a brilliant sprinter." His best time figure of 1949 was almost identical to his two year old rating: **1.31** fast. Timeform rated Abernant 8lb better than his Guineas conqueror Nimbus.

Murless' stouter-bred three year olds performed up to, or beyond, expectations during the season. Faux Tirage won the St James's Palace Stakes, before finishing third in the Eclipse, after which he was sold to New Zealand, where he was a successful stallion. Krakatao won four times at a mile, including in the Sussex Stakes. Royal Forest was the yard's Derby horse. He'd beaten Nimbus as a two year old, so after that horse won the 2000 Guineas, Royal Forest was made 7–1 favourite for the Derby. A few days later he made his seasonal debut in the Sandown Park Trial Stakes, where he routed five rivals. He was cut to 9–2 for the Derby. He handled the preliminaries well and reached the start quietly and calmly. Then there was a mishap which not even the crystal-ball gazers on the downs could've foreseen. A no-hoper put its foot through the reins at the start, and it took 20 minutes to extricate it. By then, it was as if Royal Forest had run four races. The sweat was pouring off him and his chance was gone. Nimbus won the Derby in a finish of bobbing heads; Royal Forest was five lengths behind the third-placed horse. He was put up as the short-priced favourite for the St Leger, but strained a tendon and was sold as a stallion to Argentina.

Ridge Wood brought Gordon Richards the embarrassment of perhaps the only public booing he experienced in his long career. It happened in a match. Murless rarely gave instructions to Richards, but that day he told his jockey not to make the running. The other rider had the same orders. When the tapes went up, neither horse moved. Some air-shots from the starter's Long Tom got the two horses shuffling forward, and that was about as fast as they went at any stage. The 'race' took more than twice as long as standard. Throughout, the horses and their riders were accompanied by jeering and catcalls.

Ridge Wood won five races in his build-up to the St Leger, most of them in small fields against mediocre opposition. It was a masterclass of placement by Murless. That year's St Leger wasn't the strongest of the race's renewals: the Derby form was represented by the third, Swallow Tail. He was favourite at 3–1. Next at 6–1 was Lone Eagle, winner of the Ascot Gold Vase and the Queen Elizabeth Stakes, followed by Musidora, winner of the 1000 Guineas and Oaks, at 8–1. Ridge Wood was backed from 18–1 to 100–7. Musidora and Ridge Wood were prominent from the start. The pair continued in the leading group to the entrance to the straight. With three furlongs to go, Musidora dropped away and Ridge Wood and Lone Eagle raced on together, pursued by Swallow Tail. Gradually Ridge Wood outstayed the other two, winning by three lengths.

Murless could rightly be thrilled by Ridge Wood's classic victory. It was all his own work, from picking the colt in the Doncaster sales to taking him back to Town Moor, via a softly-softly race programme, to win the race that every

Yorkshireman prizes – for a brewer from Tadcaster, Geoffrey Smith. Ridge Wood was Smith's third horse: "To think that I used to lie awake wondering if I'd spent too much money on the colt," he said. It was the culmination of another marvellous year for Murless. He didn't quite win back-to-back trainers' titles. He comfortably led in terms of races won, 66, but his prize-money total, £62,537, was behind the Newmarket evergreen, Frank Butters. In among all the winners of valuable stakes races, Murless trained The Cobbler to land a spectacular gamble in the Wokingham Handicap. He was set to carry 9st 4lb in the Ascot dash, conceding from 3lb to 41lb to 34 rivals. He was backed at 10–1 before racing. After he'd been drawn on the extreme outside of the field, he was the medium of a vast public plunge down to as low as 4–1. For half a mile, the draw seemed more of a curse than a blessing; Richards couldn't find daylight behind a bunch of horses hugging the far rail. Gradually he manoeuvred his mount to his left. By the furlong pole he was almost in the centre of the course. The gap appeared. The Cobbler breezed through it and won, unextended, by two lengths.

Of the 27 horses who Murless trained to win 66 races in 1949, 13 were two year olds. They won 25 races between them. The statistics implied that Beckhampton had a good base to build from in the following season. The statistics lied. The youngsters held out little or no hope for their three year old prospects. Five of the juveniles' 25 wins came from a single filly, expertly campaigned by Murless to win poor races at minor courses. There could be promise among the three colts with a profile of one run and one win each – until the form of their races was analysed. They'd run against donkeys. The best individual piece of form from a Beckhampton two year old was Forest Row's third in the Dewhurst Stakes. It wasn't so much that the stable didn't win any of the important first-season races; it simply didn't have horses worth running in them. When the Free Handicap was compiled, Forest Row was joint twenty-first, rated 16lb below the top of the handicap.

The following season was a crushing disappointment. Murless' total of winners fell to 47, his prize-money to £26,732. He was sixth among the season's leading trainers. There was little or nothing Murless could do about it. He was squeezing out winners at venues like Worcester, Folkestone and Wolverhampton, to keep his numbers up, but as can happen to any yard which depends on ammunition from its owners' studs, a year had come along when the bullets were blanks. He had the minor consolation of another brilliant series of performances by Abernant. His seasonal debut at Sandown provided Gordon Richards with his 4,000th winner. The flying grey went on to repeat his successes in the July Cup, the King George Stakes and the Nunthorpe. He was beaten only on soft going in the King's Stand Stakes, where the race conditions of the time required him to give 23lb (15lb more than weight for age) to a good three year old, Tangle. He failed by half a length. The trainer of the winner declared that the horse who could give Tangle 23lb 'hadn't been born.'

Assessments of Abernant are unanimous. In *Racehorses of 1950*, Timeform lifted the colt's time figure to **1.55** fast, placing him alongside the greats of any age and any distance. "An outstandingly brilliant sprinter," they concluded. On their ratings, he was the champion of his age-group in Britain as a two, three and four year old. Only Frankel has matched that in the last 65 years. James Park of *The Evening Standard* wrote that, 'Only the real champion can come out time and again and beat the watch, as Abernant did. None of the other sprinters of recent years recorded such fast times with the consistency of Abernant. When conditions were right he could set a pace which none of his generation could equal.' Tony Morris and John Randall placed Abernant first among twentieth century sprinters in *A Century of Champions*. Writing recently in the *Racing Post*, Randall has gone further, describing Abernant as, "The greatest sprinter who ever lived, [recording] a string of dazzling performances that went off the top of the handicap scale."

Noel Murless' daughter Julie Cecil remembers going into Abernant's box, lying on her back in the straw, patting his hanging-out tongue. Aged five, she was allowed to sit on his back, while he stood tolerantly, like an old hunter at the meet. When he went to the Macdonald-Buchanans' stud, he sired something over 1,000 winners, with many a grey among them. As could be forecast of a grandson and great-grandson of two scintillating speedsters, Mumtaz Mahal and The Tetrarch, he sired sprinters. As a rule, his daughters turned out better than his sons; his only classic winner was the 1962 1000 Guineas winner Abermaid.

CHAPTER EIGHTEEN

Disappointment, damp and Dewar

Noel Murless knew before the curtain rose on the 1951 season that he faced, at best, damage limitation. He described the day of the discovery that not only did he have a moderate batch of three year olds: the two year olds were hopeless. Gordon Richards tried the whole year group at the start of June:

> "Each lot worked worse than the one before. By the time we'd finished and got back to the house both Gordon and I were feeling so depressed that I decided to open a bottle of champagne. By the time we'd finished the second bottle the two year olds seemed considerably better. At the end of the third we decided there were definitely some high-class animals among them. As we downed the fourth there were classic prospects, Gordon was standing on the arm of a chair singing, as he usually does at a party, and I was laughing my head off helplessly. We sent for Herbert Blagrave to help us finish off the fifth and sixth."

Gordon's private aircraft was waiting to fly him to Shoreham, where he was staying for Epsom. His wife was waiting. The plane arrived five hours late, taxied to a halt, and Richards fell out head first. He rode three winners the following day. Murless had a whole season's suffering to endure. The two year olds were at least as bad as trials day had suggested. He managed his resources well enough to saddle 45 winners, all of them ridden by Gordon, for a total of £22,799 prize-money. He fell out of the top 10 in the trainers' list. He was also falling out of love with Beckhampton. The reasons were disappointment, damp, Darling and Dewar. Murless was a proper, courteous man but he was also ferociously competitive. He hated his career moving backwards, and he was stung by negative media coverage. The Press Association wrote:

> "The Beckhampton training establishment will have only one runner during the four days at Epsom this week. It must be a considerable time, if at all, since Britain's best-known stable has been so poorly represented at this important meeting. Almost every year it has had at least one runner in the two Classics there, and often it has provided either first or second favourite in the Derby. None of the Beckhampton three year olds has lived up to early promise, and the stable looks set for a very disappointing season."

As he cast around for the causes, Beckhampton itself was high on the list: "It was so cold and damp that I never really felt well." Murless suffered from a form of tuberculosis early in his life, and it resurfaced. His daughter Julie remembers that, "There was condensation down the walls of the house, and it didn't do his lungs any good." At the time, the Newmarket trainer Clive Brittain was apprenticed to Murless. He had a bed in the main dormitory: "It was always damp. If your bed was against the wall, the bedding was soaking wet by morning." Murless also had to cope with pain from the foot he'd injured in his riding days. It was prone to react to the weather. Then he contracted jaundice: "I feel so dreadful," he complained.

If Murless needed any reminding of the long-term effects of TB, he had only to cross the road to Willonyx House. Fred Darling's move to Kenya hadn't brought about any material improvement in his lungs, and he was bored. He came back within six months. All might've been well had he immersed himself in the Blacklands Stud and kept away from the yard – including from the fillies he had in training with Murless. Unfortunately, it wasn't in Darling's nature to leave well alone. He interfered with the training of his own horses, sending messages to Murless via Gordon Richards. He could be seen from the downs in an upstairs window of Willonyx, his binoculars focused on Murless and the gallops. 'Bloody Fred Darling,' his successor muttered. As Murless struggled during his third and fourth seasons at Beckhampton, the men's relationship soured. Darling sent his horses to his friend Jack Colling at West Ilsley.

Arthur Dewar was the last straw. He'd been an owner and breeder for more than 15 years when Fred Darling approached him with the suggestion that he should buy Beckhampton, but he wasn't a horseman. He hadn't shown any interest in the sport prior to the day when his uncle dropped Cameronian and a thriving stud into his lap. Dewar's life had been short of setbacks, and when Beckhampton's fortunes nose-dived in 1950 and 1951, he reacted badly. He seems not to have understood that a stable dependent on owner-breeders can't turn itself round in a year. He liked to dictate where his horses ran. He had a way about him that grated with people. When he inherited his uncle's goody-bag, he was asked, how did it feel? He replied:

> "I am old enough not to be excited about a million. I have handled large sums of money for so long that it's not nearly as thrilling suddenly to be a millionaire as people might think."

It happens sometimes that people begin as friends and end up unable to be in the same room. Dewar and Murless reached the second stage unusually quickly. Murless thought his landlord was difficult and unreasonable. The 1951 season turned out as expected – 45 races won and prize-money at a meagre £22,799. From champion trainer in 1948 and second-placed in 1949, Murless had dropped out of the top 10 two years later. The statistics concerning Dewar's horses told their own story. In the first two years of Murless' tenancy, he trained the winners of 33 races for Dewar, worth £18,739. In 1951, the respective tallies were 13 races and £6,112. The 1952 season held out promise of a revival. The two year olds seemed to be superior to those of the two preceding years. There were a number of lightly-raced three year olds. The best of them, Agitator, headed the Free Handicap and the winter betting for the 2000 Guineas. Better yet, he was owned, and had been bred, by Arthur Dewar. There was an opportunity to settle differences and move the yard forward again. Agitator won the Kempton Park Guineas Trial well and was a warm favourite at Newmarket in a field of 26, but finished only fourth. Meanwhile, the other three year olds were mostly winning their maiden races, but not progressing, and the juveniles disappointed.

Gordon Richards put it as diplomatically as possible: it was 'getting a little uneasy' at Beckhampton. 'Noel Murless was unsettled. Things weren't too easy for him, with the old Guv'nor fretting just across the road, and sometimes offering suggestions which he didn't want to take. And there were a few words between him and Mr Dewar.' At this juncture, Richards was asked by a prominent owner, Sir Alfred Butt, if he knew of a good trainer who might be prepared to take his horses in Newmarket, possibly with a few of the Aga Khan's thrown in? Richards and Murless 'Had a long and frank discussion about everything.' Soon after, Dewar phoned Murless and they argued. That was the tipping point. Murless at once told Richards that he was going to leave Beckhampton. The two men travelled to Paris to see the Aga Khan and his son Prince Aly. The Aga Khan agreed to send some two year olds to Murless for the 1953 season. The timing was fortuitous. Murless had a five-year lease on Beckhampton, expiring at the end of 1952. He went to Newmarket, visited Warren Place and bought it at once.

With his future secured, he gave Dewar notice. It was badly received. Dewar urged Murless not to tell anyone what was happening, and promptly wrote to Murless' other owners, in less than enthusiastic terms. Then he took pettiness to a nadir: he removed his dozen horses – from his own stable – and sent them to Druid's Lodge to be trained by Noel Cannon. It was Cannon's good fortune that Murless had been resting them during the summer months of firm and hard ground. They were big and well, and not far off being ready for a run. Cannon immediately started winning races with them. Dewar appalled Gordon Richards by telling him, "There you are! They're being trained now." The missing word was 'properly'. At least Cannon had the grace to say what marvellous condition Dewar's horses were in when they arrived from Beckhampton.

Noel Murless' five years at Beckhampton could have ended miserably; instead he had the public endorsement of the Aga Khan, followed by confirmation from his existing owners, bar Dewar, that they intended to follow him to Newmarket. Commitments included those from the National Stud – its horses now leased to Queen Elizabeth – and the Macdonald-Buchanans. A curious rationale was produced to explain his departure from Beckhampton. It was that, 'He needed to win at least £30,000 a year in prize-money to have a large enough percentage to clear his overheads.' This nonsense was accepted by a number of commentators who ought to have known better. Its implication was that Beckhampton was somehow incapable of providing him with enough income to feed and clothe his family. Yet in 1948 and again in 1949 he won over £60,000. The problem was lack of horsepower, not capacity.

Murless spent 24 years at Warren Place before passing the yard to his son-in-law Henry Cecil. By the time he stepped back in 1976 he was the best-respected member of his profession. He trained 19 classic winners – the same total as Fred Darling – and two more in Ireland. He said training was no magic art: "Just a question of hard work, observation and patience." He was remembered at Beckhampton for pottering around the yard in the quiet of the afternoon with a trug filled with carrots and dandelion leaves, getting to know his horses. Sometimes, he noticed that the occupants of adjacent boxes didn't get on; he'd move them, to minimise upset and stress. His target, always, was to create an atmosphere of calm, free from any sense of rush or urgency. Gordon Richards said that Murless, 'Only had to open the box door at night to know if the horse was right or wrong. He'd be out with the string in the morning and he could pick out one with a dull eye. He had that gift.'

The corollary to Murless' passion for spending as much time as he could with his horses was that he disliked going racing. He enjoyed seeing his horses run, but he thought the periods between the races would've been better spent in his stable yard. Instead, they provided opportunities for press men to bombard him with questions. He was a shy man, and the sight of a journalist homing in was low on his list of life's pleasures. Nonetheless, he answered questions with charm and patience. He was as considerate to his employees as his horses. Clive Brittain said, "He never forgot anyone and looked after his staff when they were sick and after they retired."

He was also capable of spotting those rare moments when the merit of a horse hadn't been appreciated by the odds-makers. For whatever reason, profile-writers queued up to claim, "He never bet," "He had no interest in betting" (*The Times*) and "[He is] totally uninterested in betting" (*The Biographical Encyclopaedia of British Flat Racing*). They were wrong. In his days with Hubert Hartigan, the yard had a horse called Wild Meadow. It made no impression in selling hurdles or middle-distance flat races. Hartigan gave it to Murless as a hack. By chance, Murless discovered that Wild Meadow was really a sprinter. He cleaned out the yard's two year olds, then the older horses. Hartigan entered him for a six-furlong seller at Stockton, and told Murless, "I'll back the horse for you." Murless thought Hartigan was planning a tenner. He had grander ambitions. He scraped together £300 (more than £18,000 today) and sent a friend to pepper the Stockton bookies. The friend backed Wild Meadow from any odds, down to 6–1. Murless was looking at a life-changing pay-out. The plot was scuppered by what Murless called, with heroic understatement, 'A somewhat moderate jockey' who got trapped on the rails, never found an opening, and finished so strongly that 'He actually pushed the bloody winner past the post!' Wild Meadow won six of his next seven races. Murless said the experience taught him there was no such thing as a racing certainty. There was a happier ending, 23 years later, when Murless was training the bad-legged but brilliant Crepello. Even before Crepello's two year old debut, he told his owner Sir Victor Sassoon that his colt would win a classic. Murless put £100 on Crepello at 66–1 with William Hill for the 2000 Guineas and Derby double. He picked up, in our money, £142,000. The Inland Revenue demanded to see the ante-post voucher. Noel Murless wasn't a punting trainer, but he did know a good thing when he saw one.

At the end of his career Murless said he'd been associated with four greats: Abernant, Crepello, Petite Etoile and Gordon Richards. Beckhampton provided two of them. He was champion trainer nine times, and he saddled over 1,400 winners. He was knighted soon after his retirement.

Fred Darling was horrified when Murless announced that he was leaving. He found retirement frustrating. His health steadily deteriorated; he spent much of his time in English and Swiss sanatoria. He kept as close a connection with racing as he could, with horses at Jack Colling's yard and the management of his stud. His doctor decided even that was over-tiring him, and he was ordered to the coast for a rest. He stayed in a hotel on the Sandbanks peninsular in Poole. Early on his first morning there, he heard the clip-clop of horses' hooves on the road below. To his surprise, it was a small string of racehorses. He'd stumbled on the unlikely training operation of the sometime bus driver Louise Dingwall. He was entranced. His recuperation was spent in Dingwall's yard, dispensing advice. Dingwall told him it was her life's ambition to have a runner in the Derby, and he, the trainer of seven winners of the race, sent her a colt to train for Epsom. The plan ended sadly – the colt was injured in a collision with a car and couldn't be saved – but it was part of a surprising development in Fred Darling's life: the martinet had softened.

The signs were clear in his changed relationship with Marcus Marsh, the nephew he'd sacked for betting without his say-so. Marsh was with Bomber Command when his plane was shot down over Holland, early in the war. In a prisoner-of-war camp at the end of 1941 he received a long-delayed letter from Fred Darling: "Have just won the Derby with Owen Tudor and I didn't have a penny on him." Food parcels and letters then arrived regularly, including in the spring of 1942, "I have one called Sun Chariot, who may prove to be the best I've ever trained." When the war ended, the gaunt Marcus Marsh was welcomed back to Beckhampton, where Darling housed him, fed him and insisted he took plenty of rest. When Marsh was recovered, he re-started his training career, supported by horses sent to him by Darling.

Darling even, at the end of his career, opened up a little to the press. Quintin Gilbey was asked by his editor to go to Beckhampton to find out what Darling's hopes were for the approaching season. The weather was miserable, with deep snow in the fields and ice on the roads. Gilbey's heart sank at the thought of driving to Marlborough. Hesitantly, he phoned. Darling had a heavy cold, and didn't want a visitor, but he told Gilbey to make some notes, and then rattled through his better-known horses, describing their condition and their targets. It was a stable tour by telephone. Gilbey's editor was delighted, and put the story on the paper's front page. There was never any question as to whether or not Gilbey actually went to Beckhampton: his expenses claim proved he had. The local newspaper reporter Bob Wise asked Darling for an interview. "He said yes, but he wasn't easy. He put you in your place. He only told me what he wanted to say. When I asked a question, he began every answer with, 'Young man.' I regarded him with a certain amount of awe."

Nineteen fifty-three was a year of celebrations. The new Queen's Coronation was held on the second of June, accompanied by news that the British expedition had made the first ascent of Everest. The racing world rejoiced in the news that Gordon Richards had received a knighthood in the Coronation honours list. It could only get better if, four days later, Her Majesty's colt Aureole were to win the Derby – and if he didn't, the alternative fairy-tale ending would be for Gordon Richards to end his long search for a Derby winner, on his twenty-eighth attempt. His mount was Pinza, a bay colt by Chanteur II out of Pasqua by Donatello II, bred by Fred Darling at the Blacklands Stud. Various mistakes and disappointments led up to the end product which was Pinza. His dam Pasqua had been bred by the wife of Darling's former owner, 'Manna' Morriss. In her first six years as a brood-mare Pasqua had only one foal capable of winning a race. In her seventh year she was barren, after which Mrs Morriss sent her to William Hill's French-bred stallion Chanteur II. No inspiration or planning was involved: she had a free nomination. Mrs Morriss entered the in-foal Pasqua in the December sales. By chance, the auctioneers sent the catalogue to Darling, who was wintering in South Africa. He liked Pasqua's bloodlines, and asked one of his owners to buy her, which he did, for 2,000 guineas. When Darling first saw her at his stud, he liked her a lot less. As soon as her large, clumsy colt was weaned, he sent the mare back to the sales. Darling wasn't impressed by her foal, either; he told a friend he had a colt with plenty of bone, who 'Might make a good 'chaser one day.' One of Marcus Marsh's owners called in at Blacklands to buy a yearling and was shown Pinza and another. He looked at the Pasqua colt's sprawling limbs and awkward action and chose the wrong one. Jack Colling and his wife Sue were shown 'a big ungainly-looking bay.' Darling told them, "He makes the place untidy. I don't think I can bear to go on looking at him. Let's go back to the mill and feed the trout!" Pinza went to the yearling sales, where Sir Victor Sassoon bought him for 1,500 guineas, and sent him to be trained by Darling's last head lad, Norman Bertie.

On the eve of the Derby, the Queen sent a message to Fred Darling. She wished him a speedy return to good health. She added that if any horse was to beat Aureole, she hoped it would be Pinza. Tens of thousands gathered outside Buckingham Palace to wave her and Prince Philip on their way to Epsom. A vast crowd cheered her progress down the course and her every appearance on the balcony of her box. They willed on her colt, Aureole. He was a good horse, but not as good as Pinza. After all the non-stayers he'd ridden, and all the times when he'd partnered the wrong horse to stay loyal to his retainers, Gordon was on a good, uncomplicated staying colt. He enjoyed that rarest of Derby rides, a wide gap down the inside turning for home, and won by four lengths from the running-on Aureole. Sir Gordon rode into the winner's enclosure looking almost glum. "When we got into the straight I knew I'd win. But why today of all days?"

Fred Darling was propped up in bed, listening to the radio commentary. Marcus Marsh reflected on his uncle's thoughts:

> "It was the straw to which he clung, the final task to be completed at the end of the day. I don't think he was scared of death, only of dying before Pinza's Derby had been run.
>
> "He had trained seven Derby winners and now he wanted to prove that he could breed one too. He wanted Gordon who had been his jockey for so long to win [the Derby] and I think too that he was propelled by a sense of destiny. He knew that Pinza was the last horse with whom he would ever be associated on this earth. So he wanted to go out on a high note. Even on his death bed, he wouldn't entertain the thought of failure."

Three days later, Fred Darling haemorrhaged and died. He was buried alongside his father, next to the porch of the church in East Kennett. There was a huge turn-out for his funeral. Sir Gordon was among those left standing outside. Prince Monolulu laid a white feather on the coffin. Darling's will included six gold cigarette boxes gifted to him by his owners and jockeys, including from Peter Beatty and Steve Donoghue. The painting of Sun Chariot was given to the Jockey Club. He left a long list of cash bequests, including to former lady friends, to his stud groom at Blacklands, and to his loyal chauffeur Bert Hampton. Marcus Marsh was left £2,000 and the Jockey Club Cup. All the domestic staff in service at Willonyx at his death received a year's wages. His long-serving yard man Jack Blake was gifted rent-free occupancy of his house for as long as he or his wife wished to live in it.

Arthur Dewar looked for a buyer for Beckhampton from the day Murless gave him notice. He found his man just up the road. It was Herbert Blagrave, the gentleman-trainer who lived at The Grange, a large property to the north east of Beckhampton, with a stable block converted from an old thatched barn. Blagrave was an enigmatic figure who combined great wealth with a determination to spend as little of it as possible on anything unrelated to his horses. He thought he might help the widowed Doris Blake by asking her to help out when he and his wife had visitors. He offered to pay her 1/6d an hour – £1.75 today. She declined. Blagrave owned, besides The Grange, a large house near Reading; the Harwood Stud near Newbury; the Mount Prospect Stud in County Kildare; and in 1964 he bought the village of Linkenholt and 2,000 acres. He employed his wife's nephew to run the Harwood Stud, but paid him such a pittance that the man could barely feed his family. Blagrave gave Ian Balding his first job, and explained to the future champion trainer that the nephew, "Wasn't paid very much, and as I was new to the job I couldn't be seen to be getting even that." Blagrave offered to pay his rent and his petrol, and £10 for every winner. Balding's mother was mystified: "It can't be a proper job without a salary; surely anyone who has a job gets a salary?"

Some rich people think everyone they meet wants to take their money. Blagrave was one of them. When the young daughter of a villager who helped out at The Grange asked him what it was like to be a millionaire – "Is it totally great?" – he replied, "I can do lots of nice things, but I'm never quite sure who my real friends are." His lifestyle was comically frugal. He seldom bought anything new, because it was liable to purchase tax; the 'nearly new' wasn't. His jackets had frayed cuffs and patches at the elbows. Maintenance at The Grange was put off until the last possible moment. Blagrave and his wife spent most of their time in one downstairs room, with a single-bar electric fire – an arrangement that can't have done much for her chronic ill-health. The cheeseparing extended to his treatment of his stable staff. One apprentice who rode his first and only winner on a horse of Blagrave's asked the trainer, "Have I got anything to come?" "Think yourself lucky you got a ride." Soon after Noel Murless arrived at Beckhampton, he put up his apprentices' wages by ten shillings a week; Blagrave told his own boys he hoped they weren't expecting him to do the same. Terry Stringer, who unlike most apprentices of the time became a successful senior jockey, rode work and winners for Blagrave. He used to be asked, “I’m a bit short this week, Terry. Can you wait until next week?” or, “I’m going to the Ailesbury Hotel tonight. I might need some cash. Will half your wages do for now?” Stringer was invited into the house one December. The Blagraves, he heard, were going to Barbados for Christmas.

> “‘Would you like a glass of sherry? It’s very expensive,’ he said, and rationed me to one glass. When I saw the bottle it was a cheap supermarket brand. But he gave me an envelope and inside was £100. That was a helluva Christmas box. Next year, after I’d ridden him one or two winners, I was counting the days, and sure enough, the conversation began, ‘We’re off to Barbados,’ and ended, ‘I’ve sent my driver round with your present.’ I couldn’t get home fast enough. I asked the wife, where is it? She replied, ‘It’s hanging in the hall; didn’t you see it?’ It was a brace of pheasants. I told her, ‘Be careful how you cook them – they’re the most expensive birds in Wiltshire!’”

He may have scrimped on many things, but Blagrave didn’t hold back where his horses were concerned. Ian Balding says: “He bred his horses at Harwood, he owned them all and he trained them.” Sir Peter O’Sullevan, whose friend Rae Johnstone rode numerous winners for Blagrave, said, “Blagrave had plenty of money, he indulged a hobby, he did his own thing. He was no mug: he had good people riding for him and he chose his staff well. He didn’t complicate it; he just fed his horses well and got them handicapped. He didn’t worry too much about the opposition.”

In his younger days, Herbert Blagrave was a noted sportsman: an enthusiastic football player, a cricketer good enough to play one first-class match for Gloucestershire, a winning rider in point-to-points and on the flat. His passion for football led to the chairmanship of Southampton FC. At the end of one season the club was relegated. The team’s star player was Mick

Channon, for years now a successful trainer, and even in his footballing days, no stranger to a stable yard. It was inevitable that Channon would ask for a transfer from his demoted club. Blagrave had a cunning plan: he gave Channon two broodmares.

> "One was barren. The other had no teeth, was difficult to get in foal and harder still to keep in foal. Eventually she produced a filly who never won a race. I suppose Herbert thought his gift would make it embarrassing for me to task for a transfer. After I realised what I'd got it didn't embarrass me one bit!"

Blagrave gave his horses all the time in the world. 'Big and well' is Mick Channon's recollection of the typical Blagrave runner, and Ian Balding's also: "He loved them to have several runs before they were fully fit, by which time they were usually well handicapped too." Balding became frustrated at what he saw as a waste: "These lovely big home-breds just weren't getting enough graft to do themselves full justice," and his verdict is borne out by the results Blagrave achieved. A haul of 350-odd winners is impressive in isolation. It's less so in the context of his taking out a trainer's licence in 1928 and holding it for over 50 years – with two studs to breed new stock, and up to 20 horses in training in any given year. On the other hand, Blagrave had a limited number of targets, principal among them Royal Ascot, and his record there was enviable. He won the Gold Vase in 1939 with Atout Maitre, a £3,000 buy from his friend and regular bloodstock provider Leon Volterra. Blagrave won the Hunt Cup three times, with Couvert in 1938 and Master Vote in 1947 and 1948 – the only horse to win back-to-back Hunt Cups. He won the 1947 Coronation Stakes with Saucy Sal, the 1950 Ascot Stakes with Honorable II and the 1951 Ribblesdale with Chinese Cracker; she might've been the best horse he trained, finishing as she did second in the 1951 Oaks after a barging match. He also had horses placed in the Derby and the St Leger.

Blagrave had a vivid turn of phrase, often based on a simile from the animal world. At Kempton he pointed to a fellow trainer: "There's Bill Marshall, clinging to the bar like a swallow to its nest." When a jockey got trapped in a pocket riding one of his horses, he described him as like, "A chicken caught in wire netting." And after sitting next to Harold Wilson in the Royal Box at Wembley, he said the prime minister resembled, "A hare lying in its form, looking out of the backs of its eyes, waiting to bolt."

Herbert Blagrave would ordinarily be no more than a footnote in racing history, but after his death his well-attested scrimping was turned on its head. He left everything to a trust which makes grants to charities helping young people, in those counties of southern England to which he was linked. In the most recent financial year it disbursed £1.6 million, and it expects to continue at that level into the future.

CHAPTER NINETEEN

The mysterious Colonel Warden

Dick Warden's life was lived mostly in the public eye – as an amateur rider, trainer, owner, Master of Hounds and bloodstock agent. Yet he was a mystery: widely known, but hardly known at all, summed up by one acquaintance as 'phenomenally elusive'.

He was born Richard Bell to British parents who divorced almost before their banns were read. His mother's second husband was a wealthy American, Bert Warden, with the result that Dick's prep school was in California rather than the Home Counties. When he was 13 his mother changed his surname to Warden by deed poll. He came back to Britain for his senior school, Harrow, where he won academic prizes in consecutive years. Re-crossing the Atlantic, he started an Agriculture course at Cornell University, but didn't complete his degree. He spent most of his time with his stepfather's relatives in Connecticut – 'racing and polo and hunting,' he said. It was a gilded youth. He described travelling to Ireland 'for pleasure – mainly fox hunting – and on business connected with horses.' Besides which, he visited a number of countries, including Argentina, 'To stay with friends and to observe horse-breeding and racing.' His stepfather had a property in the Bahamas, from where his parents' yacht sailed the Caribbean.

The lifestyle didn't encourage thoughts of a nine-to-five job, and when Warden came back to England, he enrolled at Cirencester for a veterinary course: it was clear he'd decided his livelihood was going to come from horses. Despite the wealth conferred on his mother by her second marriage, he needed an income, because she wasn't a reliable provider. He was cast in the unhappy role of remittance man, his mother controlling the purse-strings like a faulty tap, with long periods of drought followed by sudden, short streams. For most of his adult life, Warden's fortunes swung between boom and bust. The only certain time of plenty was his mother's annual sortie across the Atlantic, when her accounts at Harrods and Fortnum & Mason were activated. For that month each year, Warden's existence was transformed from hard tack to champagne and caviar.

Warden decided that bookmakers should contribute to his expenses during the fallow months. Aged only 23, he had a small string of horses in training with Ivor Anthony at Wroughton. He insisted on partnering them in their work, and dictated their running plans. He was an amateur with one or two wins in point-to-points, he'd never ridden a winner under rules, and he rode in spectacles: he was the first jockey that most punters would put a line through. In April 1931 he rode his horse Laudamus in a big-field handicap hurdle at Chepstow. None of the newspaper tipsters mentioned the horse. Unknown to them and to any bookmaker within 300 miles, Warden had men in place to work an SP commission in Scotland. Laudamus was returned at 100–6. Warden had paid for the keep of his horses for the season and more, and he struck again when another of his horses, Young Buck, ran at Newbury early in 1932. Like Laudamus, he was ignored by the tipsters in *The Sporting Life*. Warden played to the gallery in the paddock – blinking behind his glasses, stirrups at ground level. At the exit from the paddock, he leaned down and told Ivor Anthony he should bet his maximum. Warden flapped to the start like a cavalry trainee. After that it was all business: he pulled his leathers up many notches, rode a hold-up race like the coolest professional and led at the last hurdle to win by four lengths, going away. The bookmakers weren't wholly unprepared this time; the horse was only 8–1 in a field of 23. *The Sporting Life* headed its report, 'American Student's Success,' which suited

Warden perfectly. The stereotype of casual visitor was ideal for future punting. He showed how serious he was by finishing third among the amateur riders with 10 wins in the season. He had a bad accident the following year, and after a spell working at one of the Lambourn yards, he set up his own small training operation with a dozen or so horses at Barrett's farm in nearby Eastbury. He shared digs with Fulke Walwyn, who rode all the horses.

It was a scene of permanent chaos, mostly financial. Interludes of living high on the hog after a win were followed by regular visits from the bailiff. In those days the collector's instructions were to occupy a defaulter's home or office until all debts had been paid. Nothing could have prepared the man for dealing with Warden. He and Walwyn had no money; furthermore, the bailiff was a pleasant enough chap, and they didn't mind him staying. As the days passed, he found himself integrated into the household, helping with the cleaning, even cooking a meal. He withdrew, baffled, after which the landlord lost patience. It was something of a relief to Walwyn when Warden went to France as assistant to the Chantilly trainer Jack Cunnington. Not that the two men had fallen out; Warden was best man at Walwyn's first wedding, and godfather to his daughter. The problem was Warden's unreliability. In the kitchen at Eastbury, he'd say, 'I'm just going out' and disappear for a week or more, before returning as unexpectedly as he'd vanished. No one had any idea where he'd been; hunting, most likely. The men's roles reversed, with Walwyn taking up training, while Warden rode for Cunnington in amateur races in France.

Warden stayed in Chantilly for three years, a remarkably long period considering his attention span. Among his experiences was an afternoon when he fell in a 'chase, far out in the country, and pretended to be injured so as to get a ride back in the ambulance. All went to plan until the vehicle reversed up to the Red Cross hut and braked sharply. Its back door hadn't been properly shut and Warden was fired out of the back, head first, strapped to a stretcher. He claimed he was nearer death than in any steeplechase fall. Not long after, German tanks rolled into France. Warden's employer sent him south to Spain with his best filly, and the story goes that he scrambled onto the last boat leaving Bordeaux. On his return he joined up as a private in the Army. A widely-travelled Old Harrovian who spoke perfect French and good Spanish must've stood out among the rank and file at Warminster. Within weeks he was transferred to the Intelligence Corps, and after another three months the Special Operations Executive recruited him. When he filled in the SOE forms and came to the section asking for 'other interests,' he wrote:

> "Hunting, racing, all outdoor sports and country life, travelling, yachting. Casinos and nightclubs when the aforementioned are unobtainable."

Under 'Any private means?' he replied: 'Any necessary money comes from my family, who are of considerable independent wealth.' As for his physical condition, he offered: "[Have] had several accidents steeplechasing, but now fit." Many people remember Dick Warden, and he never told any of them anything about his service with the SOE. His later colleague David Minton says, "He was a secretive man. He never spoke about the war at all." The retired trainer John Dunlop adds that Warden, "Never let his left hand know what the right was doing." His friends assumed that since he was fluent in French, Warden had been involved with parachute drops into occupied France. Indeed, he joined raiding parties, but there was much more to his war record. He was involved in maintaining secrecy around the Shetland Bus, the covert small-boat crossings of the North Sea between the Shetlands and Norway, carrying agents and supplies to the Norwegian resistance. Warden was also responsible for security at the manor house in Dorset where SOE men attached to the commandos trained for raids on the Channel Islands and the French mainland. On occasion he took part in the raids himself. They were designed to force the enemy to tie up troops defending every conceivable coastal target.

For a time, Warden lectured at the Beaulieu spy school. When the local GP was called to Beaulieu, Warden 'charmingly warned him that when he stepped through the door into the house he would be entering another world and one which, afterwards, he would have to forget.' Later, Warden was responsible for SOE's liaison with MI5; and only two years after being head-hunted by SOE, he was put in charge of its operational security, which included a number of high-level interrogations. His success was confirmed when two senior German intelligence officers were captured in 1944, and overheard moaning to each other about their failure to place an agent inside SOE's headquarters. Warden's last assignment was in Paris, with a team winding down the SOE's network of agents in France.

Warden's war record shows bravery and accomplishment. He progressed from a private soldier at the start of 1941 to Colonel by the end of 1944. His superiors' confidential reports were fulsome:

> 31 December 1942: "He is alert and sophisticated. He can be trusted to carry out any job with intelligence, assiduity and resource."
> 2 November 1943: "I take an exceptionally good view of his ability and intelligence. He is very able."
> 22 December 1944: "A most live and intelligent officer whose knowledge of the world and outside interests have fitted him for the work he has performed so well."

Another report card described Warden as 'unorthodox,' which was a fair description of his post-war life as a racehorse trainer. Between his de-mob at the end of September 1945 and the start of the following flat season, Warden assembled a team of 24 horses in Newmarket at the La Grange stables. He also cleared the slate with his creditors. All through the war, he had a bankruptcy judgement hanging over him. Early in 1946 it was rescinded: 'All proved debts and costs have been paid in full.' So Warden started his delayed third season as a trainer free – temporarily – from money worries. He also had the support of Peter Wentworth-Fitzwilliam.

Earl Fitzwilliam owned 90,000 acres in County Wicklow, and the largest private house in Europe, Wentworth Woodhouse in Yorkshire. Fitzwilliam also had horses in training with Walter Easterby, and it was through Fitzwilliam that Warden met the Easterby family; they became his lifelong friends. Warden was to all intents and purposes the private trainer to the Fitzwilliam family for his first three years at La Grange. The connection ended suddenly and tragically. Fitzwilliam died in a light aircraft crash in the south of France. He was in a complicated relationship. He, a divorced Protestant, hoped to marry the widowed Kathleen Marchioness of Hartington, sister of John F Kennedy. The Roman Catholic Kennedy clan were implacably opposed. Fitzwilliam booked a plane to fly himself and Kathleen to France, in search of her father's blessing. The plane broke up in a thunderstorm.

Despite Fitzwilliam's death, Dick Warden's stable strength leaped to 45 in 1949, which made his string one of the largest in Newmarket. The reason for the increase was that La Grange was sold by Fitzwilliam's executors to a leading owner-breeder, Major Lionel Holliday; his horses were added to Warden's string. The Major was an opinionated and overbearing man, who changed his trainers frequently. One of them was Geoffrey Brooke, who found himself under attack for the running of a filly at Ripon. Not only had the filly run badly, Holliday thundered, but 'A friend of mine was there and he says she looked awful.' 'Really?' replied Brooke, 'I didn't know you had any friends.' Dick Warden didn't linger to savour the Holliday experience; at the end of that season he moved the short distance to Kremlin House. At the time of the move, he took on a young man called Jeremy Tree as his assistant. It was an unusual hiring, insofar as Tree had no racing credentials, and a physique unsuited to riding. He was, though, well connected, and a year later Warden was training 50 horses, the most that he ever did. Before long, his owners included his assistant's parents, Michael and Lady Anne Tree. He had horses from the Fitzwilliam family, and the name 'Miss M Sheriffe' appeared as an owner for the first time.

Everything seemed set fair. So many owners wanted to have horses with Warden that the 1952 season began with all Kremlin House's boxes full again.

Jeremy Tree moved to a yard nearby, holding the licence in his own name. All that Warden needed was a good winner or two, and they were thin on the ground. Ironically, one was for his own assistant: Tree's Rumpelstiltskin in the Bessborough Stakes. Warden had a keen interest in the Lincoln handicap. He saddled the second-placed horse in successive years. His first try was with Clarion III, who was backed down to 100–9 favourite to beat the largest field assembled for a British flat race: 58 runners. He nosed ahead at the furlong pole, but found one too strong. Back on the Carholme course at the start of the next season, Warden's Lincoln hope was Goldsborough. He too led a furlong out, but was outpaced. Goldsborough and Clarion III were each beaten by two lengths. Over the years, as Warden retold the story of his near-misses, the distances were whittled down to heads and short-heads.

The roll-call of Dick Warden's successes was disappointing, despite him having knowledgeable owners, plenty of horses and an equal amount of goodwill. The reason he made so little mark as a trainer was plain: his heart wasn't in it. Jeremy Tree said:

> "I don't think he was temperamentally suited to being a trainer. He was a restless character, almost impossible to pin down. Most of the time I was with him was spent trying to keep owners at bay who wanted to know where he was."

Fulke Walwyn's widow Cath says, "You could never make any plans with Dick – not even for the next day. It was hopeless." It wasn't surprising that his owners ebbed away during the 1952 season. Then it was announced that Noel Murless was leaving Beckhampton and going to Newmarket. Warden and Tree made the reverse journey. They divided Beckhampton, with Warden taking the main yard and Tree the top yard. They shared the stable office. The double move was puzzling, because Warden had made it clear where his priorities lay; the moment he heard that the scent was good and hounds were running, he was off.

Once their move was complete, the pair began the 1953 flat season with depleted resources. Tree had 14 two year olds and 10 horses aged three and over. Warden had 20 horses, half of them two year olds, and against the odds, seven of his previous owners gave him another chance. Without question, he could do the job well enough when his mind was on it. Wilf Morris joined Warden as an apprentice at Kremlin House and followed him to Beckhampton. He recalls the trainer as, 'A nice fella who treated everyone well. The grub was good and my pay compared well with most other yards.' One morning he was told to take an unraced two year old called Tormentor II up to gallops. Alongside him was the stable's head lad on a three year old who'd won a race the previous summer.

> "At the top of the gallop, Mr Warden was waiting with a racing saddle for me. I had no idea what weight was in it. He told us, 'I want you to come up to me as strongly as you can, just let them run in your hands,' and my two year old finished in front by a neck. 'Keep that under your hats,' was all that Mr Warden said afterwards."

Wilf naturally told everyone he knew, but most of them pooh-poohed his story, so when Tormentor II made his winning debut a fortnight later in a selling race at Hurst Park, he started at 100–7. Afterwards Warden gave his apprentice a big white £5 note. He had another coup a few weeks later with a moderate five year old at Chepstow, ridden by the 3lb claimer Jimmy Lindley. Both the winning horses were owned by Warden himself. As outside owners dropped away, he was increasingly left training his own few animals, with weekly bills to pay and his main income source his capricious mother. He stuck it out until the end of the 1954 season. He probably saw the light when he was called in by the stewards at Manchester over the running of one of his horses. Its jockey Manny Mercer told the veteran yard man Jack Blake that, 'I could've won by a street if my orders had allowed me to.' Blake asked Warden, "What are you keeping that one for,

Guv?" Warden tapped his nose, but he knew his scope for plotting with the horse had vanished, and perhaps his hopes for laying out the others for a touch, too. Wilf Morris brought down the curtain on Dick Warden's training career when he took Warden's last two horses to be trained by a friend in the Midlands. The inexperienced Jeremy Tree was left at Beckhampton as the successor to three of the greatest racehorse trainers: Sam Darling, Fred Darling and Noel Murless.

Dick Warden had no job and no regular income. He went to Argentina soon after. He knew the country from pre-war visits and he spoke Spanish. Other than that, no one was sure why he was there. Some of his friends assumed it was on a Nazi-hunting mission for the Secret Service. That can be discounted: he'd left SOE 10 years before and there's no trace of him retaining a connection. The only people left looking for war criminals were the Israelis; the British intelligence services had long since turned their attention elsewhere. Another explanation was that Warden had a commission to supply stallions and broodmares for Argentina's bloodstock industry. That was entirely possible. The most intriguing explanation for his presence was that he'd been invited by the president, Juan Peron, to manage and develop the racing interests of Peron's wife Evita. Warden's friend Johnny Harrington said:

> "He was in Argentina to be Peron's racing manager (*The timing was dreadful: Peron was ousted by a military coup*). Dick was planning to fly out to Uruguay in a private plane. There were two others waiting with him. Suddenly some security people barged into the room. Dick feared the worst, but they took away his fellow passengers. He was left to escape the country."

Harrington had an unsentimental view of his friend, saying, "I should think he was a terrible trainer." Warden had been on the last boat out of occupied France and the last flight out of a civil conflict in Argentina. The hedges and ditches of the Ledbury country must've been a blessed relief. He was the Ledbury Hunt's Master for five years, followed by a similar period as Master of the Vale of the White Horse. Peter Walwyn, trainer of Grundy and starter of races at the VWH point-to-point, remembers that Dick Warden 'rode like a bullet through a country.' Former VWH hunt servants say, "He was brave – especially as he couldn't see anything." At the start of one season, Warden had a new mount. The first time he asked it to clear a fence, it turned a somersault. Warden was on the ground, groaning, his glasses smashed. The local farmer took him to hospital, where they tried to keep him overnight. No, he told them as he limped out: 'I have to organise tomorrow's hunt.' Mastership was time-consuming and expensive. The full season, in which the VWH hunted three days a week, spanned five months, preceded by three months of hound exercises and cub-hunting. No wonder, as Ted Dibble of the VWH says, "Warden organised his life around his hunting. He might have to go to Newmarket for a day, but he made all his appointments on non-hunting days." As for expense, the Master supplied horses for the hunt staff. That meant perhaps 14 horses a season for the VWH at the time, and Warden 'Provided super horses, usually showjumpers who hadn't quite got to the top.' He also bought horses from the Easterbys, with a £75 ceiling. Inevitably, money was tight:

> "He was very good to the staff at the kennels and in the stables [but] there was a summer when all the volunteers who stopped up the foxes' earths were complaining they hadn't been paid for months. I told the Colonel, 'The earth-stoppers need paying.' He had a faraway look: 'Oh, I must do that sometime.'"

Warden spent a decade hunting without cease, including frequent visits to Ireland to ride with the Louth and Meath packs. He was a welcome guest in every big house, because he was a knowledgeable horseman and he had a vast fund of stories and gossip. Many an Irish country house had a room on standby for Warden, and a pair of his half-length wellington boots in the hallway. He left them like a calling-card; he was nicknamed 'Gumboots.'

The job offer came out of the blue. His hunting friend Peter McKeever had taken on the chairmanship of the Curragh Bloodstock Agency, and he invited Warden to combine business with pleasure. Apart from the war years, it was the first time in his life that Warden had enjoyed a regular salary, with the added attraction of a base above the CBA's offices in Newmarket: 'the Colonel's room.' As might be expected, Warden had his own views about buying horses. He liked animals that looked like show horses, almost irrespective of pedigree, and he was prejudiced against a tooth-grinder: 'Shoot it!' he'd bark. But the bloodstock agents David Minton and Johnny McKeever concur that Warden was an excellent judge, 'as canny as you could find.' Behind the glamour of the big sales, an agent's work can involve fairly humdrum assignments: one such was the supply of horses to Dubai's police force. 'Dark bays only,' it was stipulated. On his return to England, Warden told colleagues that he'd met a charming young Arab who might take an interest in racehorse ownership. That meeting changed racing forever, because the young man was Mohammed bin Rashid Al Maktoum: Sheikh Mohammed.

In the early years of the Sheikh's and his brothers' involvement in racing, some of the less scrupulous people in the racing and bloodstock world took them for a ride: ran them up at the sales, sold them pups. One of the Maktoums' closest associates says simply of Warden, "He was honest," and that led to a relationship with Sheikh Mohammed that lasted up to Warden's death. The first horse that Warden bought for the Sheikh was the precocious Hatta, who won four races in 1977, including the Molecomb Stakes. Warden took pains to steer Mohammed to good trainers, like Fulke Johnson-Houghton and Hatta's handler, John Dunlop. When the scale of the Maktoums' ambitions escalated, and they flew to Keeneland to buy the world's best bloodstock, Dick Warden was a key part of their team. He advised them on breeding and bloodlines, he was the bidder in the dramatic head-to-heads with Robert Sangster's syndicate, and he signed the tickets afterwards. He was described as sitting directly opposite the auctioneer, "Like an inscrutable oriental, nodding with the expressionless inevitability of a fully-wound metronome."

There were hiccups, of course, none more than when a titanic duel ended with his $10.2 million bid for a Northern Dancer colt. It was the highest price ever paid for a thoroughbred at auction. Alas, the colt was so slow that it wasn't risked on a racecourse – and then proved infertile. But the Maktoums were in a hurry, and they could afford the setbacks, however costly. Warden stuck to his belief that the quality of the horse came first; "Ideally that should be combined with good breeding, but I would never, unless ordered, buy a well-bred [but] bad individual. The stock must have a record of soundness, too. It's all fairly *pons asinorum,*[2] you know," he told a perplexed journalist.

A week after he'd been buying in millions at Keeneland, he was at a minor National Hunt sale at Doncaster. Tony Morris said it was strange to see him at such a lowly event. "Not at all," replied Warden, "I just love attending horse sales. I'll be at a sale of New Forest ponies next week." He was well into his seventies when his mother died. The doctors asked him, should they put her on a life support system? 'God, no. Pull the plug.' She had, after all, watched him take a purler at the water jump in a Grand National and asked him if it'd been necessary, 'To fall off right in front of my friends?' The outcome of his – at last – inheriting her fortune were that he segued, overnight, from the years of dodging his creditors to becoming a tax exile. He bought a house on the Isle of Man, as close as possible to the airport. It seems to have been the only home that he owned in his long, nomadic life. He spent as much time as he could with the Easterbys, and he was able to buy a few more horses for Peter Easterby to train and his son Tim to ride in amateur races. Among his better horses were Felipe Toro, who won the Portland Handicap; the durable Karenomore, who won 15

2 A problem which separates a quick thinker from a slow one

times over hurdles and fences; and Jobroke, a winner at the Cheltenham and Aintree festivals. Warden disliked Cheltenham. It took his trainer a while to persuade him to run Jobroke in the County Hurdle, "By which time the price had gone," chuckles Peter Easterby. It would be hard to imagine a cleverer owner-trainer team than Warden and Easterby. The Colonel continued to enjoy a bet, and Easterby seldom failed to deliver. The winnings would be put aside to pay for the next batch of yearlings. Warden's colours – jade green, flame hooped sleeves and black cap – were left to Tim Easterby, so there's a continuing reminder of Dick Warden on the racecourse to this day.

In his last years, Warden suffered from chronic ill health. Sheikh Mohammed stepped in and provided a plane to fly his old adviser to America and to Switzerland for treatment before Warden died, aged 82, in 1990. The valedictories from the people who knew him focus on his ability to make others laugh. John Dunlop says, "He was the most entertaining man I've ever known, the best company you could imagine. He had an amazing turn of phrase." The former Goffs and Phoenix Park director Jonathan Irwin rated Warden as, "Hysterically funny, a great character. He lit up any party – he sang for his supper. He was a lovely man, a force for good: and a wonderful judge of a horse."

True to form, Warden's last words were, "Rain has stopped play."

CHAPTER TWENTY

Sir Gordon Richards: too kind for his own good

Dick Warden's decision to quit training at the end of 1954 left an opening which was tailor-made for one man – Sir Gordon Richards. After his knighthood and Pinza's Derby, he finished 1953 as champion jockey for the twenty-sixth time. The following August he was injured when a horse reared over backwards in the paddock and rolled on him, fracturing his pelvis and breaking ribs. It was clear that he wouldn't be able to ride again until late in the season, when his owners' good horses would've been put away, and the jockeys' championship relinquished. He announced his retirement. Even before the accident he'd talked to friends about calling it a day and turning to training. The journalist Quintin Gilbey implored him to go on for another season or two. He pointed out that Sir Gordon hardly had a grey hair on his head – 'But it'll all be snow white after you've trained for two years!' Richards pressed on with his plans, including talking to Herbert Blagrave about Beckhampton. Then he was injured. Soon after, Dick Warden decided to stop training; the necessary vacancy had been created. Jeremy Tree moved into the main yard at Beckhampton; Sir Gordon took over the top yard. He was up and about in time to be at the Doncaster sales, buying yearlings.

He started his training career in 1955 with a complement of 30 two year olds. His first owners included the ship-owners Stavros Niarchos and

Basil Mavroleon, the Irish owner-breeders James and Meg Mullion, and Dorothy Paget; she provided a third of Richards' string. She was the only one of the former Beckhampton owners to support him; others had died and the rest were settled with Noel Murless at Newmarket. There was also a widespread feeling at the time that top jockeys, especially flat jockeys, didn't make top trainers. And there'd never been a jockey like Gordon Richards. He became champion for the first time in 1925, the second season after riding out his claim. In the next 28 seasons, he was champion again in every year but three. Once he lost the title by one winner, to Freddie Fox. In the other two, he was ill or injured; in 1926 he missed almost the whole season when a tubercular patch was found in his lungs. Mercifully, a long spell in a sanatorium cured him and the condition never returned. It did, though, rule him out of military service, allowing him to ride all through the war. He retired having won 4,870 races with an almost 23% strike rate. He rode over 200 winners in a season 11 times. In 1933 he set a world record of winning 12 consecutive races: the last at Nottingham one day, followed by all six at Chepstow the following day and the first five on the same course the day after.

All his records were set in an age of much less racing, no helicopters, no evening meetings, no jockeys' agents, no Sunday racing, and no all-weather courses. It's true that much of the time he was on the best horses, but he'd earned that, and he put plenty of effort into ensuring that he was fully occupied. Sunday mornings he was in the pigeon loft. Sunday afternoons he spent with the calendar of the next six days' racing. He knew where and in which races his retainer for Fred Darling would take him, and he combed the calendar for potential winners in the other races. Then he phoned owners or trainers without retained jockeys, asking for the rides on the horses he liked. Naturally, the recipients of these calls were thrilled to have him riding for them. He was probably the first jockey to hunt systematically for outside rides in this way, and he had a priceless advantage: for the first part of his career he rode at 7st 7lb. Even in his last season, aged 50, he could do 8st 2lb. He could take lightweight rides that most of the champions – from Fred Archer via Lester Piggott to Ryan Moore – could only dream about. Despite his domination of the jockeys' championship, Richards wasn't resented in the weighing room, because he didn't ask for, or accept, a ride that was rightly another jockey's. The trainers knew they could rely on his word. If he was approached to take a ride in a race in which he didn't have a booking, he said yes to the first person who asked him – and stuck to his commitment, no matter what other approaches he had. The amateur rider, journalist and breeder John Hislop said, "He was loyal. He'd never try to get off a horse, even if it was awful, to ride something better." So he managed to combine years of hegemony with universal popularity. His riding style came into the same category as Piggott's – unique, effective, and best not attempted by lesser talents. John Hislop described it:

> "He had an entirely individual style. He rode with a loose rein and sat rather upright. By modern standards he rode long, but he still kept his horses straight. He had a vigorous whip action, but hardly ever hit his horses – just flicked them or waved the whip at them. He would draw the whip and start to swing it a long way from home, even if his horse was going well. This made it difficult for the other jockeys to know how much he had in hand. Sometimes they were tricked into thinking his horse was under pressure, when it wasn't.
>
> "By his terrific strength, determination and faultless rhythm, he was able to keep horses running on after they seemed beaten, with the result that he won races which no other jockey before or since could have pulled out of the fire. He lost fewer races that he ought to have won than any other jockey of my time."

Quintin Gilbey waxed lyrical: the best sight in racing, he swore, was when he'd bet three times his limit and twice what he could afford, and Gordon was in the last furlong, two lengths clear, whip still swinging. He seldom stopped riding until he was past the post. All his strength came from his legs. He could squeeze a horse so tightly with his knees that it stayed balanced and ran straight, however much he threw the reins at it. He once jumped on the arm of his sofa, put a coin under each knee, and defied a physically much larger friend to dislodge the coins. The man couldn't move either of Richards' knees an inch.

Richards set out to recreate as much of Beckhampton's former staff as he could. Morgan Scannell, who looked after Myrobella and Big Game, was hired as head lad. Jack Blake signed up for the start of his fifth decade at Beckhampton. Others from the last years of Fred Darling's time answered Richards' call. There were 10 apprentices. His first runner was a winner, for Dorothy Paget at Windsor. She had an unraced colt in training in Ireland, The Saint, who was working well enough to win any average maiden race. She transferred it to Beckhampton and a week later Richards took it to Windsor and duly won. He deflected the praise and congratulations to its former trainer. Miss Paget hated any contact with men, but she shook Sir Gordon's hand benignly after the race. She was a large woman and he was, at a stretch, five feet tall. The photograph suggested she was sizing him up for one of her gargantuan middle-of-the-night snacks.

There were only a dozen or so winners in that first season, but that was to be expected from a rookie trainer and a stable of two year olds. What couldn't have been foreseen was that 1955 was the only year which Sir Gordon spent at Beckhampton. He laid on a party at the Waggon and Horses for his staff and their wives; his landlord Herbert Blagrave was invited. A cake appeared, with a sugar model of a horse and jockey. The colours on the jockey were those of Fred Darling. Blagrave was affronted. He owned Beckhampton: he thought the colours on the cake should've been his. Words were exchanged in public. A couple of mornings later Sir Gordon's string rode out for work to find a sign planted in their way: *Gallops Closed.* The trainer pulled it up and threw it to one side. At the end of the season he left Beckhampton and rented a yard the other side of Marlborough at Ogbourne Maizey – Bonita Stables, where he'd spent part of his apprenticeship. The kerfuffle with Blagrave did him no harm: his owners stayed with him, and his string increased to 50. One fine day he found a Marlborough College boy playing hooky, sunning himself by the side of the gallops. 'Be careful,' Sir Gordon told him: 'You can probably be seen from the school.' In time the boy became a racehorse trainer himself and took over Bonita Stables. He delighted in showing Sir Gordon 'the spot where you shooed me off.' It was Peter Makin.

Ironically, Richards' kind nature was his Achilles heel. He let an assortment of idle opportunists take advantage of him. Nelson Guest, who rode for Richards, remembers the secretary opening a ledger that showed the stable lads' borrowing. "The total book was over £700 (£15,000 today). There were lads owing £60, £80 and more – on £8 a week wages. A couple of Irish lads went to Gordon with hard luck stories. Their mothers were sick, their fathers were sick, they needed to get home. He lent them £60 each. They were never seen again."

> "There was a former jockey with debts, down on his luck. He asked Gordon to help him, and Gordon bought him a tobacconist's kiosk at one of the London mainline stations. It went on for a couple of years, but the man lost money gambling and had to sell the business. Gordon didn't get any of the proceeds, but the man was back in touch soon enough, asking to borrow a couple of thousand. Gordon showed me the letter, 'What can I do?' he asked: 'It's hard when you've ridden with them.'"

Graham Stephens, who served his apprenticeship for George Todd at Manton before riding work for Sir Gordon and for Dick Hern, insists that Richards was the best trainer he worked for, but winces at the extent to which he was 'a soft touch.' One of the lads was out partying in Marlborough. He spent all the money he had. It was a cold night and he didn't fancy the long walk back to Ogbourne. At least he was smartly dressed: Sir Gordon insisted that his staff wore suits if they went into town. The lad had a bright idea. He banged on the door of the Ailesbury Hotel and roused the night porter. 'I'm Sir Gordon's new second jockey,' he told the man: 'I'd like a bed for the night.' The porter showed him to a room, took his order for a large Scotch 'and one for yourself' and breakfast at 6 am, and 'please send the bill to Sir Gordon.' When he strolled into the yard, rested and breakfasted, the miscreant boasted to his mates about the stroke he'd pulled. Somewhere between admiration and horror, they persuaded him that he should own up to what he'd done, before the bill arrived. To everyone's astonishment, Sir Gordon accepted that the lad had been stuck in town, and paid the hotel bill without any deduction from his wages.

There was a potentially devastating instance of doping in the yard. Bert Woodage, a work rider and occasional jockey, was giving 'hurry up' powder in little twists of paper to lads taking their horses to the races. Sir Gordon found out. He was shocked; those were the days of primordial Jockey Club justice, when a trainer was held responsible for any doping in his yard, irrespective of his own innocence. When he alerted the Stewards, he was told, 'If we find the culprit first, you will be held responsible.' He called the police. Tests showed that Woodage's potions were no more potent than self-raising flour, but he got 18 months. The episode was traumatic for Sir Gordon and the lads who had to testify. Richards was forgiving, to a degree beyond sainthood. He pleaded leniency for Woodage, he paid the man's wages to his wife for all the time that her husband was in prison, and after his release he petitioned the Jockey Club to allow Woodage to return to work in racing. Quite rightly, they said no.

Sir Gordon rented Bonita Stables from Norah Laye, the widow of the trainer Rupert Laye. She was a good-looking woman, though regarded warily. She married, first, the trainer Paddy Hartigan. He fell to his death from a window of the Adelphi Hotel in Liverpool. She later married Hartigan's brother Martin. In due course he joined Paddy. She set her cap at the married Laye, who said his schedule was, 'Three days with my wife, three days with Norah, Sundays to myself.' His wife divorced him. His friends implored him not to marry Norah: 'You'll be upstairs with the first two,' they told him, but he did marry her, and sure enough the curse of Norah struck again. The yard he left to her needed plenty of refurbishment to accommodate Richards' lads. Laye was an 'old school' trainer: his horses were well looked after, but their lads lived like rats, sleeping in empty boxes or in the tack room, with horse blankets for bed-linen.

Sir Gordon rented Norah Laye's yard for nine years. Having started with 50 horses, he was soon training over 60; the Macdonald-Buchanans returned as owners, and were joined by the industrialist Michael Sobell and his son-in-law Arnold Weinstock. Richards suffered a potentially disastrous loss before the start of the 1960 season. Only days after he'd phoned Dorothy Paget to say her two year olds were potentially her best ever, she had a fatal heart attack. At the time she owned half the horses in training at Ogbourne. It said much for Sir Gordon's reputation that despite the loss of so many horses, his numbers actually rose the following season. He'd ridden many winners for Paget, but it was a loser that made the biggest impression on her – Captain Payne, after whose costly flop Richards told Dorothy Paget that Fred Darling was probably jumping off the stand. Despite the financial damage, she burst out laughing. She liked his directness. "[If she] made some more than usually outrageous statement or suggestion," wrote Quintin Gilbey, "Sir Gordon would smile and say, looking her straight in the eye, 'Miss Paget, you know you don't really mean that.' She would laugh and agree." She didn't interfere with his plans, and he trained happily for her for five years: some achievement, considering she had 15 or 16 trainers before him.

She never visited his yard, and Richards believed she didn't know where it was. Her all-consuming interest was betting, and she asked him to tell her when he was having a bet. His wagers were on a modest scale, but they gave her an indication of his confidence. If he wanted £10 on, she confined herself to a 'tiddler.' If he said £25, she loosed off one of her 'banco' bets: £10,000. If his bet was £50 – his limit – she thumped down a double banco. Many of these bets were placed in the middle of the night, long after the races had been run. William Hill kept an office open all night to take her bets. He knew she was honest, because she was often betting on a horse that'd been beaten many hours earlier. She added Sir Gordon's bets to her own, and the pair settled their account at the end of each season.

Sir Gordon came towards the end of his lease at Ogbourne at loggerheads with Norah Laye. When she presented her terms for extending his tenancy, they included doubling his rent. His second jockey Nelson Guest heard that the old stable at Whitsbury was empty. He went to have a look and was amazed to find, "Everything freshly painted, done over beautifully. The gallops were immaculate, in pristine condition. What a place, I told the Guv'nor." Richards wasn't sure: Whitsbury was owned by William Hill, and he thought his owners wouldn't like that. But Hill promised him he would operate as a valued tenant, no more or less. His owners agreed to move with him, so the 1965 season saw him in his third yard.

Richards trained one outstanding horse from Whitsbury – Michael Sobell's Reform, the winner of six of his seven races as a two year old, and then becoming what Timeform assessed as, 'The best miler in England, if not Europe.' Sadly, Reform was such an ugly duckling as a foal, with crooked forelegs, that no thought was given to entering him for the classics. He must've had an outstanding chance in the 2000 Guineas, because he won the St James's Palace Stakes, the Sussex Stakes, the Queen Elizabeth II Stakes and finally the Champion Stakes. Timeform paid a generous tribute:

> "A horse is nothing without his trainer, and Reform's record speaks volumes for Sir Gordon Richards, whose skilled and sympathetic handling transformed what was an undersized, undernourished and unwanted specimen as a yearling into a neat, powerful, handsome and courageous thoroughbred."

Three seasons later, Richards retired. Strangely for such a good-natured man, he fell out with his third landlord in a row. William Hill was master of all he surveyed, a fearless bookmaker and successful businessman, but over-accustomed to having his own way. He'd arrive at Whitsbury on a Friday evening and spend the weekend finding fault with everyone and everything. Sir Gordon was irritated, and he let Hill know. When his five-year lease ran out, Hill declined to renew it, though to allow an orderly wind-down, it was extended for one more season. At the end of it, Sir Gordon handed in his trainer's licence. For public consumption, he said he hadn't been able to find another stable with sufficiently good private gallops. In truth, his wife Margery had been pleading with him to stop training, not least because he was losing money. He never hung onto a pound note unnecessarily, thinking nothing of sending his driver up to London to buy some early-season fruit. In his riding days he liked to mix a plover's egg into brandy, as a tonic. He used to pay the Beckhampton lads five shillings per egg (close to £15 today).

It's curious that Richards had little business sense: he'd been as sharp as a pin when negotiating his retainers in his riding days. In Noel Murless' time at Beckhampton, Richards at one stage had his first retainer from the yard's owners; a second retainer from the Aga Khan; a third from the Duke and Duchess of Norfolk; and then seven other stables standing in a queue for his services – and paying for the privilege. Commercially, he could be imagined like a Formula One driver today, with a big Beckhampton logo across his chest, the Aga Khan on his helmet, and the symbols of his other retainers distributed in smaller and smaller images around his arms and torso. Yet none of this nous helped him to make money when he turned to training. He had few regrets when he took on the role of racing manager for Michael Sobell and Arnold Weinstock, and for Marcia Lady Beaverbrook, widow of the newspaper magnate. During his last season, 1970, Richards trained only for those three owners.

In 16 years Sir Gordon saddled 634 winners. If he had failings as a trainer, they were mostly of the sympathetic kind, such as allowing some of his staff to exploit him. He was also inclined to be a little soft on his horses. Reform lost only three times in 14 starts, and two of the defeats were on seasonal debuts, when he was clearly backward. He wasn't always helped by his stable jockey. Scobie Breasley was an outstanding rider, certainly in the top rank of the twentieth century. But he had an incurable addiction to the hold-up ride. In race after race, he'd drop his mount out, switch it off and aim to arrive artistically, putting his horse's head in front on the line. Every now and then it went horribly wrong. His riding tactics were nightmarish for an owner like Dorothy Paget. She'd splashed out a banco or double banco on a whiff of optimism from Sir Gordon, and there was her horse, going supremely well behind runners, a furlong to go, and *the miserable Breasley* (as she called him) *hasn't moved a muscle.* It was the same on the home gallops. Scobie was a perfunctory work-rider, replicating his racecourse antics, giving start away, waiting behind the galloping companions, joining in at the last possible moment. He wasn't helping Richards to get his horses fit.

Sir Gordon's record stands at 14 classic wins as a jockey, followed by none as a trainer. The disparity caused some to question his ability as a trainer. Sir Peter O'Sullevan saw all the best trainers over several decades; he didn't accept that Sir Gordon was a failure. "On the contrary. He did very well and he made some good horses, such as Reform. But the expectations were high. It's a hard game, and there are some savage critics. If he hadn't had the spotlight on him he'd have been accepted as a reasonable trainer. It's a big disadvantage to be the focus of attention." Sir Peter remembered Richards for his kindness, too: "When I was at the Press Association, the *Daily Express* offered me a job which would involve tipping. I told Gordon about it and said that I didn't like the idea, the pressure of finding a winner every day. 'Don't you worry,' Gordon said; 'You'll tip winners.' He called Charlie Smirke over and told him, 'Peter's worried that he won't tip a winner.' Between them they assured me that I would. It was Gordon who talked me into taking the job." That was Sir Peter's start in the national media. Years after, he read the lesson at Sir Gordon's memorial service. Nelson Guest, who rode 60 or 70 winners for Sir Gordon, later became the four-time champion trainer in Denmark. He too believes Richards was a good trainer:

"He won with nervous, funky horses that other trainers wouldn't have got onto the racecourse. I remember one owner, a childhood friend of Gordon, ran a sweetshop. He had an awful little filly, useless. Gordon said, 'These are the ones that need to be helped. Stick with it.' Well, there was a tiny race at Bath, Scobie rode, she won, and I never saw Gordon so happy. He'd done the impossible. He was as pleased as if he'd trained an Oaks winner."

CHAPTER TWENTY-ONE

"Does Jeremy Tree ride work?"

In its first 110 years as a racing stable, Beckhampton had four trainers. The next eight years saw four more: Noel Murless, Dick Warden, Jeremy Tree and Sir Gordon Richards. After Sir Gordon's dispute with Herbert Blagrave, Jeremy Tree began the 1956 season as the sole trainer at Beckhampton. Normal service was resumed. Tree held the licence for 34 years, his achievement summed up by the racing writer Richard Onslow as, "Making Beckhampton into a modern international stable, whose consistent success at the highest level has attracted a huge overseas investment into British racing."

Jeremy Tree was born with the proverbial silver spoon. He inherited connections and substantial wealth from his parents. His father Ronald was an American who naturalised and became more English than the English, Master of the Pytchley Hunt and a Conservative Member of Parliament. His mother, née Nancy Field, was an heiress to the Marshall Field department store empire and a niece of Nancy Astor.

Tree's presumed progress from prep school to Eton and Oxbridge was interrupted by the second world war. To his disgust, his father insisted that he must leave Eton for a school in New England. As soon as he was old enough, he came back to this country to join up. The British Army may not have come across an officer trainee quite like him. The author Ivor Herbert arrived at Pirbright barracks on the same day as Tree. Herbert recalls that

Tree had stolen a march by getting there early. "He lived the life of a lord. There was a Turkish rug by his bunk; a cosy eiderdown; and a large cabinet to hang his clothes." In the shooting season, a brace of pheasants hung nearby. An NCO was assigned to look after the new intake of national servicemen, but he seems to have morphed into a batman for Trooper Tree. Sometimes, when the men had an afternoon off, a chauffeur-driven car would wait the other side of the fence which enclosed the barracks. Tree would change into a suit, summon his friends, and lead the way under the wire. To negotiate the guard post at the entrance to Pirbright, Tree sat looking like a VIP in the passenger seat, while his friends, still in khaki, crouched down in the back of the car. Invariably, the important-looking vehicle, the chauffeur and the civilian were acknowledged by a salute from the guard. Then it was off to the Ritz where Tree would pay for a slap-up lunch, having cocked a snook at every possible regulation. Ivor Herbert remembers Trooper Tree as, 'Big, jolly and very clever – wonderfully generous and amusing.' Tree passed out of Sandhurst on VE Day, joined the Life Guards, and served for two years in Egypt and Palestine.

He'd been mad about racing from an early age, because of his family link to the Astors. He was a regular visitor to their stud at Cliveden, and was betting enthusiastically at prep school. The milkman used to take his wagers and his pocket money. His first selection – when he was eight – was Colombo, who finished third to Windsor Lad in the 1934 Derby. He was in his first year at Eton when his uncle Peter Beatty took him to Beckhampton to see his Derby hope, Bois Roussel. Tree was enchanted by the horse and the stable. He had £1 each way on Bois Roussel with the school bookie. If he hadn't been hooked before that day, he was after his uncle's colt won the Derby at 20–1. As soon as he left the Army, he told his father that he intended to be a racehorse trainer. Ronald Tree was horrified. He warned that there was a Labour government hell-bent on taxing the rich. Didn't Jeremy realise no one would have any money to keep a horse in training? Grudgingly, Tree agreed to try a career in the City. He hated it; he implored his father to relent. The elder Tree had an inspiration. Fred Darling had just retired: who better to knock some sense into Jeremy – to spell out the pitfalls and the disappointments? So Tree paid another visit to Beckhampton. Darling may not have tried terribly hard to follow Ronald Tree's script: Jeremy left Beckhampton more determined than ever to be a trainer.

He joined Dick Warden as pupil assistant. His two years at Kremlin House must have been hair-raising, given Warden's tendency to vanish without warning. On the other hand, it provided Tree with a rapid introduction to handling owners, managing stable staff and training a large string. The owners posed the trickiest problem: what could he say to callers who wanted to know when their horses were running, after Warden had gone walkabout without telling Tree his plans? No wonder he later replied to a question about the qualities needed to make a success of training, "Be choosy, if possible, with your owners."

Then came a family tragedy: his uncle Peter Beatty committed suicide. He had a degenerative eye condition; he'd submitted to several operations to attempt to reverse it. His surgeon told him that nothing more could be done: he would be blind. He jumped from a window of his suite at the Ritz. His will divided his estate into racing and non-racing assets. He left everything connected to racing to Jeremy, and the rest to Jeremy's brother Michael. Jeremy Tree's inheritance from Beatty comprised the 200-acre Mereworth Stud in Kent, 16 broodmares, and shares in the stallions Bois Roussel, Nearco, Migoli and Alycidon. They were, respectively, the winners of the Derby, the Grand Prix de Paris, the Prix de l'Arc de Triomphe and the Gold Cup: a choice selection.

Beatty's bequest allowed Jeremy Tree to move to his own yard in Newmarket, Lansdowne House, and he began the 1952 season there with 21 horses, owned by his mother, his friend Ian Gilmour and himself. He became friends with the Bedford Lodge trainer Jack Clayton and his wife; they introduced Tree to bridge, and the two trainers talked for hours about pedigrees. That summer the news broke: Noel Murless was leaving Beckhampton. Tree took the lease and, perhaps to provide an antidote to his own inexperience, asked Dick Warden to join him. At the start of the 1953 flat season, Tree was installed at Beckhampton with 24 horses, a couple of them sent by Herbert Blagrave to help get him started. Today he might've functioned as a permit trainer; apart from his own horses, he represented his mother, his best friend and his landlord.

In Tree's first two seasons he made a mistake which was easy enough for a young trainer switching from Newmarket to downland gallops: he tended to work his horses too hard, and some of them bled. The positives were that he had a nucleus of experienced staff to help him, men who'd worked for Noel Murless and in some cases for Fred Darling too. He also attracted new owners, including the Duchess of Devonshire and 'Porchey' Carnarvon, returning to the yard for the first time since Darling's retirement. In his third season at Beckhampton, Tree saddled his first winner of a big race, the cleverly-named colt Double Bore, by Borealis out of one of Peter Beatty's broodmares Borobella. Double Bore had been well beaten in the St Leger the previous autumn – after significant ante-post support at long odds – but had more than paid his way with three wins, the last of them in the Newmarket St Leger. Timeform described him as 'good-looking, on the small side, very game.' He improved steadily as a four year old, winning three races in succession: the Old Newton Cup at Haydock, a two-mile stakes race at Ascot, and the Goodwood Cup. He was odds on to win the Doncaster Cup, but broke down during the race, and was retired and sold to South Africa. Jeremy Tree's Christmas card that year was the photograph of Double Bore's Goodwood success. The colt had advertised his trainer's ability with three wins in successive seasons, culminating in a Cup race at a top meeting, had won the equivalent today of £245,000 in prize money, and been sold. For good measure, Tree still had his dam.

It was thought by some in racing that Tree was a wealthy dabbler, playing at horses. Nothing could have been further from the reality. Tree was deadly serious about training. Nicky Vigors, who became his first assistant trainer in 1967, and later trained successfully himself, says, "Jeremy definitely didn't do it as a hobby; it was all very professionally run." John Randall wrote in the *Racing Post*, "Jeremy Tree came from a rich and privileged background, but he became one of racing's true professionals – a quality trainer of quality horses." Jimmy Lindley, who was Beckhampton's retained rider for several seasons, says, "For a man who didn't come from a racing background, he had a lot of finesse and feeling for horses." To some extent, Tree blind-sided people who didn't know him well, with his patrician lifestyle and his generous build. He made one or two attempts to lose weight and to supervise his string from horseback. A stout hack was found, and Tree rode around for a while, but he suffered from sore knees, and the project was abandoned. This provided Mick Channon with a terrific quip. He'd applied for a trainer's licence. The Jockey Club weren't impressed by his CV. He was asked, did he ride work? When he answered no, he was told he needed more experience. As he left the room, he turned and asked innocently, "By the way, does Jeremy Tree ride work?"

One sign of Tree's seriousness was the team that he built around him. From Newmarket he lured the former head lad of the eight-times champion trainer Frank Butters. From Dick Warden came a crack work rider, Johnny Gomez, who became head lad in due course. And thanks to Carnarvon, he acquired his stable jockey. Porchey had phoned Jimmy Lindley out of the blue and without preamble said: "John Hislop has told me I should retain you to ride my horses." A retainer was agreed during the call, which ended with Porchey asking his new jockey to be at Beckhampton at six o'clock next morning to ride work. Lindley duly presented himself, to be met by a surprised Jeremy Tree, who asked, 'Why are you here?' Carnarvon had forgotten to tell his trainer. All ended well, with Tree telling Lindley soon afterwards, "You might as well ride them all." The retainer was £10,000 a year. Lindley stayed at Beckhampton for eight seasons.

During the last half of the 1950s the stable steadily grew in strength, from an average of 20 or so horses in training to the mid-30s. One cause was the acquisition of two important new owners: John Hay Whitney and Monica Sheriffe. 'Jock' Whitney came from a family steeped equally in horses and money. Tree said, "For Jock, money has three purposes: to be invested wisely, to do good with, and to live well off." Whitney's grandfather William won the 1901 Derby with Volodyovski; his mother won two Kentucky Derbys. Whitney himself hunted and played polo; it was in the hunting field that he met the trainer Ivor Anthony, who handled Whitney's best-known horse, the 1929 and 1930 Cheltenham Gold Cup winner Easter Hero. Over time, Whitney focused on flat racing and breeding. He built up a large stud, Greentree, in Kentucky; it housed 50 broodmares and half a dozen or so stallions. When Tree began to sell off the mares left to him by Beatty, three of them were bought by Whitney to found his own European stud. He knew his horses. Once, his many interests had kept him so busy that he hadn't visited Greentree for a considerable time. His stud groom paraded 31 horses for his inspection: Whitney hadn't seen any of them before. The next morning, he identified two-thirds of them on second viewing. His first trainer in England was Cecil Boyd-Rochfort, and he supported Boyd-Rochfort until his retirement in 1968. Whitney also had some horses with Gerald Balding, an occasional member of the Greentree polo team. When Balding died, Whitney moved those horses to Beckhampton. He told a dinner of the Thoroughbred Club of America why he raced in England:

> "I race [there] because I've had fun and I still do. Compared with ours, English racing is what the country store is to the supermarket. On a big day at Newmarket, 10,000 is a big crowd. And very few of them get to sit down. But sitting or standing, they appreciate the horse – as a creature of flesh and blood and spirit. What they have, and what we seem to be losing, is the personal interest in the horse."

A substantial part of the fun for Whitney was training and racing with Jeremy Tree. He settled so quickly at Beckhampton that before long he offered to buy the stable and its land from Herbert Blagrave. Whitney and Tree shared a view that racing revolved round Royal Ascot, and any Whitney horse with the requisite talent was laid out for the meeting. In 1957 President Eisenhower asked Whitney to be the US ambassador to the Court of St James's. It was a sensitive post: feelings in London were still bruised by America's lack of support for the British government during the Suez Crisis. Whitney was worried that in the circumstances it might be inappropriate for him to have a string of horses in training. He consulted the prime minister, Harold Macmillan, who assured him that, "The surest way for you to become a great ambassador would be for you to win the Derby." Whitney did become a great ambassador, but the Derby eluded him. With a new President came a new US envoy, and Whitney returned to America, but there was a week in June every year when he was sure to be in England.

Notwithstanding the firepower that Whitney brought to Beckhampton, Monica Sheriffe provided Tree's first classic winner. 'Miss Mon' was a formidable lady, born to inherit an estate near Melton Mowbray. She rode to hounds almost as soon as she could walk. Options for a high-born young woman were limited in those days. Sheriffe socialised, rode whenever she could in whatever discipline, and did her bit for good causes. She was roped in to join some society ladies who posed at the Nottingham Empire, 'In the manner of porcelain groups' at a matinee organised to raise money for charity. The scene was designed by Cecil Beaton. As for the social side, the *Spectator* noted that, "She was the organiser of much of the fun indulged in by the Prince of Wales and his set at Melton." She was celebrated as one of the finest women to hounds in High Leicestershire, riding as hard as any man, but side-saddle. She took a Melton Mowbray team to the Hurlingham Club for its inaugural women's polo match. Mowbray won 4–1. A sarcastic report described the first chukka as 'like a mounted tea party.' Heaven help the writer if Miss Mon ever caught up with him. Sir Peter O'Sullevan described her as, "Abrupt and abrasive, but engaging at the same time."

Monica Sheriffe first registered her colours in 1932: 'blue, white spots, yellow cap,' before a slight change to, 'blue birds-eye, white cap.' "Hopeless colours for a non-trier," says one of Jeremy's Tree's early assistants, though Tree did send a horse of Sheriffe's to Salisbury with 'not today' instructions to the jockey. He asked Miss Mon, did she want him to call after the race? No, she said, she'd be playing bridge. To Tree's horror, the horse won. He thought he'd better call his owner at once. He told her the bad news. "Oh fuck! Did the reins break?" Besides being decidedly forceful, Sheriffe was a skilled practical joker. To embarrass a neighbour she'd fallen out with, she had some 'stiffies' printed, with an invitation from the man's wife to a grand ball. The card went with a warning that the party was a secret, and urged its recipients not to talk about it, and not to RSVP. On the night, Miss Mon hid in some bushes with a view of her victim's front door, and was delighted to see a line of cars setting down the guests, dressed to the nines. The first arrivals found the house in darkness. Eventually the 'host' appeared in his pyjamas and dressing gown, flummoxed and furious.

Sheriffe met Dick Warden through hunting, and had a horse in training with him at Newmarket. Once Tree was settled at Beckhampton, she sent her first horse to him in 1958; she was still on the owners' roster 31 years later when he retired. She never paid an extravagant price for a yearling, and she only ever had one or two horses in training, but many of them turned out well. The first of them was Only For Life, a bay colt by Chanteur II out of Life Sentence. Tree bought him for only 1,600 guineas in the October sales. The trainer didn't buy him for his looks; "He was a plain customer with a head that looked far too big for his body. In addition he had a couple of outsize curbs. He was one of the ugliest yearling colts I ever saw." Tree did, however, know and like the family. The dam Life Sentence was out of Borobella, who'd bred him Double Bore. The colt's name was Miss Mon's salute to a trust of which she was the beneficiary, but only for her lifetime. Only For Life had two runs as a two year old, winning on his debut at Ascot; he was the outsider in a field of six, and carried 3lb overweight, but still won, running on strongly.

His reappearance was in a traditional 2000 Guineas trial, the Greenham Stakes at Newbury. He was prominent in the betting, and struck the front two furlongs out, going well. Then, reported Jimmy Lindley, he ran into a patch of heavy ground – "Couldn't you have ridden round it?" asked Tree – lost his action, and dropped away. Pundits and punters alike forgot the circumstances of Only For Life's defeat, and took account only of his finishing position. At Beckhampton, though, the Guineas was viewed with something close to confidence. Some of the colt's work had been a revelation. First there was a day when the Lambourn trainer 'Ginger' Dennistoun asked Tree, 'Can I bring a horse over to work with some of your good 'uns?' Tree supplied Only For Life and the yard's best three year old filly, Spree. Down at the start of the gallop, Jimmy Lindley heard Dennistoun telling his rider "Don't show them up. Don't beat them too far." At the end of the work, Lindley looked round. He laughs, "You needed a telescope to see Ginger's horse."

In the lead-up to the 2000 Guineas, Tree arranged a strenuous work-out on the Trial Grounds, the best of the Beckhampton grass gallops – some distance from the yard, high up on Crown land to the south of the Devizes road. It's a straight mile, rising steadily for five furlongs, where at a point called Middle Change it levels out to a slight incline for the last three furlongs. Only For Life had two galloping companions. The lead horse was a four year old, Miletus, who'd won the Kempton Park 2000 Guineas trial the previous year; he was being trained for the Victoria Cup. The other, Arise, had just won a 35-runner maiden race at Newbury by six lengths. The three work riders rode at their own weights. Johnny Dixon rode Miletus, and he was a little heavier than Only For Life's lad Alan Baker, so on the weight-for-age scale, Only For Life was at least 17lb 'wrong'. Dixon remembered Tree's instructions as, 'When you go over Middle Change, kick on.' At the start, Baker told Dixon, "Go a bit sooner. I want a good gallop." "He zoomed past me and went clear," said Dixon. Baker hardly had any money, but managed to get a pound or two on his horse at 100–1. Johnny Dixon had £10 each way at 66–1. Neither the lads nor Tree could know just how well the gallop would turn out. Cautiously, Tree phoned Miletus's owner Jock Whitney and told him, "I'm afraid your horse must have deteriorated badly – unless of course I win the Guineas." In the next 10 days, Only For Life won the 2000 Guineas, Miletus was second in a typically competitive Victoria Cup under 9st 10lb, and Arise easily defied a penalty in a maidens-at-closing race.

Tree had no crystal ball, but he was sure that Only For Life was wildly over-priced for the 2000 Guineas, and probably Spree in the 1000 Guineas as well. He backed them ante-post in each-way singles and an each-way double, to win £75,000 (£1.4 million today). He told Monica Sheriffe and his friend Simon Parker-Bowles what he'd done, and suggested they get involved. At the time Only For Life could be backed at 100–1 and Spree at 33–1. All through the morning of the race, it rained heavily at Newmarket. The going was officially soft, probably heavy. As the time of the Guineas drew near, there was panic behind the scenes. Only For Life's lad Alan Baker was on his own with his horse in the racecourse stables. He'd never been to Newmarket. He was told when he should leave the stables to walk to the saddling boxes. As the time came, and he was putting the finishing touches to Only For Life, he realised the other lads had already gone. "I was sure I was going to miss the race. I could see the grandstand in the distance, so I led my horse towards it as fast as I could. Then we came to a peat gallop. He wouldn't cross it – he'd never seen anything like it. I pulled and I pushed and eventually he gave a half-jump forwards and I lost a shoe in the peat. So there I am, in pouring rain, holding a classic runner's rein in one hand and feeling about in wet peat for my shoe." Rescue arrived in the shape of one of Tree's travelling lads.

The race was as eventful as the preliminaries. Only For Life was drawn close to the stands' side rails, and was up with the leaders throughout. From the Bushes, it was clear that the horses on the far side were struggling, lengths off the pace. One by one the runners on the near side began to flounder in the mud, and in the Dip two colts drew away: Only For Life on the rails, an Irish colt, Ionian, alongside him. Ionian took a narrow lead, seemingly going the better, but in the last half-furlong his stride shortened. By contrast, Only For

Life stayed on dourly. Strongly ridden by Lindley, he put his head in front on the post. Lindley took him into the place reserved for the second horse. Five minutes went by before the judge called the result. Lindley, Tree and Sheriffe had all won their first classic. Cue delirium in Beckhampton and Avebury and in the Leicestershire village of Goadby Marwood, home to Miss Mon. She was a popular figure, and many of the locals had backed Only For Life.

Jeremy Tree and Simon Parker-Bowles found themselves highly sought after. Tree used to tell gleefully how his bookmaker Heathorn's representative chased him all over Newmarket, trying to get him to lay off some of his bet. Parker-Bowles, whom Miss Mon called 'Punter' from that day on, was phoned repeatedly by Cyril Stein at Ladbrokes. The double didn't quite come off; Spree, a brown filly by Rockefella out of Emancipation, was home bred by his owner, James Morrison at his Fonthill Stud in Wiltshire. Morrison's horses had been trained by Noel Cannon at Druid's Lodge. When Cannon retired and the yard was sold, Morrison moved the horses the few miles east to Beckhampton. Spree had won the last two of her races as a two year old, both on soft or dead ground, so the mud at Newmarket was likely to favour her. Her seasonal return had been a promising second at Newbury to a filly who next won the Irish 1000 Guineas. At Newmarket, Spree ran into the brilliant French filly Hula Dancer, and chased her valiantly through the last two furlongs, always held, but only a length behind in second. Then she caught another tartar in the Oaks, Noblesse, before winning the Nassau Stakes. Jeremy Tree rued the bet that got away, but conceded that as it'd been each way, "I didn't do too badly." He could say that again: Monica Sheriffe gave him a Bentley – and handed £250 to Alan Baker. Simon Parker-Bowles picked up £12,000 for the place portion of his bets. He was able to buy a flat and a new car.

The season of Only For Life and Spree was Tree's breakthrough year. The precious metals magnate Charles Engelhard had horses at Beckhampton for the first time. His first act as an owner in Britain was to recruit Jock Whitney's racing manager David McCall. A friend of McCall joked, "You must be the first person who ever sacked a Whitney." Engelhard completed a quartet of wealthy owners who provided the backbone of Tree's stable strength for the next dozen years: himself, Jock Whitney, Monica Sheriffe and James Morrison (later Lord Margadale). Engelhard's first good horse came along the following season; it was a chestnut colt called Double Jump. He was bought by Tree at the September sales for 7,800 guineas. It wasn't for his looks; Jimmy Lindley, who rode him in all his races, called him, 'lean and lanky.' But Tree saw something he liked, and the colt had a marvellous temperament, not unlike Abernant's. Alan Baker broke in Double Jump, and says, "He was a pet. You could've poured a cup of tea sitting on his back."

Double Jump's first serious gallop was electrifying: he routed his galloping companions so comprehensively that Tree for one couldn't believe what he'd seen. On his debut at Salisbury he won readily, the winning margin double the judge's verdict of three lengths. He ran next in the Savernake Stakes at Newbury, where he burned off 13 opponents after three furlongs and won, hard held, by five lengths. It was the same story in the National Stakes at Sandown, and Tree and David McCall decided to run Double Jump in the Prix Robert Papin at Maisons-Laffitte. The race attracted 19 runners; Double Jump was drawn 17, on a course where a low number was thought to be essential. Facing the Beckhampton colt were all the best French juveniles to have raced at that date, and an unbeaten winner of two starts from Paddy Prendergast's stable in Ireland. Double Jump started at 5–1, brushed his draw disadvantage aside, and pulled his way to the front shortly after half way. He won unchallenged; the second and third had both won their previous starts by six lengths. The English press went into raptures: Double Jump was the first home-trained two year old to win in France for 17 years. *The Sporting Life* paid tribute:

> "Let us congratulate Jeremy Tree. Because [he] did not have to struggle quite as hard to get started as some trainers, he used to be regarded in some quarters as a dilettante, dabbling in the sport for fun. All trace of

> that unfair canard has now been swept away by several seasons of steady, consistent success, culminating last year with Only For Life's 2000 Guineas, and now carried on by Double Jump. Beckhampton is once again a powerful force in English racing and for this its popular master has good reason to be proud."

Tree and McCall were in two minds over Double Jump's next race; the options were the Gimcrack Stakes at York, or a return to France for the Prix Morny. They chose York, despite Charles Engelhard making it clear that he didn't fancy 'speechifying'. A field of the best two year olds from England and Ireland faced Double Jump in the Gimcrack. He was smartly away, made all, and decisively held off the winner of the July Stakes, Ragtime. Newmarket's Middle Park was immediately nominated as Double Jump's final race of the season. He was re-opposed by the second and fourth from the Gimcrack, Ragtime and Spanish Express; there was one other runner, winner of a modest maiden. It looked a formality for Double Jump, who was held up with the other three until they reached the Bushes. Moments later, it was clear that he was in trouble; he dropped quickly away, leaving the path clear for the horses he'd beaten at York. He was pulled up, Lindley dismounted, and the cause was clear: blood was pouring from his mouth and nostrils. Lindley says, "Double Jump was one of the best horses Tree ever had. He was the only racehorse I rode where I didn't know how fast I was going. He just floated over the ground. If he hadn't bled he might never have been beaten."

The essay on Double Jump in *Racehorses of 1964* began with an exceptional rating for a two year old: 131. It ended with a gloomy prognosis: "His prospects depend entirely on his recovery from his accident, and its non-recurrence. The outlook is not bright: the haemorrhage was severe, and once a horse has broken a blood-vessel, he's always likely to do it again." He did. He was given a long rest and brought back into training, but he bled again the first time he was galloped. He was retired immediately. Sadly but predictably, he tended to pass his infirmity on to his offspring.

CHAPTER TWENTY-TWO

The amazing Mr Grace

When *The Sporting Life* praised Jeremy Tree after Double Jump's win in France, it added the thought, 'His outlook on life bears little resemblance to that of his great but somewhat ascetic predecessor Fred Darling.' In truth, Tree's outlook and lifestyle bore little resemblance to that of any other trainer of his time, or before it. The day at Beckhampton began with two lots. Serious it might have been, but Tree never kept his humour in check for long. At the time when Pat Eddery rode most of the Beckhampton horses, he had an unavailing struggle with an animal called Two Timing. It was uncontrollable and had one speed – flat out. One morning it carted him off the gallops and over the skyline. "Oh dear," said Tree from behind his binoculars: "I think Patrick's gone for the papers. We won't be seeing him for a while." Another day, he was giving an owner a commentary on the breeding of the two year olds as they cantered past: 'That's a Crepello, that's a Nijinsky, this one's a Mill Reef,' at which moment the animal crossed its legs and fell ominously to the ground; 'No. That *was* a Mill Reef.'

First lot was followed by a magnificent breakfast. It was no place for a weight-watcher. Kedgeree, kippers, eggs and bacon, kidneys and all the trimmings were laid out in silver dishes. Jimmy Lindley says the spread was, "Unbelievable; I found it agonising sitting there trying not to eat, because I was always struggling with my weight." Second lot followed breakfast. Then

Tree would retire, reluctantly, to the stable office. His secretary was Diana Hastings, who'd worked for Fred Darling and Herbert Blagrave; she was the sister of the Kingsclere trainer Peter Hastings-Bass. Tree's first assistant, Nicky Vigors, had arrived at Beckhampton with a recommendation from a Newmarket trainer. Vigors was invited to the yard for evening stables and offered the job there and then. Tree confessed that he didn't know what it entailed, as he hadn't had an assistant before, or even thought about it.

> "Diana Hastings had her desk and bits. There was a small corner for me. Jeremy was writing furiously with his squeaky fountain pen. Scrunched-up paper was being thrown and missing the waste paper basket. I plucked up the courage to ask if there was a problem. 'I'm writing to my owners.' 'But you only have four,' I said. Tree was letting them know his training fees were going up from 18 to 20 guineas a week. The only reply came from Charles Engelhard, who thought 20 guineas *a day* was slightly excessive. Jeremy loved that."

When Vigors started his own training career, he was replaced by Andrew Simpson. One quiet day, he and Tree were filling in a quiz in *The Sporting Life*. One of the questions was, 'What makes a good owner?' There was a space below for suggestions. "Put down, 'Must live in America'," volunteered Tree. Another day, Tree asked Simpson vaguely, "Is Ribston off to Paris this weekend?" Ribston was a colt of Engelhard's who'd been a useful two year old, but failed to train on. Simpson checked, and found to his horror that because he'd forgotten to scratch the colt, Ribston had accumulated £400 or so in forfeits for the Prix du Jockey Club. Fortunately, another of Engelhard's horses earned £4,000 that weekend by finishing second in the Prix Jean Prat. Tree told Simpson, "I had to wait until rather late at night to tell Mr Engelhard. He took it well."

Andrew Simpson has happy memories of his time as Tree's assistant: "Beckhampton was a wonderful place to work, and he was a great man to work for. He was highly intelligent, bright, witty. He liked jokes and catching people out, and he didn't mind being caught out himself. He had great respect for his lads and it was reciprocated; they adored him, and the standard of the lads was pretty high." As for the horses:

> "He was getting the same families from the owner-breeders, so he knew them well. Plenty of time and manpower was devoted to gentle, gradual breaking in. They started shaggy, gradually they became less shaggy, they started cantering, there was never any hurry. Tree gave them as much time as they needed. They had no bad experiences. He knew what they'd become, he let them grow into themselves."

When Simpson moved on, having combined the roles of pupil-assistant and secretary, Tree advertised for a stable secretary only. He had two replies. One was from a pig farmer, the other from Judy Foxwell. Like Andrew Simpson, she had a forfeits oversight, costing Jock Whitney over £600: "I was frightened to death, mortified. But Mr Tree never berated me." Of course it helped Tree to know that £400 or £600 was no more than a rounding-up number on the bank balances of Engelhard and Whitney. It also helped the people who worked for Tree to know that while he didn't suffer a fool gladly, he understood humans make mistakes, and the well-intentioned ones weren't likely to repeat them.

Tree's Beckhampton was ahead of its time in its openness to visitors. Marten Julian, who has long published an annual 'dark horses' guide, found Jeremy Tree, "Approachable, a delight to talk to. He was unbelievably laid-back and relaxed, which reflected the way Beckhampton was run. I always looked forward to conversations with him. Some of the other trainers back then were aloof, reluctant." Captain Ryan Price reacted badly to any of his charges being thought 'dark': "I killed six men with my bare hands in the war, and I'm quite happy to make it seven." Some visitors demanded more attention than others. Charles Engelhard used to arrive in a helicopter, which was followed at ground level by a Rolls Royce, in case the helicopter had to put down. Jim McGrath of Channel 4 researched the first Timeform interview with Tree. Eight o'clock, he was told. He arrived with a minute to spare. Tree was pacing up and down in the driveway: 'Come on, come on. I never wait for anyone.' "My heart sank when I saw Pat Eddery's car. I thought, I'm never going to be allowed to watch the work. But Tree wasn't in the least concerned." McGrath's impression of him was, "Sharp as a tack, with a sense of humour and mischief."

Humour was certainly never far away. After winning a race at Royal Ascot, Tree took the lift down from the owners' and trainers' level. As the lift opened, a woman shoved her way out, launched herself at a litter bin, and threw up. "Oh dear," drawled Tree: "Do we think she backed the second?" One of the horses he trained for the Vesteys beat a Sainsbury-owned opponent: "Butcher beats grocer." And at Doncaster, when his head lad John Reed thought a stable fancy hadn't run very well, Tree told him, "Mr Eddery went everywhere on the racecourse apart from the ladies' lavatory, John – and he's not allowed in there."

Tree's sights were set on 'Saturday' horses. Apart from at Newbury and Salisbury, he had few midweek runners outside the major racecourses and meetings. There was seldom any need to hare back for evening stables, or to miss them. It was a procedure and to a standard that Fred Darling would have recognised, though without the tension he injected. Henrietta Knight visited Tree when she was starting to train point-to-pointers: "The horses were immaculately turned out. The lads put out their stable mats with all their tools laid out, straw rolled in front of the boxes. The unspoken message was, 'This is how it should be done.' You learn from seeing how others do it. He was a perfectionist." Tree's old friend Jack Clayton often stayed, and as they walked round the evening inspection they'd reminisce at length about pedigrees.

Once the horses had been set fair and the day's work was done, Tree changed, in the few steps across the yard to his house, from racehorse trainer into man-about-town. It was remarked that he seemed to know everybody. A visitor might find Fred Astaire was staying; he was distantly related to Tree, who suggested to his housekeeper that she might like a twirl with Fred round the dining room table. She demurred, to the chagrin of her daughter Heather, who would've leaped at the chance. If Tree was on his own, he had dinner with a decent wine, followed by a serious book, most likely a biography. He was a voracious reader, well informed about the world beyond racing, and picky about the precise use of the English language. He came across the Channel 4 and BBC presenters Jim McGrath, Jimmy Lindley and John Hanmer in a huddle at the races: "Ah, a commentators' corner – which is rather appropriate," Tree said, handing McGrath a slip of paper listing his recent mistakes, factual or grammatical. There was another list for Lindley; only Hanmer escaped unscathed. McGrath was also told: "I've been to Kempton. Your namesake was commentating. He called a horse 'Green's Fennelly.' Tell the silly boy it's pronounced *Fernley*. He was an artist."

Tree loved gossip, and he roamed far and wide in pursuit of a rumour. Occasionally, Willie Carson's phone would ring: "It was Jeremy. I'd think, 'I'm going to get some rides!' but he just wanted to find out if I'd heard some story or other." Henrietta Knight used to go to the Doncaster sales each May: "As soon as I got back, he'd want to know what happened, who was there, what they were up to. He had to be *au fait* with everyone's comings and goings." He monitored the fortunes of his friend Tim Forster, who trained a few miles away. Tree no sooner returned from holiday than he was on the phone to Jim McGrath: "Has Captain Forster had any winners while I've been away?" No, replied McGrath, it'd been bone dry; Forster hadn't had any runners. "Ah yes. All those soft-ground staying 'chasers for Towcester. There's no better judge of a slow horse than the Captain."

One evening when Tree was comfortable in his study, reading, the phone rang. It was an owner with three horses in the yard. He was bursting to tell Tree about some expensive yearlings he'd bought at Keeneland, what their breeding was, and how excited he was about their prospects. He went on at

Alan Baker

SECOND PLACE is where Jimmy Lindley directed Only For Life's lad Alan Baker after the near dead-heat for the 1963 2000 Guineas. A pensive Jeremy Tree follows the pair: he had a long-odds bet riding on the outcome. The happy ending was, Only For Life won by a short head at 33-1.

MONICA SHERIFFE was Jeremy Tree's friend, bridge partner and loyal owner. Only For Life was her first good horse, Sharpo her last. Both were bargain buys. She and Tree are pictured in the paddock at Longchamp before Sharpo's farewell victory in the 1982 Prix de l'Abbaye.

Archibald Stirling of Keir/the Turf Club

Opposite: ON THE TURF: William Grace was the Turf Club's long-serving head porter, informal banker to the profligate younger members (note "IOU" on the paper in his hand) – and Jeremy Tree's super-discreet commission agent. He was painted by Charmian Stirling.

AMBASSADOR: the diplomat and race-horse breeder Jock Whitney supported Beckhampton for many years. He inscribed the original of this cartoon to his friend Jeremy Tree: "From no-nose Whitney to no-knees Tree."

SAFE PASSAGE. Jeremy Tree holds up the traffic on the Calne road as his horses return to the 'Manna' yard after work.

KNOWN FACT (near side, ridden by Willie Carson) became Khalid Abdullah's first classic winner after the disqualification of Nureyev (white cap) in the 1980 2000 Guineas.

IN THE SWIM: Roger Charlton operated a successful equine swimming pool in Lambourn before joining Jeremy Tree. He's pictured (right) with his assistant Don Reed; the 'guinea pig' is former 'chaser Highland Brae.

'GRADUALLY he did a little less and I did a little more,' recalls Roger Charlton (right) of his time as assistant at Beckhampton to Jeremy Tree. The pair review the day's racing over one of Tree's famed traditional breakfasts.

DOUBLE DELIGHT: Pat Eddery drives out Quest For Fame (pink cap, left) to win the 1990 Derby, just three days after the same rider and owner – Khalid Abdullah – had given Roger Charlton a sensational start to his training career with Sanglamore in the French Derby.

PRINCE Khalid Abdullah has been Beckhampton's main supporter from the late 1970s until the present day. Known Fact and Quest For Fame have been his two classic winners from the yard.

Fiona Marner

SPEEDSTERS: Roger Charlton with owner John Deer's sprinters Patavellian (left) and Avonbridge, winners respectively of the 2003 and 2005 Prix de l'Abbaye. Their work together convinced the trainer that Patavellian was a good thing for the 2003 Stewards' Cup.

CITYSCAPE, ridden by James Doyle, winning the 2012 Group 1 Dubai Duty Free race at Meydan for Khalid Abdullah. It was Beckhampton's biggest prize to date, and a transformational success for Doyle.

HANDSOME is as handsome does: Al Kazeem, owned by John Deer and ridden by James Doyle, going down to the start at the Curragh before what turned out to be his last Group 1 win and last race, the 2015 Tattersalls Gold Cup.

H

TRANQUIL: the peaceful courtyard at Beckhampton gives little hint of the size of the training operation behind and around it. At first, a visitor sees only – in front and to the right – two rows of old-time cage boxes, dating back to Sam Darling's days.

Steve Dennis, F

some length. Tree's patience evaporated. He cut in: 'I'm sure they all look very nice, but what is it that you want?' The man wanted Tree to train them. "I don't think so, Stavros. Three will do until we know each other better." It would be a challenge to name any other trainer who'd swat away the horses of Stavros Niarchos. Tree continued to train for him, but only on the scale that he wanted. Every now and then he was persuaded to take a horse from a new owner. He usually regretted it, and like a finger working out a splinter, the horse and its owner would be ejected. There was an American diplomat with a fetish for facial enhancement: the man had been 'lifted' so often that his ears were close to the top of his head. And there was Arnold Weinstock; he and Tree got on well. Weinstock moved some horses from France and sent them to Beckhampton. Then his son told Tree he expected a call every Sunday morning, with a report on the horses. When he realised he'd effectively be training for the son and not the father, Tree cooled on the horses: off they went.

If Tree was going up to London on a weekday, it might be to the American Embassy as a dinner guest of Jock Whitney. The rarefied company that he kept is clear from the diaries of the diplomat and politician Sir Harold Nicholson. Besides Tree, Sir Harold's fellow guests included the Queen Mother, and the prime minister, chancellor and Army minister of the time: Harold Macmillan, Derick Heathcoat-Amory and John Profumo and their wives. Nicholson grumbled that, 'while surrounded by distinguished and charming people,' he had to pretend to be interested while the Queen Mother 'talked all but uninterruptibly with Tree about their respective racehorses.' At another of Whitney's dinners, the Queen and the Duke of Edinburgh sat down with David Ormsby-Gore – soon to be Britain's Ambassador to the United States; the Cabot Lodges, of whom it was said in their native Boston, 'they spoke only to God'; and Jeremy Tree, 'who, should the conversation flag, could be counted on to talk to the Queen about horses.'

Once or twice a month during the flat season, more often over the winter, Tree had a routine which began on a Thursday afternoon and ended with his return to Beckhampton in time for evening stables on Friday. His chauffeur drove him up to the Turf Club. He enjoyed a cocktail before heading out to dinner at White's and cards at the Portland Club, home to some of the highest-stakes bridge in London. One evening, when Tree had begun training for Prince Khalid Abdullah, he felt a tap on his shoulder. It was Bobby McAlpine of the construction family. "Please don't interrupt me when I'm playing, Bobby." McAlpine waited until the hand finished and said, "Your new owner Prince Khalid and I have a company which is costing [me] a lot of money." Tree asked: "How much do you call a lot of money?" "Three or four million and increasing all the time." As McAlpine waited patiently, another hand was shuffled and dealt. Finally Tree replied: "May I suggest that when you've lost fifteen million each, His Highness might start taking an interest?"

Jeremy Tree loved the Turf Club, and especially valued its head porter William Grace. Tree had a sizeable team organising his life, and he depended on them, because he was impractical. Asked about the heating in a lad's cottage, he countered, 'There are lots of electricity sockets, aren't there?' He had a housekeeper, a cook and butler – the fondest-remembered were Mr and Mrs Baker, dubbed 'the fabulous Bakers', a gardener and a chauffeur. None of them were as valuable to Tree as Mr Grace at the Turf Club. Grace served the club for over 50 years, having begun as a young man in the days when the members tipped out the loose change from their pockets, and the silver coins were scrubbed by the club servants, ready for collection when each member left. During his long tenure at the club, Grace placed the bets of many of the members. He saw they consistently lost money – including the trainers among them. He must've worked out which members' bets he could safely 'stick,' because he accumulated enough wealth to act as a prototype payday lender. Some of the younger members owed him four-figure sums. Occasionally, if the credit line was stretched to breaking point, Grace would invite the errant youth to, 'Just come downstairs, if it's convenient, Sir,' and in his ill-lit cubbyhole he'd show every detail of the financial embarrassment. Nothing was ever demanded: it was enough to know that Grace knew.

Grace also knew that Jeremy Tree was different. The horses Tree asked him to back usually won. Tree wasn't an everyday punter, nor did he bet heavily; £100 each way was probably his limit, but as Tree liked ante-post betting, he was getting good prices. Placing his bets through Grace gave him anonymity, and camouflage; his own bets were accompanied by other members' losers. Before long, Grace confined his own betting to Tree's horses. He told his successor as head porter, John Campbell, "You make sure you look after Mr Tree, because Mr Tree is a nice man." Campbell recalls that, "Mr Tree never gave us tips. You had to listen carefully. He'd just say, 'I've got a horse running at York.' He never said 'It'll win,' but it usually did. He knew how to train horses for big races." The club's head barman Brian Reilly calls to mind a suggestion by Tree: "Grace, I think you should come down to Goodwood." Reilly and two other staff members went with Grace to the races. Tree had two runners that afternoon; they both won. Afterwards the four drove on to Brighton, where Grace paid for dinner: "It was a good day at the office, but he would never discuss how much he won." Grace had the discretion of a father confessor. He also acted as a private office for Tree; he looked after Tree's travel arrangements, bought his airline tickets, made theatre bookings.

Tree's routine at the Turf Club included a Friday-morning phone call to the yard to check that all was well. His head lad John Reed spotted a pattern: "I learned to make a note of the first couple of horses he asked about. If they were top of his mind, it usually meant they were running soon, and as often as not, they'd win." Reed was head lad for the last eight years of Tree's training career, and he personified Tree's hot-and-cold approach to his lads' betting. Reed might as well have had a neon sign reading 'bets' on his forehead. He'd been sacked by another trainer for pinching the market; he made the episode public by taking the man to a tribunal for unfair dismissal – and winning. Tree interviewed Reed and told him, "If you can make money betting on my horses, I wish you good luck, and if you find a winner or two, please let me know." By contrast, Only For Life's lad Alan Baker had a punter who compromised Baker with some loose talk at the races; Baker found he was no longer required to ride work. David Quinn was for years Tree's travelling head lad, and highly valued, but when someone told Tree that Quinn had punters and was passing on tips, the trainer subjected Quinn to vigorous questioning.

Most stable lads bet their boots every now and then. Sometimes it comes off, sometimes not. Pearl O'Connell's late husband Denis was at Beckhampton for 42 years; she worked behind the bar at the Waggon and Horses. "One day, Den asked me to go with him to Salisbury races. He hadn't asked before and I'd never been racing before." The landlord thought this curious. He gave Pearl £10, with the request, 'If Den's backing a horse, have £5 on for me and £5 for yourself.' "I didn't know it, but Den had been putting money aside every week to back this horse. It won by a short head. We bought a new car." Another long-serving lad, Paddy Jackson, waited for the debut of a two year old of Jock Whitney's. He had £300 saved up for his wedding; it went on the newcomer. "It couldn't be beaten." It was, finishing fourth under an 'introductory' ride. It then won five races. Paddy had to borrow the wedding money from his future father-in-law. Paddy hasn't had a bet since, and he's been married for 50 years. Occasionally, too, signals were scrambled. One day at Newbury, Tree was in the paddock with a senior jockey. The man seemed distracted: he couldn't take his eyes off the odds board. His mount was drifting. He couldn't contain himself: "Why is it 12–1?" he blurted. "It's very slow," replied Tree. "Isn't it the one I rode work on the other day?" asked the jockey. When he was legged up, he became agitated, shaking his head violently from side to side, and making a gesture which looked as if he was wiping a pane of glass with his hands.

Sun Chariot's minder Dai Rees was the yard's runner for a bookmaker in Devizes. He lived in a cottage behind the Waggon and Horses. Besides the Beckhampton lads, various locals and tradespeople came to him with their bets, scribbled on odd bits of paper. Rees didn't have a telephone, so he made friends with the AA patrolman in the box at the crossroads; crucially, it had a 'phone. Unknown to the AA's management, for years they laid on a facility for Rees to relay bets to Devizes. In the summer, he spent most afternoons scuttling up and down his garden path, to and from the box. He had his own key, to get in if the patrolman was called to a breakdown. Tree knew perfectly well about the goings-on, and ignored them. If not Rees, there'd be someone else. In fact there already was; when Rees was on holiday, Alfie Button stepped in: "I made lots of money sticking some of the bets."

When Tree expected a horse to win, he told only his owners and Grace and his immediate family. His brother Michael was privy to most secrets, although he wasn't much interested in racing. It used to infuriate Tree that Michael had put only £5 each way on one of his tips – 'If that's all you're doing, I'm not going to bother in future' – while passing them on to his own friends, some of whom did bet heavily. Tree adored his nieces Isabella and Esther, and on the days when he was close to utter confidence, they were taken care of too. He opened a bookmaker's account for them before they'd reached their teens. They were at their convent school one red letter day when they won £300. Word reached the nuns, who were scandalised, but saw that good might yet come from bad: the winnings must go into the poor box. The nieces thought quickly enough to persuade the nuns that the windfall had been only £50.

One of the apprentices, Ron Bode, asked Tree to put £5 for him on one of the yard's runners. "I thought it was a good thing. I watched the race and it wasn't off a yard. So I went back to the office and I asked him, had he put the bet on? 'That's what you asked me to do.'" Bode protested that the horse hadn't been very busy. "You didn't ask me that," retorted Tree. Yet Bode also benefitted from a characteristic of Tree's that many mention: his generosity. While Bode was still apprenticed, his father died, leaving his mother in financial difficulty. "I explained the situation to Mr Tree and asked for a loan of £50. 'How will you pay it back?' I asked him to deduct £1 a week from my wages. He gave instructions to Miss Hastings to send my mother a cheque. The next week, I noticed nothing had been deducted from my next wage packet. Nothing ever was." Twelve months later and for the remaining three years of Bode's apprenticeship, further £50 cheques were sent to his mother.

Tree was famously kind to his friends' children. He treated Celia 'Cece' Knight – daughter of his bridge and croquet sparring partner, Guy Knight – like his own favourite child. He took her racing to Longchamp and Deauville, and when she was in London training to be a nurse, they went to the best restaurants. "After lunch one day we walked into an art gallery. Among the paintings on show was a Munnings of a gypsy caravan. As it happened I had a caravan myself at the time. Jeremy bought the picture and promised, 'I'll leave it to you in my will.' And he did." She rode a horse of Jock Whitney's in the first ladies' race at Newbury. To prepare for it, she rode work for Tree and another trainer. "Johnny Gomez was a great help at Beckhampton. Unfortunately I was given a riding-out saddle and the leathers were too short. I got cramp in my calves and fell off the horse after the post. I broke my C2 vertebra and spent four weeks on my back in hospital. Jeremy was absolutely mortified by my accident. His idea of a pick-me-up was to bring me caviar."

Ginny Leng, uniquely the holder of three consecutive European individual event riders' titles, tells how for the 10 years during which her horses dominated the eventing world, they were welcomed to Beckhampton. They included Master Craftsman and Welton Houdini, who won Badminton; Murphy Himself and Night Cap II, who both won at Burghley; and Priceless, a Badminton winner who for good measure was the first horse to win Burghley twice. Leng worked them twice a week on Tree's gallops. She says, "Jeremy Tree was a hero. He was incredibly kind to me. I owed him a massive amount for allowing me to use his gallops and prep my horses for the major events. Without him it wouldn't have been possible." The only 'rent' she paid was a bottle or two for Tree's gallops man, Edgar Blake. Edgar was the nephew of Fred Darling's yard man Jack Blake, with added attitude. Where his gallops were concerned, 'they shall not pass'. Tree used to field complaints about Edgar's robust handling of intruders. There was a day when the Beaufort Hunt thundered over the downs, led by a retired Admiral. Edgar drove a tractor straight at them. He cursed them loudly, fluently and at length. As the huntsmen turned, in silence, Edgar spotted a family member on a small pony at the rear: "And you, young Somerset, you should know bloody better!" The Admiral was foolish enough to tell Tree: "I'm very unhappy. Your man was bombastic, rude. I've never heard such language." "And you were a sailor?" replied Tree.

When the Queen visited Beckhampton, Edgar scandalised everyone by announcing, "I don't want to meet her. She must have better things to do than meet the likes of me." He did his best to be inconspicuous among the staff lined up respectfully outside the yard, but her car pulled up next to him, a window wound down, and a Royal voice said, "I hear you don't want to meet me." Edgar stuck to his guns: "I'm sure you've got something else to do, Ma'am."

Blake, like his uncle before him, was a Beckhampton 'lifer'. When Tree retired, there were four lads in the yard with 35 or more years' service, and another four with over 25 years. One of the reasons they stayed for so long was their affection for Tree. The present head lad Steve Raymont says, "If you did something wrong, of course you got a bollocking. He'd look at you over his half-glasses: 'Out you go.' And then it was all forgotten by evening stables. He was a proper gentleman." Former apprentice Ian Watters says, "He was a great man to work for. What I loved about the bloke was that he treated all his people just the same and all his horses just the same." Ron Bode remembers, "We were looked after like Lords. Our job was to ride and look after the horses and go the races with them. Everything else was done for us. We had fitted yard clothing from a tailor in Marlborough, and a charcoal grey suit for the races." He remembers the Beckhampton food being so good that the lads were picky about the fare provided at racecourses. The cook at the lads' canteen at Newmarket was stung by their criticism: he used to cry, "Jeremy's lads are in – get the silver out!" Pearl O'Connell, whose husband Denis worked at Beckhampton from 1965 to 2007, says:

> "No one could've wished for a better boss than Jeremy Tree. He never bawled anyone out in front of the others if they did something wrong. Every Christmas he sent round a turkey and bottles of sherry and port to the wives. The children got individual presents. When I'd been ill, there was Mr Tree at the door with a massive bouquet and a hamper. He was so kind and considerate to his workers. You'd never meet another man like him."

Tree was open-handed with his horses, too. When Nicky Vigors left to launch his own training career, Tree arranged for both Whitney and Engelhard to send him good-quality older horses from Beckhampton. Sir Mark Prescott was the beneficiary when Tree had to make room for some yearlings. There simply weren't enough boxes to go round, and Tree was forced to shed one of his owners, Major-General Sir George Burns. He asked Sir George, "Do you want the good news or the bad news?" The soldier chose the bad. "It's your filly. I'm afraid she's unathletic." Sir George wanted the good news: "Oh, I didn't say there was any good news." He recommended 'a talented young trainer in Newmarket' who'd be able to devote much more time to Sir George's filly than he could, and to get the best from her. Sir Mark acquired a wonderful owner who never gave him a moment's anxiety, save for when Sir George, well into his eighties, insisted on taking part in the ceremonial parades on Horse Guards, with a nervous Sir Mark convinced 'he'd fall off and I'd lose him.'

The most public of Tree's acts of altruism was the result of the drought of 1976, the hottest summer since records began. His gallops were baked hard. Tree had two of Jock Whitney's good horses, Bright Finish and Intermission, targeted at big end-of-season races, and he wouldn't risk them on the prevailing ground. Fate intervened when he was in Deauville; he met the young trainer Michael Stoute. The pair knew each slightly from Barbados, where Tree's parents had a home. Tree heard from Stoute that the Jockey Club had just put in a new all-weather gallop at Newmarket. "Even before I got home from France, Jeremy 'phoned to say that he was sending me the horses," says Sir Michael today; "It was a very, very generous gesture; not many people would've done that." The two men kept in touch about the horses by telephone, and when Stoute ran them, both won, Bright Finish in the Jockey Club Cup and the filly Intermission taking the Cambridgeshire. Stoute's success with Whitney's horses reaped its reward: "When Bright Finish ran, a Swedish owner thought she looked very well and as a result he sent four yearlings to me." One of the youngsters was Fair Salinia, who in 1978 became the first filly to win the Oaks, the Irish Oaks and the Yorkshire Oaks. That in turn caught the attention of the Aga Khan, and the second batch of yearlings that he sent to Stoute contained Shergar. Sir Michael says, "I'm eternally grateful to Jeremy. He helped my career enormously. And he was a really good handler of a classy horse." As for the less classy animals, "He didn't need to!"

CHAPTER TWENTY-THREE

The arrival of Prince Khalid

Four jockeys had the lion's share of the rides during Jeremy Tree's years at Beckhampton: Tommy Gosling, Jimmy Lindley, Lester Piggott and Pat Eddery. Gosling had shared the apprentice riders' championship in 1945. He rode for Beckhampton before a combination of bad injuries and weight problems led to his early retirement in 1958. His worst injury was caused by a saddle slipping. As he fell, he was kicked on the head and knocked out. When Gosling came round, he remounted, rode back to the unsaddling and drove home. Later, complaining of headaches, he was taken to hospital. He had a brain clot. By chance, a pioneer in brain surgery was visiting from the United States, and his life was saved. The incident led to the mandatory use of reinforced crash helmets.

Gosling became a trainer. He liked a plot. A friend saw him at the York August meeting and heard Gosling couldn't find a hotel. The man had a twin room and offered him the spare. The next morning he woke to a susurrus of whispered telephone calls. Gosling was talking to the owners of London taxi firms, telling them to give bundles of £5 notes to their drivers. The plan was for them to stop at every betting shop they passed and back a horse of his, running at Yarmouth. Before the start of racing at York, the friend asked a rails bookmaker, as casually as he could, what price so-and-so at Yarmouth? '14–1, Sir.' He asked for starting price. The result came through. The horse had won. Then the SP: 9–4. The jockey was an Australian with, unknown to Gosling, a large retinue of punters. The dogs had barked from Yarmouth to the Yarra Valley.

Gosling's replacement was Jimmy Lindley. In the decade from 1960 he spent eight years as stable jockey: "I had a lot of fun with Jeremy Tree. He was an easy man to work for." Lindley was a stylish jockey and a strong one. Unfortunately, the source of his strength was also his weakness; from the start of his career he struggled not to put on weight. When he was 21 in the mid-1950s, he weighed 9st 7lb, but with diets and determination he managed to get down to 8st 6lb. It took sustained effort to remain there; hence his dismay at the banquet masquerading as breakfast at Beckhampton. His first season in the yard was notable for his wins on Monet in the Stewards' Cup and Persian Road in the Bessborough Stakes, providing Jock Whitney and Jeremy Tree with their first winner together at Royal Ascot. Persian Road led two furlongs out and 'kept on well under strong handling.' Later in the season the horse won the Ebor, though Tree doubted if Lindley could do the weight; he turned to the French-based Australian jockey, George Moore. Lindley's next red-letter days were Only For Life's 2000 Guineas of and the near-miss by Spree. He recalls Spree as a hard ride: "She always went terrifically well behind horses, but pulled up the moment she hit the front. When I won the Nassau on her she practically skidded past the post." The following year he had the thrill and then disappointment of Double Jump, and then he partnered another good horse of Whitney's, Gulf Pearl, winner of the Chester Vase.

Jimmy Lindley's association with Jeremy Tree ended in a dispiriting way. Noel Murless split with Lester Piggott in 1967; he offered Lindley the position of first jockey. Lindley replied no, his place was at Beckhampton. Murless persisted: he had an exciting colt called Royal Palace, winner of the Royal Lodge Stakes the previous season, and his owner Jim Joel wanted Lindley to ride Royal Palace in all his races. Murless asked, could Jimmy get a release from his retainer to ride Royal Palace only? Lindley took the proposal to Tree, who vetoed it at once, saying, "We've four of our own entered in the Derby." Lindley thought that was a bit rich; the previous season's Beckhampton two year old colts were moderate. Nevertheless, he told Murless he had an agreement with Tree, and he couldn't accept the ride on Royal Palace. It was an outcome that reflected well on Lindley, less so on Tree: the thought 'dog in a manger' is hard to resist. Lindley had to watch as George Moore won the 2000 Guineas and the Derby aboard Royal Palace. In neither race did Beckhampton even have a runner, as Lindley had foreseen. Murless ended the season as top trainer, with 60 winners and £256,699 in prize money. Jeremy Tree finished in tenth place with £30,064 from 30 wins. Just in win percentages, Lindley's rejection of Murless' offer to be stable jockey cost him, in our terms, almost £370,000 that season – never mind the glory, and the likely additional opportunities.

It got worse. Beckhampton had two nice horses the following year, Jock Whitney's sprinter D'Urberville and Monica Sheriffe's two year old The Elk, but Lindley hardly sat on either of them. He partnered D'Urberville to an all-the-way win in the Temple Stakes, but had to watch as Joe Mercer won the King's Stand Stakes on the colt. D'Urberville was set to carry 8st 3lb, and Jimmy had no hope of making the weight. It was D'Urberville's standout performance, beating the subsequent July Cup, King George Stakes and Nunthorpe Stakes winner So Blessed by a comfortable two lengths. Tree thought on the day D'Urberville was the fastest horse he trained. As for The Elk, Lindley was in the saddle when it was withdrawn at the start on its intended debut. The following day, he had a fall. The papers said he was 'rather badly shaken,' but he'd sustained a shoulder injury. As the weeks passed, The Elk had two promising 'sighters.'

A week before York's August meeting, Jimmy was able to tell Tree the doctor had passed him fit. He was raring to ride. 'Good,' replied Tree, 'But I've booked Lester to ride in the Ebor.' "In that case," replied Lindley, "He might as well ride all of yours." So their connection ended. Today, Lindley has only good things to say about Jeremy Tree: "No trainer was more professional. Everything was done to perfection. He was a great man to ride for. He gave you terrific confidence. 'Ride it exactly how you want to.' And he understood that mistakes happen." At the time, Lindley could've been forgiven a portion of the German dish *schadenfreude* when Lester was beaten a neck on the Ebor horse, finished first in the Great Voltigeur on Charles Engelhard's Ribocarre – only to be disqualified and placed second; and was second again on Tree's other runner of the day. But Miss Mon's horse The Elk won a maiden at Doncaster, a nursery at Newmarket and what is now the Racing Post Trophy – with a jockey other than Lindley in the saddle each time. He was unlucky. He rode for another five seasons, including a year based in France, but the weight was bound to beat him in the end. Between Lindley leaving Beckhampton and quitting the saddle, Noel Murless trained five more classic winners.

For the next decade, and especially for Jock Whitney's good horses, Lester Piggott was Beckhampton's preferred jockey. Tree said Lester, "Used to come down once a year, usually at about the time of the Newbury spring meeting. It was an occasion I looked forward to with some trepidation. It was fairly obvious that all Lester really wanted to do was to find out what was any good and what he'd be prepared to ride. He used to try them all pretty highly. From anyone else it would have been quite unacceptable." "Hugely infuriating," he added, but Tree thought Piggott was a brilliant judge. One day, on impulse, he legged Lester up on a colt called Saviour. It was lethargic, flopping about at the back of the string. 'This is all right,' muttered Lester, and he was right. Saviour ran second in the King Edward VII Stakes at Royal Ascot, third in the Great Voltigeur and fourth in the St Leger. Lester provided a story which Tree loved to tell against himself. He made the mistake of telling Piggott that he'd been invited back to Eton to give a talk on racing. "What do you think I should say, Lester?" "Say you've got 'flu."

The first two prolific winners which Lester rode for Beckhampton were sprinters: Whitney's Swing Easy and Monica Sheriffe's Constans. Swing Easy was foaled in a year of fast two year olds – Cawston's Pride, Fireside Chat, Mummy's Pet, My Swallow – but ran up a sequence of four wins, including the New Stakes at Royal Ascot and the July Stakes. Piggott exercised his right as a freelance and switched to My Swallow in the Prix de la Salmandre. As he'd expected, My Swallow handled the step up to seven furlongs better than Swing Easy. My Swallow completed a clean sweep of all the top French two year old races that year; Swing Easy didn't quite stay. His final outing was back at six furlongs in the Middle Park, where he ran into Brigadier Gerard, the best horse trained in England between Tudor Minstrel and Frankel. Swing Easy was simple to categorise: a good colt, but not quite top class. On his first run as a three year old, he ran into the other champion of his generation, Mill Reef. It was in the Greenham Stakes, and thereafter he was never tried beyond sprint distances. He finished seven lengths behind Mill Reef, and then only fourth in a handicap at York. It seemed he'd be difficult to place, but he defied appearances. First he won an unsatisfactory King's Stand Stakes. He was fourth favourite at 7–1, behind a good French colt, Mummy's Pet and Cawston's Pride. The French horse swerved badly at the start, Mummy's Pet had too much use made of him, and Cawston's Pride refused to race. Swing Easy was left with an open goal. He won a valuable stakes race at Doncaster, and was awarded the Nunthorpe after being bumped and finishing second. His last race before retirement and syndication was in the Prix de l'Abbaye, where he never quite got to an older sprinter. For what he was, he won a lot of races and prize money.

"It is obvious that he won't have to improve at all to win almost any maiden race in the Calendar." That was the conclusion of the gurus at Timeform after Constans had completed his first season. In his three runs he'd twice finished placed behind the 130-rated So Blessed. As forecast, he won on his reappearance, in a supposed 2000 Guineas trial at Kempton which attracted three runners, none of whom won another race that season. At the end of it, having broken blood vessels and shown signs of breathing problems, Constans was hobdayed, and as all hopes of a stud career had been extinguished, he was gelded too. After a third season in which he made all to win a small six-furlong handicap from six attempts, his Timeform assessment had fallen from 117 to 109 and then 98. Yet he won the last three of his races as a five year old; first beating the good sprinter Jukebox – that season's Stewards' Cup winner – at a difference of only 3lb. Then he took the Rous Memorial Stakes at Ascot, finally a handicap at York under one of Lester Piggott's masterpiece rides: 'headway to lead inside final furlong, very cleverly,' reads the form book. Television retrospectives on Piggott tend to concentrate on his all-action efforts, like Roberto in the last half-furlong of the Derby or Royal Academy in his fairytale comeback at the Breeders' Cup. Arguably, he's better represented by the times he sat, sphinx-like and motionless, and produced his mount to win on the line. Lester could manhandle horses home, and he could ride in near silence, as he did on Constans at York, leading a single stride from the post. Constans started his six year old season by winning four races in a row. *Racehorses of 1971* saluted:

> "That Constans was able to win seven consecutive races and remain unbeaten for over a year is a remarkable tribute to the skill of his trainer. To pull off such a feat with the toughest and soundest of horses is difficult enough. To accomplish it with one that has been hobdayed and has also had a tendency to break blood vessels is not far short of miraculous."

Constans raced on for three more seasons, lightly campaigned, winning just one race each year. Remarkably, it was the same race, the Prix de Saint-Georges at Longchamp, ridden by Piggott each time. Jeremy Tree loved racing in France, and cottoned onto the rich prize money there before most trainers this side of the Channel. Monica Sherrife's old warrior Constans was retired after his third win in Paris. Like all her horses, he was well bought: 5,100 guineas as a yearling. He raced for eight seasons, winning 12 times from 34 starts, and his Timeform rating as a nine year old was higher than it'd been as a two year old. He was only a sprint handicapper, but when Tree looked back on his training career, and his winners of the Arc and the classics, he named Constans as his favourite horse.

Not everything went according to plan. While Constans was gathering momentum, Tree struggled with one of his greatest frustrations: Jock Whitney's US-bred Sea Pigeon, a dark brown son of Sea Bird. Whitney's American trainer doubted if Sea Pigeon would stand training on dirt, so the colt was sent to Jeremy Tree. He had misadventures from the start. Another horse on the plane from Kentucky developed an infectious disease. On arrival at Beckhampton, Sea Pigeon was sent to a nearby isolation yard. He didn't come into Tree's care until the May of his first season. He presented as an exceptionally good mover 'who was full of life and was going to be a handful to train.' Johnny Gomez was assigned to ride Sea Pigeon in all his work. The colt had another setback when he fell into barbed wire. It was late summer before he started to show anything on the gallops, apart from an aversion to starting stalls. Then it became apparent that Sea Pigeon might be the yard's best two year old. He confirmed it when he worked well on the Trial Grounds with a couple of older horses.

Finally in October, Tree got him onto a racecourse, in the Duke of Edinburgh Stakes at Ascot. He made all and sauntered home under Piggott, ears pricked. Piggott reported that Sea Pigeon was 'definitely a good horse in the making.' His three year old season began with Piggott keen to ride him in the 2000 Guineas, but another jockey had been booked. "Who?" asked Piggott. "Bill Williamson." "Is he still riding?" Sea Pigeon's prep race for the Guineas was the Craven Stakes. It was a disaster. Tree winced when he described Sea Pigeon's antics: "He ran away going to the start. They had a hell of a job getting him into the stalls – and then he just took off." He fought Williamson for six furlongs, blew up, and finished a distant seventh. Tree decided to bypass the Guineas and to concentrate on the Derby. The Dante Stakes was Sea Pigeon's next race, and again he was over-keen, and finished fourth. His chances for the Derby were reflected in his starting price of 50–1. Hopes evaporated when Sea Pigeon got stirred up in the preliminaries and pulled hard for his head on the way to post. He hung badly up the home straight, finishing seventh to Morston, beaten 10 lengths. He had two further runs that season, the second of them a deplorable flop in France: his jockey said, 'He was like a person on the edge of a nervous breakdown.' Tree had him gelded. Sea Pigeon was recuperating at a nearby stud – still colty, 'a definite handful' said the stud manager – when Tree received a letter from a northern owner offering £8,000 for the horse, to send him over hurdles.

First he went to Gordon Richards' stable near Penrith, where his regular hurdles rider Jonjo O'Neill said, "He used to be lathered [in sweat] every morning. He was a hot and agitated horse who only settled down as he got older and stronger." Nonetheless, Richards coaxed him to win four of his five races in his first term over hurdles, and three more the following season. Richards and his heavy-betting owner fell out over another horse, and Sea Pigeon was sent to the trainer associated with his multiple glories: Peter Easterby. One of the best ever dual-purpose trainers turned Sea Pigeon into one of the best ever dual-purpose horses. Easterby managed to get Sea Pigeon to relax: "Once you'd got his head right, he could beat anything." Mostly, he did – winning almost 30 races for Easterby, including two Fighting Fifth Hurdles, two Champion Hurdles, two Chester Cups and a memorable short-head victory in the Ebor. Tree found it galling. Not the hurdles wins: it's good for future business when a former flat horse does well over obstacles for its new connections. To have a 'cull' winning 15 times on the flat, including top handicaps, was another matter. It was difficult to see that Tree could've done anything different, other than turn out Sea Pigeon after gelding, and wait for a year or two. That wasn't an option: Jeremy Tree had been embarrassed by Sea Pigeon's wayward displays on the racecourse, and he needed empty boxes.

The two years during which he trained Sea Pigeon were Tree's least successful for a decade. The seasons that followed brought the good horses and the good times back, in spades. As a disappointment left the yard, the usual intake of yearlings were arriving. One was Juliette Marny, a bay filly by Blakeney out of Set Free, a half-sister to Spree. She was home-bred by James Morrison, as Spree had been, and caught the eye in her second run as a two year old, finishing strongly into second in a field of 16. In the Lingfield Oaks Trial, Juliette Marny had a hard race to wear down Harmonise by a head, receiving 5lb. The win gave Morrison's filly a chance in the Oaks – but it gave Harmonise a better one. Piggott had cast his net about for a ride. His choices included another of Tree's, Brilliantine. She was the hard luck story of the Cheshire Oaks, finding trouble in running before finishing powerfully into third. Piggott's other options disappeared, and he was left to pick between Juliette Marny and Brilliantine. The imponderables were, Juliette Marny seemed held on form, and she was – at Piggott's suggestion – wearing blinkers for the first time. Brilliantine's only win had come on heavy ground; it was forecast to be firm going at Epsom. Neither Tree nor Piggott could be sure that the blinkers would improve one filly, or that the other would act on unfamiliar going. Lester prevaricated, and tried to get Tree to make the decision. As late as noon on race day, Piggott was on the phone to Tree: "Which one would you choose?" "Leave me out of it," said Tree: "It's your choice!" The jockey picked Juliette Marny. It didn't seem likely to affect the outcome of the race; she was only sixth favourite at 12–1 in a field of 12. Brilliantine was 20–1. The close-up in *The Sporting Life* read, "Always in touch, led well below distance, quickened, readily." Or in Piggott's words, "We were never in danger." He equalled Fred Archer's tally of 21 classic wins. Juliette Marny was the first classic winner to wear blinkers.

Tree nominated the Irish Oaks as Juliette Marny's next race. James Morrison travelled to Dublin the day before the race; everyone else stayed at Beckhampton that night, and missed their flight the next day. A private aircraft was booked. The young baronet William Pigott-Brown had a runner opposing Juliette Marny. He hitched a lift, and made Tree an offer: "If you win the race, Jeremy, you pay for the plane. If I win, I'll pay." Tree, who was fairly confident he was going to be in the winner's enclosure, smiled, "I don't think so, Sir William." Only one of the fillies Juliette Marny had beaten at Epsom re-opposed; the most potent of her new antagonists was the French filly Nobiliary, who'd finished second in the Derby. There was a might-be-anything filly of Vincent O'Brien's, Tuscarora, wide-margin winner of a maiden race. Piggott could've ridden any of the three; he stuck with Juliette Marny. Tuscarora's jockey made first run from a long way out, pursued by Nobiliary from the entrance to the straight, with Juliette Marny some way back. She didn't pick off Nobiliary until the furlong pole, and had to be hard ridden to overcome Tuscarora in the last 50 yards, winning by a neck. For all that she wore blinkers, she showed herself to be consistent and courageous. In her last race, the Yorkshire Oaks, she injured a leg and was retired. She produced a number of winners, including of a Group 1 and Listed races, and her daughters included good broodmares. She was no saint: on the home gallops she dropped every rider that sat on her. Like all the difficult ones, she ended up as Johnny Gomez's ride, and the lads who knew him swear that Johnny could've sat securely on a pea. Juliette Marny's importance, beyond providing Jeremy Tree's second classic winner, was to get the yard rolling again after some quiet seasons. The next two years belonged to Jock Whitney's horses – the ones at Beckhampton, and the ones sent to Michael Stoute.

The 1976 season was notable not only for several of Whitney's horses winning a series of good races, but the more so because three of them were foaled in consecutive years by the same broodmare, Peace. She may have fallen short of the high hopes created by her debut win for Jeremy Tree, but her first three foals – Peaceful, Quiet Fling and Intermission – won eight races. Peaceful won three handicaps, including the Vaux Gold Tankard and the Old Newton Cup. Every time he won, he was ridden by the apprentice Steve Raymont. Quiet Fling won three races in his second season before finishing runner-up in the Irish St Leger. On his first start as a four year old he won the John Porter Stakes, before stepping up in class to the Coronation Cup. He may have stumbled on a weak renewal, and two of his main rivals suffered mishaps, but ridden with something in hand by Piggott, he won by half a length. Later in the year the drinks company Schweppes contacted Jeremy Tree to ask for permission to feature Quiet Fling in their annual racing calendar. It used to hang in half the pubs in Britain, a different horse for each month. Tree and Whitney were happy for Quiet Fling to be featured. Schweppes contacted Lester Piggott. He mentioned an appearance fee akin to the gross national product of a small country. The outcome was that Quiet Fling's lad Johnny Dixon was told to spruce up himself and his horse, fetch Mr Whitney's colours and have a quiet sit. He was given five pounds. Intermission won once before her transfer to Newmarket; Michael Stoute won twice with her, a handicap at Ascot, then the Cambridgeshire.

Alongside the successes of Peace's three offspring, Whitney won eight more races with two stayers, the three year old Bright Finish and the five year old gelding John Cherry. Bright Finish had one run in his first season, backward but promising. He was carefully placed by Tree to win his first four races in 1976, stepping him up in trip from 10.5 furlongs to a mile and a half and then a mile and six. After his move to Stoute came the two-mile Jockey Club Cup, in which Piggott rode the other jockeys to sleep, taking a clear lead soon after halfway and coming home eight lengths clear. Back with Tree the following season, Bright Finish was one of the sufferers in a bout of coughing at the yard, and wasn't seen out before the Yorkshire Cup, which he won, but he was out of his depth in the Gold Cup. He was sold to Australia. John Cherry was a tough and ultra-consistent horse who'd won three times over 16 furlongs as a three year old, twice more aged four, and then finished a close second in the Cesarewitch. He did even better as a five year old, winning the Chester Cup on the bridle, the Newbury Autumn Cup, and then he was tried again in the Cesarewitch. He was set to carry 9st 13lb – 7lb more than any horse before him had carried to victory. He produced a jaw-dropping performance, Piggott holding onto him until a furlong and a half from the finish, easing him into the lead, sitting still, winning by five lengths and eight. To some surprise, he was sold to the Newmarket yard of Harry Thomson Jones to go hurdling. His flat form didn't fully translate to National Hunt, though as he won two Long Walk Hurdles, he was hardly a failure. Jones ran him on the flat in the 1977 season, taking the Queen Alexandra Stakes and beating high-class stayers in the Prix Gladiateur. John Cherry was a durable and genuine dual-purpose horse, but not quite a Sea Pigeon.

Jock Whitney needed the tonic of his horses' successes. In 1976 he suffered a major heart attack. As he convalesced, he continued to send horses to Jeremy Tree, but there was nothing of any account in the time up to his death in 1982. That season, 18 horses ran in his colours. Tree was forced to plan for a stable without his friend and principal patron of over 20 years. He was boosted by the arrival of new owners: the Duke of Marlborough, Lord Vestey, the Keswick family, Lady Murless, and, renewing a long-dormant connection with Beckhampton, the Macdonald-Buchanans. Tree couldn't possibly have known it, but the most important of the newcomers – for Beckhampton and for worldwide racing – was a low-profile Saudi businessman, Prince Khalid Abdullah. Tree said years later he, 'Really hadn't wanted to start with a lot of new owners. I'd even thought of retiring when Mr Whitney eventually gave up, but when the Prince came along I thought it best not to rock the boat.'

Humphrey Cottrill was a vastly experienced former trainer. He was stewarding one day at Newbury and met Khalid Abdullah. The two men hit it off, and Abdullah asked Cottrill to look after his racing interests. Cottrill was taken aback when he discovered the extent of Abdullah's ambitions, "But I did manage to contain him for a season or two and got him going quietly." That included recommending Jeremy Tree. The Prince previously had a handful of horses in training, including with Ron Smyth at Epsom. Cottrill felt that Tree's personality and the Beckhampton set-up would suit his client. He was right. Tree went with Abdullah and Cottrill to the Keeneland sales. He'd never visited Keeneland, for all his connections to Kentucky via Jock Whitney. He and Cottrill bought one yearling at the select sale, a bay colt by the multiple stakes winner In Reality out of Tamerett. At $225,000, the colt was vastly more expensive than any yearling either man had bought before. They'd also looked carefully at a Northern Dancer colt, but decided not to bid: it was sold to Stavros Niarchos for $1.3 million. Tree was an idiosyncratic judge of a horse: he'd examine it side on, and had no interest in having it walked towards him, although other prospective buyers would want to see if the animal was offset. Essentially, Tree bought what he liked and ignored what he didn't, and at another of the sessions at Keeneland, he saw and liked a filly which he was able to buy for a relatively modest $50,000. She was to be named Abeer and became Khalid Abdullah's first Royal Ascot winner. The In Reality colt became his owner's first classic winner: Known Fact.

CHAPTER TWENTY-FOUR

Triumph in Paris

Only a few months passed between Jeremy Tree's first Keeneland sale and Abeer's win in the Queen Mary Stakes. She was Khalid Abdullah's first Group race winner. The second was another filly, Alia, who won the Princess Royal Stakes at Ascot. The third was Known Fact. It was obvious from his first pieces of work that the colt had ability, but he was headstrong. He came to hand soon enough to win a Newbury maiden in May, but ran a demented race at Goodwood, tearing off so fast that he had nothing in reserve when another horse challenged.

Tree called Willie Carson, who describes Known Fact as, "An absolute bolter. I went down to Beckhampton to straighten him out. I said, 'I'm not riding him unless I keep the ride.'" The first test of the partnership was at Newbury. "For the first two furlongs I just manhandled his head over the rails. He gradually got the message. He had to be buried; if he saw any daylight, he attacked it." The struggle between horse and jockey was so fierce that Known Fact burned himself out, finishing third. His final two year old race was in the Middle Park. He settled well in a small field, coming to lead when Carson asked him to, and winning narrowly but comfortably. At the unsaddling, the delighted Carson told Tree, "We'll win the Guineas!" His seasonal debut as a three year old was in the Greenham Stakes over seven furlongs. Known Fact finished fourth, just behind a horse of John Dunlop's, Posse. The two were the strongest finishers.

The hot favourite for the 2000 Guineas was the French-trained Nureyev, the Northern Dancer colt who Cottrill and Tree had passed over at Keeneland. He won his prep race for the Guineas by six lengths. Racegoers at Newmarket saw him float down to the start, with the most perfect action. He was drawn 1; Known Fact was in stall 4. Carson got cover behind the leaders on the stands' side. Nureyev's jockey Philippe Paquet dropped his mount to the back of the field. His options included going to his right and challenging on the outside of the field, or shadowing the rails runners and waiting for a gap. He chose neither. Instead, as the field approached the Bushes and Carson went for home on Known Fact, Paquet elected to run through the middle of the pack. Nureyev showed brilliant speed to weave through inside the last furlong, but in doing so he gave Posse a violent bump. For a few moments it seemed Carson's first run on Known Fact would win the day, but close home Nureyev wore him down to win by a neck. Meanwhile Posse recovered from being almost on the ground to finish powerfully into third. It wasn't until his rider Pat Eddery came back that the majority of racegoers knew there'd been an incident in the race. A furious Eddery said, in the hearing of all, 'Paquet nearly killed me.' A stewards' enquiry was announced. After 45 minutes the placings were revised. Nureyev was disqualified and placed last. Paquet was banned for seven days. Posse was moved up to second – and Known Fact to first. When the head-on view of the race was played, the reason for the stewards' action became clear.

The consensus was that if Paquet had made any other choice, he must've won on Nureyev. Others argued that if the race could be run again, it'd be won by Posse, who got to within a length of winning after being all but knocked over. Only a rematch between the three would provide the answers. It never happened. A week before the Guineas, the vets took a blood sample from Known Fact. They told Tree that the colt was about to get an infection, and shouldn't run; Tree decided to ignore them. Then when Known Fact was being saddled at Newmarket, Tree's assistant Roger Charlton heard a horse cough nearby. He looked, and saw Nureyev. Both colts ran when sick, or about to be. Afterwards, Nureyev had a virus which persisted through the summer. He never raced again. Known Fact developed bronchitis, and wasn't seen until Deauville in August, where he failed to act on soft ground. Meanwhile, Posse had franked the Guineas form by winning the St James's Palace Stakes and the Sussex Stakes. Then he too coughed, and was retired. Known Fact's last run as a three year old was in the Queen Elizabeth II Stakes, against the year-older Henry Cecil-trained Kris, a brilliant, consistent miler who came into the race with 14 wins from his 15 starts. Kris led at the turn into the straight, Known Fact two lengths behind. In the last hundred yards, Known Fact drew alongside Kris, and put his head, then his neck, in front. Carson says, "He was a very, very good racehorse that day." Known Fact was rated Best Miler of the year by Timeform, with a rating of 135.

Khalid Abdullah could've been forgiven for thinking that racing was an easy game, after winning a classic in his second season with Jeremy Tree. Not least, because out of his first eight horses bought by Cottrill and Tree at Keeneland, seven won races. But a little rain fell, too. A colt named Sand Hawk was, at £264,000, the most expensive yearling sold at auction in the British Isles up to the end of 1978. He'd been troubled by sore shins as a two year old and didn't run; the following year he managed a single, minor win. As for Known Fact's four year old campaign, he finished a bad last of four in his prep race for the Lockinge Stakes. Jeremy Tree said: "He ran appallingly. I could in no way account for it. We've had him tested for everything. The vet has looked down his throat, blood tests, everything else – and he's perfectly all right." Known Fact was taken out of training. Humphrey Cottrill explained stallion syndication to Prince Khalid Abdullah: how it spread risks. The Prince asked, "Why would I need to do that?" Known Fact was taken into the breeding operation that is now Juddmonte. It has ambitious standards: not all of its Group-race winning colts are retained as in-house stallions; and the ones that fall short of expectations are moved on. So it was with Known Fact. He was sold after four non-achieving years in the covering shed.

Scintillate became Jeremy Tree's fourth classic winner when she won the 1979 Oaks. She was a bay, by the miler Sparkler out of James Morrison's broodmare Set Free. Morrison admitted that originally, he didn't hold out much hope for Set Free: "Her first three foals looked like giraffes. [The first] was a slow giant who eventually won in Panama. Her second was enormous and never ran. Her third was also quite big and unhappily broke a leg." He decided to mate Set Free to smaller stallions, and the first result was Juliette Marny, by Blakeney. Three foals later came Julio Mariner, also by Blakeney, who in line with Morrison's policy to sell his yearling colts, went to Tattersalls, sold well, and won the 1976 St Leger for Clive Brittain.

There was little in Scintillate's first season to suggest she'd uphold her dam's record. On the last of her three first-season runs, the Fillies' Mile at Ascot, she kept on well to finish four lengths fourth. She won her first race on her three year old debut, in a bunch finish at Newbury. She was barely considered at 20–1 for the Oaks. The going was soft. Neither Morrison nor Tree was sure that Scintillate would stay a mile and a half, and she'd never run on anything softer than good. Pat Eddery was asked to ride a waiting race. He held her up at the back, and coming down to Tattenham Corner she could be seen travelling strongly. In the straight, Eddery let her stride out, and she moved up to the leaders with the greatest of ease before quickening to win by three lengths. Alas, she, who hadn't looked like a classic prospect before the Oaks, didn't look like one afterwards. The fillies she beat in the Oaks were a moderate lot, none of whom handled the going. Scintillate went back to the Morrison's stud in Wiltshire, and despite the attentions of good stallions, was a failure as a broodmare.

Sharpo was Monica Sheriffe's last big-race winner, and like the ones before him, he was bought inexpensively at the yearling sales. He didn't have an appealing conformation: one jockey looked at his angular hocks and said, 'He'll never see a racecourse.' Only For Life had shown the same defect, so Tree had no qualms about paying 10,000 guineas for the chestnut. Sheriffe had been playing bridge with a banker called Fred Packard. He asked her, could he have a half share in the next horse she bought? Later, she wished she hadn't agreed. It didn't take much to irritate Miss Mon, and Packard used to ask before Sharpo's races, 'What will happen to his value if he loses?' After a win, the question was, 'How much is he worth now?' He claimed it was so he could adjust his insurance cover.

Sharpo was well enough thought of at home that he started second favourite on his debut in a 22-runner late-season maiden at Newbury. He finished in midfield. After the race it was found that he'd fractured a pelvis. He was entered in the autumn sales, in case the injury made him untrainable; luckily, the horse mended and was withdrawn from the sale. The following spring the trainer was mulling over a choice of entries for Sharpo. Run in a five-furlong maiden at Bath – or the Group 2 Temple Stakes at Sandown? Had he run at Bath, Sharpo would've been the biggest certainty ever trained at Beckhampton. He travelled to Sandown with a stablemate, and all the way to the races a Manton lad who'd hitched a lift heard about this horse that 'couldn't be beat' – the other horse. Sharpo came down the box's ramp as green as grass, rearing up on his hind legs. He plainly needed the race. He started at 33–1, which didn't seem overly generous, but he belied the odds with an extraordinary performance. It took him half the race to find his feet, but he then showed rare pace to challenge and go clear, from a field that included the second and third from Newmarket's Palace House Stakes. Having only previously raced in public for two or three furlongs before injuring himself, Sharpo had thrashed Group 3 sprinters. The clockers and the form readers welcomed a potential champion sprinter, and they were right: Sharpo was the kind of sprinter who comes along every decade or so. It was a pity he was foaled in the same year as one of the best of two or three decades: Moorestyle. Timeform don't often name a sprinter as their Horse of the Year, but Moorestyle was an exception.

After Sharpo's sensational debut, he was a close second in the Cork and Orrery at Royal Ascot. He then easily won the William Hill Sprint Championship (the Nunthorpe) at York. But Sharpo also ran into

Moorestyle twice, at five furlongs and six, and was beaten each time. In the two colts' four year old campaigns, Tree made sure that Sharpo avoided Moorestyle wherever possible. He felt that Moorestyle was better at six furlongs than five, so Sharpo was campaigned at the minimum trip. It turned out to be a vintage year for sprinters: joining Sharpo and Moorestyle was the Michael Stoute-trained filly Marwell, unbeaten after five races as a two year old. At Longchamp, Sharpo won the Prix de Saint-Georges, the race which Miss Sheriffe's Constans had farmed. He disappointed in the King's Stand Stakes, finishing jarred up on the firm ground. As a result, he was a derisory 14–1 when he met Marwell and Moorestyle again in the Nunthorpe Stakes at York. Marwell was a shade of odds-on, and looked the winner when she challenged Moorestyle below the distance, but Pat Eddery had been quietly stalking, and when he pulled Sharpo out to challenge, the response was devastating: Sharpo smothered the other two horses for speed and beat Marwell by two and a half lengths with another length and a half back to Moorestyle. The first and second re-opposed in the Prix de l'Abbaye, where on his favoured soft ground Sharpo seemed to have an outstanding chance, but Marwell got first run on him, and though he made up ground rapidly, Sharpo didn't quite catch her.

Sheriffe kept Sharpo in training as a five year old, and with his main rivals retired, her colt had an obvious chance of taking the major sprinting prizes, which he did. The early part of that summer was unusually dry, and a number of races which looked at his mercy passed by before Tree anxiously let him take his chance on firm going in the July Cup. He dominated his 15 rivals in the paddock and in the race, with Eddery holding him up as long as he dared before weaving through to lead on the rising ground. He then took the Nunthorpe for the third year in succession, with the same tactics. His last race was the 1982 renewal of the Abbaye. He led just inside the last furlong to win readily by a length. Monica Sheriffe's interest in racing was largely confined to her own horses. On the flight back from Paris, John Hanmer was surprised to be poked in the back and asked, "What won the Arc, boy?"

Sharpo was Europe's top sprinter of 1982, and he was Beckhampton's best horse during that and the preceding year. In the background, the yard was quietly filling with Khalid Abdullah's horses. The Prince's ambitions – shown first at the sales, then by a rapidly-growing number of home-bred yearlings – soon outstripped Tree's capacity to house them. After Jock Whitney's death Tree helped arrange Abdullah's purchase of some of Whitney's broodmares. They included Rockfest, the third dam of Frankel and Noble Mission. Tree was Abdullah's principal trainer, and he had his choice of all the Juddmonte yearlings, but other trainers were needed to take the ones that Tree didn't want. Tree built seven new boxes in 1988, in which year he had 70 horses, his largest-ever string. Around 40 of them were Abdullah's; even so, they represented only a third of the Prince's horses in training. Inevitably, Tree made one or two poor calls. One was Dancing Brave, who Tree passed over because he was undershot, 'parrot beaked'. That imperfection never made a horse run slower, but Tree was looking at over 100 yearlings and whittling them down to a couple of dozen: "It involves some horribly difficult decisions," he said. It was frustrating when the horse won the 2000 Guineas and the Prix de l'Arc de Triomphe and much else for another stable, but Tree was delighted for Khalid Abdullah. And as he pointed out, "I've ducked a lot of bullets, very expensive yearlings which I didn't happen to like." He and Abdullah got on well. "He comes down quite often to Beckhampton. He couldn't be nicer, is enormously interested and is becoming extremely knowledgeable," Tree said. It probably helped that Tree had mixed with the highest-born of Britain and America all his life, and wasn't the slightest intimidated by wealth or status. Not many men would've asked their largest owner, on a humid day at Keeneland, "Do you really expect me to walk all the way up that hill again, just to look at a horse?" It can be imagined that the Prince found it refreshing. He says, "Jeremy Tree was to play a significant role in expanding Juddmonte's racing and breeding operations. I had the highest regard for him. He was never keen to over-rate my horses. I was particularly amused by his caution, even pessimism on occasions."

Prince Khalid's Rainbow Quest was the last top-class horse trained by Jeremy Tree. He was an imposing bay colt by Blushing Groom, a high-class French colt who finished third in the 1977 Derby. Abdullah paid $950,000 for Rainbow Quest at the Fasig-Tipton sales in Kentucky. It was the second-highest price out of almost 400 yearlings at the sale, so it could be imagined there'd be a jostle among the Beckhampton lads to look after the new arrival. Steve Raymont was at the head of the queue, and to this day rates Rainbow Quest with Al Kazeem as the best horse he's ridden at the yard. Rainbow Quest's first two runs suggested Prince Khalid's dollars had been well spent. First the colt went to Newmarket and won a 30-runner maiden. Next he appeared in another big field at Newbury, winning comfortably, eased before the line.

Rainbow Quest's final two year old race was the Dewhurst Stakes – a step straight up to the top division. The opposition was headed by Vincent O'Brien's El Gran Senor, unbeaten winner of his three races in Ireland. Nonetheless, Tree was confident of winning, and he was aghast when, after a prolonged struggle, Rainbow Quest went down by half a length to El Gran Senor, with daylight to the other runners. Rainbow Quest closed all the way to the line, allowing his trainer to hope that he might reverse the form over longer distances. The leading contenders for the 1984 Guineas included the three top-rated colts of the previous season: El Gran Senor, Rainbow Quest and Lear Fan, the last-named being, like El Gran Senor, unbeaten. The contest between the three, with a solid supporting cast, turned out to be as brilliant as had been hoped. Lear Fan set off at a fast pace to make all the running; El Gran Senor tracked him as far as The Dip and then quickened away as he liked. Lear Fan weakened and was passed by an outsider, Chief Singer. Rainbow Quest couldn't match the pace ahead of him and finished fourth. If it was any consolation to his connections, he'd run in one of the best of all Guineas, on a par with Brigadier Gerard's defeat of Mill Reef and My Swallow in 1971.

The immediate evidence of the race's quality was the time. Timeform clocked El Gran Senor's winning performance at **1.54** fast. As the season unfolded, the principals franked the form. El Gran Senor was beaten a short head in the Derby and won the Irish Derby. Chief Singer won the St James's Palace Stakes by eight lengths; beat the top sprinters in the July Cup; and reverted to a mile to win the Sussex Stakes. Lear Fan won the Prix Jacques le Marois, easily. Rainbow Quest was sent to Chantilly for the Prix du Jockey Club, where he stayed on well into third, beaten only two lengths. His next mission was a third attempt to topple El Gran Senor, this time in the Irish Derby. A new tactic was tried; Rainbow Quest was sent for home from the entrance to the straight, with the aim of stretching El Gran Senor's stamina, which had ebbed away in the last few yards at Epsom. The end result was the same: El Gran Senor came past Rainbow Quest readily enough, and beat him by a length.

Rainbow Quest was rested and put aside for the Great Voltigeur at York. Tree left nothing to chance; a pacemaker ensured a strong gallop, Rainbow Quest was settled some way off it, made ground stylishly up the straight, led two furlongs out and coasted home by three lengths. The second horse, Gold And Ivory, promptly won two Group 1s on the continent. The London bookmakers made Rainbow Quest favourite for his final outing, the Prix de l'Arc de Triomphe, but not for the first time he was tetchy in the preliminaries; he had a pronounced dislike of parades. He ran no race at all. The likely explanation was that he'd gone over the top for the season. At the start of Rainbow Quest's four year old season, Tree told Timeform:

> "[He's] done well from three to four and I couldn't be more pleased with him. We decided quite a long time ago that his first major race this year would be the Coronation Cup. Obviously if things go well [there] he'll run in all the big mile-and-a-half races. I hope he'll manage to win some of them."

Happily, it went mostly to plan. Two essentials had been identified: Rainbow Quest needed a pacemaker, so a front-running colt called August was bought from Barry Hills' yard, to be ridden by Steve Raymont. And the jockey should be Pat Eddery: no one else had won on Rainbow Quest. The pieces were in place when he picked up a weak heat at Goodwood before the Coronation Cup, which he won hard held. Two difficult assignments came next. First was a small-field Eclipse Stakes, where Rainbow Quest was running below his optimum distance against a high-class four year old mare, Pebbles. He went down by two lengths, a result put in context when Pebbles won the Champion Stakes and the Breeders' Cup Turf. Next, Rainbow Quest gave 16lb weight for age to good three year olds in the King George VI and Queen Elizabeth Diamond Stakes and was beaten by a neck and three quarters of a length. The second horse, Oh So Sharp, was that season's winner of the fillies' triple crown. Rainbow Quest's farewell was back in Paris, in the Arc. It was possibly Jeremy Tree's greatest achievement to bring back a five year old colt to the race in which he'd run lamentably the previous year, to keep him calm in the preliminaries, and to coax a lifetime best from him.

The favourite for the race was the previous year's winner, the French colt Sagace. As the Arc field turned for home, a stable companion moved obligingly off the rails, Sagace whizzed through the gap, and looked as if he'd be the fourth horse to win back-to-back Arcs. Behind him, though, Rainbow Quest had moved smoothly through the field onto the heels of the leaders. He was momentarily checked by the manoeuvre of Sagace's stablemate, but then he was in the clear, laying down the only challenge to Sagace. It was imperceptible from the stands, but in the closing stages the bandaged Sagace, perhaps feeling the firm ground, jinked left and gave Rainbow Quest a bump. Sagace's young jockey kept on driving with his whip in his right hand and his horse again hung into Rainbow Quest. There was some surprise when the hooter went for a stewards' enquiry, but Eddery had already decided on an objection:

"I'm not sure whether Jeremy had heard [the hooter]. He loved Rainbow Quest, he loved Paris, and the look on his face as I dismounted told me that, beaten or not, he'd just enjoyed one of the great training moments of his [career]. I'd seldom seen him as happy as he was that day. His horse had only finished second but he was plainly proud beyond words. I wasn't accepting defeat just yet. 'I'm going to object,' I said, receiving by way of return one of Jeremy's quizzical, old-fashioned looks."

Eddery told the Longchamp stewards the first barge from Sagace 'had been quite hard enough for my horse to lose his action and it could've cost me the race.' Tree strolled over, "In that deceptively nonchalant way of his. He was still high on the emotion of having come so close. I know he thought we had no chance of getting the race." At that moment a British journalist rushed up to them and shouted, 'You've got it!' The PMU screens above their heads were flashing the revised placings. "Jeremy was reduced to silence, but then he threw his arms around me in a great bear-hug, before turning in search of his owner."

Jeremy Tree delighted in his social routine. Any summer Sunday morning when he wasn't racing abroad was spent at his friend Guy Knight's house in Lockinge, for a ferocious game of croquet with Knight and Tim Forster and sometimes Ginger Dennistoun. Play was accompanied by much betting, cursing and laughter. Sunday afternoons were set aside for backgammon or bridge. Every Good Friday, Tree hosted a bridge party at Beckhampton. Miss Mon startled the gathering by exclaiming, "The bugger's bid four spades!" As every eye swivelled to her, she growled, "Term of endearment." The usual Sunday bridge foursome was at Ardington House, the home of a racing family, the Barings. Tree's regular companions in the quartet were Molly Baring, her lodger John Hanmer, and Guy Knight. It was in their company early in 1989 that Tree collapsed with an aneurism. He announced his retirement the week before Royal Ascot. There was a glorious last hurrah: he sent out three winners at the meeting; Danehill, Two Timing and True Panache, all in the colours of Khalid Abdullah. Tree was delighted with True

Panache, who won him his only Hunt Cup, after two second placings and two thirds. But it was Danehill who founded dynasties: he was that rarest of commodities, a stallion who consistently sired offspring of greater racing merit than his own.

Jeremy Tree's hope for Danehill was that he'd be a 2000 Guineas horse. The first part of the plan was achieved: Danehill won the Free Handicap over seven furlongs and took his place in the Guineas line-up. He expended energy chasing a top-class colt, Nashwan, and weakened to finish third. It was a similar story in the Irish 2000 Guineas, where he faded in the last furlong. Tree decided to drop him back in distance, and Danehill rewarded him with a resounding three-length win in the Cork and Orrery Stakes, in a course record time. He couldn't quite match the top sprinters in the July Cup, but signed off with a clear-cut win in the Group 1 Sprint Cup at Haydock. The astonishing contribution that Danehill has made to the breed couldn't have been foreseen from his racing record. Indeed it wasn't, because – despite Tree arguing for Danehill to be retained by Juddmonte, to add speed to its middle-distance broodmares – he was sold for £4 million to a partnership between Coolmore and an Australian stud. What followed puts him up with Hyperion and Northern Dancer as a prepotent stallion. He shuttled between the two hemispheres, covering for 11 seasons in Australia and one in Japan. He sired the winners of over 1,500 races, among them 89 winners of Group or Grade 1s. He was a multiple champion sire in Australia, England, France and Ireland. Many of his sons are themselves successful stallions, and his broodmares are just as good; one of his daughters, Kind – also trained at Beckhampton – is the dam of Frankel.

After Jeremy Tree announced his retirement, Juddmonte sent him a lavish photo album, recording the best 18 horses he trained for Khalid Abdullah. They were the winners of 25 Group races, arranged alphabetically from Abeer to Zelphi, with particular prominence for Danehill, Known Fact and Rainbow Quest. It was inscribed by the Prince's racing manager, Grant Pritchard-Gordon: "On behalf of all at Juddmonte, I would like to thank you for some wonderful memories and hope that this album will roll back the years on our association with Beckhampton. I have ordered a new album for the continuing saga!"

Jeremy Tree was a great trainer, and an uncommonly nice man. Many of his friends wrote to him with their best wishes. Monica Sheriffe noted fondly:

> "Those years were the happiest of my life with all those wonderful WINS and all the fun we had with [Jack] Clayton and the classic horse [Only For Life] – all those lovely victories in France with the old hero [Constans] and then Sharpo and "the reins breaking at Salisbury" – all such happy memories, and you are a top class trainer and friend second to none. I remember Jock saying to me one day, 'What would you do if Jeremy gave up?' and I replied I would give up too."

In among the messages was a letter from County Durham. It was from Michael Curry. His father was a miner and had followed Tree's horses until his death in 1984:

> "You became in a sense a friend of the family. My father often used to say, as he sat at the kitchen table with the racing pages, 'I think Jeremy will win us our holiday money today.' I will never forget the day when we heard that Only For Life had won the 2000 Guineas at 33–1.
>
> "Please accept, on behalf of my family and myself, sincere best wishes for a long and happy retirement, filled with contentment and pleasure – which you have unknowingly given us over the past 30 years."

Jeremy Tree took the trouble to reply. Michael Curry has kept the letter to this day. It read:

> "Thank you so much for your absolutely charming letter, which gave me great pleasure and really seemed to make 37 years of pretty hard work

seem worthwhile. I am also very glad that, if your family has been following my horses for so many years, you still have the postage to send the letter!

"I feel confident that everything here will carry on much the same, as the staff will remain and most of the owners have expressed their intention of continuing to have horses with Roger Charlton, who I am confident will be a great success, and I hope worthy of your continued interest and support.

"Should you ever be in these parts do let me know and come and see us. I send all best wishes, and again, a great many thanks for an outstandingly nice letter."

CHAPTER TWENTY-FIVE

Roger Charlton's dream debut

From swimming pool attendant to Derby-winning trainer isn't an obvious career path, but it's served Roger Charlton well. The catalyst was a horse called Highland Brae, injured out hunting. Charlton remembered reading that swimming was a good therapy for horses. At the time there were only two equine pools in England, and Charlton took Highland Brae to the nearest, at Leamington Spa. He noticed that all sorts of horses were arriving at the pool for exercise and treatment, some from a long way away. It was a 'Eureka' moment. He went on a fact-finding mission to Chantilly, where the much-respected trainer Angel Penna had his own pool. Charlton's second brainwave was to take the pool to the horses, by siting his pool in a training centre. He chose Lambourn, and bought Peter Walwyn's former yard, Windsor House. A combination of Grand National-winning jockey Tim Norman, his JCB and a retired local builder turned some of the boxes into a pool complex for the 'pal's price' of £20,000. It was finished just seven months after Charlton's visit to Leamington with Highland Brae, and it was the first pool in the country to have heated water, and drying-off boxes with infrared lamps. Having made his investment, Charlton invited trainers and the racing press to take a look; Highland Brae acted as guinea pig. The result was plenty of curious and favourable coverage, supported by divine intervention. He'd planned on horses being sent to Windsor House with leg or back problems, to exercise and recuperate without strain. So they were; what he couldn't have foreseen, when he was showing the pool off at the end of 1975, was that the following summer would be the hottest on record. Hose pipe bans extended for months. The countryside was baked to a shade of pale ochre. Many trainers' gallops were too hard for their horses to be worked. Since three minutes and 10 laps of Charlton's pool were calculated as the exercise equivalent of two steady canters, the trainers suddenly had another option. The pool was patronised by the Walwyn cousins, Fulke and Peter, and by Barry Hills and Fred Winter. Ian Balding sent horses from Kingsclere, Jeremy Hindley from Newmarket and John Dunlop from Arundel.

Jeremy Tree wasn't keen on anything new-fangled. He thought all-weather racing was no different from the dogs. Nicky Vigors shocked him at evening stables, when they were puzzling over a delicate filly with no appetite. Horse cubes had just been introduced; why not give them a try? suggested Vigors. "Certainly not! It's like eating out of tins." After Tree had won the first race to be sponsored by Vodafone, a racecourse official told him that when the prize was presented he'd be given a mobile phone. "I can't think of anything I'd like less." So it was quite an adventure for Tree when he sent his first horses to Windsor House, especially as they included a trio of his big-race hopes: Bright Finish, Intermission and John Cherry. At the end of the summer, with the sun still beating down, and having been unable to do any work with them at home, he sent Bright Finish and Intermission to Michael Stoute; but John Cherry was trained to win the Chester Cup and the Cesarewitch in Charlton's pool. Tree had already been complimentary. A two year old of his, Ground Cover, had won well at Windsor in May. He'd been aimed at Chester, but had sore shins, so he boarded with Charlton for a week's swimming. Rerouted to Windsor, he beat 19 rivals by five lengths and four. Tree insisted that Charlton accompany him into the winner's enclosure, and told the press, 'I haven't trained the horse: this man has.' That and other endorsements helped drum up business, and before long Charlton and his helpers were swimming 40 or more horses a day.

Charlton was horse mad from the age of three onwards; first on a tiny pony, then hunting from age five. His father was a farmer and permit holder. His parents' friend and neighbour Edward Courage was the trainer of the Champion Chase winner Royal Relief and of Spanish Steps, hero of a Hennessy Gold Cup and placed in three consecutive Grand Nationals. Charlton's own racing career began as soon as he reached 16 and could ride in point-to-points. He rode 'about a dozen' winners between the flags, and three under Rules. One of the three would be worth a hundred to any amateur rider, because it was at the Cheltenham Festival, riding Edward Courage's Pride Of Kentucky in the Kim Muir Handicap Chase of 1969. The only previous time he rode the horse, he was unseated in a novice 'chase at Hereford. He made no mistake at Cheltenham, beating the formidable John Lawrence (later Lord Oaksey) into second place. Charlton's mount had never been a great jumper, and various senior riders hadn't managed to win on him. The going was desperate at Cheltenham; a steward went into the weighing room to tell the amateurs to be sensible. The pace was slow, Pride Of Kentucky 'loved the ground,' recalls Charlton, 'and just jumped from fence to fence.' After the weigh-in and the presentation, he was accosted by an Irishman who asked, "Would you be the rider of the last winner?" A group of the man's ecstatic countrymen – who'd lumped on at 100–8 and better – rushed Charlton in triumph into a bar and plied him with celebratory whiskies. Charlton had wasted hard to make Pride Of Kentucky's weight. He was acutely dehydrated. The whisky went into the emptiest of stomachs. He remembered being 'on all fours' before he was rescued and driven home by his friend Charles Barnett, latterly the supremo at Ascot.

Charlton was working for the Chepstow trainer Colin Davies at the time. He had zero interest in going to university, and left school at 17 to get into racing as soon as he could. During his two years with Davies, the mighty Persian War was in the yard, winning Champion Hurdles. The stable jockey was Brough Scott, who described Charlton as, "Working as hard as any of the lads." The point came when Charlton realised that a yard far from a major training centre didn't offer him any scope to progress. His father prodded him to take a gap year, to try new things in a different environment. Davies wrote him a reference:

> "He has proved himself almost indispensable. He is a first class amateur rider, both over hurdles and fences, and only increasing weight could prevent his already excellent progress as a National Hunt jockey. He is a calm and patient horseman with good hands and a natural seat and is particularly good with young horses. He is hardworking, conscientious and absolutely reliable in every way. He has a most pleasant personality and displays tact and consideration in his relationship with the stable lads, with whom he has always got on extremely well. He has acted as my assistant trainer [this season] and I know it will be difficult to replace him."

Despite his praise for Charlton's jockeyship, Davies only provided his assistant with one ride in two years. Charlton laughs that, "Height and weight prevented me from getting many rides, and lack of ability was even more of a problem." He wasn't riding future champions: "Permit holders who didn't want to pay for a jockey would put me up on unbelievably bad horses in selling hurdles and novice chases; I didn't have any fear and would ride absolutely anything."

He decided to try his luck in Australia. He had a job lined up as a hand – a jackeroo – on an outback station, but a severe drought resulted in the offer being withdrawn. To 'assistant trainer' and 'amateur rider' on his CV were added working in a restaurant, cutting sugar cane, driving a 15-ton grain truck, finally surveying mineral claims for a firm of geologists, in the semi-desert of Western Australia. He was in a small team who lived in caravans, typically 150 or 200 miles from the towns of Kalgoorlie and Meekathara – 'place of little water.' The only available entertainment was to drive to the towns and back on dust tracks, for heroic drinking sessions. Charlton moved to Hong Kong and a job in stockbroking, helped by his employer's belief that he was an expert on Australian mining shares: "It was a bull market. It wasn't hard to make money." Back in London with the same firm, he spent two years pining for horses and racing. Then came the injury to Highland Brae and the revelatory visit to the equine pool. Charlton spied, "An excuse to get out of the City, to reconnect to racing and maybe make some money."

Windsor House was a success from Day One. In the first week, as well as the Lambourn-based horses who were walked to the pool, swam, and walked back to their yards, five of the boxes housed 'boarders' – horses sent from further afield. As word spread and the business grew, up to half the boxes were occupied at any given time. Charlton's venture was a therapeutic and commercial winner. But, walking round a swimming pool four or five hundred times a day isn't terribly stimulating. Charlton longed to train a few horses from the empty boxes at Windsor House. On reflection, he couldn't. There'd be a conflict of interest with his trainer clients. If a horse sent to him for a swimming course ran well afterwards, its owner might think, 'Well, Roger Charlton has the pool, and he trains. He might as well have my horse.' He was trying to resolve the dilemma when he met Nicky Henderson, who was looking for a yard in Lambourn. Charlton took a profit on Windsor House and was gloomily facing a return to stockbroking when Jeremy Tree said, 'Come to Beckhampton. Be my assistant.' He jumped at the opportunity. That was in 1978, and Charlton has been at the yard ever since. Tree involved him as much as possible from the start. If he had a big-race runner, or took a horse to France, there was never a question of Charlton being left at Beckhampton to mind the shop and study the *Racing Calendar*. On the contrary: 'I think you ought to come, you might meet somebody worth meeting,' he was told.

The transition was measured and deliberate. "He was brilliant to work for. He shared things. He was a great teacher. One morning we were in the tack room. He was doing the board and he asked me, 'If you were the trainer, what would you work today?' Which of course raises its own series of questions: 'Why that one? Who's going to ride which?' 'Over what distance – and on which surface?' 'Is that one lame, and do you need to book the vet?' The obvious point was, it was part of his assistant's job to be on top of those things: to look at them as a trainer would. So that did get me thinking every day, until the question was asked again. He had a very good brain, and an eye for detail. He planned carefully. He decided what was going to gallop, what was going to canter. Over time, he did a little less and I did a little more."

When Tree asked Charlton to join him at Beckhampton, he was musing about retirement. He'd planned to stay for as long as Jock Whitney had horses in training, but when Whitney died, Tree had already taken the initial consignments of Khalid Abdullah's horses. The retirement which he'd considered was postponed, not least because the Prince made it clear he wanted Tree to continue. Some assistant trainers might have chafed at their ambitions being put on indefinite hold; Charlton didn't. He'd quickly become beguiled by Beckhampton, he reasoned that he still had much to learn from Tree, whom he liked and admired; not least, the yard was developing and expanding. Tree's training problems in the arid summer of 1976 prompted him to invest at once in an all-weather gallop. He built a few more boxes. Abdullah sent him more horses. The stable was on an upward curve.

It helped that Tree travelled a lot. He'd leave Charlton with a basic outline of what horses might be running, and let him get on with their training in his absence. For the sales, Tree would send his assistant a few days in advance: Charlton would 'Look round every individual, producing a shortlist for both of us to go and look at.' Tree might scoff at the selections: "Frankly, I don't know what you see in this horse, because I don't like it." Conversely, Charlton was always searching for good conformation; within reason, Tree wasn't. Charlton would point out a defect, Tree shot back that he'd trained 'Many worse horses than that; the advantage is that this horse will be cheaper.' After Only For Life, he was never put off by bad hocks. Fifteen years on, he was happy to defy the nay-sayers and buy Sharpo, who Charlton remembers had 'Feet turned out like Charlie Chaplin,' and was lame as a yearling. "The horse was treated with much respect and ran only on ground that was suitable for him. Had he run countless times on fast ground, which was tempting, he wouldn't have stood training. It was Jeremy's patience and skill that stood out." The aspect of Tree's accumulated knowledge that most intrigued Charlton was his understanding of his horses' families. Tree would tell him, 'This family gets sore shins,' or, 'This family never gets a proper coat till the autumn,' and he was invariably right.

Charlton became Master of Beckhampton in the last circumstances he would've wished. Tree's collapse early in the 1989 season made his retirement inevitable. It was announced shortly before Royal Ascot that he intended to hand in his licence at the end of the season; Roger Charlton would take his place. Among the press tributes, *The Times* wrote in November: "With [Tree's] retirement next Saturday, the sight of his Olympian frame unsaddling yet another Royal Ascot winner will become a Turf memory, and racing will overnight be the poorer." Danehill and two other Royal Ascot winners gave Tree a memorable farewell, but at the end of the season, it didn't seem that Roger Charlton could look forward to much of an inheritance. Beckhampton had only one two year old winner in 1989. It seemed likely that Charlton's first season would be spent making the best of a bunch of moderate three year olds. Jeremy Tree's last end-of-term report to Khalid Abdullah noted that he had 'Three useful maidens in the yard, but none seemed top class.'

In common with most of the Prince's yearling colts, the trio had been entered for the Derby. Each of them had run once as two year old and each had placed: Quest For Fame and Deploy were second and third in a big-field maiden at Newbury; Sanglamore had finished second in a minor event at Leicester. His jockey Steve Cauthen said afterwards, 'He'll be a nice maiden for next year' – not an endorsement to set the pulse racing. Their respective ratings in *Racehorses of 1989* were 89p, 88p and 84p. The suffix 'p' meant 'likely to improve,' but stratospheric progress was needed for the trio to make any impression at Listed or Group race level. Timeform's top-rated two year old of 1989 had a rating of 123p – 34lb and more in front of the Beckhampton trio. More than a hundred of the first-season colts and fillies were rated above them. Unsurprisingly, Charlton hesitated before committing his owner to any further Derby entry fees. His assessments for the 'stable tour' articles in the racing press were downbeat. Sanglamore was, "Inexperienced, finishing second in a not very good maiden at Leicester. I hope he will improve." He refrained from adding that one morning late in the season, Tree had worked Sanglamore with three other two year olds. Charlton returned from the races to find a note on his desk. It read, 'Sanglamore was tailed off, he is absolutely useless. Could not go on at all.' The colt had finished 15 lengths in arrears in a gallop with moderate horses.

Quest For Fame was described as, "A big individual needing a little time." As for Deploy, he was 'A late foal, big, backward and highly strung.' For good measure, Charlton said, "My early feeling is that we're unlikely to have a classic horse." In the greater scheme of things, that was compensated for by Khalid Abdullah having a strong contender for the top prizes at another stable: it was Digression, the easy winner of the Royal Lodge Stakes, rated 116p. Charlton's debut season began with a disappointment; his much-touted Lincoln favourite Becquerel was unplaced. Then in the space of a week, Abdullah's Beckhampton three year olds all won their maiden races. The first was Deploy, at Haydock. Sanglamore won at Leicester, followed by Quest For Fame, easily, at Newbury. Apart from noting Charlton's relief at getting off the mark – "I'm glad that's out of the way" – the racing press paid the three winners little attention as future big-race winners, the more so as Quest For Fame was beaten at Newmarket on his next outing. Nonetheless, they were working well at home, and seemed to be improving from gallop to gallop. If they were to take their chances at Epsom and elsewhere, they had to be raised sharply in class for their prep races.

Quest For Fame ran in the Chester Vase. There were only three runners; one of them was Belmez, winner of both his previous races for Henry Cecil.

Quest For Fame ran well on a course unlikely to suit him, but Belmez beat him comfortably by a length and was immediately promoted to second favourite for the Derby, behind Abdullah's Digression. Sanglamore was sent to York for the Dante Stakes. The ground was soft and he relished it, winning by a length and a half and the same; the third horse had occupied that position in the 2000 Guineas, beaten a similar distance. Even so, the pundits' reactions were reflected in the headline, 'Sanglamore trial success fails to solve Derby puzzle.' The bookmakers' verdict was clear: Sanglamore was quoted at 20–1 for Epsom. Roger Charlton, who was described as, 'looking both delighted and somewhat bemused,' talked about the King Edward VII Stakes at Royal Ascot or the Prix du Jockey Club as possible targets for Sanglamore. As for the Derby, "We'll have to see what the owner wants to do" – and the owner had Digression, about whom Pat Eddery had given a favourable report: he'd worked well in a racecourse gallop at Lingfield, was in good form, and handled the left-handed incline well. Still, Charlton had plenty of cause for optimism; his two colts had finished first and a close second in two of the main Derby trials. In the space of 48 hours a week later, their prospects were transformed. News came from Newmarket that Belmez had injured a tendon, and Digression was well beaten in the Predominate Stakes at Goodwood, finishing only fifth of six. Having been 7–2 favourite for the Derby on the morning of the race, he was out to 16–1 that evening. He took his chance in the race, but significantly, Eddery switched to Quest For Fame.

Sanglamore headed to the Prix du Jockey Club. The target was decided by his uncertain temperament; he was described by his trainer as 'a quirky bugger', and Quest For Fame was thought more likely to cope with the hoopla at Epsom. It was a miserable day at Chantilly, raining heavily, and Eddery was no more than hopeful for Sanglamore: he was, "A difficult ride. He hated the stalls and he pulled too hard for his own good." It was a help that he was allowed to go into the stalls last, and another bonus when the field went a strong gallop: he was able to settle Sanglamore plumb last. "I waited until we turned into the straight and then waited a bit longer, anxious to conserve his run as late as possible. When I did ask him, we [had] a great run through and got up to beat the favourite." It was a precision manoeuvre: Sanglamore won by half a length and the same. The runner-up, Epervier Bleu, later won the Prix Niel and finished second in the Prix de l'Arc de Triomphe.

The French Derby was Charlton's tenth winner. Suddenly, it seemed that his eleventh might be Quest For Fame in the English Derby. The two colts didn't work together, but Charlton assessed them as 'Within a few feet of each other,' and there were grounds for thinking that the horses who'd run at Chantilly were a stronger collection than those lined up at Epsom. The Prix du Jockey Club had three horses who were unbeaten before the race, Epervier Bleu among them; it also contained three promising English-trained runners who as yearlings hadn't been entered for Epsom. By contrast, the Derby seemed to have a different favourite every week in the two months before the race, and of the top 10 in the ante-post market at the beginning of May, only four made it to the start. On the Sunday, one of the papers headed its Derby form guide, "18 reasons [runners] why the field might still be running on Thursday morning," mocking that "an assessment of the form is like taking a belly flop off a high board into a pool of quicksand." Its correspondent rejected Quest For Fame as, "Too slow. Never considered true Derby class until his first-season trainer began to look at the limitations of the other runners."

The writer was unlucky. A few hours after the paper appeared, Sanglamore's success in France illuminated the chance of Quest For Fame. Furthermore, the Derby hopeful had enjoyed a trouble-free preparation, including being worked twice the wrong way back down the wood shavings gallop at Beckhampton, which provided a rehearsal for the gradient and angle of Tattenham Corner. There hadn't been any full-dress trials: "He doesn't need a lot of work, he looks well," said Charlton: "He has a good chance." Before then, he had to attend to his nerves. He recently told Lewis Porteous of the *Racing Post*:

"On the Monday morning I went to the doctors in Marlborough. I explained the situation and said, 'I'm probably not going to sleep over the next few days so would you prescribe sleeping pills or Valium?' He said he wouldn't give me them, but would give me some Beta-blockers. On the morning of the Derby I woke up at 5 am and started pacing about. Between waking up and the race I'd had three, having never had one before [or since]. By the time I got to the races my heart had nearly stopped. The whole thing was a slight trance and it unfolded without me getting revved."

The Derby favourite at 9–2 was Razeen, winner of the Predominate Stakes and Henry Cecil's replacement for Belmez; next in the betting were the first and second from the French 2000 Guineas; then at 7–1 came Quest For Fame. Pat Eddery had won two previous Derbys: on Grundy for Peter Walwyn and Golden Fleece for Vincent O'Brien. He took the view that Quest For Fame – by Rainbow Quest out of a Group 1 winning filly, Aryenne – was sure to get the trip at Epsom. An outsider blazed the trail; Eddery had Quest For Fame close up all the way, going well, and when he shook the reins at his horse two furlongs from the line, the pair quickened immediately, winning by three lengths and a length and a half. Eddery said he'd never been carried round Epsom more easily: "Precious few races go so perfectly to plan as this." The merit of the race was questioned at once; it was evident that the majority of the field hadn't stayed, and their subsequent performances indicated a non-vintage renewal.

At the end of the season, Timeform rated Quest For Fame at 127, 5lb behind their middle-distance horse of the year, the Arc winner Saumarez, another son of Rainbow Quest. The verdict sold Quest For Fame short. Saumarez beat Epervier Bleu by three quarters of a length in the Arc. That horse was previously half a length behind Sanglamore; and Quest For Fame was thought the equal of Sanglamore at home. No matter. Roger Charlton, Pat Eddery and Khalid Abdullah had pulled off a Derby double that had only been achieved once, 40 years before. The other person so closely associated with the two colts couldn't be at Epsom: Jeremy Tree was recovering from a stroke. The Prince told the press, "I'll always be grateful to Jeremy for being my foundation trainer." Charlton returned to Beckhampton, saw his winner into his box, and stood drinks for his lads at the Waggon and Horses. He said that Tree had trained both the Derby winners – 'And he trained me.' Tree, typically, deflected any credit, joking that he didn't think he'd left his successor with any decent prospects: "I was quite simply delighted and there was no feeling of regret at all." Sir Mark Prescott for one doesn't believe Tree harboured angels unawares; he'd seen too many good horses to overlook two at once. Prescott reckons that Tree's stepping aside and passing on Sanglamore and Quest For Fame – instead of keeping the licence for another year, letting Charlton do the work and collecting the plaudits himself – was simply another example of Tree's generosity. His view is borne out by Tree's head lad John Reed: "I took 50–1 Quest For Fame as a two year old. I knew Mr Tree thought a lot of him."

Jeremy Tree stayed at Beckhampton House in worsening health until his death in 1993. It was a sad time for him, for the Beckhampton lads whom he'd treated so kindly, and for Roger Charlton and his wife Clare, whose children Tree adored. Charlton says, "He, who'd always been bright, clever, interesting and fun, suddenly became very depressed. I involved him as much as I could. He'd just say, 'You're doing fine, you don't need any help from me.' It's easy to interfere, but he never once did." His humour was mostly intact; Ivor Herbert saw him sitting dolefully in the lobby of a Deauville hotel and asked how he was? "Clinging to the wreckage." But in one of his last interviews, Tree said training horses "Is a wonderful life, never in the slightest bit dull. When you wake up in the morning you can be elated or depressed, depending on whether you've had a winner or not. But you're still thinking, 'Where do we go from here?'"

Sir Peter O'Sullevan remembered Jeremy Tree as, "Charming, sweet, a real personality. He hadn't a big tip for himself, but he had a good feel for the genus *equus.* He was a great trainer. He didn't over-rate his horses. He assessed them with feeling."

CHAPTER TWENTY-SIX

'A great sense of history'

"Heaven's racing centre must look like Beckhampton," wrote Paul Hayward in *The Independent* soon after Roger Charlton took over the reins. It probably does. Beckhampton is a spellbinding place. The topography can be imagined as a pair of cupped hands. Where the hands meet, below the thumbs, are the house, Sam Darling's 1890s yard and a new 20-box American barn. From the low ground inside the vee of the hands, the land rises steeply to the fingertips – the skyline of Morgan's Hill and Cherhill Down. To the right, over the Calne road and towards Avebury, is the yard that Manna's Derby paid for, and another new barn. Far out to the left is the high perch of the Trial Grounds gallops. Inside the 700-acre vee is Beckhampton's workbench: 100 or so acres of grassland, which can be configured in any number of distances and gradients. The Valley gallop swings right and then left-handed through a cleft in the downs before opening out onto 10 furlongs more of grass. The all-weather gallops are a seven-furlong woodchip put in by Jeremy Tree, and a newer five-and-a-half furlong Polytrack alongside the Devizes Road grass gallop. Roger Charlton absorbed the history and the tradition so deeply that when he succeeded Jeremy Tree, he said: "I owe it to Beckhampton, the owners, the lads and Jeremy to make a success of things." He has often returned to the theme:

> "There's the feeling everything is as it's always been. There's a sense of timelessness about Beckhampton, a great sense of history." "This is a wonderful place to train racehorses and a wonderful place to bring owners. It's very special to me."
>
> "As well as training racehorses I feel it's my job to maintain the gallops, the buildings, the whole heritage of Beckhampton." "[The] effort not only to preserve, but to make sure the place flourishes, is important. I would hate to think when I leave here [it's] all crumbling and falling down."

A first-season trainer taking over a thriving yard from a successful and popular incumbent is sure to feel pressure. It's a moot point as to whether the stellar success of his first season reduced the pressure – or ratcheted it upwards. At the time, Charlton said that there'd been no great hopes for Sanglamore at Chantilly; after the colt won, any stress was taken away from Quest For Fame at Epsom. It would've been a bonus if Quest For Fame had followed up in the Irish Derby at the Curragh three weeks later, but it wasn't to be. He ran disappointingly, but Charlton nearly won the race with Prince Khalid's second string, Deploy, who found only the supplemented 1000 Guineas and Oaks winner Salsabil too good, going down by three parts of a length. Fleet Street's sub-editors were left to rue the lost headline: 'Charlton scores hat-trick for England.'

After such a start, the pressure shifts to repeating it. New owners and their horses arrived. Charlton was given planning permission for a new American barn behind the main yard. Providentially, he put his plan to one side, because the three-month period which began on the day Deploy finished second at the Curragh was the first of five quarters in which the economy fell into recession. It was a bad time for speculative building projects. Charlton inevitably couldn't match his 1990 season; Sanglamore provided a highlight by coming back from a year off to win on his reappearance in the Group 1 Prix d'Ispahan, making all: *The Times* called it, 'An exceptional feat of training.' In his next race, Sanglamore was third in the Eclipse, before finding only the Derby winner Generous too good in the King George VI and Queen Elizabeth Diamond Stakes. The colt had ligament trouble when being prepared for the Breeders' Cup, and was retired. Quest For Fame was second in the Juddmonte International at York and third in the Breeders' Cup Turf that season before, as a five year old, winning a valuable Santa Anita handicap for Charlton and then remaining in America.

Charlton today names Quest For Fame and the Derby as his best training moment. In the years immediately following, it may have been a millstone round his neck, because of the expectations created. From 37 winners in 1990, numbers dropped by a third in 1991. During 1994 the Queen sent Charlton yearlings for the first time; he won a Tattersalls sales race with Don Corleone, delivering a huge bonus pot to his owner; and he committed to putting up the new barn. Nonetheless, he asked his wife, "Why am I doing this? It's driving me mad." The year after, he trained Cap Juluca to set a weight-carrying record in the Cambridgeshire. The three year old colt finished fifth on his debut. Three months later he won a mile maiden race at Windsor, followed by the lady riders' race at the Ascot meeting which used to be sponsored by De Beers: the winning lady got gems to go with the glory. That day, it was the future trainer Eve Johnson Houghton. Cap Juluca then ran in strongly-contested handicaps at Newbury and York, a warm favourite and making all to win for Jason Weaver in both. His last race of the season was in the Cambridgeshire. Weaver couldn't take the ride, and was replaced by Richard Hughes: it was his first ride for Beckhampton. Cap Juluca's mark had risen by 3lb after his first handicap win and another 8lb after his second. Now he carried 9st 10lb. Hughes wasn't deterred from repeating the previous winning tactics: Cap Juluca made all the running on the stands' side. Hughes reckons it was, "One of the best handicap performances for years either side, to make all in the Cambridgeshire as a three year old. It was a helluva run." Cap Juluca was periodically unsound: unraced at two, followed by the successes of his second season; and he ran only once as a four year old. It was a fine training performance to win five races in a row with him.

Roger Charlton had 70 horses in his first season. Forty-five of them ran in the colours of Prince Khalid Abdullah – colours which Arnold Weinstock helped to choose. He was in the Prince's office one day when he was asked for his ideas. He pointed to the office curtains, which were pink, green and white. The Prince had been Jeremy Tree's principal owner for 12 years and has occupied the same position all through Roger Charlton's – to date – 25 completed seasons at Beckhampton. That too is a kind of pressure: Abdullah told Charlton, "Now you are the trainer the glory will be yours, but you will be responsible for the disasters." Abdullah has other able and successful trainers on the Juddmonte roster, not only in the USA, in France and in Ireland, but several here in England as well. In Tree's day, Beckhampton had the first pick of the Juddmonte yearlings. After his retirement, the policy was modified. For a while, there was a yearlings' beauty parade. Each of the Prince's trainers was invited to mark the youngsters out of 10. Charlton was surprised to see, from the notes Cecil held behind his back, that he was marking some of the colts and fillies 15 – with stars added for good measure. He gave a nought to other perfectly good yearlings. When Charlton challenged him, Cecil insisted that it was entirely logical; he was highlighting his enthusiasm for the animals he really, really wanted. Charlton took a different but complementary tack. He focused on the group of horses which he thought were just outside the equine oil paintings – Cecil's starred 15s – and awarded them 9s and 10s, hoping the Prince and his advisers would conclude, 'Roger liked that horse,' which as like as not had been dismissed by Cecil with a nought. Nowadays, Khalid Abdullah, with input from his Juddmonte team, decides which trainer in which country gets which yearlings. No more beauty parades.

The Prince's ownership has helped sustain Beckhampton in good and not-so-good times for close to 40 years; he's also had a significant influence on the yard's riding arrangements. When Pat Eddery became retained jockey for Juddmonte, he rode most of the other owners' horses at Beckhampton, first for Jeremy Tree, then for Charlton. Eddery rode Charlton's first winner, Deploy, then the two Derby horses, and most of the yard's runners until he retired at the end of the 1993 season. When Richard Hughes replaced Eddery as Abdullah's jockey from the 1994 to 1997 seasons, he too rode many of the other owners' horses – 104 winners in all.

The extra capacity provided by the new barn at Beckhampton meant that Charlton's string rose above 100 for the first time in the mid-1990s. It was unfortunate that they didn't include many good horses. One of the few was Tamarisk, who was bought at Tattersalls for 78,000 guineas by Highclere Thoroughbreds and won a £100,000 bonus in a sales race as a two year old in 1997. He was supplemented for the Dewhurst and ran honourably in second, which encouraged Charlton to train him for the 2000 Guineas. He didn't stay the mile, and reverted to sprinting, to good effect. He was second in the July Cup before taking Haydock's Group 1 sprint in the first week of September. Tamarisk was only Charlton's fourteenth winner of the season. His final tally for 1998 was 22 winners, his lowest total in all his time training. The situation was made worse when an important owner, Ahmed Salman, suddenly took his horses away. Charlton did well for Salman over several seasons, and had won a couple of races with a nice Danehill filly, Desert Lady. He entered her for a Listed event at Deauville. The owner had other ideas. Charlton spoke to him at Ascot. The timing could've been better; one of Salman's horses with Henry Cecil had just been beaten in the King George VI and Queen Elizabeth Diamond Stakes. The men disagreed over running plans for the filly. Two days later, a box arrived to collect Salman's horses. It seemed a disproportionate response to a minor argument. Bad turned to awful. Among the departed horses was a winning two year old, Oath, who went to Cecil and won the Derby.

Charlton's string fell to 70 at the start of the following season, the prelude to three quiet years. But the racehorse equivalents of the Sixth Cavalry rode to the rescue, headed, appropriately enough, by a series of fast sprinters. The first was Harmonic Way. In other hands, the colt's first three seasons would scream 'Plot.' He won on his debut, went almost two years and 16 races without a win, and then won the 1999 Stewards' Cup under a nerveless ride from Richard Hughes. It was notable, first for his riding with a 'jockeycam'; second for the consternation among the horse's connections when he sprang a 'last-to-first' plan on them in the parade ring. The field would go lickety-split, he said, and the horse would enjoy running through them late on. "Do you really have to drop him out *last*?" asked Charlton. The form book notes, 'Rear stands' side, good headway over one furlong out, ridden to lead inside [final furlong].' The camera on Hughes's helmet gave a dramatic view of Harmonic Way's snipe-like passage to the winning line. Hughes remembers it as, "A fun ride." At Royal Ascot the following year, he provided an identikit masterclass in the Wokingham: 'Held up last far side, smooth progress from two furlongs out, shaken up and effort one furlong out, led last 100 yards, soon clear, impressive.' Harmonic Way was evidently a mid-summer colt, as well as ideally suited by waiting tactics: twelve months on, he won a Listed sprint at Windsor, getting up on the line to short-head his stable companion Tamarisk – who'd been sold for stud duties, proved infertile, and found his way back to Beckhampton via an insurance company. Harmonic Way recorded the last of his five wins in the Group 2 Cork and Orrery Stakes, ridden by Steve Drowne.

Drowne was in the saddle for the next Beckhampton sprinter to graduate to Group company: Patavellian, bred by his owner John Deer at his Oakgrove Stud near Chepstow. Deer had half-brothers in training with Charlton: Patavellian and Avonbridge. Patavellian arrived as a four year old maiden in 2002, rated 65. The following year, the two year old Avonbridge sprang a 20–1 surprise in a Lingfield maiden race and followed up in a nursery handicap at Goodwood and a Listed race at York. Meanwhile, Patavellian had stretched his losing run to 11 races; it was only in the autumn that he won a modest 0–65 handicap at Chepstow. He wore first-time blinkers, and the headgear transformed Deer's horse's outlook. Patavellian followed up on the same course in a Class E stakes race, both over seven furlongs, and then won again in a handicap at Newmarket. The official end-of-season ratings seemed to reflect their respective abilities: Patavellian was 95 – having won his first race off 64; Avonbridge was 117. In 2003, Patavellian won a minor race at Windsor over six furlongs and was then the medium of a huge gamble in the Wokingham. It didn't quite come off: he was second in his group and fifth overall, unsuited by the firm ground. Tried once more over seven furlongs – his breeding suggested he ought to be at least a 10-furlong horse – he won the Bunbury Cup, all out by a short head, his stamina visibly ebbing. He'd been favourite for both races, and was backed as soon as a market formed for the Stewards' Cup. On the morning of the race the Pricewise column in the *Racing Post* recommended Patavellian at 5–1 and a monumental gamble ensued. The race had another heavily-supported runner, Fire Up The Band, who started at 7–2 with Patavellian 4–1. Steve Drowne waited with Patavellian until the two-furlong pole, where he pushed on, opened up a clear lead and won by three lengths. The *Racing Post* reported that, "The good thing beat the other good thing, with the winner looking like one of the best things to have graced the Goodwood cavalry charge in its 163-year history."

After the race, Charlton said, "Mission accomplished." He revealed that, "For me, I was quite bullish… He's always worked like a better horse than we've seen so far. He's extraordinary. Avonbridge is rated 117 and they work together, so I'm not surprised by how he did it." Patavellian picked up a cut during the race, which ruled him out of targets like the Ayr Gold Cup, but when he was back in full training, John Deer had a suggestion for Charlton: the Prix de l'Abbaye. Charlton had another target in mind, a Group 3 at Newmarket. The Abbaye would be Patavellian's first attempt at five furlongs; the likely heavy ground was another unknown. Neither stopped him winning, having led from half-way. He was lucky to avoid the season's best sprinter, Oasis Dream, who was withdrawn because of the going, but there was no fluke about Patavellian seeing off the other Group 1 sprinters. After the race Charlton said, "All credit to the owner, who insisted on running him when I told him it was impossible." And, wistfully, "He would've been a good thing in the Ayr Gold Cup, wouldn't he?"

Two days before the Abbaye, Charlton had seen his best two year old win the Middle Park at Newmarket. It was Khalid Abdullah's Three Valleys – the colt picked by Richard Hughes as the best horse he rode for Beckhampton. His assessment was based on a spectacular victory – 'win' hardly does it justice – in the Coventry Stakes. It was his second run, after a debut success in a small race at Nottingham. Some of the other horses in the 13-runner field for the Coventry had passed sterner tests: Three Valleys was only fourth favourite at 7–1. Hughes knew he had the race won after two furlongs. Three Valleys quickened right away, still on the bridle, to win by eight lengths in a course record time for a two year old. He drifted to his right in the last half-furlong, but still equalled the winning distance of Mill Reef 23 years earlier. Charlton then ran Three Valleys in the Group 1 Phoenix Stakes at the Curragh; he disappointed in finishing third behind two Aidan O'Brien horses, One Cool Cat and Old Deuteronomy. A physical explanation was found; the colt had mucus in his lungs. He was treated with a respiratory drug, and the problem was contained. He turned round the form with Old Deuteronomy by six lengths in the Middle Park, which he won on his next appearance, quickening readily when asked, and beating the winner of the Gimcrack by three quarters of a length. Three Valleys' last race of the season was the Dewhurst, in which he finished a close second to an outsider.

A few weeks later there was a sensation: Three Valleys had failed a routine dope test after the Middle Park. Traces of the drug clenbuterol had been found in his samples. At a later hearing, he was disqualified. It was an embarrassing and damaging episode, particularly as Charlton and his vet had followed the drug manufacturer's guidelines. Ironically, Three Valleys' treatment with clenbuterol continued between the Middle Park and the Dewhurst, yet his samples after the Dewhurst tested negative. There was no happy ending. Three Valleys ran in a small-field renewal of the Craven Stakes the following season, beaten five lengths by a colt he'd finished ahead of in the Dewhurst; he was allowed to take his chance in the 2000 Guineas, but finished far back in the field. He was sent to the USA, where in nine runs spread over three seasons for trainer Bobby Frankel, Three Valleys won – of all things – a claiming race, followed eventually by a Grade 3 at Monmouth Park. It wasn't what'd been hoped for, the day he won the Coventry Stakes.

Among Roger Charlton's other two year olds in 2003 was Kind, a filly by Danehill out of a Rainbow Quest mare, Rainbow Lake. She seemed likely to be a miler, but after a few runs she was kept to sprint distances and won five races in a row at three years, followed by another at four. Kind's six wins came from 13 outings, and though she tackled Group company, her 'black type' successes came in Listed races at Hamilton and Nottingham. She was no world-beater, but she's turned out to be a golden broodmare, the dam of Frankel, by Galileo; his full brother Noble Mission; and the winners Bullet Train, Joyeuse and Morpheus. Kind serves as an illustration of the ebb and flow of fortune in racing. Ordinarily, Henry Cecil might've expected to train Kind, as he'd won three races with her dam, including a Group 3. But when Kind and that year's other Juddmonte yearlings were allocated to their trainers, Cecil's yard was under a cloud; Kind went to Beckhampton. A few years on, Charlton was enduring a quiet year while Cecil was resurgent, so Kind's first Galileo colt went to Newmarket, to make racing history.

In the meantime, Charlton had repeated the stable's wins in the Haydock Sprint Cup, the Cambridgeshire and the Prix de l'Abbaye. The Haydock race was the culmination of the single season in which Charlton trained the four year old winner, Tante Rose. She'd won twice from 10 starts for another yard when she was sent to a dispersal sale. She was sold to a Beckhampton owner, Bjorn Nielsen, for 350,000 guineas, and won all her three starts for him. She went briskly through the gears from a Listed race at Haydock and a Group 3 at York to the Group 1 Sprint Cup, where Hughes produced her fast and late to beat the previous year's winner Somnus, with Patavellian a whisker behind in third. *Racehorses of 2004* described the race as, "A triumph for [Charlton], who has had few peers with his handling of sprinters of late." For good measure, Charlton revealed after Tante Rose had won that she and Patavellian had been housed in an isolation yard: everything else at Beckhampton was coughing its head off, and the yard hadn't had a winner in the preceding three weeks. The following year saw Blue Monday win the Cambridgeshire, and John Deer's Avonbridge, a wonderfully game, consistent colt, took the Abbaye. After his trio of wins as a two year old, Avonbridge won again at three and four. He was earmarked for stud duties at the end of his five year old season, but more than justified the decision to keep him in training by winning the Palace House Stakes, finishing second in the July Cup, and then prevailing in a bunch finish to the Abbaye, beating his stable companion Striking Ambition, with Patavellian in fifth, beaten only a length. The race featured its usual traffic problems, and Avonbridge had come through the field from a long way back. The klaxon sounded for a stewards' enquiry; at one stage it seemed to Charlton that he might lose both first and second places. To much relief came the announcement: *Le résultat est maintenu.* Avonbridge stands today at the Oakgrove Stud.

By the second half of the 1990s the yard was back up to 95 or 100 horses and all was set fair. Then came a blow beyond the control of any trainer: the deep recession which began early in 2008 and continued through to the middle of the next year. The most visible impact on Beckhampton was the loss of the 11 horses running in the colours of Martin Myers. He was, "A wonderful man to train for. He loved racing. It was good fun having his horses," says Charlton, but the banks withdrew funding support from Myers' property company, as they did from many firms. The horses' ownership was linked to Myers' business, and Charlton had to spend costly and unproductive time dealing with administrators and lawyers. Eleven boxes empty overnight is one thing: a general downsizing of owners' strings and a lack of orders for yearlings is worse. A rare bright spot in a tough year was Charlton's third win in the Stewards' Cup, this time with Genki. Most of the race was invisible to anyone but the jockeys; a sea mist hung over the course. Genki and Steve Drowne appeared, in the lead, about a furlong out.

Beckhampton started 2010 with only 65 boxes filled, Charlton's smallest ever string. Among them, however, was a yearling colt from John Deer's stud: Al Kazeem, by Dubawi out of Kazeem, by Darshaan. He turned out to be the best horse trained so far by Roger Charlton, and he led the stable back to Group 1 glory and full strength. Charlton has a distinct preference for the sort of horse he prefers to train: not necessarily a colt or filly; neutral as to sprinter, miler, middle distance or stayer. What he most likes is to train older horses. Al Kazeem was retired in 2015 after six seasons at Beckhampton, a testament to his own temperament and durability as well as to the ability of Charlton and his team to go on improving horses through their racing careers. It began in typically low-key fashion with only two runs as a two year old, winning a one-mile maiden at Newbury, "Travelling well and finding plenty." At three, he made all the running to win the London Gold Cup, a handicap that often produces Group-class horses; was second in the Great Voltigeur to Sea Moon, who was later placed in the St Leger and the Breeders' Cup Turf; and then second in two Group 3s at Newbury. At the end of that campaign, Deer received some serious offers for his colt. One from Hong Kong was accepted, but, amazingly in view of what the horse went on to accomplish, a vet turned Al Kazeem down because he didn't like the shape of his feet. It was the second time that fate smiled kindly on John Deer: when Al Kazeem was a yearling he was backward, which resulted in Deer holding him back from the sales: "He wouldn't have made the price I thought he was worth, so I decided to keep him."

Al Kazeem started his third season's racing by easily winning the Group 2 Jockey Club Stakes, hanging left when clear of his field but running on strongly. It transpired that he'd suffered a stress fracture of the pelvis. After six weeks in his box and a long rest he came back into training as a five year old. He began the season by winning the Group 3 Gordon Richards Stakes at Sandown, and then set up the sequence for which he'll long be remembered, winning three Group 1s in six weeks, ridden each time by James Doyle. The first was at the Curragh in the Tattersalls Gold Cup, taking on the Aidan O'Brien-trained Camelot, winner of the previous year's 2000 Guineas, Derby and Irish Derby. Charlton said after the race that "We couldn't possibly come [here] thinking we were going to win," but he obviously had a plan: Camelot followed a pacemaker; Doyle followed Camelot. The pacemaker led to the two-furlong marker, where Camelot struck for home. A furlong out, Doyle challenged, and it was evident that Al Kazeem was going more strongly than Camelot. At the line, the Beckhampton colt was well on top, winning by a length and a half. In the post-race interviews, the word 'Arc' was mentioned more than once: it's the race that Charlton would most like to win. But, he added, 'there are a lot of Group 1s before then.' The next was the Prince of Wales's Stakes at Royal Ascot, and it provided one of the most exciting races of the season.

Camelot was expected to improve from the Curragh, and was made favourite at 5–2 over Al Kazeem at 11–4. Two more Group 1 winners, the Nassau Stakes winner The Fugue and a French colt, Maxios, were on 13–2. The William Haggas-trained Mukhadram was 14–1; he belied those odds with a bold display of front running under his rider Paul Hanagan, who made a sudden move off the final bend, quickly going three lengths clear. Among the riders behind, Doyle reacted first. At the furlong post Mukhadram's lead was still two lengths, but Al Kazeem whittled it down to a length, half a length, drew level, and in the last few strides Doyle forced him ahead. Before the race, John Deer had asked Doyle, how many winners had he ridden at Royal Ascot? If he was taken aback by the reply, "None," he would've been encouraged by the follow-up: "But don't worry – I'm just about to." Oddly enough, no one had thought to ask Doyle about his experience of riding the Curragh before the Tattersalls Gold Cup. Something had been nagging at Roger Charlton. During a euphoric taxi ride back to Dublin airport, he asked, 'Had you ridden the course before, James?' Well, no. Doyle had ridden once in a five-furlong sprint on the straight course, and had gone for a run the full distance of the race that morning, but a ride on the Curragh's round course? No. Who knows what might've transpired, had John Deer asked, three or four days before the Tattersalls Gold Cup, 'How well does our jockey know the Curragh, Roger?'

The third of Al Kazeem's Group 1s was the Eclipse Stakes. He was reopposed by Mukhadram and The Fugue, and O'Brien sent a new challenger from Ireland, the Queen Anne Stakes winner Declaration Of War. The race was a near repeat of Ascot: Mukhadram made the running and Al Kazeem wore him down in the last furlong. Unfortunately, Al Kazeem hung right and squeezed his rival; Hanagan had to snatch his mount up and lost momentum, which allowed Declaration Of War to pass him for second. The outcome created much controversy; the best horse had won, and he kept the race, but the connections of Mukhadram were entitled to feel hard done by. The difference between finishing second and third was about £45,000. Doyle was handed a five-day ban for careless riding. Al Kazeem ran a little bit below his best in three subsequent starts; The Fugue and Declaration Of War both reversed previous running with him. Then Al Kazeem was half-way down the field in the 'Arc'. And then he was syndicated to stand at Sandringham Stud.

CHAPTER TWENTY-SEVEN

The most beautiful place in England

The former England cricket captain Mike Atherton told in his autobiography how his left-arm bowler Phil Tufnell moaned that the incomparable Australian leg-spinner Shane Warne was, "Ruining my career." Atherton reflected that having Warne's peak years overlapping with his own captaincy hadn't been terribly good for *his* career, either. Beckhampton's biggest prize-winner had the bad luck to race under the shadow of the mighty Frankel. In any other year, Prince Khalid Abdullah's Cityscape would've received more attention and plaudits than he did. Cityscape, by the champion miler Selkirk out of Tantina, was another of the older horses that Roger Charlton enjoys training; and like Al Kazeem, Cityscape's best performances came after recovery from injury.

Cityscape's first season was in 2008. It was a typical lightly-raced Beckhampton two year old's progression. An arresting wide-margin win in a Salisbury novice against six previous winners was followed by placing in a better grade at Newmarket, and finishing a close second in the Group 2 Royal Lodge Stakes at Ascot. The injury came in the 2000 Guineas behind Sea The Stars. Cityscape missed the rest of the season, but resumed in 2010 with wins in a Listed mile race at Haydock and the Group 3 Joel Stakes at Newmarket, by seven lengths. It was at this point in Cityscape's career that he began to be inhibited by Frankel. The two colts were in the same ownership: it made no sense for Juddmonte to have Frankel serially beating

Cityscape, as he would've done. The outcome was that Frankel lorded it over English racecourses; Cityscape went on a world tour, which may be why he didn't fully get the recognition he deserved. *Racehorses of 2011* devoted nine lines to Cityscape and 11½ pages to Frankel. That was after a season in which Cityscape finished third to the top-class Canford Cliffs in the Queen Anne Stakes, won Group 3s at the Curragh and St Cloud, and went down by the narrowest of margins in two Group 1s: the Premio Vittorio Di Capua in Milan (beaten a short head) and the Hong Kong Mile at Sha Tin (beaten a neck). By way of consolation, Cityscape picked up £363,000 in prize money in Hong Kong.

After Richard Hughes and Juddmonte went their separate ways, Hughes rode freelance, but increasingly for his father-in-law Richard Hannon. The first-jockey position at Beckhampton was filled by Steve Drowne. He was associated with all Cityscape's early successes. Then he had the extreme misfortune of a misdiagnosed illness which prevented him riding for, effectively, an entire season. Roger Charlton had a Group 1 in mind for Cityscape at the start of 2012, and he was forced to plan for a replacement jockey. Given the prize-money on offer in his target race, he could've taken his pick of the internationally-known riders without a mount. Instead he chose a somewhat forgotten young Englishman who'd arrived at Beckhampton in 2011, with few expectations beyond riding work on good horses. The race Charlton was planning for was the Dubai Duty Free at Meydan; the young jockey was James Doyle. He rode over 70 winners in 2006, his last season as an apprentice, but as can happen when apprentices ride out their claim, Doyle struggled. He had 41 and 53 winners in the following seasons – hardly a disaster, but when the totals fell below 30 in each of the next two years, he considered taking a plumbing course, to learn a trade to supplement his dwindling riding fees and prize-money income. Thanks to an introduction from the horse whisperer Gary Witheford, and an appeal or two from his trainer mother Jacqui, James Doyle was given an opening to Beckhampton by Roger Charlton. Perhaps a crack would better describe it: he'd be welcome to ride work, but Steve Drowne was the jockey in place, and Doyle shouldn't expect rides.

> "I went to Beckhampton to get more confidence and to sit on better quality horses. I never thought I'd see or be involved with a place like it. I was blown away by that first morning riding work – the views, the quality of the gallops."

Doyle's enthusiasm reaped its reward when he won on his first ride for the stable, a horse of Khalid Abdullah's, Newton Lodge, running at Sandown. Not long afterwards, Doyle rode three winners for Charlton over two days at Newbury. He was on his way, riding more and more winners for Beckhampton – and as he started to be noticed, for other trainers too. In the 2011 season he overhauled the total of winners that he'd achieved back in 2006. As a result, he was offered a job riding in Dubai over the winter. "I saw Roger as almost a mentor," says Doyle. "He thought Dubai was a good opportunity for me." So Doyle began in Dubai that November, earning the praise, "[He] has been something of a revelation, winning 23 races" from the racing writer of *Gulf News*.

The impression Doyle was making and the local track knowledge he'd acquired weren't lost on Charlton. He rang Doyle early in March 2012 to tell the jockey nothing had been decided, but he was in line for the ride on Cityscape in the £1.9 million-to-the-winner Dubai Duty Free on the last day of March. Doyle was handed a return ticket to Heathrow, and rode Cityscape in an unnoticed gallop at Kempton Park. The lead horse was a Beckhampton secret, Marzante, a modest performer on the track but a 'morning glory', a super-reliable work horse who's led all the best Beckhampton horses of the last few seasons. His BHA rating is in the mid-70s. Doyle rates Marzante a 110 horse on the gallops: he recalls that day's work by Cityscape as, "Astonishing."

> "It was electric. We went a mile and must have finished the best part of a furlong clear of Marzante. Cityscape just kept on quickening and I'd never experienced a horse doing that."

Doyle flew back to Dubai to put in the hours in the gym, and to study the form and running styles of the other runners in the Dubai Duty Free. What transpired was like the Kempton Park gallop: astonishing. Cityscape had travelled over well, without losing any weight. Doyle had a confidence-booster from Charlton in the paddock – "You know what you're doing: I'll leave it to you" – and gave Cityscape what, over jumps, would be called a young man's ride, which it was. He kept close to the pace, took the lead over three furlongs out and then asked his mount for maximum effort two furlongs from home. Cityscape quickened twice, as he had in his trial, bounded clear to win by a little over four lengths, and claimed Beckhampton's biggest-ever purse. The photograph of the presentation showed Charlton with Abdullah's racing manager Teddy Grimthorpe, both jubilant. Lord Grimthorpe was identified in a *Gulf News* photo-caption as 'Grim Thorb.' He wouldn't have cared: the moment was the polar opposite of grim. Doyle looked stunned. It was a life-changing moment – more prize-money than he'd won in his 300-plus previous winning rides put together. "I was hopeful, not confident, but I had an inkling that he could do something special," says Doyle. Roger Charlton topped up his Polytrack gallop, and built a handsome conservatory in which to welcome his owners.

After winning at Meydan, Cityscape was twice second in Group 1 races to the Ballydoyle-trained Excelebration: at Royal Ascot in the Queen Elizabeth II Stakes, and at Deauville in the Prix Jacques le Marois. Excelebration was a top miler who had a regular rear view of Frankel; his two defeats of Cityscape, by one and a quarter lengths and by three lengths, show how Cityscape, although overshadowed by Frankel, was lucky to be in same ownership, so that he was campaigned to avoid him. Cityscape's other notable run was in Canada, in the Woodbine Mile, where he finished third to Wise Dan, that year's Breeders' Cup Mile winner. At the start of the following season, Cityscape ran down the field in the Lockinge Stakes, after which he was taken out of training. Juddmonte had not long before added Cityscape's half-brother Bated Breath – a high-class sprinter trained by

Roger Charlton – to their stallion roster, so Cityscape was sold to a syndicate to stand in Gloucestershire.

"He was the springboard, the horse that put me on the map," says James Doyle. Just a year after his career's relaunch at Beckhampton, Doyle was retained by Juddmonte, so that as well as riding Al Kazeem, he rode Prince Khalid's Noble Mission in Lady Cecil's yard and Kingman for John Gosden: all Group 1 winners. That in turn attracted Godolphin's attention to Doyle.

The precedents for colts returning to racing after a spell as a stallion aren't encouraging. Breeders had flocked to Al Kazeem, but the results of his first covering season showed him to be sub-fertile. Not infertile – he sired 26 foals – but not getting enough mares in foal to continue with the original syndication. An insurance claim was made on behalf of his shareholders, and John Deer bought him from the insurers. Deer himself had sent three mares to Al Kazeem: all were barren, though he subsequently acquired one of the 26 in-foal mares. Meanwhile, Deer sent his horse back to Beckhampton to be trained for the 2014 season. Hopes for Al Kazeem's racing future were muted. Roger Charlton was concerned that he'd be difficult to handle: "I expected him to shout and stand up on his hind legs" – to behave like a stallion. That he didn't is in part a reflection of the tranquillity of Beckhampton and his returning to the same box, the same groom and the same work rider.

Al Kazeem was soon back in his familiar place at the head of the string, working with his previous enthusiasm. After a win in a Group 3 at Windsor he ran in the Irish Champion Stakes, finishing fifth, but only a neck behind his old rival Mukhadram, suggesting he was getting close to his previous form. He was again in midfield behind Treve in the Arc, though several lengths closer to the winner than the year before, and then ran in the Champion Stakes at Ascot. He was ridden by George Baker, with James Doyle – now the retained jockey for Juddmonte – on Noble Mission, Frankel's full brother. The pair went hammer and tongs at each other from two furlongs out. Al Kazeem went down by a neck, despite every effort from the horse and his rider. As a seven year old he started the 2015 season by winning in France, before returning to the Curragh and an emotional repeat win in the Group 1 Tattersalls Gold Cup. Sadly, he picked up a joint injury, and a few weeks later his owner decided to retire him and take him back to his stud. The statistics from his season at Sandringham point to his suitability for maiden mares: he got 45 per cent in foal, as against 18 per cent of mares previously barren, or with a foal at foot, though John Deer cautions on the reliability of one year's data. It's likely that other breeders will be happy to take a chance on Al Kazeem's fertility. Few horses match his profile of class, guts and durability. Whatever transpires, the Oakgrove Stud manager Tim Lane promises that Al Kazeem will be a strong contender for the title of 'World's most pampered pet'. Roger Charlton said when the horse's retirement was announced that bringing Al Kazeem back twice, and winning Group 1s each time, "Is the greatest training feat of my career – and yet he made it so easy for me."

Richard Hughes says, "Beckhampton brings you back in time when you step into the courtyard." So it does. It's intimate. A visitor might think, where are all the horses, because the first sight, in front and to the right, is of two short rows of Sam Darling's nineteenth century cage boxes, eight to a side behind their retaining walls, cool in summer, warm in winter. High up in the boxes is a sprig of holly. Charlton isn't yet sure if he believes in it, but a cattle man swore to him that holly keeps ringworm away, 'So why not try it?' The visitor will see that Beckhampton evolves and develops. A flock of sheep has been deployed to clear scrub below Cherhill Down. Hundreds of beech trees have been planted: Charlton continuously adds back to Beckhampton's landscape. There are constraints. The yard and its lands are so hedged in by areas of special scientific interest and outstanding natural beauty, not to mention the world heritage site at Avebury, that it's hardly possible for the trainer to put one breeze block on top of another. Go on another stable visit, perhaps to Jonjo O'Neill's Jackdaws Castle, and there's an indoor school the size of an aircraft hangar. In foul weather, O'Neill's horses walk a few yards from their boxes and turn left then right, for circuits and figures of eight, under cover. At Beckhampton, the horses are rugged up to work in whatever weather is thrown at them, as they've been since Billy Treen's days.

A successful racehorse trainer is an amalgam of many different attributes. Horse management is only the tip of the iceberg. It's necessary also to buy horses well and sell them well; to find and keep owners; to recruit and retain good staff; to balance the books. The management of a large downlands estate requires a particular sub-set of skills. Roger Charlton has done much more than his original target of 'keeping it going.' He has, with one or two boulder-sized bumps in the road, steered Beckhampton into its nineteenth decade with every box in the yard filled and every hope alive. He also has a better business brain than most, having successfully set up and run his Lambourn swimming pool.

A television camera focused on Charlton as he watched Al Kazeem fight his way past Mukhadram in the last yards of the Prince of Wales's Stakes. As James Doyle finished the race off, the cameras showed Charlton puffing his cheeks out with relief and a fleeting smile. It was at a Royal Ascot, by no means the first, when many winning connections hugged, danced and cavorted in the paddock. Had it not been for the limitations imposed by middle age and morning dress, they might've done cartwheels. That isn't Charlton's style. Down the years, various commentators have tried to analyse him. The journalist and author Alastair Down wrote that Charlton, "Does not bat very high up the order for the Incurable Optimists XI." Charlton's friend Luca Cumani has said, "No one believes it, but Roger is a great worrier and gets very tense. He hides it brilliantly." Certainly the trainer tries not to wear his heart on his sleeve; among the compliments Jeremy Tree's former staff pay to him is that he never, ever raised his voice. The same is likely true of Roger Charlton. Fatalism is part of his make-up: he says, "Sometimes your number just comes up," but he works hard to minimise the element of chance. Most trainers with large strings have a form expert to help them place their horses; Charlton does his own form study and targets his horses himself. James Doyle was astonished to find that he was sometimes being 'jocked up' by

Charlton on Weatherbys' racing administration website at 11 or 12 o'clock at night. "Roger is the most thoughtful trainer I've ridden for," says Doyle: "He doesn't run a horse unless he thinks it can win. He plans carefully and he thinks about every aspect of the horse." What's more, he adds, "The team there is incredibly tight. They put the same amount of thought in."

Charlton has said that a conversation with Sir Henry Cecil during the late trainer's battle with cancer brought about a personal reassessment. In effect, if Sir Henry could maintain his optimism and determination during a long, brave struggle and debilitating treatment, what excuse did he have for appearing pessimistic? Downright optimism may be too much of a stretch: "I don't like to be over-optimistic; you're heading for a fall." Then again, at times a tinder-dry humour lurks behind the self-deprecation. Archie Stirling was one of Charlton's first owners. He had a share in a horse which he says was: "Good-looking but useless. When I asked Roger how it was, he replied cheerfully, 'It seemed fine when I passed it on my hack this morning.'"

Charlton recently had a gripe on his website about the handicapper's treatment of his progressive stayer Quest For More. It was being trained for the Northumberland Plate. First it was put up 6lb for finishing second; then at Goodwood the horse won by less than a length and went up 8lb. "For a staying race this is ridiculous and defies handicapping principles." Quest For More won the Northumberland Plate, comfortably. "I'm not a very good trainer. I thought [it] couldn't win. I know nothing," was Charlton's follow-up.

A few seasons ago, he handled a promising colt of Khalid Abdullah's called Top Offer. He was a bitter disappointment, regressed, was gelded and had a wind operation. Eventually he was sold to a small yard in Surrey. His new trainer Peter Crate remarked on Charlton's kindness in sending him Top Offer's medical notes. After much hard work, Crate coaxed a little race at Lingfield out of Top Offer. Charlton wrote in his blog:

> "The much-publicised Top Offer [made] an impressive debut at Newbury in August 2011, and became a leading contender for the 2000

> Guineas – probably due to the over-optimistic and hyping trainer. Top Offer is now trained by Peter Crate and won his second race, rated 62, in July [2014]."

Roger Charlton's most extreme show of pessimism – almost in the Captain Tim Forster class – is his oft-repeated fear that Beckhampton's land might one day become a site for motocross. A pitch 'n' putt golf course is only a little way behind in his nightmares. Neither seems likely, for as long as it's so valued and admired by the people who work, visit, or have horses trained there. Lady Rothschild was among Charlton's first owners. She sends him home-bred yearlings from her Waddesdon Manor Stud. She says, "I go to Beckhampton every moment I can, for the gallops or for evening stables. On a fine morning on top of the downs, it's the most beautiful place in England," her words echoed by John Deer: "It's a remarkable estate. On a summer morning on the high ground, looking back towards the stable, it's magnificent."

Of Lady Rothschild's horses in the yard over the years, the best have been Mince, who won eight races, including a Group 3; Spout, who won five times, the last four in Listed or Group 3 races; most recently, Thistle Bird. She retired in 2014 after eight wins and six places, moving up through the gears during 20 races over four seasons in training. She won the Group 3 Princess Elizabeth Stakes in 2013 and 2014, and ended her career in glory in the Group 1 Pretty Polly Stakes at the Curragh, ridden by George Baker. Lady Rothschild mentions her fondness for the stable's lads and lasses. They contribute to what a former pupil-assistant, Ed Walker, calls "A happy yard, a happy place." Walker is now a successful trainer in his own right. He went to Beckhampton on a placement from a course at Cirencester's Royal Agricultural College; at the end of it, he was invited to join Charlton full time, doing "Everything from mucking out to representing Roger at the races – a terrific grounding." He talks of 'a great place to work: the gallops are second to none, always in great nick.' The point is echoed by another former assistant, Tom Grantham:

> "It's a lovely yard to work in, a special place, steeped in history, with fantastic gallops. The Trial Grounds are gorgeous." As for the trainer: "He always did the job properly, there was never a stone unturned, but he was always ready to try something new. He gives his horses plenty of time, they'll always improve for a run."

Richard Hughes says, "Roger is a great man through good and bad. We're all good winners; Roger can be a good loser as well." Hughes meant it in the context of a man's reaction to the heads and short heads that separate defeat and victory. When it comes to betting, Charlton certainly hates losing. Accordingly, he bets in small stakes, seldom on Beckhampton horses. That might be tempting providence.

John Deer has had horses at Beckhampton for 15 years. They've included Patavellian, Avonbridge and Al Kazeem, whose four Group 1s were, "A fantastic outcome for a small breeder." He says that he and Charlton are, "Aligned in that the interest of the horse comes first – it's paramount." Lady Rothschild values Charlton's "Integrity, loyalty and friendship." Her son Nat Rothschild says he, "Under-promises and over-delivers." That's a characteristic shared by the Masters who went before Charlton. They could look over his shoulder and recognise much from their days: Treen and Woolcott the old inn and the core of the stabling; Sam Darling his re-building of the bottom yard and his meticulously maintained gallops; Fred Darling would see the yard Manna paid for; Noel Murless would frown to see, most winters, water rise up through the floor of the Beckhampton House cellar. Jeremy Tree would be pleased to note horses still working up his woodchip gallop.

Continuity is the key. Khalid Abdullah and Lady Rothschild have trained with Charlton since he took over from Tree. Judy Foxwell has worked in the office for 44 years; Heather Bufton has helped in the house since her mother worked for Fred Darling. The never-forgotten Dai Rees served Fred Darling, Noel Murless and Jeremy Tree: he was an anchor-man, connecting good horses to good horses across generations, regulating the speed of thousands of early morning gallops from the back of the lead horse. The same role is filled today by Steve Raymont; barring a few years with Godolphin in Dubai, he's been at Beckhampton for over 40 years. Roger Charlton says Raymont "Knows the gallops far better than I do." Continuity is represented also by the appointment of Charlton's son Harry as assistant trainer.

The play remains the same, but the cast is constantly renewed. Each October, yearlings arrive at Beckhampton from the sales. In December or January, more are sent from the owner-breeders. Beckhampton's boxes will be filled again. The lads will have a fresh spring in their step. The search for the next champion begins.

Beckhampton's Honours Board of Classic Winners

YEAR	RACE	HORSE	TRAINER	OWNER	JOCKEY
1839	Oaks	Deception	Billy Treen	Fulwar Craven	John Day
1868	2000 Guineas[1]	Formosa	Harry Woolcott	William Graham	George Fordham
1868	1000 Guineas	Formosa	Harry Woolcott	William Graham	George Fordham
1868	Oaks	Formosa	Harry Woolcott	William Graham	George Fordham
1868	St Leger	Formosa	Harry Woolcott	William Graham	Tom Chaloner
1870	Oaks	Gamos	Harry Woolcott	William Graham	George Fordham
1897	2000 Guineas	Galtee More	Sam Darling	Jack Gubbins	Charles Wood
1897	Derby	Galtee More	Sam Darling	Jack Gubbins	Charles Wood
1897	St Leger	Galtee More	Sam Darling	Jack Gubbins	Charles Wood
1898	St Leger	Wildfowler	Sam Darling	Harry Greer	Charles Wood
1901	Oaks	Caps And Bells II	Sam Darling	Foxhall Keene	Milton Henry
1902	Derby	Ard Patrick	Sam Darling	Jack Gubbins	Skeets Martin

1 Dead-heated with Moslem

YEAR	RACE	HORSE	TRAINER	OWNER	JOCKEY
1907	2000 Guineas	Slieve Gallion	Sam Darling	Harry Greer	Billy Higgs
1916	St Leger	Hurry On	Fred Darling	James Buchanan[2]	Charlie Childs
1922	Derby	Captain Cuttle	Fred Darling	Lord Woolavington	Steve Donoghue
1925	2000 Guineas	Manna	Fred Darling	Henry Morriss	Steve Donoghue
1925	Derby	Manna	Fred Darling	Henry Morriss	Steve Donoghue
1926	Derby	Coronach	Fred Darling	Lord Woolavington	Joe Childs
1926	St Leger	Coronach	Fred Darling	Lord Woolavington	Joe Childs
1931	2000 Guineas	Cameronian	Fred Darling	Arthur Dewar	Freddie Fox
1931	1000 Guineas	Four Course	Fred Darling	Lord Ellesmere	Charlie Elliott
1931	Derby	Cameronian	Fred Darling	Arthur Dewar	Freddie Fox
1938	2000 Guineas	Pasch	Fred Darling	Henry Morriss	Gordon Richards
1938	Derby	Bois Roussel	Fred Darling	Peter Beatty	Charlie Elliott
1940	New Derby	Pont l'Evêque	Fred Darling	Fred Darling	Sam Wragg

2 Became the first Baron Woolavington in 1920

YEAR	RACE	HORSE	TRAINER	OWNER	JOCKEY
1941	New Derby	Owen Tudor	Fred Darling	Reginald Macdonald-Buchanan	Billy Nevett
1941	New Oaks	Commotion	Fred Darling	Arthur Dewar	Harry Wragg
1942	New 2000 Guineas	Big Game	Fred Darling	King George VI	Gordon Richards
1942	New 1000 Guineas	Sun Chariot	Fred Darling	King George VI	Gordon Richards
1942	New Oaks	Sun Chariot	Fred Darling	King George VI	Gordon Richards
1942	New St Leger	Sun Chariot	Fred Darling	King George VI	Gordon Richards
1947	2000 Guineas	Tudor Minstrel	Fred Darling	Arthur Dewar	Gordon Richards
1948	1000 Guineas	Queenpot	Noel Murless	Sir Percy Loraine	Gordon Richards
1949	St Leger	Ridge Wood	Noel Murless	Geoffrey Smith	Michael Beary
1963	2000 Guineas	Only For Life	Jeremy Tree	Monica Sheriffe	Jimmy Lindley
1975	Oaks	Juliette Marny	Jeremy Tree	James Morrison	Lester Piggott
1979	Oaks	Scintillate	Jeremy Tree	James Morrison	Pat Eddery
1980	2000 Guineas	Known Fact	Jeremy Tree	Khalid Abdullah	Willie Carson
1990	Derby	Quest For Fame	Roger Charlton	Khalid Abdullah	Pat Eddery

Acknowledgements

Her Majesty Queen Elizabeth II's permission to make use of correspondence from the Royal Archives is gratefully acknowledged. Thanks to the senior archivist at Windsor Castle, Pamela Clark, for finding and sending me letters between Fred Darling and the Royal household. Other archivists who've helped include David Rymill at Highclere Castle; he unearthed the betting books and racing-related correspondence of 'Porchey,' the sixth Earl of Carnarvon. James Towe at Chatsworth sent letters from Victor, the ninth Duke of Devonshire, to his wife, discussing his horses in training with Sam Darling. Alia Campbell at Diageo provided a file on the life and business career of James Buchanan, Lord Woolavington. The letter that ended William Graham's turf career is in the Nicholson Distillery archive at Hackney Library. Thanks also to the Harrow School archivist Angharad Meredith and to Dr Bill Teatheredge, curatorial researcher at the Munnings Art Museum.

Other researchers have been captivated by Beckhampton and its history; several have provided me with their notes and photographs. David Acock has done more than most to study the yard and its best horses: his notes are on Roger Charlton's website. Willie Lawson hails from the Blake family, which provided several yard men to Beckhampton in the last century: he told numerous good stories. Ed Tomlin and John Saville both recorded conversations with people who worked for Fred Darling, and lent the tapes. Roger Day, the historian of the Marlborough district, has written about Darling's Home Guard platoon, and provided wartime photos of the stable and the gallops. The late racing journalist and author Richard Onslow wrote an unpublished monograph – *The History of Beckhampton House Stable* – which served as the basis for the booklet which was published for the yard's last open day.

Michael Darling provided two unpublished images from Sam Darling's time. Gillian Rowlands has a fund of stories from her father Dai Rees's 50 years at Beckhampton. She also kindly provided contact information for other stable lads who worked with Rees. Ron Blake's family has links to Beckhampton, from Fred Darling's time onwards. Peter Willett gave me his impressions of Darling and his last champion racehorse. John Cherry and Patrick Eyre made useful suggestions. Rachel Evans at Christie's supplied the image of the gold cigarette box which Darling received from Peter Beatty. Brian Rickard has the photo of the Beckhampton Home Guard. David Hues of Galtee More Farm lent the map of the land which Fred Darling sold – and the accounts book which shows the wartime damage caused locally by tank manoeuvres.

Herbert Blagrave shunned the limelight. For bringing him to these pages, my thanks to Ian Balding, who was briefly Blagrave's assistant trainer; to Mick Channon, who Blagrave was determined to keep at Southampton FC; to Terry Stringer, who rode winners for Blagrave; to Gretchen Rawlings, who did office work at The Grange; to Heather Peak-Garland, for the Blagraves' lifestyle; and to Jo Wells of the Blagrave Trust.

Dick Warden's erratic early years in Lambourn were recalled by Cath Walwyn. Fred Judge helped piece together Warden's wartime service in the SOE. The years Warden spent hunting and horse-dealing were recalled by, in Ireland: Gerald Delamere, the late Johnny Harrington, Jonathan Irwin, Sonia Rogers and Simon Walford. John Walsh kindly sent photographs. Peter Walwyn, Ted Dibble and Sidney Bailey recalled Warden's Mastership of the VWH. David Minton and Johnny McKeever described Warden the bloodstock agent. Peter Easterby recalled his owner and family friend. John Leat outlined Warden's role in the Maktoum family's entry into British racing. Wilf Morris was Warden's last apprentice. John Dunlop and others told me about Dick Warden's humour. Thanks also to David Arbuthnot, Tim Preston, Tim Roots and John Waugh, for their help with the portrait of a man who combined the Scarlet Pimpernel and Macavity: forever daring and forever missing.

Noel Murless' time at Beckhampton began brilliantly and ended sourly. His daughter Julie Cecil has been a great help in explaining why. Thanks to Murless' former employees Clive Brittain, Cliff Lines and Mick Leaman for adding to the story.

Nelson Guest rode as Sir Gordon Richards' second jockey; Graham Stephens was one of the work riders. They've given insights into a trainer who perhaps didn't ask enough of his horses or his staff. Peter Makin filled in the background to the Ogbourne stable, where he has trained with distinction. He also recalled Jeremy Tree, looking lost in Waitrose in Marlborough, trying, 'To show my new Portuguese butler how to do the shopping.'

A long and varied cast are united in affection for Jeremy Tree. Beginning with those lads and apprentices who worked for him, and their spouses, my thanks go to: Alan Baker, Ron Bode, Alfie Button, the late Johnny Dixon, Paddy Jackson, Pearl O'Connell, Steve Raymont, John Reed, David Quinn and Ian Watters. Thanks also to Tree's assistant trainers Nicky Vigors and Andrew Simpson.

Sir Mark Prescott and Sir Michael Stoute told from their own experience how disinterested Tree could be when he acted on his owners' behalf. Jimmy Lindley and Willie Carson both rode a classic winner for Tree: their contribution is much appreciated. Grant Pritchard-Gordon kindly talked about Tree's contribution to the development of Khalid Abdullah's interest in racing and breeding. Andrew Gosling told me about his father Tommy, Tree's first stable jockey. My thanks at the Turf Club go to Sandy Malcolm, and to John Campbell and Brian Reilly - both of whom worked with William Grace, who placed Tree's bets. Judy Foxwell and Heather Bufton recalled their long service to Beckhampton.

Simon Parker-Bowles was one of Tree's closest friends. He's been a fund of stories, and of introductions to others, Rhydian Morgan-Jones among them. Tree was a director of Parker-Bowles's St James's restaurant, Green's. Among those who've given me an owner's perspective on Tree are Hughie

Morrison and James Swartz. Vicky Westropp made available the photo albums of her godmother, Monica Sheriffe.

Jeremy Tree's nieces Isabella Tree and Esther Cayzer-Colvin provided their account of how he set them up with a bookie's account while they were at school and won them £2,000 or so in our money. Guy Knight was one of Tree's closest friends: my thanks to his daughters Henrietta Knight and Lady Vestey for their kind contributions. Thanks also to Michael Curry for sending me the letter that Tree wrote to him after his retirement. From the pressroom, Claude Duval, John Garnsey, John Hanmer, Marten Julian, Jim McGrath, Howard Wright and the late Bob Wise all helped with stories and suggestions. Ivor Herbert told of the early Army career of Trooper Tree.

Roger Charlton is the primary source for information about Jeremy Tree and his stable management. He's also offered unstinting help and encouragement: showing me round the yard and its gallops; lending me Richard Onslow's 1995 monograph; giving access to his own and Jeremy Tree's scrap books; providing the 1882 plan of the yard and other illustrations; patiently answering innumerable questions; and suggesting other people to talk to and other information sources for me to follow up. This book wouldn't have been possible without his goodwill and support, and that of Clare Charlton and the Beckhampton office team.

Charlton's own career is a work in progress, with over 1,000 winners to date. For his story so far, my thanks to his owners John Deer, Martin Myers, Lady Rothschild and Archie Stirling. James Doyle and Richard Hughes talked about their respective spells riding for Beckhampton. Tom Grantham and Ed Walker supplied the assistant trainer's perspective. At the *Racing Post,* Steve Dennis sent me the photographs from his June 2014 feature on the yard; James Hill helped with research. Thanks to them and to Tim Cox, whose racing library is both a labour of love and an incomparable research resource. In the same vein, Tony Morris's and John Randall's ratings of the twentieth century's best horses supply a basis from which it's possible to make realistic judgements about their respective merits.

The late Sir Peter O'Sullevan was kind enough to reminisce over lunch across decades of Beckhampton's history. He was then 95. He shared a glass of Chablis, followed by a bottle of decent red. Back in his flat, he produced two balloon glasses big enough for a baby's bath and half-filled them with Calvados, continuing to talk in perfectly-formed quotes about Beckhampton's trainers, owners and jockeys ("Charlie Elliott was a disastrous punter. Most of them are"). With the exception of Fred Darling, he didn't have a bad word to say about any of them. Truly, 'A very parfit gentil knight.'

Alan Chester, Anthony de Freitas and Philip Malcolm kindly read and critiqued the book at draft stage. Julian Brown at Racing Post Books is a sympathetic and soothing publisher.

Last but as always not least, my wife Heather has put up with months of drawn study blinds and 'Silence' notices, with utmost good humour and tolerance.

Bibliography

Allison, William: *Memories of Men and Horses* [1922]
Armstrong, Walter: *Wrestliana* [1870]
Atherton, Michael: *Opening Up* [2002]

Balding, Ian: *Making the Running* [2004]
Browne, Capt TH: *History of the English Turf* [1931]
Bull, Phil: *Best Horses of…* [1942 to 1947]

Captain X: *Tales of the Turf* [1940]
Carnarvon, Earl of: *No Regrets* [1976]
Carnarvon, Earl of: *Ermine Tales* [1980]
Childs, Joe: *My Racing Reminiscences* [1952]
Clark, Neil: *Stranger Than Fiction; the Life of Edgar Wallace* [2014]
Colling, Susan: *Jack of his Own Trade* [1993]
Corbett, Henry: *Tales and Traits of Sporting Life* [1864]
Cunningham, Cyril: *Beaulieu, the Finishing School for Secret Agents* [1998]
Curling, Bill: *The Sea Pigeon Story* [1982]

Darling, Sam: *Sam Darling's Reminiscences* [1914]
Day, Roger: *Look, Duck and Vanish* [2011]
Day, William: *Reminiscences of the Turf* [1891]
Dixon, Sydenham: *From Gladiateur to Persimmon* [1901]
Donoghue, Stephen: *Just My Story* [1924]
Donoghue, Stephen: *Donoghue Up!* [1938]

Eddery, Pat with Alan Lee: *To Be a Champion* [1992]

Felstead, S Theodore: *Racing Romance* [1949]
Fitzgeorge-Parker, Tim: *Great Racehorse Trainers* [1975]
Fitzgeorge-Parker, Tim: *The Guv'nor* [1980]
Fitzgeorge-Parker, Tim: *Roscoe the Bright Shiner* [1987]

Galtrey, Sidney: *Memoirs of a Racing Journalist* [1934]
Gilbey, Quintin: *Champions All – Steve to Lester* [1971]
Gilbey, Quintin: *Queen of the Turf, the Dorothy Paget Story* [1973]
Good, Meyrick: *Good Days* [1942]
Good, Meyrick: *The Lure of the Turf* [1957]

Hamlyn, Geoffrey: *My Sixty Years in the Ring* [1994]

Jackson, Robert: *Gordon Richards: First!* [1952]

Kent, John: *The Racing Life of Lord George Cavendish Bentinck* [1892]
Khan, EJ: *Jock – the Life and Times of John Hay Whitney* [1981]

Lambie, James: *The Story of Your Life* [2010]
Lambton, George: *Men and Horses I Have Known* [1924]
Langtry, Lillie: *The Days I Knew* [1925]

McAlpine, Bobby: *One Shot at Life* [2012]
Marsh, Marcus: *Racing with the Gods* [1968]
Morris, Tony and Randall, John: *A Century of Champions* [1999]
Mortimer, Roger: *The History of the Derby* [1962]
Mortimer, Roger, *Twenty Great Horses* [1967]
Mortimer, Roger; Onslow, Richard; Willett, Peter: *Biographical Encyclopaedia of British Flat Racing* [1978]

Nightingall, Arthur: *My Racing Adventures* [1901]

Oakley, Robin: *Clive Brittain, The Smiling Pioneer* [2012]
Onslow, Richard: *The Squire* [1980]
Onslow, Richard: *The History of Beckhampton House Stable* [1995, unpublished]

Parslew, Patricia: *Beckhampton, Time Past and Time Present* [2004]

Richards, Gordon: *My Story* [1955]
Rickman, Eric: *Come Racing with Me* [1951]

Scott, Brough: *Henry Cecil – Trainer of Genius* [2013]
Saville, John: *Insane and Unseemly* [2008]
Seth-Smith, Michael: *Steve* [1974]
Seth-Smith, Michael: *Knight of the Turf* [1980]
Sharpe, Graham, with Mihir Bose: *William Hill* [2014]
Sim, Andrew: *English Racing Stables* [1993]
Stukeley, William: *Abury (*sic*) A Temple of the British Druids* [1743]

Taunton, Thomas H: *Portraits of Celebrated Racehorses* [1887]
Todd, Bob: *My Racing Memories* [1947]

Welcome (Brennan), John: *Fred Archer* [1967]
Welcome (Brennan), John: *Irish Horseracing* [1982]
Wright, Howard: *Bull – The Biography* [1995]

Annuals

Cope's Racegoers Encyclopaedia [1936 to 1962]
Horses in Training [from 1925]
The Bloodstock Breeders' Review [1912 to 1948]
The Racing Calendar
Timeform, *Racehorses of…* [from 1948]
Raceform

Newspapers and Periodicals, including:

Baily's Magazine

Bell's Life

Cork Examiner

Daily Mail

Daily Telegraph

Empire News

Limerick Chronicle

Licensed Victuallers' Gazette

Morning Advertiser

Morning Herald

Sporting Times

The Evening Standard

The Graphic

The Independent

The Irish Field

The Marlborough Gazette

The Morning Post

The Racing Post

The Racing Times

The Sporting Chronicle

The Sporting Life

The Sporting Review

The Sportsman [the Pink 'un]

The Times

The Westmorland Gazette

The Winning Post

Truth

Wiltshire Times

Index

INDEX

INDEX

INDEX

INDEX